The Ethnography of Reading

The Ethnography of Reading

EDITED BY

Jonathan Boyarin

UNIVERSITY OF CALIFORNIA PRESS

Berkeley   Los Angeles   Oxford

"Loud Cows" copyright © 1992 by Ursula K. LeGuin

University of California Press
Berkeley and Los Angeles, California

University of California Press
Oxford, England

Copyright © 1993 by The Regents of University of California

Library of Congress Cataloging-in-Publication Data

The Ethnography of reading / edited by Jonathan Boyarin.
    p. cm.
  Includes bibliographical references and index.
  ISBN 0-520-07955-8 (cloth : alk. paper).—ISBN 0-520-08133-1
(alk. paper)
    1. Books and reading. 2. Literature and society. 3. Literacy.
I. Boyarin, Jonathan.
Z1003.E87 1993
028'.9—dc20   92-34690
                                    CIP

Printed in the United States of America

1 2 3 4 5 6 7 8 9

The paper used in this publication meets the minimum requirements of American
National Standard for Information Sciences—Permanence of Paper for Printed Library
Materials, ANSI Z39.48-1984 ∞

CONTENTS

MOOOOOOOOVE O-VER

here come   the LOUD COWS   right NOW!

Moooooving throoough the silences,

MOOOOOing in the libraries,

LOUD COWS in the sacred groves — (shh! don't wake Daddy! -)

MOOO-OOO-OOOVE along there,

MOOOOVE along, JUMP! over the

MOOOOOOOON!

LOUD cows
LOUD cows
loud SOWS loud sows now
mouthing sounds — HEY!
it is aloud!

Ursula K. LeGuin - 1990

Loud Cows

It's allowed. It is allowed, we are allowed SILENCE! □
It is allowed — it is allowed — it is aloud SILENCE! □ □
It used to be aloud. □
             ♪ SI-EEE-LENTSSSS. □
    I-EE AM   THE   AWE ⟋ THOR ⟍
    REEED MEEE IN SI-EE-LENT AWE ⟍.

                              But — it's aloud —
                               it is aloud —

           A word is a noise a word is a noise
            a word is a noise a noise a noise —
                                         AWW. □

The word is aloud, the word is a loud thing.
The loud word is allowed, aloud to be, the loud word allows to be,
              it allows as how. □

                    Guns have ssilencers.
                    Guvvments have ssilencers.
                    SSo do Pri-vate SSec-tors.
              Words are to be-have.
              To lie si-lently on pages being good.
              To keep their covers over them.
              Words are to be clean.
              To be seen — not — heard. SILENCE!
       Words are the children of the Fathers who say SILENCE!
              who say BANG! you're DEAD. □
                                      But..

the Word is longer than Daddy   and louder than bang,
and all that silent words forbid DO·NOT·NO·TRESPASS·KEEP·OUT·SILENCE!
and all that silent words forbid,   loud words allow to be. □

      All, all walls fall. I say aloud, all walls all fall.
           It is aloud, it is allowed to be loud
           and I say it is aloud loudly,
           loudness allowing us to be us —— SO ⟿

ONE

Introduction

Jonathan Boyarin

Nothing is more commonplace than the reading experience, and yet nothing is more unknown. Reading is such a matter of course that at first glance, it seems there is nothing to say about it.
—TZVETAN TODOROV, QUOTED IN HOWE, THIS VOLUME.

The contributors to this volume have all given reading a second glance, and find much to say about it. Their investigations take us beyond the simple rubric of "literacy," which was once understood as an evolutionary advancement in the generalization, abstraction, and reliable transmission of otherwise evanescent and changeable oral communication. They all throw into question the assumption made a few decades ago, at the beginning of anthropological studies of literacy, that we could safely posit a "'central difference between literate and non-literate societies'" (Goody and Watt 1968, cited in Goody et al. 1988). We are now coming to recognize a much more complex interplay of different forms of human communication, from lullabyes to hypertext and beyond. Likewise all of their essays make it clear that the question of causality—whether it is "writing itself that makes a difference" (1968/1988), or writing is merely part of a larger context—will not get us very far, not only because reading is as much part of literacy as writing, but also because "writing" and "reading," unlike the speed of light, are hardly constant at all times and places.

At the origin of the collection lies my own experience as part of a collective reading group—a yeshiva study class described in my own contribution to this book. I was inspired to come to the yeshiva by the example of my older brother, who had successfully entered the world of traditional Jewish reading as an adult. Lacking the philological skills he had acquired, however, I remained somewhat of an outsider even though I wanted to be "in the book." One way to enrich my experience, and to reassure myself of my own intellectual worth in a situation where I was relatively incompetent, was to remind myself that in addition to being a novice Talmudist, I was a certified professional ethnographer.

In "writing up" this experience for a professional audience, I found it necessary to counter the lingering anthropological prejudice that literate cultures were somehow less authentic, less "anthropological," than cultures that relied strictly on oral communication. As I began reading the current scholarly literature, I found that I was not the only researcher questioning the very distinction between oral and literate cultures. I reasoned that, no matter how famously prominent texts may be in Jewish life, the situation of "living textuality" I found at the yeshiva could hardly be unique to Jewish culture. Comparing the place of texts in various cultural situations might also be one way to counter, and to help explain, the persistent isolation of Jewish culture as a research specialty in anthropology (Boyarin 1991).

I tested this hypothesis by organizing sessions on the ethnography of reading in 1989 at the conventions of the American Anthropological Association and the Modern Language Association. In addition to the inherent interest of the topic, I saw it as one way to build what many scholars realize are needed bridges between cultural anthropology and literary studies. One indication of both the promise and the lag in this synthesis is that the MLA session was sponsored by the "Division on Anthropological Approaches to Literature"—a body whose name reflects an older concept of the *application* of anthropological theory and method to the study of something that still remains set apart as Literature, rather than what we are working toward in the essays here—the collaborative exploration of a shared human field. On the other hand the broader rubric of "cultural studies," institutionally problematic as it still is, for now finds more of a place in literature than in anthropology. It is as if the anthropologists, seeing themselves in terms of the vanishing primitive, still felt some need to preserve their "integrity" and thus delimit their field. Meanwhile the people at the MLA take language use in the broadest sense, anywhere in the world and by anyone in the world, as their legitimate field of inquiry. My impression, in fact, is that the distinctions between the approaches of anthropologists and literary scholars in these essays is not so much methodological as chronotopic—between those who are learning how to include textuality as one of the fields of interaction they study in the present, and those who are learning to see fields of interaction shaping and surrounding the textual remains of the past. Being interdisciplinary may be "very hard to do," as Stanley Fish (1989) has contended, but it is hardly impossible—as Elizabeth Long proves especially clearly here by combining the social history of reading with a fieldwork report.

This does not mean that the disciplinary gap is or should be wholly closed prematurely, for to do so might foreclose some insights that the respective general orientations of anthropology and literature have to offer each other. Thus Jim Baker's stark portrayal of the question of meaning in reading as collective recitation, where comprehension per se is not the issue, should pose a particularly compelling challenge to the still-prevalent literary tendency to analyze reading in terms of disembodied decoding of inherent meanings. Baker's evocation of the particular power of reading *names* leads him to the larger insight that "the claims we might make of knowing about (comprehending) things by way of generalizing principles can never be divorced from the persuasive efforts, at a social interactional level, of acknowledging (apprehending) what particulars there are worth knowing and remembering." On the other hand, literary scholars are a type of native informant, professionally concerned with not only practicing but understanding the topic at hand in this collection. Thus there is a particular poignancy to the way Susan Noakes traces the modern ideology of masterly critical reading to a representation of Jesus reading in the Gospel of Luke. This kind of ability to commit oneself to strong readings—rich, daring, and innovative interpretations—while simultaneously acknowledging and examining the contingency of those readings, should encourage more anthropologists to look for similar double optics (Bleich 1988) in the reading situations they study.

As I explained in introducing the AAA session, my title was inspired by two sources. The first was the landmark collection *Writing Culture* (Clifford and Marcus 1986): I noted that while anthropologists and critics had taken to the analysis of ethnography as a cultural practice, they needed similarly to examine reading "out there" in ethnographic context. Much attention has been paid in the last several years to the insight that literary methods and questions can provide concerning the implication of anthropology in power-laden representations of difference. Yet we have only begun to explore how the kind of attention to the shifts of meaning in context that characterize the best ethnography can complement the new sense literary scholars have of reading as culturally and historically determined.

The second inspiration was the pioneering work done in the 1970s on the ethnography of speaking (Bauman and Sherzer 1989), an idea I found as stimulating when I was an undergraduate as I hope the present collection will be to students and more advanced scholars today. Aside from its focus on something that almost all human beings do, rather than on a comprehensive and objectified representation of a "primitive culture," this was an important early exploration of the notion that social practices could be compared by anthropologists as processes carried out by active subjects and not merely enactments of a superorganic structure.

Like those earlier volumes in their respective spheres, this collection is intended to help nurture our understanding of reading so that it can better fulfill the empowering critical function we all like to ascribe to it. Let me mention here some of the things I have learned about reading from these papers, a few of which have already been suggested. Almost all of the contributors to the panels and to this book focused in one way or another on the way that orality and textuality, far from being opposite poles, interact

in complex, multidirectional ways. Furthermore, most of the essays share
the task of dissolving the stereotype of the isolated individual reader, showing that not only is all reading socially embedded, but indeed a great deal
of reading is done in social groups. Some accomplish this by starting with
that ideology and then developing their ethnographies as a departure from
it (Howe, Long); others through the sheer eloquence of their counterexam-
ples (Digges and Rappaport). Third, the set of essays together question the
still-prevalent notion that societies progress along a universal sequence
from orality to literacy.

We have learned to read ethnography in much the same way as we read
literature (even if it is true that ethnography cannot be reduced to a genre
of literature, as Fabian [1990] insists). Readers of this collection should
therefore be alert to the contributors' occasional use of words that echo
other, earlier or intercultural, meanings and thereby hint at connections of
which the authors themselves might not even be fully aware. Thus Greg
Sarris ends most tellingly, speculating on whether it is possible for a non-
Indian reservation teacher to "position herself as a learner, and in a way
students and parents can tell." The last word doesn't only mean
apprehending, discerning the position the teacher has reached; it also suggests a renewed ability on the part of the Kashaya students and teachers to
speak, to tell their stories in a new way, something the entire essay has been
about. The implicit double meaning of "tell" resonates with Nicholas
Howe's interpretation of the Old English *raedan* as implying both the giving
of oral counsel and the comprehension of runic symbols, and also with
Mack Horton's remark that in Old English the word "tell" itself meant
both "to count" and "to narrate."

There are many such points of contact evident in the different situations
described in these essays: between Sarris's struggling Kashaya Pomo readers and Howe's struggling Anglo-Saxons; among Horton's description of
the interaction of rewriting and rereading in the structure of *The Tale of
Genji,* Fabian's report of the reoralization and retranscription of a native
history, and my own discussion of Talmudic commentary; between Long's
account of the increasing association of ephemeral reading with the frivolous female body, and Digges's and Rappaport's emphasis on the disembodied authority of the colonial writ as opposed to the integrated rituals by
which native communities marked land claims; between Baker's discussion
of the contrasting pair *al-Kitab* (the Book) and *al-Quran* (the Recitation),
and Daniel Boyarin's remark that *kithvei haqqodesh* (Holy Scripture) appears
in Hebrew alongside *Miqra,* which he glosses as "reading"; or again, between Daniel Boyarin and Howe, who both use classical Rome as a contrastive backdrop.

The last two examples, in fact, suggest that the essays have much to
teach not only us, but each other. Neither Boyarin nor Baker remarks on

the semantic and etymological parallelism in the Hebrew and Arabic terms. Furthermore, whereas Daniel Boyarin stresses the lack of a semantic overlap between the ancient Hebrew verbal root "*qr'*" and our modern English "reading," it seems there is much more overlap between "*qr'*" and Anglo-Saxon "*raedan.*"

There are also points of implicit controversy within this volume, which should prove equally fruitful for debate and further research. One such set of contrasting assertions pits Long's charge that the "grim" aspect of reading in the West can be traced "back to that original author, the transcendant patriarchal God who was, in the beginning, the word," and my own insistence that this charge of monologic phallogocentrism does not adequately characterize the dynamics of authority and interpretation in Rabbinic Judaism. I hope readers of this collection will find many other such affinities, controversies, and points of mutual enrichment.

The example of "*qr'*" and "*raedan*" aptly illustrates the concern here for reuniting textuality and orality within a shared field. Thus Horton refers to "the dynamic between Japanese orality and Chinese orthography," but rather than maintaining these as two separate sites of communication, he goes on to detail with remarkable precision the shaping of literary reception in Japan by this very dynamic. Fabian's essay in particular confounds our lingering sense of an evolutionary development from simpler, oral societies to more complex literate ones, by detailing the way that a "native" text— produced within an intricate matrix of colonial relations—had to be reoralized before it could be received and interpreted by European anthropologists, in a situation where "the traditional distinction between ethnographers who write and natives who talk can no longer be maintained."

However much we may speak of the interactive relations between the spoken and the written, the heard and the read, no one should forget that they are distinct techniques, or imagine that there is a happy, anarchistic relation of "free play" between written and spoken language. Several of the essays detail the relations of power within which the distinction between the oral and the written is continually "reinscribed," as academic theorists like to put it. Sarris does so in an especially effective way by weaving together the insights available to one born into a culture, the insights available to a sympathetic outsider who comes with a set of critical, comparative questions, and the complex tensions between those two positions. And certainly there is evidence in his essay of loss of meaning, both in the "translation" from oral to written forms, and more strikingly, in the translation from one set of conventions about the relation between orality and literacy to another set—the latter a phenomenon documented by Horton as well. Digges and Rappaport, exploring along with many other scholars today the cultural technologies of colonialist legitimation, show that even when the colonized gain access to literacy, their attempts at counterlegitimation are often easily thwarted. Such vital new insights into the relation between the oral and the textual show what can be learned in the space between a processual distinction and an objectivized dichotomy.

Another dichotomy that is bridged by all these essays is between "theory" and "description." Even though all of the pieces here focus on well-defined places and times, and none is primarily organized around a theoretical or comparative issue, they contain exhaustive discussion of current theoretical debates about oral and written language in society. Fabian's essay begins with an account of the relation between changes in the politics and theory of anthropology on one hand, and that discipline's view of orality and literacy on the other.[1] Long provides a comparable review of sociologists' and literary historians' studies of changes in modern Euro-American ideologies and practices of reading.

It may be impossible to combine chronological depth and ethnographic detail with the range of representative "voices" we have come to demand from intercultural collections like this one. Thus Fabian, Digges and Rappaport, or Baker along with Horton, as fine as their essays are, are not intended to represent reading on entire continents. The very richness of the ethnography, with its attendant respect for local particularity, dispels any notion that such adequate representation could be achieved within a single volume. Horton notes that "it was perhaps unfortunate from an orthographic point of view that Japan was closer to China than to Rome, for the Latin alphabet would have been far better suited" to the purposes of those who created a Japanese written language—thus making it obvious that there can be no question of a generalized "Asiatic" relation between oral and written language. Nor is Sarris's essay intended to represent reading among "U.S. minority groups." But studies that fully respect what Clifford Geertz calls "local knowledge" provide richer access to other situations than could be accomplished by simply cataloging every identity that should properly be represented. Sarris's careful diagnosis of the failure of "culturally relevant" reading materials to connect to the lives of Kashaya Pomo schoolchildren should be attended to by anyone concerned with the promise and difficulties of "multiculturalism" as a value or as a solution.

Similarly my hope is that critical insights like those afforded by Howe and Long, concerning the inseparable relation between the development of reading as a practice and an ideology and changing relations of power along lines of class and gender in European history, will open further creative cracks in the monolithic notion of a literate "Western civilization." Several of the essays suggest, in response to the question quoted in the first paragraph of this introduction, that we will not get very far with a simple notion of "reading" as a technology or practice independent of social context, since close examination of the nearest lexical equivalents of "reading" in other times and places reveals the very particular set of expectations our own modern European notion conjures up.

Here we have, of course, not speech but another book, and since the format of this book is quite standard, it will doubtless be read and judged by the same conventions applied to other secular scholarship in the modern European tradition. Yet, despite the erudition and insight of my coauthors, I trust there is little danger that "the ethnography of reading" will become a code word for any new orthodoxy in theory or in research practice. Johannes Fabian's essay—the closest of all to a programmatic overview—ends with an acute reminder that as we concern ourselves with the ethnography of reading we are doing precisely what we study. Therefore, "reflections on the current place of reading in anthropological (or literary) studies of literacy should neither be elevated nor dismissed as 'meta'-problems." This insight points ironically to one of the gaps that persist even in this collection—we still need an ethnography of that "solitary reader" whose stereotyping we decry, but who we spend much of our waking time being. Sarris acknowledges this as he recalls sitting in the UCLA library, reading a transcription of Kashaya legends for the first time, and gradually beginning to realize that it wasn't necessarily the case that "university people weren't Indian and what was Indian wasn't in books"—that he was himself becoming "a university person who is Indian."

Several of the essays similarly acknowledge the prevalence of solitary reading in our own academic contexts, only to shift our attention immediately to more exotic topics like Anglo-Saxon England. And, even while contextualizing "scripture," a number of the essays still focus on texts which are unquestionably canonical in various traditions—the Talmud, the Quran, the Gospel, *The Tale of Gengi*. As an anonymous reader for the publisher of this book noted, "Most of the papers deal with the reading of important work—literature or sacred texts—not with reading as a daily activity, and of routine stuff—the newspaper, mail, reports, scholarly articles, and yes, even, for example, my reading of this manuscript." We can take the point, even while demurring from the implicit judgment that this manuscript does not constitute "important work!" It is doubtless true that more time is spent by more people on reading the daily newspaper than on reading the Talmud and *The Tale of Gengi* combined.

The issue is not whether it is inappropriate to focus on the reading of canonical texts, or reading in distant locales or long-ago times. The danger that this outside reviewer correctly hinted at was that the focus of this particular volume might obscure other areas that demand the same kind of critical attention. Several such lacunae can be identified briefly. The first, as just suggested, is precisely reading as a generalized technology within the academic world (not just in classroom settings). A second is the current

crisis in the teaching of mundane reading skills not only on Indian reservations, but in schools that badly serve millions of immigrant children and
children in poor neighborhoods throughout the United States—children
who may never have the opportunity to learn who the Anglo-Saxons were
or where Zaire is. Finally we should be aware of the important way in
which "reading" is also an unreflective, tactile, and not only cognitive response to the presence of all sorts of fragmentary, conventionalized, or tele-
graphic texts within our everyday world: "'Not what the moving red neon
sign says—but the fiery pool reflecting it in the asphalt'" (Benjamin
1978:85–86, quoted in Taussig 1991:151). As Michael Taussig claims, this
image should make us more aware that when we devote so much effort to
historicizing "reading" we not only demystify that rubric; we reinforce it
as well.

For all these reasons, I hope that these essays and the questions they en-
gender will be read, talked about, and written about not as "definitive" but
as challenges to the still-prevalent notion that there is a bifurcation, analogous to that between orality and literacy, between the real world and the
world of scholarship. Perhaps this notion is a heritage of the monastic conception in which, as Long writes, "the scholar-anchorite is allowed at most
a distant view of the sensuous delights of earthly intercourse." Yet even
where it *is* grounded in an explicit ethos of renunciation, scholarship, like
speaking and listening, like reading and writing, is a way of being in the
world. Scholarship, like language, is inseparable from both dialogue and
domination, and most often contains an admixture of the two. Can the
ethnography of reading, as a reflexive stance and as a positive rubric, prove
a rewarding tool for the detection of domination and the enhancement of
dialogue? These essays suggest that it can and will.

NOTE

1. Perhaps because his theoretical overview is limited to work by anthropologists, Fabian does not cite Derrida's *Writing and Difference* (1976), which is certainly
an important source for this reexamination of the way orality and literacy "con-
taminate" each other.

REFERENCES

Bauman, Richard, and Joel Sherzer, eds.
    1989   *Explorations in the Ethnography of Speaking*. 2d ed. New York: Cam-
    [1974]   bridge University Press.
Benjamin, Walter
    1978   "On the Mimetic Faculty." In *Reflections*, pp. 333–336. New York:
    [1934]   Harcourt, Brace, Jovanovich.

Bleich, David
   1988   *The Double Perspective: Language, Literacy, and Social Relations*. New York: Oxford University Press.
Boyarin, Jonathan
   1991   "Jewish Ethnography and the Question of the Book." *Anthropological Quarterly* 64:14–29.
Clifford, James, and George Marcus, eds.
   1986   *Writing Culture: The Poetics and Politics of Ethnography*. Berkeley: University of California Press.
Derrida, Jacques
   1976   *Of Grammatology*. Baltimore: Johns Hopkins University Press.
Fabian, Johannes
   1990   "Presence and Representation: The Other in Anthropological Writing." *Critical Inquiry* 16:753–772.
Fish, Stanley
   1989   "Being Interdisciplinary Is So Very Hard to Do." *Profession '89* 15:22.
Goody, Jack, et al.
   1988   "Selections from the Symposium on 'Literacy, Reading, and Power,' Whitney Humanities Center, November 14, 1987." *Yale Journal of Criticism* 2:193–232.
Taussig, Michael
   1991   "Tactility and Distraction." *Cultural Anthropology* 6:147–153.

TWO

Placing Reading:
Ancient Israel and Medieval Europe

Daniel Boyarin

Reading for pleasure is an extraordinary activity. The black squiggles on the white page are still as the grave, colorless as the moonlit desert; but they give the skilled reader a pleasure as acute as the touch of a loved body.

—NELL, *LOST IN A BOOK*

INTRODUCTION

Robert Alter's book, *The Pleasures of Reading in an Ideological Age* is a vigorous description of (and defense of) the European practice of reading literature for pleasure. I hasten to add that this "pleasure" does not mean a hedonistic experience, but rather one of affective identification with the characters, an experience understood in our culture to be gratifying, but nonetheless edifying and improving of the reader. Alter identifies several of the distinctive features of this practice: "Very few people will take the trouble to read a novel or story unless they can somehow 'identify' with the characters, live with them inwardly as though they were real at least for the duration of the reading" (Alter 1989:49). If we pay close attention to this statement, we will see that it conjures up several features of our reading practice. It assumes that reading is a voluntary act; people can choose to do it or not (Nell 1988:2). Accordingly, it must cause some kind of pleasure to the reader or he or she will abandon the activity (Nell 1988:8–9). Second, the pleasure is produced by an affective identification between the reader and the characters in the story, a sympathy between the real reader and imaginary people and their imaginary adventures (Nell 1988:39). Third, at least ideally, the pleasure of this identification is produced when the reader is in private and can "forget" reality in the illusion of the reality of the characters and their story.[1]

   "Reading" as spoken of and described in the Bible has none of these features. The Torah names the function of its reading as a speech act. It declares of itself that its intention is, "it shall be with him, and he shall read in it every day of his life in order that he will learn to fear the Lord his God, to keep the words of this Torah and to perform the commandments" (Deut. 17:19). Reading is not a voluntary act, nor one that is supposed to produce pleasure. It is not an excitation of the emotions or sentiments but simply a demand that the reader fulfill the obligations that the read document contains. This is not a claim of lack of literary value and beauty in the biblical text. To our ears and eyes, the poetry of Jeremiah is full of such poetic value; nevertheless, it can hardly be said to have attempted to persuade or seduce its hearers with its poetry. There is nothing *dulce* in the *utile* of Jeremiah. It should be made absolutely clear that I am not invoking a positivistic content-form distinction; indeed, I am asserting that the very notion of form is a historicizable practice and not a given of language.[2]

In an extraordinarily suggestive recent interview, the French Jewish poet and theoretician, Henri Meschonnic spoke about the biblical term "Miqra," the word that best translates the English word "reading." Meschonnic's central claim is that reading means something entirely different in biblical Hebrew because the written text is always read orally:

> Keeping the tie between writing and reading is in the biblical name of *Mikra* itself. In a manner very characteristic of our European languages, the biblical corpus is called *Writing*. . . . I think that to say *Writing*—holy Writing, Writings, from *Scriptura* onward—makes the texts thus named enter culturally into a field radically different from the Hebraic, Jewish field, in the sense that to say *Writing* or *Scriptura* is to conceive fully an opposition, finally, of the subject and the social, of writing and reading, of the act and the word. . . . In the Hebraic field it is completely otherwise: the very term *Mikra*, which designates the biblical corpus, etymologically and functionally at the same time, signifies *reading*—not reading as we speak of reading by contrast to writing. *Mikra* assumes the gathering during which one reads or has read the texts in question, and since this reading is done out loud, the notion conjoins, indissolubly to my understanding, orality and collectivity in reading. (Meschonnic 1988:454)

There is great insight in Meschonnic's remarks. However, since Meschonnic's claim that *Scriptura* is unknown in Hebrew is exaggerated—we do find, after all "kithvei haqqodesh" (Holy Scripture) as a title for the Bible—the relevant distinction seems to be not the designation of the Bible as the Writing or the Reading, but the fact that the word "reading" means, as well, the Bible. In other words, the point is not to situate the text in Jewish culture in the metaphysics of the reading-writing opposition, but to situate reading in that culture in its sociocultural semantic field. "Reading," in ancient Jewish culture signifies an act which is oral, social, and collective, while in modern (and early-modern) Europe it signifies an act that belongs to a private or semiprivate social space.

By studying the structure of the semantic affinities and fields of the Hebrew words for "reading," I hope to show that they do not belong to the same lexical categorization of practices that reading does in modern European culture. However, that alone would leave my investigation open to the sort of theoretical questions posed by Keesing:

> To what extent are conventional metaphors, and the schemas they express, constitutive of our experience? Do varying schemas, whether of emotion, time, causality, social relationships, and so on, reflect contrasting modes of subjective experience, of thought and perception—or of simply different conventions for talking about the world, as creatures with our human brains and sensory equipment and bodies experience it? There is no simple answer. (Keesing 1987:386)

In order, therefore, to corroborate the findings from this semantic inquiry, I will analyze biblical narrative texts that describe scenes of reading; the descriptions of practice coincide with the semantics of the words involved. Then, I will interpret some European scenes of reading, which through contrast will point up how different "reading" is in the two cultural formations. In the last section of the paper, I will attempt to shed some light on an important critical debate vis-à-vis biblical narrative from the perspective developed in my main argument.

THE BIBLE: "READING" AS A SPEECH-ACT

A semantic analysis of the distribution of the root *qr'* in biblical Hebrew reveals the following points. The root encompasses a range of meanings including "to call," "to proclaim," "to summon or invite," and "to read." It will be immediately observed that the whole semantic field to which these glosses belong is that of speech acts and not of passive reception. And indeed, as I shall argue, "reading" in biblical Hebrew is a speech act. It nearly always means "to read aloud to someone," as confirmed by the complements "in the ears of PN"[3] or "before PN." In all of these cases the activity described is the reading of some kind of a message and its communication or proclamation to an audience. The following verses will point up the force of *qr'* in the Bible:[4]

1. "And the Lord *called out* to the Adam and said to him 'Where are you?'" (Genesis 3:9)
2. "And the angel of the Lord *called out* to him from the heaven and said, 'Abraham, Abraham.' And he said, 'Here I am.'" (Genesis 22:11)
3. "And now, *call out* in the ears of the People, and say, 'Whoever is afraid and terrified, let him sit and watch from the Mountain of Gilead!'" (Judges 7:3)
4. "And he took the Book of the Covenant, and he *read* it in the ears of the People, and they said, 'All that the Lord has spoken, we will do

and we will obey.' And Moses took the blood and sprinkled it on the People and said, 'This is the blood of the Covenant, which God has enacted with you with regard to all of these words.'" (Exodus 24:7)

5. "When all of Israel come to appear before the Lord, your God at the place which he shall choose, *read* this Torah in the presence of all of Israel, in their ears. Gather together the People, the men, the women and the children and the stranger within your gates, in order that they hear and in order that they learn and they fear the Lord your God and watch to perform all of the words of this Torah." (Deuteronomy 31:11)

6. "And you shall come and *read* out the Scroll which you have written in accord with my dictation." (Jeremiah 36:3)

We learn several things from this very partial list of verses with *qr'*. First of all, in every case, the usage indicates an oral act, an act of the speaking of language. Second, the usage of *qr'* when there is a written text present is virtually identical to that when there is no written text present. From the point of view of the semantic structure of Hebrew, this is not even polysemy, but simply the same meaning. Thus, comparing example 3 with 4 and 5, we are hard-pressed to find any reason from the Hebrew to translate the verb differently in the latter cases than in the former one. I think it might not be going too far, indeed, were we to translate "call out (or proclaim) this Torah"![5] The Rabbis seem, at any rate, to have understood this point well, for they commented on example 6, "Was Barukh used to speaking out in the presence of Jeremiah?"[6] Finally, all of these acts of speaking in which the verb *qr'* is used are immediately followed by the desired or actual result of the performance of the speech act in the performance of the listener. Looking into the semantic affinities of the root *qr'*, then, certainly seems to suggest that for the biblical culture, reading occupies a different place in the social world than it does for us, so different that it is nearly an entirely different practice.

When we begin to look at narrative scenes of reading—both prescriptive and descriptive—in the Bible, we will find the semantic analysis strengthened by the accounts of our informants, as it were.[7] In all of the Hebrew Bible, there is no unequivocal usage of *qr'* in the sense of "to read to oneself," no place where someone is described as silently (or even orally) consuming a text alone and/or without immediate public consequences.[8] Although in Deuteronomy 17:19, we are told that the king must write for himself a copy of Deuteronomy, and "it shall be with him, and he shall read in it every day of his life in order that he will learn to fear the Lord his God, to keep the words of this Torah and to perform the commandments," we can learn what this "reading" would have been like from the description of the first occasion in which a king "read" this scroll:

[8] And Hilqiahu the High Priest said to Shafan the Scribe: I have found a
Scroll of the Torah in the House of the Lord, and Hilqiahu gave the scroll to
Shafan and he read it. . . . [10] And Shafan the scribe told the king, saying:
Hilqiahu the Priest has given me a Scroll and Shafan read it before the king.
[11] And it happened that *when the king heard* the words of the Scroll of the
Torah, he rent his garments. [12] And the king commanded Hilqiahu the
Priest and 'Ahiqam the son of Shafan and 'Akbur the son of Mikiah and Sha-
fan the scribe and 'Asaya the king's servant, saying: [13] Go seek the Lord for
me and for the people and for all of Judea with regard to the words of the
Scroll which has been found, for the wrath of the Lord which has been kin-
dled against us is great, because our ancestors did not obey [lit. hear!] the
words of this Scroll to do all that is written for us. [14] And Hilqiahu the
Priest . . . went to Huldah the Prophetess . . . and she was sitting in Jerusalem
in Mishneh and they said to her. [15] And she said to them: Thus has the
Lord the God of Israel said, Go tell the man who sent you to me: [16] Thus
has the Lord said: I hereby bring evil to this place and upon its inhabitants—
all of the words of the Scroll *which the King of Judea has read*. (II Kings 22:8 ff.)

We can learn several things about the ethnography of reading in ancient
Israel from this scene of reading. This event is portrayed by the Bible as the
founding moment for the practice which Deuteronomy—the very Scroll
which was discovered in the Temple—prescribes, so we can take it as a
model for that practice. The scribe reads the Torah before the king and his
attendant councillors of various types, and then the king is declared to have
"read" the Scroll. According to Deuteronomy he is expected to respond to
its import immediately, and according to the Kings text, that is exactly
what happens. "Reading" is a proclamation, a declaration, and a summons.
Even though the original reading, that of the scribe itself, here described in
verse 8 seems to have been a silent reading, it is quite clear that it is preparatory for the real reading, that is, the public, oral proclamation and receipt
of the message that the Scroll contains.[9] Each of the readers has to act, and
the act of each is contingent on his social function: the scribe, having read,
must read to the King. The King, having read, must send men to seek the
Lord. As claimed by Meschonnic's text,[10] the noun form, "miqra" means
both the "reading" and the "Holy Assembly" at which the reading takes
place. Moreover, even this last sense of "miqra" has a double meaning,
because it refers to the summons to come to the convocation as well as
the calling out or reading that will take place there. The text, "Miqra"
is the place one is summoned to and the place that summons. To dramatize the difference in structure between that culture and ours, I would
claim that the field of our social practice which most nearly fits that of *qr'*
in the biblical culture would be "preaching" or even "adjuring" and *not*
"reading."[11] It is certainly significant that in English there is a synchronic semantic opposition between "reading" and "lection"—the reading

of the Bible in church or synagogue—, while in biblical usage, of course, no such opposition exists. Reading in that culture is a public, oral, and illocutionary speech-act, an act, moreover, which when successful always has perlocutionary effect. And this is the only type of reading of which the Bible knows. There simply is no other word in biblical Hebrew which conveys the sense of processing and receiving written language, and there are no scenes described in the text which indicate private reading.

The above scene of reading is doubled in the famous incident described in Jeremiah 36. Exactly one generation after the discovery and reading of Deuteronomy described in Kings, the king and the people have been backsliding. God commands Jeremiah to "take a scroll and write on it all of the words that I have spoken to you about Israel and Judea and all of the nations, since the day when I first spoke to you in the days of Josiah and until now. . . . Perhaps the House of Judea will hear of all of the evil which I intend to do unto them, and will repent each one from his evil ways, and I will forgive their sin and their transgression" (1–2). The prophet, of course, performs as commanded. He has his scribe Barukh write down all of the words in a book, which is then read before all of the people, before the king, the son of Josiah and all of his councillors, the sons of the very same officials described in the Kings story. The emphasis on citing the genealogies of the persons—note that in the Kings story the officials' genealogies are *not* given—seems intended to establish that this scene is a (reversed) antitype of the former one.[12] The reading of prophetic text, as that of the Torah, is expected to function as the speech-act of command, and its intended perlocutionary effect is obedience—as opposed, for example, to an illocutionary act of exhortation whose intended effect would be persuasion. In this case, however, the speech-act does not have the desired perlocutionary effect. The king defies the warning in the scroll that has been read to him. The experience is, however, so threatening that he has the scroll burnt bit by bit as it is read to somehow neutralize its power. Once again, we see, that even when disregarded, the act of reading is public, social and illocutionary, not private and subjective in nature:

> And it was in the fifth year of Yehoyakim, the son of Josiah, the king of Judea in the ninth month, they called [*qar'u*: Note that this is the same verb as the one used for the reading! The root is *qr'*.] a fast before the Lord, all of the people of Jerusalem and all of the people who come from the cities of Judea in Jerusalem. And Barukh read [*qara'*] in the book the words of Jeremiah in the temple in the office of Gemaryahu, the son of Shafan the scribe, in the upper court, near the entrance to the gate of the new House of the Lord, *in the hearing of all of the People.* (9–11)

After this reading, the text is brought before the king and all of the rest of his councillors, once more identified as the sons of the very ones who heard the first reading of Deuteronomy as above. When the scroll is read before them, "When they heard these words, each man was very afraid, and they said, *we will tell the king, all of these words.* And they asked Barukh, saying, 'tell us, how did you write all of these words from his mouth?' And Barukh said to them, 'He called-out [*qara'!*] all of the words, and I write them on this scroll'" (16–18). The same root is used to signify the calling of the fast which is the setting for the reading, Jeremiah's oral declamation of his prophecy, and the scribe's reading out of that prophecy to its destinators.

> And the king sent Yehudi to take the scroll and he took it from the office of Elishama the scribe and Yehudi *read it in the ears of the king and in the ears of all of the princes who serve the king.* And the king was sitting in his winter house in the ninth month and the fire-place was burning before him. And it was, that as Yehudi read three or four columns he ripped them with a razor and threw them into the fire that was in the fire-place until the entire scroll was consumed in the fire on the fire-place. And the king and all of his servants who heard these words were not frightened and did not rend their garments. (21–25)

In its very description of the *failure* of the speech-act and in its explicit contrast between this event and its type in the previous generation, we have further evidence for how "reading" was conceived as a practice in the biblical culture. We see clearly that it was a social and public practice, more akin to a court's sentence than to anything like the practice of private, recreative self improvement and ethical growth that we conceive it to be. The concept of a silent and private reading and that of the aesthetic pleasure of being taken up in an imaginative world (Alter 1989:49), even only for a moment, is simply excluded from possibility both by the semantic structure of the language and by the actually described practices of reading in the text.

"READING" WITH THE RABBIS

When we turn to rabbinic literature, the texts of the Talmud and midrash, we find that the situation is somewhat more complicated, but still much the same picture will emerge. There are more relevant terms in this linguistic field. In addition to *qr'*, also *drsh*, *grs*, and *'yn* belong to the semantic field, which can be generally characterized as the processing of written language. The last two can be dealt with very briefly, for neither of them have anything to do with interpreting the marks on the page as text or discourse, *grs* meaning to repeat over and over again and thereby memorize, while *'yn* denotes merely the physical process of training one's eyes on the writing. Thus, one who translates the Torah in the synagogue is required not to *'yn* in the Torah, because the onlookers might err and think that his translation is actually written there.

Beginning once again with *qr'*, we find that in addition to the biblical usages of "to call, to invite, to summons," it has several senses relating to the processing of texts in the Hebrew of the rabbinic period. The first is, as in biblical Hebrew, to read scriptures aloud in a communal, ritual setting. The sememe of "aloud" is attested in the contrast between what is written and what is read, as in the type of interpretation called "al tiqre," that is, do not read what is written but read (pronounce) it differently, or in the Massoretic distinction between the "kᵉthiv" and the "qᵉre," that is the "written and the read." Although certain words are written in the text, one is commanded to "read" them differently. Thus, for example, everywhere that the Holy Name of God [the Tetragrammaton] is written, we read "The Lord." Since this is not an injunction to emend the text, "qᵉre" here cannot mean that which is read in our sense of "to read," for to read something other than what is written is an oxymoron in our culture. It is only because reading means oral recitation of the text that this distinction between the written and the read can mean anything at all. *qr'*, in this sense, is typically used for the public, ritual reading of a portion of the Torah at every synagogue service.

The second sense of *qr'* in rabbinic Hebrew is to perform certain biblically ordained rituals which involve the recitation of passages from the Torah, once again out loud. Thus the daily recitation of "Hear O Israel, the Lord our God, the Lord is one," is designated "reading the Hear O Israel." The third sense attested for this root in rabbinic Hebrew is to study scripture. Even in this last sense, the verb does not cover the ground of our "to read," because a different root is used for the study of Mishna, as we clearly see in the following text: "And Rabbi Shefatia said that Rabbi Yohanan said, 'Anyone who *reads* Bible [qore'] without a melody or repeats Mishna [shone] without a song, of him Scripture says, *And also I have given them bitter laws'* (Ezekiel 20:25) ['B *Megillah* 32a]." The semantic dominant of *qore'* here is not reception of a text, but participation in the religious act of studying scripture. Indeed, to this day, the study of religious texts in traditional Jewish societies is typically carried out in pairs called *"hevrutot"* or in small study conventicles[13] and the term "reading the Talmud" simply does not exist in any Jewish language, while "reading the Bible" still exclusively means reading it out loud in the ritual setting. One could fairly say that "reading" in the European sense just does not exist in that traditional culture.

If we attempt a sememic analysis of all of these usages of *qr'* in this state of the language then, we notice that:

1. They all belong to the field of religious practice.
2. Most of them, indeed, belong to the semantic field and the social sphere of prayer.

3. They are all activities carried out in public places.
4. They are all speech-acts, not only performed out loud, but having some illocutionary; or perlocutionary force.[14]

The second important root for us to consider in the context of rabbinic Hebrew is *drsh*, the verbal root from which "midrash" is derived. However we characterize that special style of interpretation, what it does is interpret narrative texts, and therefore is close to what we call "reading." In this context what is important for us is, however, not what kind of reading it is in the sense of how it interprets texts, but rather what kind of social practice it is in the sense of what social settings it takes place in. Again we will find that the social setting of *drsh* is public and religious exclusively.

The two situations in which we find the practice of *drsh* are the study house, called the House of Midrash and the synagogue. In the first situation, we truly have an activity that seems closest to what we mean by "reading a text," that is perusing it carefully and trying to make sense of its various linguistic levels. However, the project is undertaken always as part of a dialogical encounter. Thus, a typical situation involves a claim made by a given Rabbi, which is challenged by his fellows, and to which he answers, "I am reading [doresh] a verse from the Torah."[15]

The second setting of *drsh* simply involves what we would call "lecturing" or, once again, "preaching." The rabbi stands in front of a congregation and interprets for them the lection of the day with a view, of course, that they assimilate the messages intended and act on them. Thus there are subjects about which one is enjoined not to *drsh* at all. Again the contrast between *drsh* and "reading" can be sharpened by pointing out that while "reading" is typically understood as consumption (except in very special institutional settings like MLA meetings), *drsh* is *always* production of text. Clearly, *drsh* also, while covering some of the ground of "to read" does not provide a semantic fit.

Summing up the results of this brief semantic analysis, we can conclude that the structure of the semantic field which includes the practices analogous to what we call "reading" was entirely different in the Hebrew of the biblical and talmudic periods. In this light, there was simply no word in that language at all which meant what we mean by "reading a book," that is, the essentially private, individual consumption of narrative with the effect of and for the purpose of "pleasure."

EUROPE: READING IN THE SOCIAL SPACE OF THE EROTIC

Reading in the Bible and Talmud occupied the public social spaces of the forum, the synagogue, the House of Study, and the court. In contrast, there

are two privileged social sites for the practice of reading in Europe in Late
Antiquity, the Middle Ages, and the Early Modern period: the study and
the bedroom. Horace, in a famous and much discussed passage, refers
already to "reading and writing which I like to do in silence" (*Sat.* 1.6:122–
3). The silent and private study of a sophisticated Christian like Ambrose
also belongs to the tradition of studious, private reading.[16] Monastic reading of saints' lives grows out of this tradition as well.[17] This sort of private
reading, whose architectural trajectory takes it from the monk's cell to the
scholar's study has a powerful ascetic element.

More revealing for our purposes here is the pervasive association of reading in the West with the private social spaces and meanings of the erotic. In
order to evoke this moment of Western culture, I now will take a lightning
tour of several of the most privileged scenes of reading in our European
tradition. First, of course, is Augustine for any inquiry into European reading. Augustine is describing his early education and remarks, "Better indeed, because more certain, were those first studies by which there was
formed and is formed in me what I still possess, the ability to read what I
find written down and to write what I want to, than the later studies where
in *I was required to learn by heart I know not how many of Aeneas's wanderings,
although forgetful of my own, and to weep over Dido's death,* because she killed
herself for love, when all the while amid such things, dying to you, O God
my life, I most wretchedly bore myself about with dry eyes"[18] (Augustine
1960:56 [emphasis added]). Now, on the one hand, it is quite clear that this
text does not record an experience of the practice of reading for pleasure
that our culture knows. Augustine is *required* to do these things, including
weeping (apparently in the classroom) for Dido. One suspects, as have earlier readers of Augustine, that it was at least as much Dido's representation
of Africa as her dying for love that produced this school requirement to
weep over her fate (Brown 1969:23). Be that as it may, there can be very
little doubt that Augustine's story is one of the major sources of the practice
of affective identification, and particularly affective identification with a
female character, which is so emblematic of our reading practice. It is
important to note as well that Augustine is drawing an implied contrast
between the perverted ludic reading of his youthful education and the
converted reading of his later life, between the weeping for Dido and the response to *tolle, lege.*[19]

It seems to me that it is not overinterpretation to see this affective
identification as a development out of the cathartic identification with the
characters which was earlier the mark of the tragic theater, and indeed
Augustine's description of theater-going is not altogether different from
his description of reading the *Aeneid* in school (Augustine 1960:78).[20]
This interpretation is supported as well by explicit notations in Aristotle
himself:

> In the next place, [tragedy is in fact the better form] because it has everything
> that epic poetry has, and has in addition an element of no small importance
> in its music, which intensifies our pleasure in the highest degree, then also
> it has the advantage of vividness *both when read and when acted. (Poetics* 26,
> Aristotle 1982:78, emphasis mine)

It is, moreover, Aristotle as well who is among the first who speak explicitly
of "pleasure" as the telos of literature (*Poetics* 4, Aristotle 1982:47). We can
locate, then, one historical source of "reading" in the pleasurable catharsis
of ancient theater as theorized by Aristotle in the *Poetics*. However, we have
not yet located the source of the strong association of reading pleasure and
erotic experience in our culture.

A vital necessity for this move to take place is the transferral of reading
from public to private spaces. Thus with regard to one of the poetic genres
of the Middle Ages a recent scholar remarks:

> Despite its high degree of self-reflectiveness, the *canso* remained public in that
> it was performed. Hermeticism for the troubadors was not possible in the
> same way as it was for, say, Mallarmé. A modern poet can occasion a private,
> silent confrontation between himself and his reader through letters on a
> printed page. But the troubadors worked within a tradition that was largely
> oral. The *cansos* which they composed were destined to be sung by a *jongleur*
> before a number of people. There was, then, an unavoidable tension between
> the private realm created by the song and the public setting in which it had to
> be verbalized. One way in which the troubadors reduced this tension was to
> use *senhals*, or pseudonyms. In giving secret names to the *personae* of the *canso*,
> the poet discouraged connections between the men and women mentioned in
> his song and those assembled in the audience. (Poe 1984:15)

It follows that in order for such connections to be promoted by a reading
practice and not discouraged by it, a private setting (not necessarily
individual—"alone together" works fine) had to be invented for reading.
One very important viaduct of this transition would seem to be the *Vidas* of
the Provençal troubadours. These were prose biographies of the troubadors
who composed the *cansos*. They seem to have developed when the *cansos* became collected into volumes called *chansonniers*, which from the thirteenth
century were produced for private reading (Schutz 1939). They thus serve
as a double transitional moment in the "erotic" formation of European
reading, as a transition from oral, public to written, private and as a transition from poetry to prose as well. We have here a specific site of origin for
an erotic connection between the book, its author, its protagonist and the
reader, an eroticized connection which is central to our notion of ludic reading. As a modern commentator on reading for pleasure evokes it, "Reading
for pleasure is an extraordinary activity. The black squiggles on the white
page are still as the grave, colorless as the moonlit desert; but they give the

skilled reader a pleasure as acute as the touch of a loved body" (Nell
1988:1). This is, in itself, an extraordinary comment, if only for the way
that it testifies to how naturalized the sense of reading as erotic experience
has become in our culture.[21]

Another crucial moment in the history of European reading is the story
of Hèloïse and Abelard, which marks the site of a cross or a juncture between the two traditions of reading that Augustine represents. On the one
hand the reading of this couple belonged to the tradition of reading as
monastic study, but on the other hand it quite obviously activates the
Augustinian *Aeneid* topos of reading as erotic experience as well. Indeed
Abelard in his autobiographical *Historia calamitum*, admits almost to a
willful manipulation of these commonplaces (Abelard 1974:66–67). This
hybridization (or contamination) will find its fullest flowering, however, in
Dante.

Perhaps the most famous "scene of reading" in European literature, and
a crucial one for the association of reading with erotic experience, is the
narrative of Paolo and Francesca in *Inferno*, Canto v (127 ff.). The text both
alludes to earlier eroticized scenes of reading, Augustine and Dido,[22] and
Hèloïse and Abelard (Dronke 1975), and forms a distillation of the history
of European reading. Encountering the pair, Dante (the pilgrim narrator) is
told:

> One day, for pastime, we read of Lancelot, how love constrained him; we
> were alone, suspecting nothing.[23] Several times that reading urged our eyes to
> meet and took the color from our faces, but one moment alone it was that
> overcame us. When we read how the longed-for smile was kissed by so great
> a lover, this one, who never shall be parted from me, kissed my mouth all
> trembling. A Gallehault was the book and he who wrote it; that day we read
> no farther in it.
>
> While the one spirit said this, the other wept, so that for pity I swooned, as
> if in death, and fell as a dead body falls. (Dante Alighieri 1970:55–56)

This is a text which explicitly thematizes a scene of reading for private ["we
were alone"] pleasure ["to pass the time away"], but as we can easily see, it
renders precisely that practice thoroughly problematic as well.

The crux of the problem, and indeed of the text, is Francesca's charge
"Galeotto fu 'l libro e chi lo scrisse." How can the author and his book be
accused of having caused the downfall of Paolo and Francesca? One possibility would be to understand Dante as indicting a certain type of literature
as socially dangerous, much as Flaubert would do centuries later. However,
this reading seems excluded by the fact that Dante in other places indicates
approval of the Romances, precisely the texts that the couple were reading
here.[24] How can its author, then, be referred to as a Galehot? Put somewhat differently, although the situation of these illicit lovers is comparable

(and has intertextual connections) with the narrative of Hèloïse and Abelard in the *Roman de la Rose* (Dronke 1975:131–135), no one to my knowledge has accused the book that they were *studying* or its author of leading to the downfall of *that* couple. This innovation is Dante's, and it is a crux. The question, of course, is to what extent is Francesca's claim that she was seduced by a book to be relied upon. Some critics [Dronke refers to them as the "hawks"] have understood that Dante is merely indicating here Francesca's Eve-like dissembling, an attempt to mislead the pilgrim and justify herself, reading his text as referring to a topos of feminine misreading (see Musa in Dante Alighieri 1984:119 and see Hatcher and Musa [1968:107–108]). However, the swoon of pity on the part of the Pilgrim militates against this reading. Although the pilgrim pities other sinners (and indeed expresses pity for Paolo and Francesca's fate even before hearing their story), in all the *Inferno* there is no such extravagant expression of identification with the plight of the condemned as here. His pity can only have been so aroused, I would argue, if he accepted (at least in part) Francesca's argument that the book and its pious author were in fact Panders and she and Paolo thus innocents.[25]

How then can the book and its author be accused of pandering? The question is even stronger according to the view of some Dantean commentators that the book that Paolo and Francesca were reading was the Cistercian[26] prose *Lancelot*, an anti-Romance, one in which the love of Lancelot and Guinivere is presented grotesquely (Hatcher and Musa 1968: 108) and with an awful end. On that interpretation, the trouble that Paolo and Francesca got themselves into was not at all because they were reading the wrong texts. Susan Noakes is one of the adherents of this interpretation. She concludes, "In short, the prose *Lancelot* cited by Dante had transformed the Lancelot story (already condemned by the Papacy a hundred years before the *Commedia* was written) into a religious attack on chivalrous values, showing that adulterous love brings only unhappiness. Paolo and Francesca are thus depicted as reading a text designed expressly to keep potential adulterers out of Hell" (Noakes 1988:44). Noakes, in contrast to Musa, doesn't read this as dissembling on Francesca's part so much as denial and lack of insight, " 'Galeotto fu 'l libro e chi lo scrisse,' expresses an appalling blindness that she has carried with her into Hell, for it is she and Paolo (rather than a textual or authorial panderer) who have undone themselves by misreading a work written to edify them" (Noakes 1988:46). The pilgrim faints, on this account, in terror at the "evidence of readerly blindness." Both of these exegeses have in common that the author is *wrongly* accused of pandering.

I would like to suggest a different interpretation, namely that even if the text that Paolo and Francesca were reading was the pious prose Lancelot (and all the more so if they were reading Chretien), the text and its author can be *justly* accused by Dante of causing the evil that befell Paolo and Francesca, because of the very scene of reading which it presupposes—even against its overt intentions. Francesca emphasizes that the reading was private and "to pass the time away."[27] I speculate, therefore, that notwithstanding the pious contents of a text, Dante is suggesting that the very practice of reading for pleasure can be morally dangerous.[28] This interpretation is supported by the swoon of the pilgrim as a sign of moral identification between him, Paolo, and Francesca. How so? The privacy and intimacy of the very act of reading of the anti-Romance covertly supports the practices of Romance, even as it overtly attacks them. Put another way, the way that the text wishes to achieve its effects is by stimulating and exciting the reader, and that is indeed what it did. Because the text is intended to seduce the reader to the moral life, it necessarily excites him or her, and the effect that it has willy-nilly is a seduction.[29] The similarity between the pragmatics of reading the Romance and that of the anti-Romance is stronger than the oppositions of their semantics and sufficient, indeed, for the text and its author to be condemned as panderers.

As Noakes argues, Dante's narrative can be understood on the background of the *newly emerged practice of private reading for pleasure* (Noakes 1988:42). This historical shift has been best documented by Paul Saenger (1982), who concludes most relevantly for us, "the habit of private silent reading among laymen seems to have begun at least a half-century earlier in Italy than in northern Europe. Dante's *Inferno* and *Paradiso* were intended to be held under the eyes of the lay reader"* (Saenger 1982:410). Thus if one of the intertexts of Canto v is assuredly the tale of Héloïse, another is such texts as Guillaume de Saint Thierry's exhortation against silent (and thus, private) reading even of scripture (Saenger 1982:390). On this view, then, Dante announces here precisely the blurring of the two moments of private reading, the ascetic and the erotic, because of the social practice and space which they share. The moment of this blurring is most clearly marked, I suggest, by "that day we read no farther in it," almost surely an echo of Augustine's "I had no wish to read further" at the climax of his conversion by the book (Confessions viii:12). The cell can be a bedroom, and holy literature read in a *boudoir* can be erotic. Indeed, I would argue that the very ambiguity of the nature of the text that the lovers are reading is a thematization of the perceived moral ambiguity of "reading for pleasure."[30] Dante is aware that this practice is not necessarily conducive to uplifting and moral behavior on the part of its practitioners no matter what they read. It is, after all, Francesca's identification of herself with the

---

*Erich Auerbach, *Literary Language and its Public in Late Latin Antiquity and in the Middle Ages*, trans. R. Manheim (London 1965) 299–302. [Note in Saenger's text—Ed.]

heroine that got her into all that trouble, as pointed out by Mazzotta (1979:169). "The new privacy afforded by silent reading had dramatic and not entirely positive effects on lay spirituality. Private reading stimulated a revival of the ancient genre of erotic art" (Saenger 1982:412). Note that this will be the case whatever Paolo and Francesca were reading, for even while the prose *Lancelot* thematically exhorts against the values and practices of Romance, *a fortiori* of erotic literature, as act of communication it works by indirection—seduction. The theory of *dulce et utile* is explicit in medieval poetics, including, of course, Dante's. The pilgrim, Dante, is panicked by the thought that given the reading practices of his time and place the same accusation might be leveled against him, and indeed, he was right, for the bitter, almost Sartrean irony of "as you see, he never leaves my side" has actually often been read by Romantic readers, themselves half in love with Francesca, as love conquering hell! (Dronke 1975:127, see Hatcher and Musa 1968:107).[31] This mistake too was, of course, only possible because of the reading practices of our Romantic culture, and indeed of Dante's. Well might the pilgrim faint: If even so pious an author as the Cistercian who composed the prose *Lancelot* can be rightfully accused of being a Galleoto, what will be said of his intentions and his text which also will be read in such a culture?[32] Dante's text, then, can be said to be a historical sign of the rise of reading as a practice in the modern sense in the centuries just before his writing.

A final step in the distancing of reading from public, ritualistic, and con-trolled space to private, ludic, eroticized space is the development of the practice of reading in bed. Two of Chaucer's scenes of reading are very much to the point here. The first is his *The Book of the Duchess*, which both opens and closes with the insomniac protagonist reading in bed and pro-ceeds to a romantic dream (Chaucer 1986) and see Boitani (1982:140–149). The other is, of course, *The Parliament of Fowls*, once again the dream of a reader who after reading in bed falls asleep and proceeds to a dream whose thematics are explicitly concerned with the erotic (Boitani 1982:169–183). Nell documents convincingly how preeminent the bed is as a privileged site for ludic reading even now (Nell 1988:250).[33] Carrying out the sort of ethnographic characterization that I did for the Bible and Talmud suggests that here reading occupies a sociocultural space entirely different from the one that it did in the biblical and rabbinic culture. Rather than being speech-act, public, and liturgical in nature, reading is passive, private or semi-private, and belonging to the sphere of leisure and pleasure.

"READING," "HISTORIOGRAPHY" AND "THE BIBLE AS LITERATURE"

This analysis of the pragmatics of reading in Ancient Hebrew may help us get a clearer take on a recent debate in biblical hermeneutics. An important new development in the interpretation of the Bible is the application of literary canons of reading to its prose narrative. Two of the most subtle and skillful of practitioners of this criticism are surely Robert Alter (1981) and Meir Sternberg (1985). Both of them treat the art of biblical prose, showing through myriad examples how we can derive great aesthetic pleasure from an appreciation of such devices of linguistic art as repetition, variation, echoing, irony, and the like. The question at hand is, what historically justifies such a practice? Or indeed, is the practice justified? Some have argued, after all, that in truth it is not, because it is in the very nature of the biblical discourse to battle against such "trivialities" as aesthetics and literary art. To be sure, both Alter and Sternberg are sensitive to the theoretical problems that their critical/hermeneutic practice raise. I, for one, am convinced that their reading practice is justified by the profound effect that it has on the richness of our perception of the biblical text.[34] While I find their *practice* telling, however, I find its theoretical grounding in both of their works much less so for reasons that I will now adduce. That is to say, using a talmudic apophtegm: I am in accord with their practice but not their theory. I wish, nonetheless, to suggest that the practice of reading the Bible *as literature* (I use this disdained terminology advisedly—see below) can be reestablished on another theoretical footing, provided in part by the ethnography of reading approach here adumbrated.

I will begin by setting out the terms of the issue as Alter and Sternberg themselves laid it out. In his comprehensive work on biblical narrative, Alter has defended the thesis that, "prose fiction is the best general rubric for describing biblical narrative" (1981:24). Among the criteria that Alter applied are the signs of intervention on the part of the narrator in the presentation of the story, namely, the conventionality of narrated events and other signs of verbal artistry. In a recent paper Alter (1992), has further elaborated and exemplified his thesis. He argues from three "test-cases" (1992:5) that, "If virtually every utterance of biblical narrative points toward the imperative concerns of covenant faith, it is also demonstrably evident that virtually every utterance of biblical narrative reveals the presence of writers who relished the words and the materials of storytelling with which they worked, who delighted, because after all they were writers, in pleasing cadences and surprising deflections of syntax, in complex echoing effects among words, in the kind of speech they could fashion for the characters and how the self-same words could be ingeniously transformed as they were passed from narrator to character or from one character to another" (Alter 1992:9–10). I find Alter's identifications of "pleasing cadences" and all the rest persuasive, but here's also the rub.

Sternberg disagrees strongly with Alter's description of biblical narrative, claiming that it must be understood as historiography. What is relevant in the distinction between historiography and fiction is the truth claims which the text makes as a function of its discourse—certainly not

our judgment of those truth claims, nor our judgment of the plausibility of
the evaluation of the events which the text presents (Sternberg 1985:33–
34). Sternberg argues that the fact that the "narrative . . . illegitimates an
thought of fictionality on pain of excommunication," makes it impossible
for us to understand it as anything but historiography. It seems to me
doubtless as well that Sternberg has also put his finger on something important here. Our understanding of biblical narrative must at some level take
into account the evidence that many people, including very likely its authors and first audiences did believe in its literal truth. I believe that the
"ethnography of reading" approach adumbrated in this paper will give us a
way out of the dilemma thus created by showing that the terms of the debate should be recast. Rather than talking about what biblical narrative is
or is not, we should be talking about strategies and pragmatics of reading in
different cultural moments.

In a recent essay, I have argued against Sternberg's position that biblical narrative is historiography, to the effect that *since biblical narrative does not
generally verify its factual claims by referring to evidence, but in fact at nearly every
moment presents its data as that of an omniscient narrator*, from the point of view of
our own time and our conventions of writing-reading, it belongs to the
genre of fiction and not historiography (Boyarin 1990). Indeed Sternberg
reads the Bible in essentially the same way that Alter does, providing also
illuminating readings of verbal artistry. His critical practice thus shows that
the Bible's narrative reads like fiction. (The fact that much historiography
is written like fiction does not obscure this argument; when historiography
tells what goes on in the mind of a character, we read it as more or less
plausible historical fiction.) All of his comparisons to various discursive
strategies in texts closer to us in time and place are to fictional texts, and
this is not accidental. Sternberg complains against the terminology of reading "the Bible as literature" (or of "literary approach to the Bible"), unless
they are taken as shorthand for "reading the Bible as the literary text that it
is" (Sternberg 1985:3), but historiography is not the typical case of literary
text for our culture. Indeed, when we read Gibbon in a literary way, precisely what we are doing is reading historiography as literature. He suggests
that when we read the Bible we must suspend disbelief, but that also is
an argument for its fictional status—not historiographical! When we read
ancient historiography, we may enjoy its style and wit and be fascinated
to learn what people thought about the world once, but we do not ask
ourselves to suspend disbelief. Such suspension of disbelief is a practice
which belongs in our culture to the reading of fiction, not of historiography.
Indeed, the "suspension of disbelief" is one of the prime mechanisms of
"reading for pleasure." Since the major discursive gesture that Sternberg
finds, the omniscient narrator, and its concomitant requirement of the reader that she or he "believe" this narrator, belongs in our literary system ex-

clusively to fiction, I think that Alter is right when he asserts "prose fiction is the best general rubric for describing biblical narrative."

Here I would like to propose that there is a real contradiction or tension in the very practice of literary criticism of the Bible, which Sternberg senses and which produces his problematic. As convincing as Alter's readings are, they seem also to be missing something by referring to the texts as fiction. Sternberg is surely right about something here; after all we don't excommunicate people for not believing in the literal truth of fiction. Sternberg, in fact provides one argument which I take to be very similar to the one I am promulgating here when he says that the Bible "internalizes its own rules of communication, whereby the remembrance of the past devolves on the present and determines the future" (Sternberg 1985:31). However, this suggests exactly that my own discourse is prone to very much the same contradictions as his, for I seemingly assert at one and the same time with Alter that the Bible is prose fiction and with Sternberg that fiction (and indeed "literature") is an irrelevant concept for the language cum reconstructed culture of the Bible. If reading, as we know it, did not exist in the biblical culture, then certainly neither did "literature," *a fortiori* fiction! We seem, then, to be caught in an adamant aporia.

It seems to me that cognitive anthropology will offer us possible avenues of rescue from the horns of this dilemma. In recent years a great deal of very important theoretical and descriptive work has been done in cognitive anthropology. One important area of research in this branch of ethnography has been based traditionally on the study of semantic fields in various languages, with the understanding that they are informative of ways of world making of the respective cultures.[35] Before getting into the substantive argument, I think it is necessary to spend a little time assessing the current status of this method. Holland and Quinn have put the question in the following way:

> It has been colleagues from the more materialist traditions in anthropology, and indeed from some of the ideationalist traditions within the discipline as well, who have been at pains to point out the limitation of a research program for validating cultural models solely on the basis of linguistic behavior. These anthropologists observe that people do not always do what would seem to be entailed by the cultural beliefs they enunciate. . . . Do cultural models, they want to know, influence more than talk, and if so how? (Holland and Quinn 1987:5)

For the type of research engaged in here the question is even sharper, since we have virtually no access to the culture other than what people said. Can linguistic behavior teach us anything significant concerning behavior in cultures about which we know very little other than their written and material remains?[36] Do linguistic cultural models reveal anything more than the "talk" of the ancient culture?[37] Recent work suggests that they do, but we must seriously nuance and qualify what precisely it is that they reveal. As Holland and Quinn put it, "culturally shared knowledge is organized into prototypical event sequences enacted in simplified worlds. That much of such cultural knowledge is presumed by language use is as significant a realization to anthropologists as to linguists. For the latter, these cultural models promise the key to linguistic usage; *for the former, linguistic usage provides the best available data for reconstruction of cultural models*" (Holland and Quinn 1987:24, emphasis mine).

One way out of our aporia of biblical narrative which claims to be historiography but looks like fiction would be to regard this as a particular instance of a familiar ethnographic problem, one that could be defined as the gap between what a culture says about its practice and its observed practice. A classic instance of this in the literature is the "long-standing debate in social anthropology over the reported disparities between Nuer descriptions of their kinship system and Nuer kinship behavior 'on the ground'" (Holland and Quinn 1987:5–6). Now one way of resolving this debate in the literature is Holy's which Holland and Quinn discuss. He argues for a solution based on Caws's two types of native or folk models, "representational" and "operational." "The former are indigenous models of their world that people can more or less articulate; the latter are indigenous models that guide behavior in given situations and that tend to be out of awareness. Representational models, from this view, are not necessarily operational nor are the latter necessarily representational; thus inconsistencies between what people say and what they do need not be cause for puzzlement" (Holland and Quinn 1987:5–6). Following this reasoning, what we have in the case of biblical narrative is a similar situation where the Bible's representational models (what they say) deny both at levels of semantic organization and of explicit representation the existence of a category like fiction or indeed literary art while their operational models (what they do) certainly presuppose such categories. This is a formalizable way of talking about the distinction between explicit and implicit poetics in literary theory.

I would like to take this distinction a step further and suggest that we need to historicize the very opposition of fiction and historiography. My claim in brief is that it is from the point of view of *our own* practices of reading that biblical narrative reads as fiction. That does not imply, in any way, that for the biblical culture itself, fiction is a relevant category, nor, for that matter, need we assume that historiography is a relevant category for the biblical narrator. Indeed, I would argue that the whole theoretical debate between Alter and Sternberg is nonessential, precisely because we cannot assume an ahistorical organization of cultural productions into the genres familiar from our own. In this way I hope to account for the evident fact that the practices of both critics are virtually identical in principle. Both read the Bible *as* didactic fiction. There are other genres and possible organizations of textual cultures than history : : fiction. Just to take an obvious example, in many cultures myth makes truth claims every bit as serious as those of historiography in ours, and indeed, disbelief in myths might well lead to excommunication or worse in some cultures, but that certainly does not define them as historiography.[38] On the other hand, while myths are emphatically not fictions, certainly not madeup narratives for the production of pleasure, for us, the practices of reading fiction may be the only ones available for the reading of myths. We must accordingly make a sharp distinction between reading strategies and practices which we adopt vis-à-vis given texts from other cultures and the assumption that the rules and practices of those cultures were the same as ours. The evidence cited above suggests, therefore, that whatever pleasure biblical narrative may produce for us, when we read it for the aesthetic values that we find in it, producing pleasure was the farthest thing from the minds of the authors of that narrative.

This point can be honed by examining another claim of Alter's.

One should add that the very act of writing in one respect makes the writer more craftsman than communicator, for he is directed in the first instance not to his—necessarily, eventual—audience but to the medium of words, which has its own intricate allure, and which he works and reworks as a sculptor models his clay, to produce the pleasing curve, the intriguing texture, the satisfying symmetry. (Alter 1989:79)

I dare suspect that Jeremiah would have been horrified at such a description of his practice, however much we may find "intriguing texture and satisfying symmetry," in his rhetoric. Communication and not craft was his primary (if not only) aim, and any craft involved was only to serve that aim. An analogy may be helpful here. We in Metropolis read the statuary of Others in accord with the practices of our culture as art. We find genuine aesthetic value in precisely "the pleasing curve, the intriguing texture, the satisfying symmetry" of what was for that Other perhaps a god— sometimes an icon and producer of terror—directed certainly in the first instance to its audience for its function and not at all to the medium or to the beauty that we legitimately, nevertheless, find there. Indeed, it is not uncommon that the very statues that we place in museums were in their original cultural contexts normally hidden entirely from sight! Thus, reading the Bible as fictional art may indeed be the only way appropriate or available for many of us to read it, without requiring us, however, to assign that meaning to it in its original cultural context or contexts.

As Sweetser (1987:49) has shown "fiction" in our culture is part of an intricately structured cultural model, in which such entities as jokes and white lies also have a place. What possible reason is there to assume that the model of this general area of culture in ancient Israel was anything like in ours? To be sure, cognitive anthropologists no longer assume radical discontinuity between human cultures in basics such as emotions, but in the details there certainly are significant differences (Keesing 1987:374, 386). Thus the Rabbis *do* have a category that means something like "fiction," that is, they have a term for narratives which are not referentially "true." The term is "parable," that is *"mashal."* The concept of true versus false stories was, therefore, part of their sociomental world. But let us just imagine how different "fiction" would feel if the only fiction we knew of were *romans à thèse,* "authoritarian fictions," in Susan Rubin Suleiman's phraseology!

Both Alter and Sternberg read biblical narrative appropriately for our cultural context as if it were fiction. That is the only way we can read texts (I can hear somebody saying, "What do you mean 'we', white man?') that tell us what went on in the hearts of men, women, and angels and report private conversations with all their psychological nuances. For the Talmud, however, it was precisely these features that "proved" Divine intervention in the authorship. I cannot, therefore, accept Sternberg's claim that the Bible is "not just an artful work; not a work marked by some aesthetic property; not a work resorting to so-called literary devices; not a work that the interpreter may choose (or refuse) to consider from a literary viewpoint or, in that unlovely piece of jargon, as literature; but a literary work" (Sternberg 1985:2). I believe that the semantic/ethnographic analysis performed here supports the view that reading and indeed literature are the historically generated practices of a particular culture, and not the one in which the Bible was produced. Indeed, Alter's, "prose fiction is the best general rubric for describing biblical narrative" is valid, if when he says, "for describing" he means, "for us in our culture, given our practice of 'reading', to describe." I suggest then that by engaging in literary reading, that constructed (but not less valuable for that) practice of European culture, that precisely what we are doing is *reading the Bible as literature.*

NOTES

This paper was originally delivered in earlier versions at a conference at Bar-Ilan University on the occasion of the retirement of Prof. Harold Fisch in November, 1989 and at the MLA session on the "Ethnography of Reading" in Washington, D.C. in December of that year and is being published in the volumes generated by both conferences. I wish to thank all of the respondents at those meetings as well as Robert Alter, Piero Boitani, Jonathan Boyarin, Joan Branham, Ken Frieden, Steven Fraade, Dell Hymes, Chana Kronfeld, Ellen Spolsky, Brian Stock, and an anonymous (and very nasty) reader for the University of California Press for their helpful comments. The section of European reading and the erotic was presented at a colloquium titled "Is Reading a Universal?" at the Townshend Center for the Humanities at Berkeley on November 13, 1990, and some important final revisions were incorporated in response to the discussion thereafter.

1. Alter emphasizes, of course, that a reader who is psychologically normal never really forgets that he or she is reading a fictional story. To imagine that anyone claims otherwise is to set up a straw man (Alter 1989:50).

2. Thus, for example, while modern critics discover exceedingly "artful" word-play in Jeremiah 36 (a text that I will be analyzing below), there is very little reason to suppose that the author/s of Jeremiah had any aesthetic (that is, ludic) intentions. The paronomasia serves not to delight and thus win over the hearer/reader but only to increase the effectivity of the speech-act, or, at any rate, this is a strong possibility. On the wordplay of Jeremiah 36, see now the paper of J. Andrew Dearman (1990). His paper was published too late to be fully integrated into my text, so the reader will find some overlap in the discussion of Jeremiah 36 below.

3. For non-Semitists let me explain that PN is a convention referring to unnamed persons; it stands for "personal name."

4. Emphasis is added in all translations from Hebrew throughout this chapter.

5. Dearman also translates Jeremiah 36 "proclaim the words of the scroll" (1990:405).

6. *Sifre Bamidbar* 52.

7. Robert Alter has argued (personal communication) that my "informants" are not clearly a random sample of the culture, as they are all centered around the Deuteronomistic school with its very heavily didactic tendency. He questions whether such documents as J and E would share D's concept of reading. However, since J and E do not seem to ever mention reading at all, it is hard to argue from silence. Moreover, I believe that there is other corroborating evidence for my analysis of reading in the Bible which is not from the Deuteronomists per se. See, for instance, the description of a scene of reading in *Nehemiah* 8, although it could be argued that this late text reflects the devolutionary influence of Deuteronomy, and that argument would have some merit. On the importance of the Deuteronomistic connections of Jeremiah 36, see now Dearman (1990:403–404) and passim and especially (420); and on the Nehemiah passage (409, n. 16). Moreover, we have not only evidence from "informants" but also the report of an ancient "ethnographer," Hecataeus:

> At all of the gatherings of the people, the High Priest explains the commandments of the Torah, and the people listen with such willingness that they immediately fall on their faces and bow to the High Priest who reads and expounds to them.

The caution remains, nevertheless, important. We have, at best, only partial data for any culture that we know only through literary remains, and allowance must be made, as sophisticated, recent critiques of ethnoscience teach us for variation, diachronic development (expressed as synchronic variation), ideological interests and cultural conflict (Keesing 1987:371 and especially 388: "Models are created for the folk as well as by them.").

8. There are, to be sure, cases in which the orality of the reading is not explicit. However, even in those cases we find that the act of reading is accompanied by perlocutionary force—that is, it demands an action in response. The following example will make this clear:

And the King of Aram said, "Go and I will send a scroll [*sefer*, the same word that refers to a scroll of the Torah, or the Book of the Covenant!] to the King of Israel," and
he went and he took with him ten talents of silver and six thousand golden coins and
ten suits of clothes. And he brought the scroll to the King of Israel which said, "And
now, with the coming of this scroll to you, I have sent to you Na'aman my servant.
Cure him of his leprosy!" And when the King of Israel *read* the scroll, he rent his
clothes, and said "Am I God that I can kill and revive? For this one has sent to me to
cure a man of leprosy, but indeed, he is seeking a cause against me." (II Kings 19:5–7)

Since there is no more reason to believe that this king was himself literate any more
than the king-protagonists of the texts that I will presently discuss, it is very probable that "when the king had read" means here "when the king had heard the reading of," just as it does explicitly in the next text cited in the body of the paper.

9. That is, *a perlocutionary effect*!

10. In that text, it is Alex Derczansky (Meschonnic 1988:454) who makes this
point explicitly, but it is already contained within Meschonnic's remarks. I think it
best to read that "round table" as a single dialogical text, a fiction with several
voices.

11. Dell Hymes's remarks: "Perhaps, in other words, *qr'* indicates a type of communicative event (a mode of communication, a way of 'speaking', using 'speaking'
figuratively, in the sense of my chapter in R. Bauman and J. Scherzer, *Explorations in
the Ethnography of Speaking* (Cambridge, 1974, 1989). A certain configuration, or set of
relations, among participants and text and channels" (letter to the author, Spring
1991).

Prof. Hymes's remarks seem right on the mark.

12. For a general literary comparison of the two chapters see Isbell 1978 and see
now Dearman (1990:409).

13. See Jonathan Boyarin 1991 for an ethnographic description of such a contemporary conventicle—not, to be sure, an entirely typical one, but then none is.

14. For an illuminating analysis of liturgy as a speech-act, whose perlocutionary
force is to convince of the "truth" of the unprovable, see Rappaport 1976.

15. Gerald Bruns is one of the few theorists who has connected the social situation of midrash, that is its dialogical setting, with its hermeneutic practice. He has
also clearly talked about how midrashic, "understanding always shows itself as
action in the world" (Bruns 1987:629–631). See also David Stern 1988, who has
addressed the social setting of midrash importantly.

16. See discussion in Knox (1968:423), however the Horatian text cited in
Hendrickson (1929:187) seems to contradict the interpretation that Horace enjoyed
silent reading. In any case, he does refer here to reading as a pleasure. Notice that
I am decidedly not claiming that "silent reading" was unknown or impossible in
the Ancient World. In spite of the celebrated astonishment of Augustine at finding
Ambrose reading silently, this might very well reflect just his backwater origins.
Moreover, the practice of "reading for pleasure" can be an oral one in which the
reader murmurs to himself or herself, and it is possible for readers to read certain
kinds of documents silently even when the general practice is for narrative to be
read publicly and orally. Knox makes it abundantly clear that reading silently was
certainly possible for the Ancients.

17. Private reading was developed especially among the Cistercians. See below
n. 26.

18. *Confessions*, Book 1, chap. 13. I am using the translation of John K. Ryan (Augustine 1960). There is another moment in this text which Jonathan Boyarin has called to my attention, namely the contrast between reading/writing and memorization with Augustine's valorization of the former over the latter.

19. This is one, then, of a series of binary oppositions which structure the *Confessions*, which are, of course, in that work set out temporally. See now the reading of Jill Robbins in her work (Robbins 1992), chap. 2. What Augustine figure as perversion and conversion remains a synchronic structure in European culture, just as do Vergil and the Bible.

20. Book 3, chap. 2.

21. There is a serious problem with Nell's book. From this formulation, it would seem that the reading practice that leads to this kind of erotic pleasure is a trained one, that is not a given of being human. This "skill" would seem to be supremely cultural, like the erotic arts of ancient Indian culture for example. However, it is clear from other places in the book that the skill involved is the purely technical one to "rapidly and effortlessly assimilate information from the printed page" (Nell 1988:7). This skill is more analogous to the ability to remove a partner's clothing than anything else. Now, I can testify from personal experience that while I believe that I can rapidly and effortlessly assimilate information from a printed page, I do not share the pleasure of ludic reading, so something else is clearly required. Not being able to partake of that erotic experience in reading fiction, I have a feeling sometimes of inadequacy that would lead me to seek a reading therapist, who would presumably provide me with a surrogate book. More seriously, the very cultural precariousness of ludic reading as a practice is attested to by many teachers, including, most eloquently, Robert Alter:

> Perfectly earnest, reasonably intelligent undergraduates, exposed for the first time to the fantastic proliferation of metaphor in Melville, the exquisite syntactic convolutions of the late Henry James, the sonorously extravagant paradoxes and the arcane terms in Faulkner, are often simply baffled as to why anyone should want to do such strange things with words, and to make life so difficult for a reader. (Alter 1989:78)

Complaints such as this, and they are legion, testify eloquently, sometimes against the manifest intention of their authors, with how much cultural effort is the practice of ludic reading constructed even today.

22. "Further, in both scenes [Augustine and Dido, Paolo and Francesca] the act of reading is disclosed as an erotic experience" (Mazzotta 1979:168).

23. Or "innocent of suspicion" (Musa).

24. For Dante's positive remarks on the Romances, see *Purgatorio* 25:118–119 and *De Vulgari Eloquentia* I,10:2. Prof. Boitani supplied these references.

25. Against the argument that the pilgrim's reaction here is occasioned by his "falling in love" with Francesca is the fact that his pity is explicitly engendered by both of the figures and in particular by Paolo's weeping.

26. This is a particularly interesting datum in light of the fact that the Cistercians particularly emphasized pious reading as a monastic practice, as pointed out in a recent lecture by Brian Stock.

27. Or "for our delight" (Dronke 1975:127); the Italian has *per diletto*.

28. Since writing this, I have become aware that my reading is anticipated in large part by Mazzotta (1979:166 ff.).

29. Much has been written on the narrative text as seducer. Most recently, several articles in Hunter 1989 deal with this theme.

30. Note that this reading also disempowers an easy division of reading by genre, e.g., into fiction and nonfiction.

31. Indeed, Dronke himself, while he does not share, of course, the ideology of the Romantic readers, proposes, nevertheless, a version of this reading (127 n. 29). Ironically, my reading implicitly answers Dronke's question that, "Did it ever occur to Dante, I wonder, that for some later readers Francesca's words might become as inflammatory as the tale of Lancelot and Guinivere had been for her and Paolo" (Dronke 1975:116–117)? My reading suggests that Dante thematizes an answer to this very question. Dronke does suggest that Dante saw an analogy between the prose *Lancelot* and his *Vita Nuova* (127).

32. This is a culture, after all, which has finally produced a text like the recent film, *La lectrice*, in which a young and attractive woman hires herself out to read *belles lettres* to people in intimate surroundings with predictable results.

33. See also his comment on a nineteenth-century homology between the "degenerative physiological" effects of habitual masturbation and those of prolonged reading (Nell 1988:29–30).

34. This is not to claim, of course, that I agree with all they say, either on the theoretical level or on the level of "practical criticism." See Boyarin 1990.

35. Immediately below I will discuss recent thinking on this subject. We no longer think that we have access to the true world picture of other cultures through semantics, however something remains valid nevertheless. At any rate, the semantic division of the world *is itself practice and worthy of analysis and "thick description."* For a definitive statement of an early and positivistic stage of this type of research, see the collection of Stephen Tyler (1969).

36. The alerts of Keesing (1987:387) against relying on inadequate field knowledge of languages are even more to the point here, but what else can we do?

37. "Early efforts sought to describe the semantic structure of lexical domains. If analysts could recover or reconstruct what one needed to know in order to label pieces and portions of the world correctly in the native's own language, it was reasoned, then the resulting model would capture an important part of those people's culturally constructed reality" (Holland and Quinn 1987:14). But "The semantic structures recovered in these earliest analyses did provide insight into the organization of some domains of the lexicon. However, the organization of lexicon was soon recognized to offer only limited insight into the organization of cultural knowledge." (Holland and Quinn 1987:14).

38. Dell Hymes remarks in a letter of October 5, 1990:

> I think it would be true to say that many American Indians heard performances of myths, and thought about them in between performances as both enacting a message and as pleasurable. In some groups some kinds of stories would be framed as not true, not necessarily true. Among the Nootka of British Columbia for example, what we typically call "myths" can be referred to in English as "fairy stories." They express truths about the world but whether they happened or not is not essential. What *are* true, and history, are the accounts (equally mythological in important part to us) of how the privileges of a lineage were acquired by an ancestor. Those are known to be true because they have been recited, exactly, from one generation to another.

The very fact that Prof. Hymes refers to different practices of reception of "myths" among different groups only proves my main point that genre is a set of culturally specific practices; however, I would continue to dissent from his characterization of the lineage accounts as history. Just as in the biblical case, the belief in the referentiality of the narrative does not constitute it as historiography, given my argument that historiography is a particular discursive practice developed in European culture for particular sociocultural functions. Even the very appeal to memory or oral tradition as authority and not documents is a fundamentally different practice, as is also the pointing out of a pillar of salt to validate the story of Lot's wife.

Because I fear that I may still be misunderstood here, I want to make it absolutely clear that my purpose is *not* to privilege "Western" culture and its signifying practices over those of "others." Quite the opposite, my point is to disrupt that privilege, making it clear that what others do with stories of their pasts is not failed (or even successful) historiography but a different practice of storytelling of the past. An example may make my point clearer. I recently attended the lectures of a colleague on Ancient History. In a review session, he asked the students what the beginning date of the course's purview was and the correct answer was 2500 B.C., because that is when the first *contemporaneous document attesting to a state occurs.* We have buildings and other material remains from people much earlier, of course, than 2500 B.C., but what we say about them is not historiography. We can easily see how culture-bound the practice of historiography is, and we do others no favor by seeing their practices as something like ours—but not quite. Once more, none of this has anything to do with the referential truth or falsity (historicity!) of events represented in any practice of telling the past. Non historiographical practices of communal memory may often be more "true" than the reconstructions of historians.

REFERENCES

Abelard, Peter
  1974   "Historia Calamitum." In *The Letters of Abelard and Heloise*. Ed. and
                trans. Betty Radice, pp. 57–106. The Penguin Classics. Harmonds-
                worth, Middlesex: Penguin.
Alter, Robert
  1981   *The Art of Biblical Narrative*. New York: Basic Books.
  1989   *The Pleasures of Reading in an Ideological Age*. New York: Simon and
                Schuster, Touchstone.
  1992   "Biblical Imperatives and Literary Play." In *The World of Biblical
                Literature*, pp. 25–47. Basic Books: New York.
Aristotle
  1982   *Poetics*. Trans. James Hutton. New York: W. W. Norton.
Augustine
  1960   *The Confessions of St. Augustine*. Ed. and trans. John K. Ryan. New
                York: Doubleday, Image.
Boitani, Piero
  1982   *English Medieval Narrative in the 13th & 14th Centuries*. Trans. Joan
                Krakover Hall. Cambridge: Cambridge University Press.

Boyarin, Daniel
　　1990　　　"The Politics of Biblical Narratology: Reading the Bible Like/as a Woman." *diacritics* 20 (Winter):31–42.

Brown, Peter
　　1969　　　*Augustine of Hippo: A Biography*. Berkeley: University of California Press.

Bruns, Gerald
　　1987　　　"Midrash and Allegory." In *The Literary Guide to the Bible*. Ed. Robert Alter and Frank Kermode, pp. 625–646. Cambridge, Mass.: Harvard University Press.

Chaucer, Geoffrey
　　1986　　　*The Book of the Duchess*. Ed. Helen Phillips. Durham, England: Durham and St. Andrews Medieval Texts.

Dante Alighieri
　　1970　　　*The Divine Comedy*. Vol. 1, *The Inferno*. Trans. Charles Singleton. Princeton: Princeton University Press.
　　1984　　　*The Divine Comedy*. Vol. 1, *The Inferno*. Trans. Mark Musa. Harmondsworth, Middlesex: Penguin.

Dearman, J. Andrew
　　1990　　　"My Servants the Scribes: Composition and Context in Jeremiah 36." *Journal of Biblical Literature* 109 (Fall):403–421.

Dronke, Peter
　　1975　　　"Francesca and Hèloïse." *Comparative Literature* 27 (Spring):113–135.

Fisch, Harold
　　1988　　　*Poetry with a Purpose*. Indiana Studies in Biblical Literature. Bloomington: Indiana University Press.

Hatcher, Anna, and Mark Musa
　　1968　　　"The Kiss: *Inferno* V and the Old French Prose *Lancelot*." *Comparative Literature* 20:97–109.

Hendrickson, G. L.
　　1929　　　"Ancient Reading." *The Classical Journal*. 25:182–196.

Holland, Dorothy, and Naomi Quinn
　　1987　　　"Culture and Cognition; Introduction." In *Cultural Models in Language & Thought*. Ed. Dorothy Holland and Naomi Quinn, pp. 3–43. Cambridge: Cambridge University Press.

Hunter, Dianne, ed.
　　1989　　　*Seduction and Theory: Readings of Gender, Representation, and Rhetoric*. Urbana: University of Illinois Press.

Isbell, Charles D.
　　1978　　　"II Kings 22:3–23:4 and Jer. 36: A Stylistic Comparison." *Journal for the Study of the Old Testament* 8:33–45.

Keesing, Roger M.
　　1987　　　"Models, 'folk' and Cultural: Paradigms Regained." In *Cultural Models in Language & Thought*. Ed. Dorothy Holland and Naomi Quinn, pp. 369–393. Cambridge: Cambridge University Press.

Knox, Bernard M. W.
　　1968　　　"Silent Reading in Antiquity." *Greek, Roman and Byzantine Studies* 9:421–435.

Mazzotta, Giuseppe
1979   *Dante: Poet of the Desert: History and Allegory in the Divine Comedy.*
        Princeton: Princeton University Press.
Meschonnic, Henri
1988   "Poetics and Politics: A Round Table." With Alex Derczansky,
        Olivier Mongin, and Paul Thibaud. *New Literary History* 19
        (Spring):453–467.
Nell, Victor
1988   *Lost in a Book: The Psychology of Reading for Pleasure.* New Haven: Yale
        University Press.
Noakes, Susan
1988   *Timely Reading: Between Exegesis and Interpretation.* Ithaca, N.Y.: Cor-
        nell University Press.
Poe, Elizabeth Wilson
1984   *From Poetry to Prose in Old Provençal: The Emergence of the Vidas, the
        Razos, and the Razos de Trobar.* Birmingham, Ala.: Summa Publica-
        tions.
Rappaport, Roy A.
1976   "Liturgies and Lies." *International Yearbook for Sociology of Knowledge
        and Religion* 10:75–104.
Robbins, Jill
1992   *Prodigal Son/Elder Brother.* Chicago: University of Chicago Press.
Saenger, Paul
1982   "Silent Reading: Its Impact on Late Medieval Script and Society."
        Viator 13:367–414.
Schutz, Alexander
1939   "Were the *Vidas* and *Razos* Recited?" *Studies in Philology* 36:565–570.
Stern, David
1988   "Midrash and Indeterminacy." *Critical Inquiry* 15(1):132–168.
Sternberg, Meir
1985   *The Poetics of Biblical Narrative: Ideological Literature and the Drama of
        Reading.* Indiana Studies in Biblical Literature. Bloomington: Indi-
        ana University Press.
Sweetser, Eve E.
1987   "The Definition of a Lie. An Examination of Folk Models Under-
        lying a Semantic Prototype." In *Cultural Models in Language &
        Thought.* Ed. Dorothy Holland and Naomi Quinn. Cambridge: Cam-
        bridge University Press.
Tyler, Stephen A.
1969   *Cognitive Anthropology.* New York: Holt Rinehart & Winston.

THREE

Gracious Words:
Luke's Jesus and the Reading of
Sacred Poetry at the Beginning of the
Christian Era

Susan Noakes

> . . . *no other portion of the New Testament provides such a compact, thorough and explicit example of early Christian hermeneutics.*
> —TIEDE, *PROPHECY AND HISTORY IN LUKE-ACTS*

On January 6, 1991, an Ecumenical Worship Service was held to commemorate the beginning of the inaugural week of Governor-elect Arne Carlson. As the parent of a child scheduled to sing with one of the several choirs participating in this event, I had an opportunity to observe firsthand the particular nature of efforts made to connect religion and politics. The Most Reverend John Roach, Roman Catholic Archbishop of Saint Paul and Minneapolis, who participated with other clergy in the Service, tried hard to build a rhetorical framework in which Carlson could emerge as a leader (though I can't help suspecting he would have rather stuck with the Democratic incumbent, a Catholic). The Archbishop presented what the printed program called "A Prayer for a New Leader," based on Luke 4:14–19. I will quote this Biblical text from the Revised Standard Version (1952):

> And Jesus returned in the power of the Spirit into Galilee, and a report concerning him went out through all the surrounding country. And he taught in their synagogues, being glorified by all.
>
> And he came to Nazareth, where he had been brought up; and he went to the synagogue, as his custom was, on the sabbath day. And he stood up to read; and there was given to him the book of the prophet Isaiah. He opened the book and found the place where it was written,
> "The Spirit of the Lord is upon me,
> because he has anointed me to preach good news to the poor.
> He has sent me to proclaim release to the captives
> and recovering of sight to the blind,

38

to set at liberty those who are oppressed,
to proclaim the acceptable year of the Lord."

Implicitly and explicitly, the Archbishop made several connections between these five verses and the Carlson inauguration. Following Christian tradition, he placed Carlson in Jesus's footsteps, expressing the hope that he would accomplish a kind of "imitatio Christi" within the political realm. The passage's two allusions to a leader who is imbued with the power of the Spirit suggest, in this context, that Carlson is (or could be or should be) similarly Spirit-endowed. And then, most specifically, there is the catalog of elements in the leader's mission, the listing of "constituencies" whose needs the new leader is called to address.

I was distracted from the Archbishop's remarks by "baggage" I had brought with me to the Service. I knew that what he presented was not an entire episode from the Gospel, but only the very beginning of one. Especially distracting was my awareness that the rest of the episode did not provide a good omen for Carlson's success. Indeed, the episode depicts very rapid decline in the popularity of a "new leader": at first warmly received, Jesus goes on to enrage his fellow townsmen with his interpretation of the passage from Isaiah and only narrowly escapes from their attempt to throw him over a precipice. No doubt it was good taste for Archbishop Roach to leave all this out, once he had linked Jesus to Carlson. On the other hand, perhaps his choice of episode was prophetic: just one short month after the inauguration, Carlson is being castigated for the "Reorganization" of Minnesota (meaning he is slashing state services to the poor and oppressed).

Though I recognize that the Archbishop followed ancient Christian example (even Jesus's) in treating just part of an episode, it is my purpose here to examine the episode in its entirety.[1] It presents a "scene of reading"[2] that long ago took on paradigmatic force for European culture, a force the effects of which are felt today less in the realm of political leadership than in the inculcation of modes of reading. Here is what Archbishop Roach omitted:

And he closed the book, and gave it back to the attendant, and sat down; and the eyes of all in the synagogue were fixed on him. And he began to say to them, "Today this scripture has been fulfilled in your hearing." And all spoke well of him; and wondered at the gracious words which proceeded out of his mouth; and they said, "Is not this Joseph's son?" And he said to them, "Doubtless you will quote to me this proverb, 'Physician, heal yourself; what we have heard you did at Capernaum, do here also in your own country.'" And he said, "Truly, I say to you, no prophet is acceptable in his own country. But in truth, I tell you, there were many widows in Israel in the days of Elijah, when the heaven was shut up three years and six months, when there came a great famine over all the land; and Elijah was sent to none of them but only to Zarephath, in the land of Sidon, to a woman who was a widow. And there were many lepers in Israel in the time of the prophet Elisha; and none of them was cleansed, but only Naaman the Syrian." When they heard this, all in the synagogue were filled with wrath. And they rose up and put him out of the city, and led him to the brow of the hill on which their city was built, that they might throw him down headlong. But passing through the midst of them he went away.

In this essay, I wish to consider how this "scene," and more generally the type of reading depicted in the New Testament as being practiced by Jesus, may be understood as a model for a type of reading widespread in the Christian Era. Developed by the Fathers of the Church, and above all by the medievals, this model is, I would contend, carried into the present by their heirs in modern literary criticism. My concern here, then, is not with the "historical Jesus," a figure about whom I have no scholarly competence to write; no historian of early Christianity, I am simply a lay person long conversant with Christian writings and many of the issues they raise.[3] My interest here, as a student of literary, especially hermeneutic, theory, and a medievalist, is more general than that of a New Testament scholar would be. I hope examination of this "scene" will make it possible to better understand the later Christian reading culture, broadly defined, which resulted from the style of reading adopted by Jesus and his early followers.[4] Luke makes this "scene of reading" the starting point of Jesus's public ministry. It is also, I would argue, an influential early step toward the formation of a particular approach to reading within Christian culture. In this broad framework, then, how can Luke's depiction of Jesus's reading activity be characterized?

It should be borne in mind that the skillfully engaging narrative which is the Gospel of Luke as a whole[5] seeks to make a particular point about reading, especially about reading of the "Old" Testament. This point is crucial to the Christian designation of the Hebrew scriptures as "old," that is, in some way set apart from the present. While all New Testament writers argue that various aspects of Jesus's life conform to the prophecies of the Hebrew scriptures, Luke broadens and deepens this notion of symmetry between Jesus's life and a reading of the scriptures in order to make it into a central Christian doctrine.

In the volume on Luke in *The Pelican Gospel Commentaries*, G.B. Caird (1963:34) outlines succinctly the substance of those passages which display Luke's keen interest in this subject. Luke "introduces the idea of fulfilment [of the Hebrew scriptures] into contexts where it was not present in his source" (cf. Luke 18:31 with Mark 10:33). Luke also "repeatedly affirms that this method of scriptural interpretation had its origin in Jesus himself, who found in the Old Testament the blueprint of his own ministry (4:21 [a verse from the passage under discussion here]) and taught his disciples how to use the Old Testament as Christian scripture (24:27, 44)." Most important, as the two verses just cited from chapter 24 indicate, Luke asserts (and indeed structures his whole narrative to show) that "Jesus fulfilled not just a few isolated promises made by the prophets, but the whole tenor, purport, and pattern of Old Testament teaching and history. In particular, he fulfilled the Exodus and Passover." When Luke depicts Jesus asserting, in the Nazareth synagogue, that the Spirit of the Lord has "anointed" him to preach good news to the poor, he makes Jesus claim a kind of kingship, a position as the "Messiah" (Caird 1963:38). This claim derives indispensable support from the ambitious approach to the reading of the Hebrew scriptures which Luke proposes.

To be sure, neither Luke nor Jesus invents this approach out of nowhere. Rather, it is an application of traditional Jewish methods of interpretation made with special urgency within a particular cultural and political framework. Drury (1976:4 *et passim*) emphasizes the dual roots of the Lukan approach to the interpretation of the Hebrew scriptures in Luke's admiration for the techniques used by the writer of the Book of Deuteronomy, for whom a "dialectic of prophecy and fulfilment was . . . history's sustaining rhythm" and in his sophistication in the techniques of *midrash*, interpretation of ancient writings which brings them into dialogue with later problems they do not address directly. How Luke develops these traditional approaches to reading, particularly in the Nazareth synagogue scene, and the way his development of them then affects subsequent Christian culture will be my special concern.

To better understand the "scene of reading," which is at issue here, it will be useful to recall the essential elements of its immediate literary context.[6] First, it follows directly Luke's account of Jesus's forty-day temptation in the wilderness. Like Matthew, Luke foregrounds Jesus's activity as a reader during this earlier episode, too: during his period of temptation, Jesus responds to each of the devil's challenges with a quotation from scripture, introduced by the formula "It is written. . . ." For example, when the devil offers him "all the kingdoms of the world" if he will worship the devil, Jesus answers by quoting Deuteronomy 6:13–14: "And Jesus answered him, 'It is written, "You shall worship the Lord your God, and him only shall you serve."'" Luke is showing that Jesus rejects "the various popular conceptions of Messiahship" (Caird 1963:38, 86). In addition to this relatively obvious goal, however, Luke's temptation narrative accomplishes another: Jesus's ability to quote even when he has no book to read from suggests, just before the synagogue scene, that he is well-versed in scripture.[7] If in the Nazareth synagogue scene, as Drury (1976:66) puts it, "scripture . . . is, together with Jesus who reads it and enacts it, the leading actor," this "actor" has already played a prominent role in Luke well before Jesus's return to his home town.

Second, the Nazareth reading episode precedes, or, to use a more properly literary concept, introduces, Luke's account of Jesus's earthly ministry, as I mentioned earlier. Its introductory function within the structure of the pair of books, Luke-Acts, is well set forth in the influential interpretation of Hans Conzelmann (1960).[8] He sees particular significance in Luke's displacement of the episode to this important introductory position from the place where the (earlier) Book of Mark had located it.[9]

Stating succinctly what he takes to be Luke's guiding hermeneutic principle, the basis for his contextual interpretation of this episode and consequent displacement of it, Conzelmann writes: "when [Luke] has discovered the redemptive significance of an event, he can go on to deduce from it the 'correct' chronology, which means, among other things, that he can begin to modify Mark" (1960:33).[10] Concerned above all with context, Conzelmann argues that the story as Luke presents it has two main points, which reinforce one another. The first derives from Jesus's implied interpretation of the Isaiah passage, asserting that he is himself the fulfillment of it and brings to his hearers the moment of deliverance. The second derives from the episode's placement at Nazareth, among Jesus's kin and fellow townspeople. This geographic placement provides the vehicle for Jesus's rejection of those to whom he should, according to tradition, be closest (in v. 24 he asserts: "no prophet is acceptable in his own country"), and for the Nazarenes' consequent wrathful and murderous rejection of him.[11]

As Conzelmann sees it, the overall import of the episode, in the Lukan context which makes it the introduction to Jesus's ministry, is that the ministry that Jesus is about to begin will be directed not toward those who can claim some special affiliation with him by birth (whether as members of his immediate family, natives of his village, or fellow Jews), but rather toward those who respond to his call. For Conzelmann, this sets the dominant theme of the Gospel according to Luke:

> One belongs to Jesus only by call and discipleship. If the preaching of John the Baptist destroyed the possibility of a call based on descent from Abraham, now the ministry of Jesus carries this a stage further: one can be a "relative" of Jesus *sola gratia* [only through the agency of God's grace]. The special features of Luke are the explicit emphasis to the point of polemic and the particular relation of word and deed in the call of the disciples. (37)[12]

At issue in this "scene of reading," and especially in Jesus's assertion in verse 21 that " 'Today this scripture has been fulfilled in your hearing,' " then, are two concerns crucial to the welfare of the infant Church.

First, in very concrete terms, the Church must be protected from claims that its legitimacy and mission derive from a blood relationship between its members and Jesus's "family," whether this concept be interpreted to mean the immediate circle connected with James, the extended family at

Nazareth, or the entire ethnic group of all Jews. By means of the Nazareth synagogue episode, Luke lays the foundation for rejecting a theology and an ecclesiastical structure based on ethnic and geographic claims. In this he makes what is, for his time, a prudent choice.[13] Assuming that Luke writes after Titus's successful siege of Jerusalem and the destruction of the Temple (cf. Luke 21:21), it would be reasonable for anyone keenly interested in the preservation and future development of the fragile community which was the early Church to argue that its authority did not derive from leaders connected with the Temple. Reluctance to affiliate with the losing side being a widespread human sentiment, it is reasonable to suppose that it would be unwise, in the last quarter of the first century A.D., to define Christian identity as based in prior Jewish identity. Drury (1976:11) remarks: "As a new religion, Christianity depended on conversions for its existence. The story of its growth, as told by Luke, turns upon them. They are the subject of many of the famous parables peculiar to him." The more Luke can do to attenuate the connection between Christianity and Jews as an ethnic group, the more he will be able to contribute to the growth of the Church. In this sense, then, it may be useful to look at Luke's Gospel as an instance of political rhetoric, that is, a text which intends to define a group, in part by establishing who belongs to it and who does not. The Nazareth "scene of reading" would thus be Luke's Jesus's first political act.

Luke demonstrates his concern for the early Church's welfare in a second way here when he focuses this political act on a mediating element capable of extensive adaptation in the unstable imperial environment.[14] Luke lifts his argument out of the vexed domain of contemporary politics and places it squarely in the more manageable realm of books. For the Jews as a people with a prominent role to play in the eastern part of the Empire, for Jewish practices, and for the Temple, Luke substitutes what is intimately associated with yet distinguishable from all of these: the Hebrew scriptures.[15] Respected even among non-Jews for, among other things, their antiquity, the scriptures become the basis for a hermeneutic practice which is among the cornerstones of Christianity.[16]

Ecclesiastical politics, then, has a major impact upon the hermeneutics represented by the Nazareth "scene of reading." Nonetheless, the specific situation within which Luke's depiction of Jesus's reading occurs is regularly overlooked, as Jesus's reading practice here is made normative, that is, applicable to many different situations in later Christian culture.[17] This transformation of a reading practice specific to a particular historical situation into one for which universal claims are made is accomplished, among others, by patristic commentators who take this scene to constitute Jesus's fulfillment of one of the roles necessary for a priest, the role of "lector" (reader).[18] In order to better understand the implications of this transformation, it will be useful to consider just what kind of "lector" Jesus is in this passage. Once his character as "lector" is understood, it will be time to consider the remainder of the passage, including the rest of Jesus's sermon and the Nazarenes' violent reaction to it.

What kind of "lector," or reader, is Jesus in this passage? Luke uses the comments of those present, the Nazarenes and Jesus, to stress explicitly three characteristics of Jesus's activity as the reader of an extract from a very difficult poetic vision. First, he is better prepared to act as reader than the Nazarenes expect a local carpenter's son to be, as the preceding episode of scriptural struggle with Satan has also demonstrated. The ambiguity of their reaction may well indicate other senses as well in which his reading performance does not appear to the Nazarenes to be congruent with this known identity. Second, his commentary on his reading ("Today this scripture has been fulfilled in your hearing") is taken by the community to be constituted of words which are "gracious," causing in the community a response of "wonder." Third, Jesus makes special claims for the character of his reading: his reading of the passage has "fulfilled" it. Jesus emphasizes the special character of this "fulfillment" with special temporal language: "today" and "in your hearing."

The long-lasting influence of this "scene," however, does not come from aspects of the drama that can be captured by such surface description. The heart of the drama is a struggle about authority. Though this struggle is, in historical terms, an echo of the struggle for power between Jerusalem and diaspora Christians in Luke's day, in the more immediate terms of the drama Luke writes it is a struggle about authority to read. When the scroll is passed to Jesus, the community is according him the same level of authority to read granted to any male member of the community who has attained a certain basic educational level. Jesus is not depicted as claiming a special authority for himself as reader on the basis of some new method of interpretation which he introduces. Indeed, the methods he uses here, and the methods of interpretation used throughout the New Testament, are the same ones long used by earlier generations of Jews (see Conzelmann 1973:140). What Luke's Jesus does, however, is reorient these traditional methods in a different direction, creating a different kind of authority for reading. The earlier framework was provided by the self-understanding of the Jews as the people called by God to faithfulness to the Torah. The new framework, derived in this text from the self-understanding of the early Christians as the people truly called by God to faithfulness to Jesus, is built upon an understanding of Jesus as the Son of God.

Luke's Jesus claims to be a reader with a unique relationship to the author of the text he is to read. He thus claims a special authority to present an interpretation which is not just one good one among many others: it is claimed to be the *right* one. Luke's Jesus is thus presented as having the authority to stop the process of the interpretation of the Hebrew scriptures.

This makes the worshiping community centered on his person and the call to be faithful to him more important than the worshiping community centered around the Temple. The statement Luke has him make, "Today this scripture has been fulfilled in your hearing," marks the beginning of the history of the institution which Luke seeks to nurture (see Conzelmann 1960:36; van Unnik 1966:24).

The word translated in the RSV as "fulfilled" marks a crucial concept here. It designates the prophetic poetry of Isaiah as incomplete. In itself, this designation is quite consonant with Jewish tradition: prophecy is by definition a statement awaiting future fulfillment. What makes Luke's Jesus's statement so arresting, however, is the assertion that the incomplete portion of Isaiah is now finished; what has remained empty there has been filled up.

This concept thus shifts the focus of interest from Isaiah's text to Jesus. If Luke's Jesus's assertion is accepted, then, the poetic text, in a subtle way, loses something of its fascination and its power. In the view of someone who accepts his claim, Isaiah's sacred poetry is, without Jesus, rhetoric, that is, a linguistic structure with the primary goal of persuading people of the veracity of something which is not evident or present. Isaiah's text becomes truth, a linguistic structure with the primary goal of naming something evident or present, only when read through the optic of Jesus's interpretation. Luke here draws upon a concept closely related to the well-known Pauline contrast between the "letter (which) killeth" and the "spirit (which) giveth life" (2 Corinthians 3:6), a contrast which, once again, is a product of the conflict between factions in the primitive Church. Luke's Jesus claims not merely that there is a meaning hidden in Isaiah's prophetic poetry (presumably a widespread notion in the contemporary Jewish community), but that he, and he alone on earth, is able to disclose it.[19] Luke presents Jesus as having unique authority to disclose what the text "really means" and to limit the moment in which a correct interpretation can be enunciated to this moment only ("today").

This hermeneutic gesture is fundamental to Christianity. Indeed, the assertion of an authority which provides a definitive interpretation of a poetic, and thus essentially ambiguous, text takes on a life in Christian culture which goes far beyond the bounds of Christian theology. This is not to deny that the broad tradition of Christian theology has been quite able to envisage other hermeneutic possibilities for reading Jesus's relation to the Hebrew scriptures (e.g., through typology, or employing process theology). With the establishment of the Church as an institution, however, the meaning of the reading of Hebrew scripture is redefined for those whose literacy is shaped by this institution.

Luke's central idea, that responsiveness to the call of Jesus as Messiah supersedes fidelity to the Temple and the Law, shapes his depiction of the reading of Isaiah's poetry and creates (together with the parallel idea urged by Paul, mentioned above) a pressure always present in a culture molded by Christianity. Luke interprets the import of Jesus's teaching in conformity with this central idea, giving it a higher priority in his writings than any other aspect of Jesus's "good news."[20] In this way, a depiction of reading born in a particular situation of political and religious crisis assumes a normative character, with a range of consequences wholly unrelated to this originating situation.

It is now time to consider more fully those consequences as they affect the professional reader, the literary critic, today. The Lukan and Pauline[21] approach to the reading of the Hebrew scriptures, and especially to that of prophetic poetry, has long shaped the reading of secular literature, not only because Western education is rooted in the Church but also because the discipline of literary criticism originates in medieval efforts to interpret what is in many ways the most challenging of sacred Hebrew poetic texts, the Song of Songs. No doubt there have been many professional readers of poetry since Jesus's time, many "lectors," who have wished they could assert that they have "fulfilled" the poem they have read and could note in their readers "wonder" rather than, say, incomprehension or criticism. The desire to accomplish a kind of "imitatio Christi" has long shaped certain of the practices of this group. To satisfy this desire, it is necessary to claim a special authority based on a privileged understanding of a poem's author,[22] which in turn justifies an implied assertion that the critic's interpretation of a poem constitutes a kind of "fulfillment" of it.

Yet there is, I think, more for literary critics to learn from Luke's "scene of reading" than such a lesson in expansion of the ego. Luke's Jesus's poetry reading is, in a quite different way, paradigmatic for literary critics in that it defines a *limit* for literary interpretation: it shows what literary interpretation *cannot* do, even though literary interpretation always moves toward this limit, or "fulfillment" of the text, as if seeking congruence with it. There is something about Jesus's reading that other poetry readings simply cannot achieve.

In general, literary interpretation, as practiced in the United States during much of this century, necessarily figures the text as incomplete, partially empty, waiting to be "fulfilled" by extratextual events. Interpretation itself is preeminent among such events, the condition which makes possible the application to the text of other events. It is the vehicle that focuses onto the text questions and concerns that are connected to the text in no other way.

Just as the special quality of Luke's Jesus's reading does not come from his unusual degree of familiarity with scripture, though this feature is, to be sure, a necessary prerequisite to what he does, neither does the professional literary reader's authority stem primarily from the great familiarity with the text which she or he must certainly have. Rather, what is essential to such a reader's interpretation is the most important feature of the Nazareth "scene of reading": Jesus's special identity as Messiah, which makes possible his claim about the temporal relationship between what he reads and his reading of it, the claim that his reading is the last correct one, the definitive interpretation.

In contrast, in what might be called "ordinary" reading, as it is still conventionally taught in high schools and colleges, it is supposed that the reader looks backward in time to try to establish contact with the authoritative character of the text; the text does not look forward to, and await, the reader. The reader is subordinate to the text and seeks something from it, to be brought forward to the present, often in the form of an inference as to a general rule of judgment or behavior. There can be no incontrovertible proof or congruence between the reading and what is read.

Here I am confounding, for a purpose, two senses of "reading." In the first sense, "reading" is Jesus's articulation of characters copied onto a scroll in a context in which such performance is much prized. In the second sense, "reading" is the exposition of the meaning of the passage so articulated. Jesus's brief sentence is presented as an adequate exposition, indeed the only adequate exposition, of the Isaiah passage. One of the peculiarities of the "scene of reading" in Luke is that these two senses of reading, articulation and exposition, which are normally distinct, are, in this unique situation, merged to become one. Indeed, this convergence is, in the context of Christian doctrine, one way of explaining the "graciousness" of Jesus's words.[23] Because Jesus is, according to claims which he makes in the Gospel narrative and which the Gospel writer accepts, specially anointed by "the Lord," he is congruent with the "me" of the text, and thus his articulation of it is a performance of what the words describe: preaching, proclaiming, freeing, and so on. Jesus's identity with the "authority" of the Book permits him to make a perfect exposition of the poetic text simply by the act of enunciating it.[24] There is no need to lay out a fourfold structure, to explicate metaphor, to deconstruct. The enunciation of the passage is its own explication.

The scene of reading described by Luke is, then, categorically different from the one I have described as "ordinary." It represents a goal toward which professional readers, who seek to perform readings that are more than "ordinary," aspire, in a form of self-delusion required by their profession. In reality, there are only two possible hermeneutic cases: Jesus's, and the "ordinary" one.

In the "ordinary" case, where no "anointed" reader is involved, the text is taken to be completed, perfect, integral: something which always already has its own meaning prior to any intervention by a reader. The reader, in this "ordinary" scene of reading, is the one who is defective, incomplete, imperfect, because he or she lacks a perfect understanding of the text. The reader seeks to fill up this gap or remedy this imperfection, through study of the text. In the unique "scene of reading" presented by Luke, on the other hand, the value of the terms is inverted. Here the reader is perfect, knowing all not only about scripture but also about everything else. He is not seeking through His reading to remedy some defect, some ignorance, in Himself. Rather, He reads in order to render perfect a defective text. The passage from Isaiah has, in the terms set up by the gospel narrative, been until the moment of reading "unfulfilled," that is, incomplete, lacking something.

The inversion of the correlation between the pair reader/text and the pair complete/incomplete (or "fulfilled"/empty) is accomplished along a temporal axis. In what I have been calling the "ordinary" scene of reading, what is complete, integral, resides in the past, the "authoritative" time frame of the text's composition. Incomplete understanding, imperfection, resides with the reader, in the reader's present. In the Luke story, to the contrary, it is the reader Jesus who is perfect and who points out that, until his reading-performance of it, the Isaiah text was imperfect, that is (etymologically) uncompleted, lacking its fulfillment. The significance of this actuality is underlined by Jesus's temporal stress: "*Today* this scripture has been fulfilled *in your hearing*."

Let me now step backward from the terms set up by the Lukan "scene of reading" to try to describe what is going on here in more general terms. The reader, in the case of "ordinary" reading, perceives a verbal representation and seeks through it to know what is represented. In the episode from Luke, the reader enunciates aloud the verbal representation and through this enunciation or performance seeks to reveal that he is himself what is represented. In the first or "ordinary" case, the reader looks forward (in the future) to understanding what was meant in the past. In the second or Lukan case, the reader affirms in the present that he is the future to which the (past) text looked forward. Whereas in this latter case the expectation of meaning which is part of the character of every sign resides with the text, looking forward to its fulfillment, in the former or "ordinary" case the expectation of meaning resides with the reader, who looks to the (past) text in hopes of understanding it at some moment in the future.

In the case of "ordinary" reading, the reader encounters the representation of an object and, in the semiotic model delineated by Charles Sanders Peirce, selects from an infinite array of interpretants, that is, other representations of the same object, that which may most readily be determined to refer to the object in the same way that the first-mentioned representation does.[25] Although the interpretant belongs to the same class as the first representation (that is, the class of representations) and although it represents the same object, *it can never be identical* with the first representation;

its *difference* from this first representation is a condition of its function as an interpretant.

It may be useful to convert into Peircian terms elements of the Lukan "scene of reading" which I have proposed, in order to provide a model of what literary interpretation seems to move toward but can never attain. The verbal representation is the scriptural passage from the Book of Isaiah. The interpreter, Jesus, in asserting that he is himself the object represented by the text, is offering himself as interpretant, that is, the abstract entity which the text produces in order to mediate its relationship to its object. Now, in "ordinary," that is, nondivine, semiosis, while the interpretant and the representation are the same kind of thing (they are both representations), they are necessarily different instances of representation, standing to each other in a necessary relationship of nonidentity. But in the case of Luke's Jesus's activity as "lector," interpretant and object become one and the same (that is, "Jesus"), thereby essentially changing the character of the relation between the verbal representation (that is, the Isaiah text) and the interpretant. Whereas in the "ordinary" case the verbal representation and the interpretant may seem to move toward identity but never find it, and whereas they necessarily have to be described in temporal terms as the prior representation and a subsequent representation, in the limit case found in Luke the text and its interpretant are asserted to be one: that is, if one accepts the claim made by Jesus, the text is "fulfilled,"[26] and the temporal separation between verbal representation and interpretant is erased.

These two cases, "ordinary" reading and Luke's Jesus's reading, differ in still another significant way. This difference concerns the dynamism of the interpretant. The literary interpreter (unlike Jesus) must consider a range of interpretants in his or her efforts to "understand" the literary text, that is, to locate the interpretant which best satisfies the interpreter's desire to conceive an interpretant that repeats as closely as possible the act of representation which is the text. In the effort to satisfy this desire, he or she will set up a dynamic relationship among multiple interpretants, substituting one for the other in succession.[27]

These interpretants, to be sure, themselves become signs, undergoing a kind of metamorphosis. Nothing is static in this quest for a satisfactory relation between interpretant and text except the goal, which, in general terms, remains always the same, that is, identity between these two, a goal which, therefore, always remains beyond reach of the merely human reader. Perhaps one can in part account for the frequent neglect of the concept of interpretant among literary interpreters by reference to a notion of semiotic frustration: the dynamic character of the interpretant reminds literary interpreters of the perhaps distasteful fact that the desire for identity between interpretants and text is never to be "fulfilled." Literary interpreters are not messiahs. That each interpretant is transformed into a sign which then pro-

duces its own series of interpretants, and so on infinitely, is a concept that
Peircian semiotics proposes to literary interpreters, and which literary interpreters must, because of the requirements of their profession, silently reject.

It is more difficult, however, to ignore the role played by the dynamism
of the interpretant in the case no longer of the individual interpreter but
rather of the interpreting community. The last thirty years' experience of
the enrichment of literary interpretation underscores that aspect of the interpreting community which is most pertinent to my argument here: that
community has emerged as one of great diversity, and has for the most part
come to understand itself as diverse. The dynamic character of the interpretant is the foundation for that diversity, and insofar as one understands this
diversity as enrichment rather than chaos, it becomes possible to acknowledge the utility of this dynamism rather than to try to cover it over or to
debate it out of existence.

To be sure, the interpretant has most often been treated, by Peirce and
by later semioticians, in relation to synchronic rather than diachronic contexts. Yet even when considered as part of a synchronic process of sign-
production, the interpretant is necessarily described in temporal terms: the
text is the first or prior representation while the interpretant is the second
or subsequent representation. An important task now facing the community of professional readers in this country is, I think, the development of
an understanding of how the concept of the interpretant functions in that
very substantial realm of literary interpretation that is diachronic, which
seeks to understand now what was written in a long-ago "then." Such
an understanding would provide a foundation for a sorely-needed new
theory of literary history, without which the current intense, indeed vicious,
debates about what is tellingly called the literary "canon" must remain
inconclusive.

Luke's "scene of reading," then, may serve as a kind of mnemonic recalling what literary interpretation cannot be. The erasure of temporal distance
asserted in the Luke story provides an ideal which literary interpretation
often holds out for itself, but which cannot be attained—at least without
divine intervention. Acknowledging the temporal dimension of the nonidentity of interpretant and object in secular literary interpretation is a
necessary move, and one which, if it must give up the prospect of "fulfilling"
the text, at least offers in return for this sacrifice the prospect of a clearer
understanding of what goes on when one serves, today, in a secular context, as "lector."

It is now time to return to consider the conclusion of Luke's "scene" of
reading, the portion Archbishop Roach tactfully omitted in his meditation
in honor of Governor-elect Carlson's inauguration. Between verse 22, where
Luke reports that all the Nazarenes at the synagogue "spoke well of" Jesus
and wondered at his "gracious words," and verse 23, where Jesus begins to

put words in their mouths and launches a sermon calculated to offend them, there occurs a shocking rupture.[28] From a proverb in Mark Luke creates a drama about the relation between prophet and homeland, a drama which culminates in an attempted mob killing. This drama looks both backward, to the hostile treatment of Elijah and Jeremiah, and forward, to the rapid change from Palm Sunday to Good Friday and the Crucifixion.[29] To be sure, Luke has prepared Jesus's announcement of the opening of election to the Gentiles in the infancy chapters, specifically in Simeon's song and prophecy.[30] But in Luke's Nazareth synagogue, such obscure hints become a manifesto. Moreover, the manifesto is not couched in positive language, describing the adding on of the Gentiles to the previously elect nation; instead, Luke has Jesus recall, quite menacingly, two instances from the Book of Kings in which God's grace is accorded to Gentiles rather than Jews.

Why does Luke add to Jesus's reading and announcement the rest of the "scene"? Why does he stage this particular drama, with such disturbing details from Kings (absent from both Mark and Matthew)? Are the requirements of literary structure, the backward glance at the persecuted prophets and the forward look to Jerusalem and Calvary, a sufficient explanation? Is Luke's principle goal here to identify Jesus with Elijah, by making him adopt some of Elijah's tactics (cf. Drury 1976.147)? Does verse 22 convey such a hint of scepticism on the Nazarenes' part as to explain Jesus's reaction?[31] Some scholars (e g , Drury 1976:11) see here the beginnings of the hardening of Luke's attitude toward the Jews in Acts.[32] Why should this beginning occur here, founded on a "scene of reading"?

As I have tried to show, the context for Luke's careful creation of this drama is the political struggle within the primitive church, a struggle intimately bound to differing approaches within that church to the reading of the Hebrew scriptures. The outline of this struggle, as it appeared to Luke, is apparent to anyone who peruses Acts.[33] But when this political struggle vanishes, largely as a result of the destruction of the Temple and the attendant dispersal and discrediting of the Jerusalem rigorist faction, the "scene of reading" Luke has created endures, to become a cornerstone of Christian reading practice.

Conversion becomes a central Lukan theme in large part in order to support Christian reading practice as a contributing factor in the growth of the early church (cf. *supra*, 13). Had the church continued to be dominated by the rigorist group, conversion would have been accomplished differently: it would presumably have left the authority of the Law and the Temple intact and at the center of the Church's belief. But the group to which Luke belonged had instead to replace this authority with a different one which did not come solely through Jewish tradition, practice, and scripture, but rather directly from God. Hence the story Luke presents of the conversion of Saul (thenceforward Paul) in Acts 9, which emphasizes that Jesus's message has come to Paul miraculously, directly from God, and not through scripture. Though Luke's polemic is in many ways more guarded than Paul's (that is, he does not use Paul's emphatic rhetoric about letter and spirit), it still clearly summons converts to look to Jesus's authority as the key to the correct reading of Hebrew scripture.

NOTES

1. Cf. Tiede 1988:101–102: "The complexity of the Nazareth episode itself invites attempts to divide it. The devastating turn from the glorious proclamation at the beginning to the harsh oracles and near murder at the conclusion has caused many interpreters to stop with v. 21 or 22a."

2. I adapt the phrase from Clayton Koelb (1982), who uses it to play on Jacques Derrida's notion of "the scene of writing."

3. I cannot even claim a thorough familiarity with Luke scholarship, which in recent decades has become a vast field. For a scholarly orientation to the foundations of this recent controversy, especially since the 1953 publication of the German original of Conzelmann 1961, see van Unnik (1966), who remarks (16): "in 1950 no one could have foretold that in the next decade Luke-Acts would become one of the great storm centers of New Testament scholarship, second only to that of the 'historical Jesus.'" For a more recent concise overview of currents in Luke scholarship spanning the nineteenth and twentieth centuries, see Tiede 1988:22–25. Van Segbroeck 1989 lists about 3000 scholarly monographs and articles on the Gospel of Luke published between 1973 and 1988. The studies I have selected to work with have been primarily book-length contributions, and thus ones which frame the Nazareth episode within a thoroughly developed approach to the Gospel of Luke as a whole; I have also preferred studies which are strongly influenced by redaction criticism, which emphasizes the role of the Gospel writers as interpreters of earlier oral and written tradition and is thus readily intelligible to a student of secular literary history.

4. I have discussed elsewhere (1977; 1988, esp. 30–33; 1990) the concept of historically distinct reading styles, and their relation to ideologies.

5. Van Unnik 1966:21 also points out that much of the scanty information we have about the early Christian church "is furnished by Luke and Luke alone." This underlines the significance of the way Luke treats reading, specifically the reading of the Hebrew scriptures, for the later development of the Church and of education, an institution shaped by the Church.

6. To be sure, this "scene" calls for more than just literary contextual study: also important are the history of Jewish worship practices and geographic setting. For a concise introduction to the former, a very complex matter, see Caird 1963:87. The noted Luke scholar Conzelmann (1960, esp. 31–38) highlights the importance of this episode in a detailed analysis emphasizing the significance of geographic elements.

7. This has already been suggested in Luke's "infancy narratives," unique to

his Gospel, where the twelve-year-old Jesus amazes the doctors in the temple at Jerusalem with his questions, his answers, and his understanding (2:41–52).

8. Conzelmann's reading has played a defining role in Luke-Acts scholarship in recent decades; that is, much of this scholarship, whether elaborating on this reading or taking issue with it, moves forward from Conzelmann's interpretation, as from a fundamental point of departure. Conzelmann's reliance on analysis of literary structure as he makes his argument creates an argument which is particularly persuasive to someone of my background. I have nonetheless, in preparation of this essay, tried to make myself aware of objections which specialists have raised to his widely accepted argument. For example, Minear 1966, esp. 121ff., takes issue with Conzelmann's "conjectural reconstruction of Luke's editorial policy," objecting particularly (123) to Conzelmann's choice of Jesus's reading at Nazareth as one of two pivotal points in his interpretation.

9. In Mark 6, 1–6, the episode in the Nazareth synagogue occurs after the ministry has been well-established by much teaching and the performance of many miracles. In Mark, Jesus's rejection "in his own country" immediately precedes the sending forth of the twelve, which is widely interpreted in Christian tradition as signifying the establishment of the Church. (Many scholars, to be sure, do not interpret the Gospel of Mark itself as envisioning the establishment of a Church; they would see it as a book written in expectation of a rapid Second Coming. Given the delay of this Coming, it would fall to Luke, then, to create a history for the Church as a contribution toward its founding. See van Unnik 1966:24, building upon Conzelmann's studies.) Most of the details Luke's narrative provides in presenting this episode are not to be found in Mark. Conzelmann 1961:35–36n summarizes the differences between the two versions. The material Luke adds in vv. 17–20 and 25–27 comes primarily from the Septuagint (Drury 1976:66). While most scholars see the Luke episode as an elaboration upon the episode in Mark, this view is not universal. Tiede (1980) remarks, pp. 21–22: "The general assumption of Luke's literary dependence upon Mark rests very gingerly upon the meager verbal correspondence and disparate sequence that exist here between Mark and Luke. The lack of close parallels certainly cautions against describing Luke's account in terms of the 'modification' of his Markan source."

10. Drury (1976) makes a similar point in a different way, explicating Luke's statement of intention (1:3) to write "in order" or "consecutively." The Greek adverb so translated might better be rendered, he argues, as "in historical order." He compares Luke to a modern historian who might choose to focus on "economic or social forces" as the guiding principle in the ordering of historical bits and pieces into a historical narrative. For Luke, instead, the dominant principle is "the force of God's will for mankind worked out in prophecy and its fulfilment."

11. Note that Jesus is quoted as using a proverb to suggest that he is *a* prophet, but not "*the* prophet expected in the last days": Moule 1966:162.

12. Conzelmann relates the polemical character of that aspect of the episode which stresses rejection of kindred to "disputes in the primitive [Christian] community, in the course of which declarations such as Acts xiii, 31 were made (N.B., in a speech by Paul)" (1960:38). An understanding of such post-Crucifixion disputes between "the called," meaning especially the disciples, first led by Peter, and Jesus's

family, is essential to historical interpretation of Luke, and especially of the "scene" of reading in Nazareth. A concise basic introduction to these disputes is provided by Kee, Young and Froehlich 1973, esp. 133–137, including the role of Jesus's family in the Jerusalem Christian community around the time of the destruction of the Temple, and 150, 154, 156–157, 391, including the struggle over the role in the Church of the Jewish rigorist faction centered at Jerusalem and headed by Jesus's brother James. See also Conzelmann 1973:55–56, 109–112 on the "wide-ranging hypotheses . . . connected with the person and career of James." Van Unnik 1966:25, situating Luke in a post-Pauline moment in the history of the early Church, describes the complex character of the Church's relation to Jewish law at this moment and asserts that "Luke wanted to show . . . that Christianity without the Jewish law was intended by the Lord." This places Luke in the challenging position of using the Hebrew scriptures, which convey and, from one viewpoint, embody the Law to show that the Law has been superseded.

13. He also, to be sure, joins Paul in making an important contribution to the ancient history of anti-Semitism. Indeed, his triumphalism, as it has emerged in the scholarship of recent decades, has led some Christian scholars to urge its removal from the canon: see Tiede 1988:24.

14. I am thinking of the fall of Nero, the subsequent civil war among army factions and generals competing for the imperial throne, and attendant economic difficulties.

15. As noted earlier, Luke is certainly not the first Christian writer to found Jesus's claims in scripture, but he develops this strategy much more fully than Mark.

16. One might contrast the fate within Luke's text of Jesus's phrase "to preach good news to the poor" with "Today this scripture has been fulfilled in your hearing." Both phrases resonate in Luke (and the former is still the crux to many Christians, as it seems to have been to Archbishop Roach), but it is the implications of the latter which Luke presses most insistently.

17. Here I intend the phrase "Christian culture" in a very wide sense. I understand contemporary Western education, secular though it is claimed to be, as the product of a continuous development since its founding by Alcuin and Charlemagne, and thus still shaped in important ways by Christian goals. I do not mean to use this phrase to deny the multiculturalism of many Western societies, but simply to designate something important about the history of what has long been the dominant element in Western education; this seems useful even if it is agreed that this dominant role is fading.

18. For a discussion of this priestly office, see Hastings, Selbie, and Lambert, vol. 2, s.v. *lector*.

19. The Lukan theme of disclosure of the divine plan is treated in some detail by Tiede 1980, especially p. 30, where he traces Greek words related to disclosure throughout Luke's Gospel. This semantic discussion lays the groundwork for Tiede's argument, p. 32, that Luke is propounding a notion of the "ignorance of the faithful," substantially different from the Markan theme of the ignorance of the messianic secret, and that this notion serves Luke as a literary technique for alerting the faithful reader to strive to move beyond such ignorance by attending to the disclosure of the divine plan as Luke's narrative unfolds.

20. On the interrelation between writing and the creation of a sense of crisis, see de Man 1967, which informs my approach to Luke's "scene of reading."

21. In recent years, and especially in the last decade, scholars have questioned the traditional view that Paul understood Jewish Law, as presented by the scriptures, to have been replaced by Christian faith. For a discussion of the several viewpoints which have emerged, see Daniel Boyarin's treatment of "Circumcision and the Erotic Life of God and Israel" in D. Boyarin 1993.

22. Much as I have claimed in treating Luke.

23. On classical and Christian traditions of the "graciousness" of words, Noakes 1988:66.

24. The best known locus for the congruence between Jesus and "the Word" is, to be sure, the beginning of the Gospel according to John: "In the beginning was the Word, and the Word was with God, and the Word was God."

25. A more detailed account of the interpretant is provided in Noakes 1985, esp. pp. 109–111.

26. Again, the famous Johannine formulation of the Logos, cited above (n. 23), may apply here.

27. Noakes 1988:207–214 explicitly discusses the impact on literary theory of the neglect of the interpretant concept; the entire book deals with this issue implicitly, in its argument that the ground of (professional literary) reading lies *between* exegesis and interpretation and that mediating terms rather than dichotomous ones must be sought to describe it.

28. For a reading by a New Testament specialist who acknowledges fully the character of the rupture, see Tiede 1980:20: "Yet even the most unsophisticated reader is likely to be caught short by the shocking contrast between the two halves of the story. Just when he has announced [his] program, Jesus appears to turn on his audience and precipitate their hatred. In response to their words of apparent approval (4:22), Jesus predicts their rejection ('you will say'), putting hostile words in their mouths and indicting them with prophetic precedent. The juxtaposition is so sharp that it tests the adequacy of any considered attempt to explain, expound, or interpret the text."

29. Drury 1976:86–88 provides a particularly rich commentary on this example of Luke's narrative skill: "The Deuteronomic historian has taught Luke the value of spacious development and how to link and control it. . . . The Jesus who reads the book in the synagogue is the adult development of the boy who sat among the doctors. . . . The whole scene at Nazareth is the prototype of similar scenes in Acts where Christians will preach the gospel and meet with a hostile, even violent response. There is . . . a hint of the resurrection in 'but he passing through the midst of them went his way.'"

30. As Drury (1976:11) points out, in the former, Luke 2:29–32, Simeon calls the infant "a light to lighten the Gentiles"; in the latter, vss. 34–35, with an obscurity typical of prophecy, he tells Mary the child is "set for the fall and rising again of many in Israel; and for a sign which shall be spoken against. . . ."

31. Tiede 1988:108–109 points out that Luke depicts the Nazarenes' question about the relation between Jesus's remarks and his parentage as couched in slightly less adversarial terms than it had been in Mark's depiction; that is, identifying him as Joseph's son rather than simply Mary's does not raise the question of the legit-

imacy of his parentage. But in the context of the episode as a whole, I think, the effect is not so much to exculpate the Nazarenes from charges of insulting verbal behavior (why should Luke want to do this if he is prepared to dramatize their violence as physical a few verses later?) as it is to erase troubling allusions to Jesus's illegitimacy from his source. Luke, in providing the infancy narratives, has already shown keen interest in addressing questions about Jesus's parentage.

32. Tiede 1980:7n points out that to distinguish Christians from Jews "tends to reinforce a distinction which would have been alien to the experience of many first-century Jews in this messianist movement. In Luke-Acts, the process has already begun by which in later eras 'Christianity' and 'Judaism' will define their identities largely by mutual exclusion. But in the community which Luke portrays as believing Jesus to be messiah . . . , those of Jewish heritage regard that belief to be the mark of their fidelity to the religion of Israel." See also Tiede 1980:135 n.23. There is no question, however, that this "scene of reading" becomes legible, from a later viewpoint, as a justification for anti-Semitism.

33. The struggle between the "Greek" or diaspora Jews and the Jerusalem Jews for control of the earliest church is evident first of all in the grumbling of the "Greeks" over the less favorable treatment accorded their widows (6:1). The conflict is reported more explicitly in Acts 11, where the Judaean Christians reproach Peter for preaching to and eating among the uncircumcised, and he responds in part by recounting a vision in which God himself dispenses him from observance of the dietary laws. It is the principal topic of Acts 15, which describes the Council at Jerusalem where Peter and Paul, among others, debate with those Christians among the Pharisees about whether Gentile Christians are obliged to be circumcised and to observe the Torah.

REFERENCES

Boyarin, Daniel
   1993   *Carnal Israel: Reading Sex in Talmudic Culture.* Berkeley and Los
                 Angeles: University of California Press.
Caird, G. B.
   1963   *The Pelican Gospel Commentaries: The Gospel of St. Luke.* London: Adam
                 and Charles Black.
Conzelmann, Hans
   1961   *The Theology of St. Luke.* Trans. Geoffrey Buswell. New York: Harper
                 & Row.
   1973   *History of Primitive Christianity.* Trans. John E. Steely. Nashville:
                 Abingdon Press.
de Man, Paul
   1967   "The Crisis of Contemporary Criticism." *Arion* 6:38–157. Revised
   [1971]   and reprinted as "Criticism and Crisis." In *Blindness and Insight:
                 Essays in the Rhetoric of Contemporary Criticism,* pp. 3–19. New York:
                 Oxford University Press.

Drury, John
1976   *Tradition and Design in Luke's Gospel: A Study in Early Christian Histo-riography*. London: Darton, Longman & Todd.
Hastings, James, John A. Selbie, and John C. Lambert
1912   *A Dictionary of Christ and the Gospels*. 2 vols. New York: Charles Scribner's Sons.
Keck, Leander E., and J. Louis Martyn, eds.
1966   *Studies in Luke-Acts: Essays Presented in Honor of Paul Schubert*. Nashville: Abingdon Press.
Kee, Howard Clark, Franklin W. Young, and Karlfried Froehlich
1973   *Understanding the New Testament*. 3d ed. Englewood Cliffs, N.J.: Prentice-Hall.
Koelb, Clayton
1982   "'In der Strafkolonie': Kafka and the Scene of Reading." *German Quarterly* 55:511–525.
Minear, Paul S.
1966   "Luke's Use of the Birth Stories." In *Studies In Luke-Acts: Essays Presented in Honor of Paul Schubert*. Ed. Keck and Martyn, pp. 111–130.
Moule, C. F. D.
1966   "The Christology of Acts." In *Studies In Luke-Acts: Essays Presented in Honor of Paul Schubert*. Ed. Keck and Martyn, pp. 159–185.
Noakes, Susan
1977   "Self-Reading and Temporal Irony in 'Aurélia.'" *Studies in Romanticism* 16:101–119.
1985   "Literary Semiotics: Towards a Taxonomy of the Interpretant. *American Journal of Semiotics* 3:109–119.
1988   *Timely Reading: Between Exegesis and Interpretation*. Ithaca, N.Y.: Cornell University Press.
1990   "Hermeneutics, Politics, and Civic Ideology in the *Vita Nuova*: Thoughts Preliminary to an Interpretation." *Texas Studies in Literature and Language* 32:40–59.
Revised Standard Version
1952   *The Holy Bible, Revised Standard Version, Containing the Old and New Testaments*. New York: Thomas Nelson & Sons.
Tiede, David L.
1980   *Prophecy and History in Luke-Acts*. Philadelphia: Fortress Press.
1988   *Augsburg Commentary on the New Testament: Luke*. Minneapolis: Augsburg Publishing House.
Van Segbroeck, F.
1989   *The Gospel of Luke. A Cumulative Bibliography 1973–1988*. Collectanea Biblica et Religiosa Antiqua 2. Brussels: Koninklijke Academie van Belgie.
van Unnik, W. C.
1966   "Luke-Acts, A Storm Center in Contemporary Scholarship." In *Studies in Luke-Acts: Essays Presented in Honor of Paul Schubert*. Ed. Keck and Martyn, pp. 15–32.

FOUR

The Cultural Construction of Reading in Anglo-Saxon England

Nicholas Howe

> *The house was quiet and the world was calm.*
> *The reader became the book; and summer night*
>
> *Was like the conscious being of the book.*
> *The house was quiet and the world was calm.*

In these lines from "The House was Quiet and the World was Calm" (1972:279), Wallace Stevens offers a particularly modern description of reading as a private, meditative transaction between reader and book. The act of reading becomes a scene in which the reader is alone, distanced from the claims of domestic and public life. What is read is specifically a book, that is, the material form texts assume in a world shaped both by the technology of printing and by Romantic notions of the self. Thus, as Stevens says, the book as an object possesses "conscious being." Under these conditions, the poet's claim that "the reader became the book" expresses a sense of causation that turns on the double meaning of "become": the reader takes on the form of the book by suiting or complimenting it. The act of reading imposes a trance-like concentration on the reader so that "The words were spoken as if there was no book." A characteristically Stevensian trope, the "as if" of this line asserts its opposite, the inescapable presence of the book in the scene of reading. This concentration is necessary because the reader "wanted much most to be/The scholar to whom his book is true." Stevens closes the poem by claiming audaciously that "truth in a calm world . . . Is the reader leaning late and reading there."

With its chastened, even mundane, diction, "The House was Quiet and the World was Calm" asserts our shared belief that we read best alone, at night, becoming our book, desiring to be the perfect reader we honor as the "scholar." In this way, the poem would have seemed incomprehensible to a medieval reader shaped by classical practices and texts as they were absorbed into Christian culture. For it is precisely the quiet and solitude of Stevens's reader that would have disturbed a medieval reader accustomed to reading as a public, spoken act performed within what Brian Stock calls a "textual community":

> What was essential for a textual community, whether large or small, was simply a text, an interpreter, and a public. The text did not have to be written; oral record, memory, and reperformance sufficed. Nor did the public have to be fully lettered. Often, in fact, only the *interpres* had a direct contact with literate culture, and, like the twelfth-century heretic Peter Waldo, memorized and communicated his gospel by word of mouth. (1990:37)

As the inclusion of orality proves, Stock's use of community is not primarily, if at all, metaphoric; it refers to an actual group of readers, listeners and interpreters. Under these conditions, reading and interpreting texts has the social effect of creating a community in which "individuals who previously had little else in common were united around common goals." Such a community depends upon but also in turn creates "a general agreement on the meaning of a text" (1990:37).

This sense of reading as a communal act, so hauntingly alien to Stevens's poem, may be taken as a useful model for considering reading as a performative event in Anglo-Saxon England because it introduces the necessary dimension of shared cultural practice.[1] Later I will suggest that Stock's idea of a textual community holds for Anglo-Saxon England by examining the etymology of such Old English words as the noun *ræd* and the verb *rædan*, and also by considering various Anglo-Saxon depictions of the scene of reading.[2] But first I want to complicate Stock's concept of textual community by examining a counterexample that in its deviation from cultural norms of reading helps us to understand better the nature of these same norms.

As Augustine describes his long journey to conversion in the *Confessions*, he frequently interposes descriptions of his rhetorical and philosophical education. These passages usually center on his encounters with great figures and, more particularly, with them as readers. Thus Augustine explains his break with the Manicheans as dating from his discovery that he had read more widely than had Faustus, the famous teacher of that sect (*Confessions*, V. 6–7). It thus seems perfectly natural that as he approaches conversion in Milan, Augustine should describe the reading practices of Ambrose, the great Catholic bishop of that city. What surprises us, however, is that Augustine does not identify the works read by Ambrose but rather describes the silent and self-contained manner of his reading. In those moments when Ambrose was not fulfilling a public role, Augustine tells us, he would refresh his body by eating and his mind by reading. But, and the full force of Augustine's *sed* must be registered, Ambrose read silently: *sed cum legebat, oculi ducebantur per paginas et cor intellectum rimabatur, vox autem et lingua quiescebant* "but when he read, his eyes followed the pages and his heart pondered the meaning, though his voice and tongue were still" (*Confessions* VI.3; 1989, I:272). Augustine is careful to specify that Ambrose would read silently to himself even when others were present and might have approached him in conversation. This practice seemed so unusual to Augustine and others around him that they debated about (*discedebamus*) it and offered possible explanations for it. Perhaps Ambrose read silently so that those around him would not be able to interrupt him with questions about the meaning of the text before him. That is, Ambrose read silently to avoid functioning, in Stock's term, as the *interpres*. Or perhaps, Augustine suggests, Ambrose did so to spare his weak voice for necessary public occasions. In the end, Augustine can only assert that Ambrose must have had some good reason for reading silently.

This last comment in no way lessens Augustine's wonder at the sight of a man reading silently. For his is the wonder of a man who had spent his first forty years or so in reading aloud and in public diverse works on Roman rhetoric, Manichean doctrine, Neoplatonic philosophy, and Christian theology. This sense of wonder belongs, then, to a man who believed that the way to the truth was through the written word as performed or interpreted within a community. Whatever spiritual beliefs he held and discarded, Augustine never lost that faith in the written text. To suggest that Ambrose would have appreciated "The House was Quiet and the World was Calm" might be foolishly anachronistic, yet it reminds us not merely of the obvious point that conventions of literacy are culturally determined but also of the more necessary point that not all members of a community subscribe to such conventions at all times. Still, to the extent that he portrays Ambrose as a reader not unlike the scholar of Stevens's poem, Augustine does establish the terms of his own practice as a reader within a textual community: that it should be the speaking aloud of the written text in the company of others so that they might interpret its meaning. That such a community would produce discordant babble rather than interpretive dialogue holds only if we assume that it had no protocols for reading as evident as the signs admonishing "Silence!" in our libraries.[3]

To move from Augustine's *Confessions* to the Old English *ræd* and *rædan* means encountering quite different conventions of culture, language, and literacy. Without denying these obvious differences, it becomes easier to make this move if we recognize that these words and their cognate forms in other Indo-European languages first denoted the act of giving counsel through speech. Recent scholarship on medieval literacy, as exemplified most imaginatively in M. T. Clanchy's *From Memory to Written Record: England, 1066–1307* (1979), Brian Stock's *The Implications of Literacy* (1983), and Rosamond McKitterick's *The Carolingians and the Written Word* (1989), also offers some assistance for considering reading practices in Anglo-Saxon England (see also Crosby 1936; Bäuml 1980). Two very recent books, both learned and subtle, focus more specifically on pre-Conquest England: Katherine O'Brien O'Keeffe's *Visible Song: Transitional Literacy in Old English Verse* (1990) and Seth Lerer's *Literacy and Power in Anglo-Saxon Literature* (1991).[4] O'Keeffe develops a range of innovative techniques for examining manuscripts as evidence for Anglo-Saxon literacy, while Lerer draws productively on contemporary literary and literacy theory to construct a vision of that culture's "literate imagination" (1991:195). Yet since neither constructs its argument by examining what Anglo-Saxons as members of textual communities might have meant by *ræd* and *rædan*, or by absorbing the work of contemporary ethnographers, the following study will be something of a foray into unexamined territory.[5] Perhaps the most useful of all guides for this foray is Tzvetan Todorov's salutary observation that: "Nothing is more commonplace than the reading experience, and yet nothing is more unknown. Reading is such a matter of course that, at first glance, it seems there is nothing to say about it" (1980:67). As Todorov goes on to demonstrate, there is indeed much to say about reading literary texts. Similarly, there is much to say about the word *reading* itself, despite the fact that it seems so utterly transparent in meaning.

The significance of *rædan* can be measured both by its complex etymology and by the range of its primary meanings, because together they establish that it denoted a variety of necessary functions within Anglo-Saxon culture. In his *Indogermanisches Etymologisches Wörterbuch*, Julius Pokorny classifies the old English *rædan* with other forms sharing the Indo-European root *rē-dh-*, *rō-dh-*, *rə-dh-*, including Sanskrit *rādhnóti*, *rādhyati* "to achieve or accomplish" and the Common Germanic **rēdan*. Important Germanic cognates include Gothic *garēdan*, Old High German *ratan*, Old Saxon *rādun*, Old Norse *rāða*, and Old Frisian *rêda* (1959, 1:59–60). As the etymological note in the second edition of the *Oxford English Dictionary* explains, these Germanic cognates share the principal meanings of "to give advise or counsel," "to exercise control over something," and "to explain something obscure," such as a riddle (*OED*, s.v. *read*). This note adds further that only Old English and, perhaps following its lead, Old Norse extended the meaning of "to explain something obscure" to mean "the interpretation of ordinary writing." "Ordinary writing" must be distinguished from the original and specialized meaning of the Old English *writan* "to cut a figure in something" (Bosworth-Toller, s.v. *writan*, I; Lerer 1991:142, 167), and more specifically, "to incise runic letters in stone." These runic inscriptions do not belong to the category of ordinary writing, and thus deciphering them would have fallen under one of the original senses of *rædan*, namely, "to explain something obscure."

The transition from reading something that is obscure, such as a runic inscription, to reading a written text in Old English or Latin—the "ordinary writing" of the *OED*—is crucial to the semantic development of the Modern English *read*. But this transition must be set in a semantic context rather different from that provided by the *OED*. Among the cognates discussed by Pokorny under the root *rē-dh-*, *rō-dh-*, *rə-dh-*, but not listed in the *OED*, are a group of words that designate various forms of speech: Welsh *adrawd* "to tell or narrate" and *amrawdd* "conversation, discourse"; Gothic *rōdjan* "to speak"; Old High German *rātan* "to consult or confer with"; Old Norse *rēða* "to speak." This set of words makes explicit what lies implicit in the other cognates listed above: that the giving of counsel, or the exercising of control, or the explaining of something obscure could only have been a *spoken* act in the cultures that used these various languages before the introduction of writing. More specifically, these words are alike in denoting speech acts that posit an audience or, in the term used in this study, a textual community. In diverse ways, giving advice and solving riddles depend on a shared set of beliefs and body of knowledge. As these functions are performed through the medium of speech rather than writing, they become public means for creating and then enlarging the bounds of a textual community.[6]

The various senses that cluster around the Common Germanic **rêdan* share these two crucial features. With them in mind, it seems slightly more comprehensible that the English word *read* acquired the sense of "to comprehend a written text." Unlike *raten*, its cognate in German, *read* has not remained within its original senses. It has instead been extended to occupy the semantic category that in Gothic is divided between the two verbs **rê-dan* and *lisan*, and in Modern German between *raten* and *lesen*. As a result, the English word for comprehending a written text has no etymological basis in the idea of collecting or gathering together letters and words to form the text as a whole, as do *lisan*, *lesen*, or the Latin *legere*. That our word has no metaphoric underlay of gathering or harvesting is quite surprising, whether one considers the linguistic relations between English, Gothic, and German, or the cultural influence of Latin on English during the formative Anglo-Saxon period.[7]

Why then did the Old English not use the very common word *gad(e)rian* "to gather" as a calque, or morphemic translation, for the Latin *legere* but instead reserved it for translating the Latin *collegere* "to collect" (see, for example, Zupitza 1966:176)? What conditions led speakers of Old English to conceive of comprehending a written text in ways that had not to do with gathering but rather with offering counsel or solving a riddle? The answer to these questions lies in the very nature of the medieval textual community as a group bound together by the reading aloud of texts to listeners for the purpose of interpretation. In a culture unaccustomed to the written text, the act of reading would have seemed remarkably like solving a riddle. For it meant translating meaningless but somehow magical squiggles on a leaf of vellum into significant discourse, even and most remarkably into sacred scripture. What was alien, opaque, seemingly without meaning becomes familiar, transparent, and meaningful when read aloud by those initiated in the solution of such enigma (see further, O'Keeffe 1990:21). Without the dimension of oral performance, reading of this sort could not be perceived by nonliterates as the solving of a mystery. The squiggles must be made to speak.[8]

The same sense of decoding appears in our contemporary use of *read* in nontextual senses, as when we speak of "reading a situation" (where reading means "interpretation" or "solution") or of "profiting from someone's reading of a situation" (where reading edges toward meaning "advice"). In such instances we are not, as might seem the case, offering a metaphorical extension of *read* from a textual to a nontextual context but rather reasserting the primary senses of the word—to solve a riddle and thereby offer advice, counsel, learning. When we speak of reading ordinary writing we are thus using one of the metaphors we live by to describe a text as an enigma that must be solved or made to yield up its meaning. Our use of reading in this sense has, I suspect, little if any conscious metaphoric intent even when appearing in the title of a work of literary analysis that promises to decode a text, such as Edward B. Irving's fine *A Reading of Beowulf*.

In tracing out the semantic development of *redan* in Old English, it is useful to begin with a poetic collection of proverbial sayings and conventional knowledge that bears the modern editorial title of *Maxims I*.[9] This poem of more than 200 lines contains dozens of maxims about virtually all aspects of human experience. The poem is especially valuable for our purposes because it presents its contents as conventional or normative. As it describes the desired order of things in the culture, *Maxims I* offers this series of statements: "Counsel should go with wisdom, the right with the wise, good with the good" (*Ræd sceal mid snyttro, ryht mid wisum, / til sceal mid tilum*; Krapp and Dobbie 1931–1953, III:157, 11.22–23a). This sequence establishes the relation between counsel (*ræd*) and the moral virtues of wisdom and goodness. Later in the poem, *ræd* is set in opposition to *yfel* "evil" so that counsel becomes the most helpful and evil the least helpful of human attributes (*Ræd bið yttost / yfel unnyttost*; 160, 11.118b–119a). The public utility of counsel demands, in the poet's vision, that it be spoken aloud and shared: "A man should speak counsel, write secrets, sing songs, earn fame, express judgment, be active daily" (*Ræd sceal mon secgan, rune writan, leoþ gesingan, lofes gearnian, dom areccan, dæges onettan*; 161, 11.138– 140). The poet announces that giving counsel is an oral, public act and further defines that statement with the following and contrasting statement that associates writing with runes, whether in the literal sense of the runic alphabet or the metaphoric sense of secret knowledge (see Lerer 1991:10– 17). In an oral culture, to give counsel is of necessity to speak and thereby to create community. This belief is explicitly stated by the *Maxims*-poet, but the poem in which we read that statement is itself confirmation that *ræd* as counsel or advice must be exchanged through speech if it is to exist in a nonliterate community.

Ræd and its derivatives are also used in the Latin-Old English glossaries to translate various forms of *consulere* "to consider, take counsel, consult." Thus, we find the Latin phrase *consulo tibi* glossed by the Old English phrase *ic ræde ðe* "I counsel you" (Wright-Wülcker 1884: col. 170.3) and *consulta* by both *rædas* (col. 374.23) and *geræding* (col. 383.25). The Old English *rædbora* "advice-bearer" is used to gloss the Latin *consiliarius* "counsellor" (Wright-Wülcker 1884: col. 539.1 and Zupitza 1966:301) and also the Latin *jurisperitus* "one skilled in law" (col. 424.5). Similarly, the Old English *rædgifa* "advice-giver" could be used to gloss the Latin *consiliator* "counsellor" (col. 170.6). This evidence is particularly useful because it derives from glossaries that record the linguistic interface between literate Latin culture and preliterate English culture. For Anglo-Saxon gloss-writers to use *ræd* and the like to translate *consulere* and the like establishes that the Old English word could often have the same sense of counsel as a public act as did the Latin world.

While most uses of *ræd* and related forms in Old English texts refer to the giving of advice, a significant number of others denote the more specific act of explaining something obscure or solving a riddle. As a major genre of the wisdom literature so loved by the Anglo-Saxons, the riddle had considerably higher intellectual standing in early medieval England than it does today (Bloomfield 1968; Howe 1985). Thus the act of solving a riddle was seen as valuable because it provided illumination, knowledge, even advice. Many of the Old English riddles found in the Exeter Book are expressed in the first-person and conclude with this challenge to the listener: "Say what I am called" (*Saga hwæt ic hatte*; Krapp and Dobbie 1931–1953, III:180–210, 229–243). These riddles quite literally demand an oral solution. In others, the challenge takes the form of "Read what I mean" (*Ræd hwæt ic mæne*; 229; see also Riddle 59, 11. 15–19:210). As a genre, the riddle announces itself as a statement that must be solved or read. Thus Ælfric (c. 955–1020) in his *Grammar* glosses the Latin *ænigma* "enigma" with *rædels* "riddle" (Zupitza 1966:33). In another Latin-Old English gloss, *rædels* appears beside four Latin words: *coniectura, opinatio, estimatio, interpretatio* "conjecture," "opinion," "estimation," "interpretation" (Wright-Wülcker 1884: col. 209.5) which are alike in suggesting responses to or readings of something obscure or enigmatic. This sense of *rædan* is not limited to interpreting texts, though that is perhaps its most common use. In his "Homily for Palm Sunday," Ælfric describes a blindfolded Christ who is challenged by the Jews to guess or "read" who is touching him: *heton hine rædan hwa hine hreopode* "they commanded him to read who was touching him" (Thorpe 1846, II:248). In this example, the blindfolded Christ becomes a personified representation of those acts which require one to read the obscure or difficult as a means of proving one's intellectual or spiritual authority.

With this sense, we reach the end of the semantic field occupied by such cognates of the English *read* as the German *raten*. The extension of the English word to mean the interpretation of ordinary writing draws on the senses that have already been surveyed and also, I would argue, a context that can be situated quite precisely. While my survey of the Old English uses of *rædan* to mean the interpretation of writing is far from exhaustive, one interesting trend emerges from even a few examples. Put simply, the need to translate the Latin *legere* seems to have provided the decisive impetus for the semantic extension of *rædan* in this direction. Ælfric's practice in translating the Heptateuch from Latin into Old English near the end of the tenth century provides a neat example for this development of *ræd* and *rædan*. In translating Exodus 18:19, *sed audi verba mea atque consilia* (*Biblia Sacra*: 60), he offers *ac gehyr min word ond minne ræd* "but hear my word and my counsel" (Crawford 1922:258). Here, as one would expect, *ræd* is used for *consilio*. In translating Exodus 24:7, *legit audiente populo* (*Biblia Sacra*: 65), however, Ælfric offers the extended sense of *rædun. rædde his boc þam folce* "he read his book to the people" (Crawford 1922:272). As I shall discuss in a moment, Ælfric's addition of *boc* "book" to *rædan* signals his understanding that he is using the Old English verb in an extended and potentially confusing manner when it translates *legere*. He thus offers the explanatory, if seemingly redundant, *boc* to help gloss this extended meaning for *rædun*.

As centers for the copying, illuminating, and interpreting of written texts, as well as the teaching of students, monasteries were quite obviously the place where the need to develop an Old English word to designate the reading of such texts was most pressing. And while Latin was the language of the monastic ideal, the vernacular had its obvious uses in the education of the young and the daily life of those monks unable to attain a working fluency in Latin (Auerbach 1965:283–284). One of the chief practices of monastic culture also contributed to the extension of *rædan* to translate *legere*, namely, the practice of reading works aloud, especially during meals (see Ong 1982:74–75; Lerer 1991:8–9). Thus chapter 38 of the *Benedictine Rule*, easily the most important of early medieval monastic rules, prescribes that there should only be holy reading during meals: *Mensis fratrum aedentium lectio deesse non debet* (Chamberlin 1982:48); or, in the tenth-century Old English version of the *Rule*: *Gebroðra gereorde æt hyra mysum ne sceal beon butan haligre rædinge* "nothing but holy reading should be recited to the brothers while they are at their meals" (Schröer 1888:62). That this *lectio* or *ræding* will be drawn from a written text is established by the subsequent references in the Latin text to a *codex* and in the Old English to a *boc*. In this brief passage from the *Rule*, we see not merely the practice of reading described but also the pressing into service of a form of *rædan* to translate a form of *legere*. Related uses of *ræd/ræding* "reading" to translate *lectio*, and of *rædere* "reader" to translate *lector* appear elsewhere in the Old English version of the *Rule* (Schröer 1888:18, 33–35, 62–63). The same translation practice may also be found in a variety of Old English works that offer glosses of Latin, such as Byrhtferth's *Manual* of the late tenth century (*ræding* = *lectio*, Crawford 1929:100–102, 182; see Wright-Wülcker 1884: col. 129.37) and Ælfric's *Grammar* (*ræding* = *lectio*, Zupitza 1966:206). In his *Grammar*, a work designed to lead young students from Old English to Latin, Ælfric three times glosses the masculine *lector* with *rædere* and the feminine *lectrix* with *rædestre* (Zupitza 1966:48, 71, 299). The last example of this gloss is particularly noteworthy because it occurs in a list of ecclesiastical officials ranging from the *patriarcha* = *heahfæder* "patriarch" to *laicus* = *læwede mann* "layman." This use of *rædere* to mean *lector* refers specifically to the church functionary who would read aloud to the spiritual community.

The Old English *Benedictine Rule* is the translation of a Latin work, Ælfric's *Grammar* is meant for the teaching of Latin, and Byrhtferth's *Manual* digests a great deal of information from Latin texts. Each of these English works therefore offers an implicitly bilingual context, which allows readers to better understand the semantic extension of *rædan* and the like to translate *legere* and the like. In works intended to promote the growth of literacy, especially within monastic culture, there would be little need to gloss or otherwise announce the relatively new and quite technical sense for *rædan*, if only because the Old English works using the word in this manner were themselves being read aloud within a textual community of monks and students. We may see here the coalescence of the important earlier meanings of *rædan* as they concern spoken discourse, the giving of counsel, and the interpreting of obscurity, for all three are contained within the reading aloud of a work of scriptural or didactic value written in a code accessible only to the initiated.

In other Old English works of a more popular character, we find writers glossing this new sense of *rædan*. In addition to the example cited earlier from his version of the Heptateuch, we find these representative examples in the works of Ælfric (c. 955–1020): *swa swa we on bocum rædað* "as we read in books" in his *Life of St. Swithin* (Needham 1966:78); *swa swa hit geræd on godspelle* as the gloss for *sicut legitur in evangelio* "just as it reads in the Gospel" in his *Colloquy* (Garmonsway 1965:39); and *we rædað on Cristes bec* "we read in Christ's book" in his "Homily for Shrove Sunday" (Thorpe 1846, I:162). In *The Blickling Homilies*, a popular work of the tenth century, the necessity to explain that *rædan* can mean to read a written text leads the homilist to a very explicit, even redundant, statement: *þonne we gehyron Godes bec us beforan reccean ond rædan, ond godspell secggean* "when we hear God's book explained and read to us and the gospel spoken" (Morris 1880:111; for similar examples, see pp. 15 and 161). This passage offers a brief but vivid sketch of a textual community in which God's book is heard because it is read aloud and then interpreted. All of the primary senses of *rædan* cohere in the homilist's use of the verb but in ways that still seem to have required explanation.

As the reading of written texts became more common and thus less enigmatic, the need to gloss this new sense of the verb must have diminished. A work such as Ælfric's *Grammar* points to a future in which literacy will become a more widespread and necessary skill. It is thus thoroughly appropriate that the forms Ælfric uses to illustrate first, second, and third person singular verbs should be *ego lego ic ræde, tu legis þu rætst, ille legit he ræt* "I read, you read, he reads" (Zupitza 1966:127–128). It is grammars of Latin written for English students that will create the necessary context for this new sense of *rædan* and make it primary over time. That this new sense of reading is still not quite ours, though, is made clear by four pages in Ælfric's *Grammar* devoted to an obsessively complete conjugation of the passive verb in Latin as exemplified by *legor* "to be read." Ælfric defines the passive *legor* as *Ic eom geræd on sumum gewrite sum ðing to donne*, literally "I am advised in this writing to do something" (Zupitza 1966:182). I would suggest that Ælfric's use of *rædan* here can be taken as meaning both "advise," and thus as belonging with the phrase "to do something," and also as meaning "read," and thus as belonging with the phrase "in this writing." That is, one is advised to do something by reading. More generally, there could be no better example of a passive verb than this to offer students who were themselves being read to and who were struggling to understand the obscurities of Latin as a written language. As Lerer observes, "Literacy for Ælfric is thus a social practice as much as it is an intellectual skill" (1991:56). In this same spirit, Byrhtferth explains in his *Manual* that he is writing for the benefit of *unge mynstermen* "young monastic students" and bids *þa boceras ond þa getydde weras* "scholars and learned men" not to be impatient with his elementary exposition (Crawford 1929:132). The Old English noun *bocere* can mean "scholar," "author," "grammarian," "Jewish scribe" (*Dictionary of Old English*, s.v. *bocere*) but most basically it means one who can *read* books (Lerer 1991:130–131, 201; for Bede as *breoma bocera* "famous scholar" see Krapp and Dobbie 1931–1953, VI:27). As these examples demonstrate, *rædan* belongs to the category of key words described by Raymond Williams: "they are significant, binding words in certain activities and their interpretation; they are significant, indicative words in certain forms of thought" (1985:15; Williams does not discuss *read* or any related form). *Rædan* belongs at the very center of the profound cultural changes that characterize Anglo-Saxon England because in no small measure they were made possible by this new idea of reading.[10]

Etymology and linguistic usage do not alone define cultural practice. To understand what reading meant to Anglo-Saxons—frequently but not always clerical males (Wormald 1977)—we need to see how they functioned within their various speech communities. We need, in other words, to ask what they did if we are to gain some sense of how the word *read* continued its semantic development to include meanings that refer specifically to comprehending a written text. There survive in Anglo-Saxon works at least two vivid descriptions of reading within textual communities. Quite fortunately these passages describe individuals of widely different class and background: the cowherd Cædmon as told about by Bede in his *Ecclesiastical History of the English Church and People* (731), and King Alfred as told about by Asser in his *Life of Alfred* (893). As the great religious history of the Anglo-Saxons and as the period's fullest political biography respectively, these two works are culturally central and command serious attention. In each we see the act of reading described in ways that the etymology of *rædan* can only hint at. Yet that etymology provides a necessary reminder that reading was conducted under largely oral conditions. In considering these passages from Bede and Asser, it is helpful to follow Carlo Ginzburg, as he discusses the reading practices of the French peasantry in the late eighteenth century, and ask: "To what extent did the prevalently oral culture of those readers interject itself in the use of the text, modifying it, reworking it, perhaps to the point of changing its very essence?" (1982:xxii).

The story of Cædmon provides a classic case for studying reading practices in a culture of restricted literacy. As a cowherd in the service of a monastery, Cædmon lives on the periphery of a literate community but he also functions each day within the established practices of his own oral culture. Indeed, the miracle associated with Cædmon could only have occurred in a setting that allowed the oral and the written to coexist and even to permeate each other. Bede relates that Cædmon would, from a sense of his own lack of talent, quietly withdraw from the banqueting hall when his turn to sing a song and play the harp approached. Put another way, Cædmon withdraws from the most established social ritual of his vernacular community. One night, after leaving the hall, he retires to the cowbarn and falls asleep to a dream in which someone calls to him by name and orders him to sing a song. Cædmon replies that he cannot sing, the authority figure repeats his command, and Cædmon asks what he should sing about. After being told to sing of God's Creation, Cædmon recites a vernacular poem that he had never heard before and that now goes by the name of "Cædmon's Hymn" (Krapp and Dobbie 1931–1953, VI:105–106). The nine-line poem that we have seems to be only a fragment of Cædmon's first creation, but it clearly observes the strict metrical, alliterative, and stylistic conventions of vernacular Old English poetry and is also orthodox in its Christian theology.

The next morning Cædmon tells the reeve and then the abbess of the monastery about his dream. All agree that Cædmon has been divinely inspired with the gift of poetic composition. For modern scholars, particularly those interested in oral composition, this story contains in the person of a monastic cowherd the great cultural encounter of Anglo-Saxon England between the native, vernacular culture of a Germanic people and the Mediterranean, Latin culture of the Catholic Church. In this encounter, Cædmon becomes a Christian hero by turning traditional poetics to the new and urgent purpose of propagating the faith (Hanning 1966:88). In doing so, he seems to preserve a necessary place for orality in a culture where religious authority was increasingly defined by those who could read the written text of the Latin Bible. For scholars of a vernacularizing bias, the story of Cædmon demonstrates the survival of a traditional, indigenous poetics in the face of the cultural invasion of Christianity. The subjects of that poetry may be new, but its oral technique and audience remain largely unchanged. Framed within the narrow terms of poetic composition, this line of argument makes good sense. If we enlarge the frame to consider the ways in which Cædmon found subjects for his poetry, however, then we must conclude that his story marks the end of pure orality in Anglo-Saxon England and initiates a complex interchange between oral poetics and written texts (O'Keeffe 1990:46; Lerer 1991:42–60).[11] More particularly, his story establishes that this new interchange could take place within the bounds of a textual community precisely because it was sufficiently flexible to include cowherd as well as cleric, vernacular as well as scriptural language.

Bede's account of Cædmon does not end with his "Hymn," as some strict oralists might prefer. Bede goes on to explain that the abbess and monks of the monastery set Cædmon a test to determine if his miraculous gift were limited to the creation of one short poem or could extend to other compositions: "They then read to him a passage of sacred history or doctrine, bidding him make a song out of it, if he could, in metrical form. He undertook the task and went away; on returning next morning he repeated the passage he had been given, which he had put into excellent verse" *exponebantque illi quendam sacrae historiae siue doctrinae sermonem, praecipientes eum, si posset, hunc in modulationem carminis transferre. At ille suscepto negotio abiit, et mane rediens optimo carmine quod iubebatur conpositum reddidit* (Colgrave and Mynors 1969:417– 419). In the Latin, the crucial verb to designate the monks' action is *exponere* "to set forth, to expound" because it makes clear that they did not simply read aloud a scriptural passage (unfortunately not identified by Bede) but also interpreted it. The initial stage of this exposition depended, either implictly or explicitly, on translation from Latin to the vernacular. While we cannot know whether the monks read the texts aloud first in Latin and then translated them into Old English, or simply paraphrased them into the vernacular, it remains evident that the members of this textual community recognized that they were functioning in a bilingual context. It may well be that the distinction between vernacular and Latin is at least as consequential for studying reading in Anglo-Saxon England as is the more obvious distinction between orality and literacy. For this distinction determined the sociolinguistic character of the community, especially in matters relating to its members' communicative responsibilities. As the monks expound the text to Cædmon, they incorporate him within their community and also determine that his role will be to expound the text in a different manner to a different audience. The nature of Cædmon's divine gift is thus clearly limited to his ability to transform written text as it is read aloud to him into Old English verse for oral delivery. To stress the obvious, what is not at issue is the question of Cædmon's inability to read ordinary writing. Miracles, it would seem, need only extend so far.

Having satisfied the monks of his ability, Cædmon is admitted yet more fully into the textual community. He takes monastic vows and continues to compose poetry. More specifically, he sang (*canebat*) stories taken from Genesis, from Exodus, and from elsewhere in the sacred scripture. He sang as well about the Life of Christ, from His birth to His ascension, and thus drew on the New as well as the Old Testament. While we have Old English poems on virtually all of these subjects, none can be ascribed on internal evidence to Cædmon. Still, it is not surprising that other Old English poets should have taken for their subjects the same biblical stories as did Cædmon. For these subjects reveal the Old English poets' understanding of the textual community to which they have been admitted: one in which they must disseminate the central canon of the evangelical church.

Unlike the divinely-inspired substance of his "Hymn," the subjects of Cædmon's later poems were very much the result of human intervention. Bede explains that the monks continued to read to Cædmon and instruct him: "He learned all he could by listening to them and then, memorizing it and ruminating over it, like some clean animal chewing the cud, he turned it into the most melodious verse: and it sounded so sweet as he recited it that his teachers became in turn his audience" *At ipse cuncta, quae audiendo discere poterat, rememorando secum et quasi mundum animal ruminando, in carmen dulcissimum conuertebat, suauiusque resonando doctores suos uicissim auditores sui faciebat* (Colgrave and Mynors 1969:418–419). To the question why the monks did not teach Cædmon to read, one might respond that it would have been a waste of everybody's time. Less facetiously, one might say that the question itself reveals a misunderstanding of the nature of an early medieval textual community. Established as he was within the monastery, Cædmon had no need to read alone and to himself. Indeed, his particular responsibility to transform Latin text into Old English verse emphasized the skills of oral performance rather than of reading comprehension. We must also ask if the entire question of Cædmon's inability to read is not at least partially anachronistic in its assumption that this ability be defined strictly by our own cultural practice as readers who exist in only the most tenuous of communities. Put in another way, one that considers ends rather than means, we can argue that Cædmon was literate in matters of scriptural knowledge. As Stock cautions, "Literacy is not textuality" (1983:7). The question then becomes one of asking what Cædmon could not do as a poet because he could not, by our standards, read for himself. The only possible answer, I would suggest, is that he could not have existed apart from his community. And yet, if that were to have happened, Cædmon could not be described as a poet because he would have no audience or community to whom he could recite his oral compositions. The point holds both ways. Separate Cædmon from his community as defined by those who read to him and he could not find the content of his poems; separate him from his community as made up of those who listened to him and he would not retain his communal validation as a poet.

The terms of this argument may also be reversed to ask what it means that the monks of Cædmon's monastery could read, as we use the term. For even here, in considering reading as a skill reserved to an elite group pledged to spread the divine truth as contained in a Latin text, we see that reading retains its earlier cultural features. Even for this elite, reading necessarily involved the element of oral delivery, of reading aloud, and also of giving counsel or advice or, in the story of Cædmon, subject matter. To read meant to expound to other members of one's textual community. However we examine reading in Anglo-Saxon England, we cannot escape the ethnographic dimension of a community bound together by common texts. Quite simply, no Anglo-Saxon learned to read in order to read alone, late at night, in a quiet house and a calm world.

One might of course counter that we can only know about Cædmon and his textual community because we can read about it in Bede's *Ecclesiastical History*, the most learned and polished of all Latin works written in Anglo-Saxon England. In other words, we know of Cædmon only because Bede could write and expected his fellow Anglo-Saxons to read so that they could learn the religious history of themselves as a people. To this, one can only respond that Bede knew the precise nature of his own textual community. Though he lived a monastic life from early childhood, Bede did not restrict the benefits of literacy to those who belonged to that community and who could read. As he closes the preface to his *Ecclesiastical History*, he requests the prayers of those who read his work or who hear it read: *legentes siue audientes* (Colgrave and Mynors 1969:6). Both readers and listeners belong in a community at once textual and spiritual, written and oral, in which intellectual and spiritual life is created through the communal interchange of reading.

This sense of reading as a communal act informs the intellectual life of King Alfred (fl. 871–899) as told by his friend and teacher, the Welsh cleric

Asser. While Alfred seems to have learned to read the vernacular at the relatively advanced age of twelve, he revealed from early childhood a powerful ability to memorize Old English poetry (Stevenson 1904:19–20). Thus Asser describes the young Alfred memorizing an entire book of Old English poetry (*Saxonicum poematicae artis librum*, Stevenson 1904:20) so that he might win it from his brothers in a competition sponsored by their mother. While Asser's text is somewhat murky at this point (Keynes and Lapidge 1983:239, n. 48), it is evident that Alfred did not himself read this book but rather memorized its contents after it was read aloud to him. To that extent, he reminds us of Cædmon, but Alfred did learn to read English in his teens and, far more impressively, Latin at the age of thirty-nine. Asser explains that Alfred learned to read and interpret Latin on a single day through divine inspiration (*divino instinctu legere et interpretari simul uno eodemque die primitus inchoavit*, Stevenson 1904:73).

At this moment, we are reminded that Asser's *Life of Alfred* owes no small debt to the conventions of hagiography (see Lerer 1991:61–96). Nonetheless, Alfred's mastery of Latin was a remarkable achievement, even if we explain it not by divine inspiration but by his life-long presence within a textual community. For Asser tells us that the most striking characteristic displayed by Alfred throughout his life was that of reading aloud or listening to others read aloud at all times and under all conditions (*Nam haec est propria et usitatissima illius consuetudo die noctuque, inter omnia alia mentis et corporis impedimenta, aut per se ipsum libros recitare, aut aliis recitantibus audire*; Stevenson 1904:67). If Alfred did learn to read Latin in a day, it was because he had spent much of his life preparing to read, as we mean the term, by listening to others read communally. Taken in this way, Asser's *Life of Alfred* records Alfred's knowing absorption of the ideas and workings of a literate culture—that is, of written texts in Old English and in Latin—before he could read for himself through membership in a textual community. Alfred, by the available evidence, never learned to write in either Latin or Old English. As Katherine O'Brien O'Keeffe puts it tellingly: "A man and a king at a transitional moment in the shift from orality to literacy, he does not write but orders Asser to do it for him" (1990:84).

Alfred's belief in the cultural importance of reading both English and Latin shaped his educational program for his own children as well as the Anglo-Saxons as a people. Given Alfred's own belated formal education, there is something very poignant in Asser's description of the school attended by his children, both male and female, and of the books in Latin and in English that were assiduously read. The principles that guided the education of Alfred's children in their small and seemingly informal school (Stevenson 1904:300, on *schola*) found fuller and more influential expression in the program of translations advanced by Alfred in the 890s. After defeating the Danes in 878 and consolidating his rule over the southern portion of

England granted to him under the terms of the Treaty of Wedmore, Alfred devoted himself to educational reform. In his famous *Preface* to the Old English translation of Gregory's *Pastoral Care* (c. 890), Alfred delivers an impassioned if perhaps hyperbolic lament on the wretched state of intellectual life in England on his ascent to the throne in 871 (for translation, see Keynes and Lapidge 1983:124–126). No one south of the Thames, Alfred claims, could then translate from Latin into English and few elsewhere on the island could do so. Those who served God at that time could not profit from the available books because they were written in Latin rather than English.

Although Alfred struggled to improve the teaching of Latin in England, he also sponsored a program of translating crucial Latin works into English. These works may not have been numerous, but together they contained the core of Latin Christianity: Gregory the Great's *Pastoral Care* and *Dialogues*, Orosius's *History Against the Pagans*, Boethius's *Consolation of Philosophy*, Augustine's *Soliloquies*, and Bede's *Ecclesiastical History*. Whether Alfred translated any or all of these works is far less important for our purposes than is his accomplishment of creating an intellectual and, it should not be forgotten, political climate of stability in which they could be translated. Moreover, as C. L. Wrenn has observed, Alfred's "impetus must have caused the writing of other prose translations in his later years" that have since been lost (1967:222; see further, Frantzen 1986). The importance of this translation program for the practice of reading in Anglo-Saxon England can hardly be overestimated, for it brought into the vernacular textual community a body of Latin learning in history, philosophy, and theology that would otherwise not have been accessible even to those who could read ordinary writing in the vernacular. Alfred's exemplary kingship thus extends far beyond his youthful military success. As a ruler, he was one of the lucky few to have known what to do with the peace he won in battle. Most remarkably, he recognized that his nation's political and spiritual well-being depended on a dynamic, inclusive, and thus increasingly vernacular textual community. By reading aloud to others or by hearing others read aloud to them, members of such a community might emulate the virtuous and shun the wicked as Bede had urged in the preface to his *Ecclesiastical History*. Arguably the greatest of Alfred's accomplishments was to place reading in all of its various senses—the understanding of written texts but also the giving of counsel and the understanding of obscure matters—at the heart of public life.

For all that one wishes, no study of reading in Anglo-Saxon England can end with the visionary Alfred and that last brilliant decade of his reign. Instead, one must close with the name of another Anglo-Saxon king, one not blessed with Alfred's love of learning. The last king to rule Anglo-Saxon England before its conquest by the Danish King Cnut in 1014 was the un-

fortunate Ethelred, literally "Noble Counsel" but nicknamed by later generations "The Unready." He was not, as one might think from this epithet,
unprepared; rather, he was more immediately Ethelred "No Counsel"
(*un* + *ræd*). Sir Frank Stenton has described Ethelred as a "king of singular
incompetence" (1971:395). To the extent that we think of him merely as
unprepared, we mitigate his incompetence, for he was guilty of a far greater
failing in an Anglo-Saxon king. He took no counsel and had no sense of his
political role within the textual community. He betrayed his name and
earned his epithet: Noble Counsel, No Counsel.

Much more could and should be said about reading in Anglo-Saxon
England. A comprehensive semantic-field study of words relating to reading
in Old English, Latin, and Old Norse would be the obvious next step, particularly if it were responsive to the larger ethnographic and sociolinguistic aspects of the topic.[12] Yet even this preliminary study makes clear
that reading in Anglo-Saxon England cannot be understood by any facile
opposition of orality and literacy. To quote Brian Stock one last time:
"There is in fact no clear point of transition from a nonliterate to a literate
society" (1983:9; see also Goody 1987:293; O'Keeffe 1990:190–194). That
no such point of clear transition can be located in Anglo-Saxon England is
vividly illustrated by the linguistic evidence, especially when the key words
are not considered only in isolation but also are placed within a larger
ethnographic context. This intertwining of language and social practice
provides a powerful methodology for countering what James Clifford
(1986:118) has called "ethnographic pastoral," the belief that there was
once a golden age of orality before the corrupting force of literacy made itself felt. As he acutely observes, "in the West the passage from oral to literate is a potent recurring *story*—of power, corruption, and loss" (118). It is
also a story, as we are now coming to realize, that has too often distorted
the practice of those who study orality and literacy either ethnographically
or historically. If we are, more specifically, to understand the complex
range of human acts that speakers of English have over the centuries designated as reading, we must avoid constructing visions of a lost past, just as
we must avoid assuming that reading is tied inextricably to our modern and
highly literate conventions. For all that we become Wallace Stevens's
"scholar" as we study—alone, by ourselves, too often late at night—the
historical and semantic development of reading, we should remember that
rædan originally referred to a public, spoken act within a community.[13]

NOTES

1. For striking parallels with reading practices in ancient Jewish culture, see
Daniel Boyarin 1993.

2. I follow the standard practice of using Anglo-Saxon to designate the period of English history from the fifth through the eleventh century, as well as the people of that period, and of reserving Old English for the Germanic vernacular spoken then. Any consideration of the linguistic communities of Anglo-Saxon England would ideally include Latin and the Scandinavian dialects introduced during the period as well as Old English.

3. For a portrait of such a modern textual community and its conventions of interpretive dialogue, see Jonathan Boyarin 1993.

4. These books appeared after I completed the first draft of this study. I have learned a great deal from them and have sought to integrate their findings into my work, while also recognizing the striking similarities in argument and evidence between their work and mine.

5. Lerer (1991:236–237, nn. 23, 24) offers a few suggestive comments on *ræd* and also quotes the etymological discussion in the *OED s.v. read*, but he does not pursue the linguistic and ethnographic issues advanced in this study.

6. A textual community is of course embedded in a larger speech community. In the case of Anglo-Saxon England, one might argue that the most important textual communities were not those that used only Old English or Latin, but rather those that used both of these languages for the purposes of reading.

7. That the English *read* lacks this underlay also suggests that the development of *lesen* and *legere* may not be quite as natural or inevitable as seems at first glance. But that is a problem for another study.

8. A similar process can be seen in the derivation of *glamour* from *grammar*. As the knowledge of written signs, grammar acquired an occult or magical aura and thus, over time, gave rise to *glamour* in the sense first of enchantment and then of bewitching beauty (*OED*, *s.v. grammar*).

9. Where possible, I offer a date for the Anglo-Saxon works cited. Quite frequently, however, these dates are very approximate and should be treated with extreme caution. They are rarely so accurate as to sustain a chronologically precise argument for the semantic development of a word.

10. For the remarkable level of literacy and learning among the educated elite of Anglo-Saxon England, see Lendinara (1991). For the practices of Anglo-Saxon readers, especially those of vernacular works, see O'Keeffe 1990:155–187.

11. For general studies of orality in Anglo-Saxon England, see Opland (1980) and Foley (1988:65–74). For a more specialized study on orality and pectorality, see Jager (1990).

12. No such study is cited in the recent and thorough survey by Strite (1989).

13. As is apparent, I write as a medievalist rather than as an ethnographer. But it is a pleasure to acknowledge my debt to ethnographic works that have shaped my thinking about reading: Basso (1974), Clifford (1986), Sherzer (1977), Tedlock (1983), Wagner, Messick, and Spratt (1986), and Goody (1987). For assistance and conversation about the topic of reading, I thank Jonathan Boyarin, James N. Comas, Morris Foster, Georgina Kleege, and Fred C. Robinson. I must also thank Daniel Donoghue and Antonette diPaolo Healey for kindly reading an earlier version of this study.

REFERENCES

Auerbach, Erich
1965   *Literary Language and its Public in Late Latin Antiquity and in the Middle Ages.* Trans. Ralph Manheim. New York: Pantheon Books.

Augustine
1989   *Confessions.* 2 vols. Trans. William Watts. Cambridge, Mass.: Harvard University Press.

Basso, Keith
1974   "The Ethnography of Writing." *Explorations in the Ethnography of Speaking.* Ed. Richard Bauman and Joel Sherzer, pp. 425–432. Cambridge: Cambridge University Press.

Bäuml, Franz H.
1980   "Varieties and Consequences of Medieval Literacy and Illiteracy." *Speculum* 55:237–265.

Biblia Sacra
1965   *Biblia Sacra.* Madrid: Biblioteca de Autores Cristianos.

Bloomfield, Morton W.
1968   "Understanding Old English Poetry." *Annuale Mediaevale* 9:5–25.

Bosworth, Joseph, and T. Northcote Toller
1882–1898 *An Anglo-Saxon Dictionary.* 3 vols. Oxford: Oxford University Press.

Boyarin, Daniel
1993   "Placing Reading: Ancient Israel and Medieval Europe." In *The Ethnography of Reading.* Ed. Jonathan Boyarin. Berkeley and Los Angeles: University of California Press.

Boyarin, Jonathan
1993   "Voices Around the Text: The Ethnography of Reading at the Mesivta Tifereth Jerusalem." In *The Ethnography of Reading.* Ed. Jonathan Boyarin. Berkeley and Los Angeles: University of California Press.

Chamberlin, John, ed.
1982   *The Rule of St. Benedict: The Abingdon Copy.* Toronto: Centre for Medieval Studies.

Clanchy, M. T.
1979   *From Memory to Written Record: England, 1066–1307.* Cambridge, Mass.: Harvard University Press.

Clifford, James
1986   "On Ethnographic Allegory." In *Writing Culture: The Poetics and Politics of Ethnography.* Ed. James Clifford and George E. Marcus, pp. 98–121. Berkeley and Los Angeles: University of California Press.

Colgrave, Bertram, and R. A. B. Mynors, eds.
1969   *Bede's Ecclesiastical History of the English People.* Oxford: Clarendon Press.

Crawford, S. J., ed.
1922   *The Old English Version of the Heptateuch, Ælfric's Treatise on the Old and New Testament and his Preface to Genesis.* Early English Text Society, O.S. 160. London: Oxford University Press.

1929   *Byrhtferth's Manual*. Early English Text Society, O.S. 177. London: Oxford University Press.

Crosby, Ruth
1936   "Oral Delivery in the Middle Ages." *Speculum* 11:88–110.

Dictionary of Old English
1991   Fascicle B. Ed. Ashley Crandell Amos, Antonette diPaolo Healey et al. Toronto: Pontifical Institute of Mediaeval Studies.

Foley, John Miles
1988   *The Theory of Oral Composition: History and Methodology*. Bloomington: Indiana University Press.

Frantzen, Allen J.
1986   *King Alfred*. Boston: Twayne Publishers.

Garmonsway, G. N., ed.
1965   *Ælfric's Colloquy*. London: Methuen.

Ginzburg, Carlo
1982   *The Cheese and the Worms: The Cosmos of a Sixteenth-Century Miller*. Trans. John and Anne Tedeschi. New York: Penguin.

Goody, Jack
1987   *The Interface Between the Written and the Oral*. Cambridge: Cambridge University Press.

Hanning, Robert W.
1966   *The Vision of History in Early Britain: From Gildas to Geoffrey of Monmouth*. New York: Columbia University Press.

Howe, Nicholas
1985   "Aldhelm's Enigmata and Isidorian Etymology." *Anglo-Saxon England* 14:37–59.

Irving, Edward B.
1968   *A Reading of "Beowulf."* New Haven: Yale University Press

Jager, Eric
1990   "Speech and the Chest in Old English Poetry." *Speculum* 65:845–859.

Keynes, Simon, and Michael Lapidge, trans.
1983   *Alfred the Great: Asser's Life of King Alfred and Other Contemporary Sources*. Harmondsworth, Middlesex and New York: Penguin.

Krapp, George Philip, and Elliott Van Kirk Dobbie, eds.
1931–1953   *The Anglo-Saxon Poetic Records*. 6 vols. New York: Columbia University Press.

Lendinara, Patrizia
1991   "The World of Anglo-Saxon Learning." In *The Cambridge Companion to Old English Literature*. Ed. Malcolm Godden and Michael Lapidge, pp. 264–281. Cambridge: Cambridge University Press.

Lerer, Seth
1991   *Literacy and Power in Anglo-Saxon Literature*. Lincoln and London: University of Nebraska Press.

McKitterick, Rosamond
1989   *The Carolingians and the Written Word*. Cambridge: Cambridge University Press.

Morris, R., ed.
    1880   *The Blickling Homilies of the Tenth Century.* Early English Text Society,
                O.S. 73. London: Trubner.
Needham, G. I., ed.
    1966   *Ælfric: Lives of Three English Saints.* London: Methuen.
O'Keeffe, Katherine O'Brien
    1990   *Visible Song: Transitional Literacy in Old English Verse.* Cambridge:
                Cambridge University Press.
Ong, Walter J.
    1982   *Orality and Literacy: The Technologizing of the Word.* London and New
                York: Methuen.
Opland, Jeff
    1980   *Anglo-Saxon Oral Poetry: A Study of the Traditions.* New Haven: Yale
                University Press.
Pokorny, Julius
    1959   *Indogermanisches Etymologisches Wörterbuch.* 2 vols. Bern and Munich:
                Francke Verlag.
Schröer, Arnold, ed.
    1885–1888   *Die angelsächsischen Prosabearbeitungen der Benedictinerregel.* Cassel:
                Wigand.
Sherzer, Joel
    1977   "The Ethnography of Speaking." In *Linguistic Theory: What Can It Say
                About Reading?* Ed. Roger W. Shuy, pp. 144–152. Newark, Del.:
                International Reading Association.
Stenton, Frank
    1971   *Anglo-Saxon England.* 3d ed. Oxford: Clarendon Press.
Stevens, Wallace
    1972   *The Palm at the End of the Mind: Selected Poems and a Play.* Ed. Holly
                Stevens. New York: Vintage.
Stevenson, William Henry, ed.
    1904   *Asser's Life of King Alfred.* Oxford: Clarendon Press.
Stock, Brian
    1983   *The Implications of Literacy: Written Language and Models of Interpretation
                in the Eleventh and Twelfth Centuries.* Princeton: Princeton University
                Press.
    1990   *Listening for the Text: On the Uses of the Past.* Baltimore: Johns Hopkins
                University Press.
Strite, Vic
    1989   *Old English Semantic-Field Studies.* New York: Peter Lang.
Tedlock, Dennis
    1983   *The Spoken Word and the Work of Interpretation.* Philadelphia: University
                of Pennsylvania Press.
Thorpe, Benjamin, ed.
    1846   *The Homilies of the Anglo-Saxon Church... Containing the Homilies of
                Ælfric.* London: Ælfric Society. Reprint, New York: Johnson Reprint
                (1971).

Todorov, Tzvetan
1980   "Reading as Construction." In *The Reader in the Text: Essays on Audience and Interpretation.* Ed. Susan R. Suleiman and Inge Crosman, pp. 67–82. Princeton: Princeton University Press.

Wagner, Daniel A., Brinkley M. Messick, and Jennifer Spratt
1986   "Studying Literacy in Morocco." In *The Acquisition of Literacy: Ethnographic Perspectives.* Ed. Bambi B. Schieffelin and Perry Gilmore, pp. 233–260. Norwood, N.J.: Ablex.

Williams, Raymond
1985   *Keywords: A Vocabulary of Culture and Society.* Rev. ed. New York: Oxford University Press.

Wormald, C. P.
1977   "The Uses of Literacy in Anglo-Saxon England and its Neighbours." *Transactions of the Royal Historical Society,* 5th ser. 27:95–114.

Wrenn, C. L.
1967   *A Study of Old English Literature.* New York: Norton.

Wright, Thomas, and Richard Paul Wülcker, eds.
1884   *Anglo-Saxon and Old English Vocabularies.* 2d ed. 2 vols. London: Trubner.

Zupitza, Julius, ed.
1966   *Ælfrics Grammatik und Glossar: Text und Varianten* (Berlin: 1880). Reprint, with preface by Helmut Gneuss. Berlin: Weidmann.

FIVE

Keep Listening:
Ethnography and Reading

Johannes Fabian

THE STUDY OF LITERACY AND THE NEGLECT OF READING

Nothing human is supposed to escape anthropology's attention. Yet reading, an activity on which many humans spend more time than on eating, having sex, or participating in rituals, has not been among the rubrics of standard ethnographic research and writing. Why this should have been so is a question to be asked, now that reading seems to become a topic of ethnography. In the first part of this paper I want to show that answers may be found if we begin to think about the ways in which literacy has been approached in our discipline.[1]

There is a story which goes like this: In the beginning, anthropologists (and their predecessors) studied the invention/origin and diffusion/ evolution of systems of writing. This was taking literacy literally. Later it was realized that literacy might be looked at more broadly, not just as a "technology" but as a social practice that involves more than using a script. And finally the idea appeared that literacy may be a political-ideological complex which is involved in the exercise of power, in the maintenance of inequality, and in imperial designs. This opened up a global perspective. Literacy, it was realized, had a real presence in much of the world—not as popular mass literacy but as something that belonged to the aura of religious and secular power—when those who began to propagate mass literacy in the service of the scriptures, at home, and in the newly conquered parts of Africa and America, invented "orality." It has been said that the Reformation was the one event that offered, by combining the power of the scriptures in the vernacular with that of the printing press, the incentives for the spread of generalized literacy (Harbsmeier 1989). Then, at the latest in the eighteenth century (Gusdorf 1973), orality took its revenge; it became a weapon of "critique" (bible criticism, literary criticism). Orality (and aurality) became epistemological issues in the nineteenth century; Herder and Humboldt built their theories of language and, indeed culture, on speech and sound (rather than writing and sight). Orality went into the foundations of modern anthropology—where it remained buried. Above the ground, the seeing eye became the root metaphor of knowledge. The observing gaze delivered the material; visible order created by classification provided its meaning.

When anthropology became established academically toward the end of the nineteenth century and began to study systematically "peoples without writing," orality was usually regarded as little more than that which remains when literacy is subtracted from a culture: a sign of a lower stage of evolution. Oral peoples were depicted as intellectually rather dim; their thoughts were said to be short-lived due to the absence of means to preserve them; their capacity to organize major work projects or to govern large populations and keep records on them were deemed limited. In short, they were the kind of people who "cried out" (orally) for the blessings of literacy.

While thus orality was used as a means to establish distance from one's own place, whereby distance implied inferiority given the prevailing equation of evolution with progress, there was some lingering envy, inherited from the romantics. Orality makes peoples verbose and lively, great entertainers and performers, free from the constraints of script and scripture. Still, except for serving anthropology by demarcating its territory, orality as nonliterateness continued to lead a shadow life; it remained the dark side of what was brought to light about human history.

Then came Walter Ong and others. They cast doubts on the blessings of literacy within our own culture by showing how the promotion of the graphic and the visual had depersonalized language and speaking. Worse, they found that most of what had for centuries been regarded sound pedagogical method had in fact been invented in order to make knowledge a matter of internalizing signs, graphs, and diagrams (which fitted the printed page), rather than disputing about matters that matter in live dialog: An interesting discovery (of Ramus and his works by Ong), and a productive critical position (and a very popular one in the form in which it was propagated by Marshall McLuhan). Still, it took decades before it was appreciated widely by anthropologists.

Then came Jan Vansina with a book on oral tradition—at a time when the idea that there was history only where there was writing became less and less accepted. Initially at least, he convinced as many people as he did because he offered a "method" whereby oral tradition "there" could be pro-

cessed such that it would meet more or less (mostly more) the same standards as those held in esteem by historians "here." (Vansina came again, a
generation later, but it was a different book.)

Then Jack Goody and others showed two things: (1) "Traditional"
(speak: oral) societies were much more involved with, touched by, literacy
than had previously been assumed; therefore processes of transition deserve
above all our attention. (2) Literacy in the narrow sense, writing, has been
but part of a graphic "technology" whose development had its own "logic"
and ran its own course with a necessity that seems to distinguish major
technological advances. One can see an element of contradiction between
these two assertions: The first one wants to dismantle received ideas about
absolute barriers between literate and illiterate societies; and that was good
because it undermined claims to superiority on the part of the former. The
other asserts an inner, necessary connection between literacy and "domes-
tication"; and that is bad, because it somehow excuses the domination of
illiterate by literate societies when it makes the effects of literacy an inevitable outcome of technological evolution. But, if there is contradiction, it is
only in ethical terms; logically and, ultimately, historically, the two theses
envisage two sides of the same coin, the coin being the victorious march of
technological progress.[2]

Then Brian Street, Goody's most thorough critic, argued that he failed to
realize that literacy was but in part a matter of technology; whatever technology was available could become effective (or not) depending on whether
literacy emerged as an ideology. As ideologies varied greatly so did practices of literacy, and attempts to understand links between literacy and imperial projects are not well served by ignoring these differences.

There runs a line through this somewhat fictionalized sketch of anthropological concerns with literacy: From the invention of writing as a material,
visible, lasting token of speech and as something achieved for humanity
as a whole, through literacy as a mark on the scale of technological evolution, to literacy as social and political ideology serving special interests.
Undeniably, this trajectory has resulted in increased sophistication about
the ways humans have with writing; the questions asked and the answers
given became more and more encompassing to a point where "literacy"
research now takes its place on the same theoretical level as, say, the
study of religion, law, or modes of production. The price of such theoretical
progress, however, seems to have been a dematerialization of the object
of research—much along the same lines that led to the dematerialization
of language in linguistics. There are probably many ways to show how dematerialization worked. One is to consider how the fascination with signs
and symbols, in short, with representations (going back to the medieval
idea of nature as a "book") favored "mirror" theories of knowledge.[3] Else-

where (Fabian 1983) I have tried to show how this in turn encouraged a "visualist" bias both in the choice of the sources of empirical knowledge and in its presentation.

Studies of its social history in the West show that reading acquired its modern, almost exclusively ocular conception not too long ago. As a result of changes that affected especially the role of the body reading underwent, as one author puts it, a "loss of sensuousness." I am referring to a study by Schön (1987) which is limited to literacy in German but probably applicable to most Western societies. Following, rather selectively, Norbert Elias and Michel Foucault he situates the crucial changes—the immobilization of the body, the end of reading aloud, solitary reading, reading as consumption, and others—in the eighteenth century. This richly documented and methodologically sophisticated treatment (and others like it; see the references) should be required reading for those who embark on ethnographies of reading. One may surmise that the disembodiment of reading described by Schön is all the more pervasive because it precedes encounter with other cultures. It shapes attitudes and habits in Western bourgeois ethnographers that limit their imagination and capacity to ask concrete and interesting questions about reading as a social practice.[4]

All this has a long and complicated history; the point of at least evoking it is to suggest that the absence of concern with reading as an activity (not just as the logical complement to writing) may be indicative of what I called dematerialization and that, conversely, attention to reading may provide a much needed corrective for our views of literacy.[5]

LITERACY AND THE WORK OF ANTHROPOLOGY

Wherever one stands in current anthropological debates there is no escaping the realization that investigating literacy is part of the phenomenon anthropology tries to comprehend. Critical anthropologists—anthropologists who reflect on the practice of writing as part of the process whereby knowledge is produced—could not fail to realize that they may themselves be servants and handmaidens of imperialist literacy and some began to agonize about a dilemma which seemed to be: either not to serve literacy, that is, stop writing and stop being anthropologists, or go on writing and contribute to the oppression of those they write about. Most settle for going on with writing, critically. The best argument I can think of for not giving up goes roughly like this: that one can take sides for or against literacy is an illusion; literacy is, for better or worse, a global phenomenon and, at least on that global level, there is no boundary to cross, no inside to be opposed to an outside. Sides can be taken only in concrete antagonistic situations of conflict or of domination/submission and, given the conditions that prevail, taking sides will have to be done (if it is not to remain a purely personal moral gesture) publicly, that is by acts which, sooner or later, involve the use of literacy. This, I realize, does not dispose of the dilemma; it may help us, though, to recognize its true nature.

It would be wrong to assume that anthropologists who think of themselves as social scientists, and most of them probably do, are habitually plagued by what I called the "critical dilemma." Still, it is fair to say that critical self-awareness was propelled to a new level by a "literary" turn in anthropology, a turn affecting even those who did not take it. Reams were written about the ethnographer as a writer and about ethnographies as texts.[6] It has largely gone unnoticed that this new awareness did little to change one of the oldest convictions of a scientific approach—namely that speaking and listening, important as they are in conducting research, are, as it were, left behind as the ethnographer's work proceeds from research to writing. To be sure there is talk of locution and rhetoric in ethnographic writing, of devices to capture an audience, but all this is discussed in a rather abstract, derivatory sense; hardly anyone literally means "speaking" when discussing rhetoric, nor is a literary audience really envisaged as a group of listeners. Writers can be dumb and readers deaf as long as literacy is imagined to exist on a plane of signs, above, outside of, or apart from the agitations of voice.

Be that as it may, a generation of anthropologists emerged which could no longer maintain the illusion of clear distinctions between literate and illiterate societies even if they wanted to. Almost all ethno-graphers (even those who work in the "interior" of Africa, Melanesia, or South America) now face people-writers: "natives" who use literacy for their own projects of survival; and that the label they attach to themselves is in Greek, ethnographers ought to know, may be expressive of their intent to hold on to old privileges (claimed in times when they wrote and the others talked). It does not absolve them from coming to grips with a situation in which literacy is routinely, not exceptionally, shared by anthropology and its objects.

Interestingly, a similar breaking down of barriers seems to go on in the one guild from which the high priests of literacy are usually recruited. Literary critics and linguistic text experts have begun to argue that "orality" has never been exorcised even from the most "literary" texts. Much of what texts have to tell us, they now say, can be understood only by listening to them while reading them.[7]

Those who have had experience with literacy outside of domains that are more or less rigidly controlled by specialized institutions (schools, churches, administrations) are beginning to realize that imperial designs have been served, inadvertently or not, by thinking of literacy mainly as the capacity to *write* while neglecting that any literacy can of course only have the insidious effect we ascribe to it when what is written is also *read*. When literacy ceases to be understood as the one-way activity of in-scribing this must have consequences for the global assessment of literacy as an instrument of domination; such a change of perspective should therefore also be considered with regard to the writing work done by ethnographers. The ethnographer's "critical dilemma" should then appear in a different light. I now want to explore how ethnographic work with written texts may, paradoxically, help us to subvert the dictates of literacy to the extent that we concentrate on reading.

WRITING AND READING: A REPORT FROM ETHNOGRAPHIC RESEARCH

Since the mid-sixties I have carried out research on various aspects of urban-industrial "culture" in the Shaba region of Zaire. Being committed to a language-centered approach, I have sought my data mainly in the form of recordings in the common language of the area, a variety of Swahili. Like many other ethnographers I have been doing my work with a notion that analyzing and interpreting my field material required, above all, transposing it into *writing*. At least this is what is foremost on our minds when we "write up" our research. We are of course aware that, while we write, we also read—to check, correct, edit (all that in the service of writing). Why even ethnographic work conducted in terms of a language- or speech-centered approach should be fixed on writing is a question which deserves some thought. I would hypothesize that it is due to a lingering epistemology that stipulated that seeing and observation were the most important or at any rate most reliable sources of ethnographic knowledge. "Saving the oral" then requires making it visible. Although it has been said that anthropologists ought to approach the cultures they study as "ensembles of texts" (Clifford Geertz), when we consider *reading* as part of the ethnographer's work we usually do not think of the people or phenomena we intend to de-scribe (after all this is supposed to make us different from historians who do their research in archives and other depositories of writing). We read our colleagues' writings because we want to learn from them or argue with them; perhaps we study some written documents that come in handy for dealing with historical context, demography, economics and all those wider aspects that cannot be known from face-to-face interaction. The people we study are usually not read, at least not before the ethnographer has transformed their utterances into written texts.

Paradoxically, it was struggling with a text written and "published" in Shaba Swahili[8] which made me realize more clearly than before that producing an ethnographic text, here taken in the narrow sense of a spoken text, is not limited to, and does not come to an end (even provisionally) with, a successful trans-scription of recorded speech. The reason is elementary, once we think about it, yet it may have complex consequences regarding our conceptions of the ethnographer's task. Writing ("scription") is inseparable from reading. The kind of writing that occurs in transcribing recorded speech from tapes is never just a straightforward transposition from acoustic signals to graphic signs. It is an activity which is geared to, guided and constrained by, the aim to make the transcript *readable* according to criteria which are always relative to culturally and historically specific situations (of both, the source and the "target" text).[9]

In this regard, there is little difference between the efforts and competences required to transcribe a recorded text and those one needs to read a text written in the kind of literacy that speakers of Shaba Swahili—a language which during its colonial history has been denied access to official literacy (Fabian 1986)—employ when they write their language. Both kinds of activity, even though one may be seen as graphic encoding, the other as decoding, require an ability to recreate the oral performance of speech. A special kind of ethnographic work, namely discussing and conversing about what is written or read is therefore required no matter whether the task is transcribing and thereby producing a text, or understanding/translating a text. I shall now report and discuss two instances of such work.

When I began work on an ethnography of conceptions of power in Shaba popular culture (Fabian 1990b), my starting point was an intriguing proverb-like saying ("Power is eaten whole") but most of the "material" consisted of recordings of a play constructed around that saying and performed by a group of actors.

When I worked on the final version of the texts presented in that study (in the original Shaba Swahili and an English translation) I had the privilege (and luxury) to have my friend Kalundi Mango, a native of Lubumbashi, literally at my side. His contribution was not only to help me fill gaps and correct errors (this affected perhaps less than 5 percent of the work previously done by myself). More importantly, the conversations and occasional heated disputes we had about "correct" transcriptions and translations made me realize that both acts, establishing the text and translating it, are to the core dialogical. Such an insight may be obscured by the fact that this phase of ethnography is usually carried out in the absence of informants with whom we can negotiate signs and meanings. To be carried out successfully, making and translating ethnographic texts in the absence of interlocutors still calls for (the substitute of) an inner dialog in which the anthropologist who writes ethnography must *listen* and match recorded sounds and graphic symbols with communicative competences, memories, and imagination. (And, of course, with that body of knowledge that gets deposited in ethnographies and lexica. Good dictionaries are always both.) In this sense all ethno-graphy is ethno-logy—recuperation of the spoken word (logos) through reading as "re-collecting" (legein).

The situation I am reporting here is perhaps not typical; much work based on recordings is done with the help of native speakers who "assist" the ethnographer by transcribing and often also translating the spoken texts. There is much professional lore about the problems of working with interpreters and native assistants, but only recently have these problems been recognized for what they are: integral parts of the production of ethnographic knowledge—hence epistemological problems and not just a practical nuisance or a minor issue in methodology.[10] And that is what I am trying to argue about the role of reading.

The same Kalundi Mango played a crucial part in the project I alluded to above: The *Vocabulary of the Town of Elisabethville*, a written text, typed and mimeographed.[11] It is presented in a kind of uncontrolled literacy that makes reading the document, let alone translating it, a forbidding task. Because the author did not have at his disposal a system of standardized rules for writing Shaba Swahili his text is characterized by erratic segmentation on both morphemic and syntactic levels. Very often word and sentence boundaries are not marked or not clear, at least not immediately. More than an inconsistent orthography and a confusing punctuation, this makes the original text very difficult for a foreign reader and, I should add, may pose problems when working with a native reader. Lack of consistency in writing is matched with inconsistency or, put positively, much freedom in reading. In the kind of literacy we meet here the written text is approached as but one *aide mémoire* between one oral realization and another without ever commanding the sort of reverence our kind of literacy pays to texts. This, rather than indifference or incompetence, is yet another reason why native speakers are notoriously "unreliable" as transcribers of language recordings. More than "a little training" is required to do what really involves a profound reorientation toward the kind of "disembodied literacy" that is the product of our culturally postulated distinctions between writing and speaking.

Yet before some kind of agreement on segmentation is reached translation of substantial parts of the document remains impossible. With untiring help from Kalundi Mango a relatively simple and elegant solution was eventually found although not without many compromises, as we shall see presently: Kalundi Mango was asked to read the text aloud and this was recorded (1986 in Lubumbashi). The intonation patterns and other prosodic features on the recording made it possible to mark syntactic segments in the written text. Many passages remained doubtful and had to be corrected later with the help of semantics. Morpheme and sentence boundaries became clarified when we proceeded to translating the text.

The next step was to ask Kalundi Mango (who, like many speakers of Shaba Swahili, is used to writing this language mainly for the purpose of private correspondence) to rewrite the original in what he felt was the manner he and other Shaba Swahili speakers like him would currently choose (1987 in Amsterdam). The results of that experiment were rather more problematic than expected. As could have been foreseen, Kalundi Mango showed too much respect for the written text and achieved only a partial transposition of the original into a version in current Shaba Swahili.[12] Nevertheless, his transcript became the starting point for establishing a Shaba Swahili Version of the *Vocabulaire* (1988 in Amsterdam). The latter is the result of re-reading aloud Kalundi's typed text together with him, word by word and sentence by sentence, and of negotiating a mode of transcription that is at least moderately uniform. Thus the Shaba Swahili Version is really a *re-oralization of the written original*.

To give an idea of what this accomplished, here are the first few sentences of the *Vocabulaire* in their three versions:

Original:
abali ya wazungu kwakutufikia mu inchi ya Afirika na mu Congo (Mukongo) yetu na pia bakatufikia na sisi wa toto wa Katanga ya mashariki ni:mwaka gani?

Shaba Swahili Version:
Habari ya wazungu: kwa kutufikia mu inchi ya Afrika: na mu Congo: mu Congo yetu: na pia bakatufikia na sisi watoto wa Katanga ya mashariki/ ni mwaka gani?

Translation:
Concerning the news of the Whites arriving in the country of Africa, in the Congo, in our Congo, and especially when they arrived among us, children of East Katanga. Which year was it?

COMMENT

- The word *abali* is a possible but not a frequent variant of ECS *habari* (with *h* before *a* deleted and alternation between *r* and *l*).
- The Shaba Swahili Version has after *Katanga ya mashariki* a tone pattern indicating a full clause. This suggests that the phrase beginning with *habari ya wazungu* and ending with *yetu* is proleptic and best translated as "Concerning, etc.," making it a sort of heading.
- Connective *kwa* should be separated from *kutufikia*; the prefix *wa* should be joined to *toto*.
- The expression *mu Congo* (locative particle + name of the country) is followed by (*Mukongo*) (prefix *mu-*, indicating person, singular, + generalized ethnic term). The parentheses make it look like a repair due to insecurity about writing. This "complication," however can be disregarded when the text is read because both forms have the same phonic realization.
- The end of the first phrase after *mashariki* is not marked in the original while the colon between *ni* and *mwaka* is not motivated.

Notice that this is not one of the difficult passages. Still, as the comments show, a direct translation from the written text would have had to be justified with numerous notes and explanations most of them based on the editor's/translator's ability to recognize Shaba Swahili *speech* in the graphic signs of the original.

The experiences made in this preparatory phase eventually determined the presentation of our edition of the *Vocabulaire*. The original was produced in facsimile. The oralized Shaba Swahili Version appears, on facing pages, with the English translation. For reasons that pertain to this discussion of ethnography and reading, I eventually decided to present the oralized Swahili and the English texts under the common heading "translations." This began as a defensive move when a historian friend reacted with what I felt was excessive discomfort to the oralized version. To him it was a threat to the original and authentic text, a false limb not needed by readers who are speakers of Shaba Swahili and never to be used by most readers of this edition of the *Vocabulaire*. His reaction (or, at any rate, my perception of it) reflects an approach to written texts which builds the authority of its interpretations on *keeping the act of reading invisible*, or rather inaudible. As I have argued and tried to exemplify, oralization, that is, recourse to audible speech, actual or imagined, is an essential part of our ability to read texts. Yet our "ideology" of literacy seems to put a taboo on revealing what we actually do when we read, for fear that oralization might subvert the authority of the written text.[13] Such an attitude may be described as a kind of textual fundamentalism (shared by many text-oriented anthropologists and true believers in the scriptures). Any fundamentalist notion of a text's authority, I submit, is false for at least two reasons: It obscures the nature of authorship (that is, of the process of writing) as well as the nature of reception (that is, of the process of interpretation and translation which occurs whenever we read a text). It is a falseness that becomes particularly insidious in the case of ethnographic texts, which are most often produced/ transcribed as well as translated/interpreted by the same person. Fundamentalism should be avoided whenever texts are approached ethnographically even if they were not transcribed by the ethnographer but already collected in written form. Thus, if we return to the example of work on the *Vocabulaire*, the oralized Shaba Swahili Version needs to be included in the presentation of texts inasmuch as it is a record of a phase in the process of *reading* the original text.[14] It is a phase that consists of negotiating signs and signification either with native speakers or with the ethnographer's own competence, most often with both. It would be especially ironic to keep that part of our work under our hat if we remember that anthropologists turned to texts in the first place because they realized that there is no such thing as naked data in cultural research. Why commit the same error, once removed, by pretending that there could be such a thing as the naked authenticity of texts?

Even if ethnographic reading of texts such as the *Vocabulaire* is still some-what exceptional compared to the sort of work described in the first of our two examples, we can now formulate a general lesson that will add an im-portant point to what has been said so far about ethnography and reading.

Apart from its extraordinary content, it was its literary, or more spe-cifically, its graphic form that made the *Vocabulaire* such a challenge. I referred to it as an instance of "grass-roots literacy," that is, of the appro-priation of a technique of writing by speakers of Shaba Swahili which was relatively free from the ideological and technical constraints that charac-terized literacy taught to the same speakers in other languages (French, some regional languages, and a variety of Swahili spoken by no one but considered fit for literacy). From the results—in this case the written text—we can infer that it is a literacy which works despite an amazingly high degree of indeterminacy and freedom (visible in an erratic orthography, a great disdain for "correct" word and sentence boundaries and many other instances of seemingly unmotivated variation). These negative characterizations should not obscure what really determined the peculiar shape of this document. It was the attempt to read the *Vocabulaire* that made us discover the immediacy and indeed primacy, not of orality in some vague general sense, but of *oral performance*. As we have learned from the ethnography of speaking, such performances come in specific forms re-flecting cultural definitions of speech events. Texts that document performances/events carry their semantic meaning not only in linguistic units up to the level of the sentence; participants, setting, topic, genre, chan-nels etc., and relations between these components, all have significations which a competent reader must be able to understand.[15]

The *Vocabulaire* is a text whose representation in writing cannot be con-ceived as mere encoding in graphic signs, certainly not in signs that exist—except physically—as a system apart from the utterances they represent. Consequently, reading such a text is not achieved by the mere ability to de-code graphic signs. It demands a capacity to reenact or recreate the oral performance that is the source of the text. To return once more to the topos of the notoriously unreliable native assistant as transcriber and translator of ethnographic texts: what is negatively deplored as lack of exactitude should be seen positively as expressive of a great degree of freedom which the native speaker enjoys both as a writer and a reader.

Interpretations of ethnographic texts that pretend to require nothing but a decoding of sign systems must eliminate or, rather, hide constitutive acts of understanding that are communicative and dialogical. These acts de-mand attention to how a text sounds and not just to what it looks like. A rehabilitation of reading in the sense I have tried to give to the term should make such ethnographic hiding games unnecessary.

Incidentally, there is much to be learned about the ethnography of read-

ing from the struggles of philologists with early writing systems such as
Sumerian (Larsen 1987) and Greek (Svenbro 1987, 1988). The early Greek
practice of *scriptio continua*—writing without what I have been calling
segmentation—necessitated recourse to orality in reading, and about the
cuneiform system Larsen makes a statement that is echoed by my observations on the *Vocabulaire*:

> From the beginning, the cuneiform system as used for the writing of Sumerian
> texts was basically a logographic system in which signs stood for words; syllab-
> ic values for signs were used to indicate only the absolutely essential gram-
> matical elements, which has the effect that Sumerian writing was really a
> mnemotechnic device, and that the texts were not meant to represent fully
> any spoken message. A text gave cues, so that for instance a literary text must
> be understood *as an aid to an oral performance*. (Larsen 1987:219; emphasis
> mine)

What I had to say about the necessity of oralizing texts such as the *Vocabulaire* may be compared to the following observation by Svenbro:

> Reading aloud is part of the text, it is inscribed in the text. At first this may
> seem a paradoxical proposition. How can an audible [*sonore*] act be part of a
> silent fact? How can one be comprised by the other? . . . the Greeks . . . wrote
> in *scriptio continua*, that is, without intervals between words, which, as experi-
> ence shows, makes reading aloud practically necessary. It is in this way that
> audible reading is part of the text which is incomplete, unfinished by itself.
> Therefore the text is more than the sum of the alphabetic signs of which it is
> made up: these signs are to guide the voice through which the text will take
> on a body—an audible body. (Svenbro 1988:54; my translation)

This brief excursion into ancient philology should not create the impression
that I see recourse to orality in the ethnography of reading also as returning
to an older, or earlier practice. Such an evolutionary perspective is irrelevant to the practices I try to understand (and certainly to those who are
involved in them).[16] A much more fruitful approach has been adopted and
exemplified in a recent paper by Kenneth George. With acknowledgments
to Brian Street he advocates a position which holds "that oral and textual
practices exist as mutually shaping *contemporaries* embedded in social,
ideological, and historical contexts." (1990:19; my emphasis)

CONCLUSIONS

> Should someone, in the future, read this fairy tale in print and doubt that it
> could have had such an effect, he should take into account that man's true
> vocation only is to act effectively [*wirken*] in the present. Writing is a misuse of
> language, to read silently for oneself is a sad surrogate of speech. (J. W. von
> Goethe, *Dichtung und Wahrheit*[17])

If this essay makes a contribution to an emerging "ethnography of reading" it does so by articulating questions and tentative insights that result when seemingly narrow, specific problems of routine ethnographic work with texts are placed in very broad historical and theoretical contexts. The narrative I offered in the first section can now be continued and concluded. The discovery of "reading" as both a subject and a mode of ethnography has been linked to the discovery of orality. We can now add some precision to that insight.

A first discovery of orality was made due to the *absence of written texts* (that is, of ethnographic and historical sources or documents). A key notion that developed from that discovery was the "oral tradition" which, we begin to realize, has really been a program of methodologizing the oral by imposing on it forms and criteria that assured (in Foucault's terms) its "passage" into literate discourse.

A second discovery of orality is now taking place which is due to the *presence of written texts*. This discovery is based on the realization that a reading of ethnographic texts demands attention to speech and oral performance. Linguists and literary critics have prepared a field of inquiry that should now be entered by ethnographers. In discussing problems with reading I faced in two projects based on texts I have only given some general and rather disconnected indications of issues that need to be addressed in detail and as systematically as it has been done, for instance, by D. Tedlock in his proposals to deal with the "spoken word" (1983) or in J. Vansina's reappraisal of "oral tradition" (1985).

Whatever shape or direction this work will take it will have to be carried out with an awareness of the historical and, indeed, political nature of anthropological inquiry into literacy. The point is this: I argued that two discoveries of orality have been made, one forced on us by the absence of written texts, the other by the presence of them. However, we must keep in mind that "written texts" may be an equivocal and confusing notion. The texts of Western ethnographic discourse and the texts produced by autochthonous, grass-roots literacy, although both are written, cannot be "read" unproblematically as members of one and the same class. Apart from relations of power and submission that determine all reading, we also need to consider the specific relations that exist between elitist and popular literacy (which are not identical, but may overlap, with relations between literacy in Western and non-Western languages).

Perhaps it is useful to recall in conclusion that, although it raised some very general questions, this paper has concentrated on an issue that is primarily reflexive. What, we asked, is the role of reading in the production of ethnography? Not for a moment do I pretend that this exhausts the agenda of an ethnography of reading. Other practices of reading need to be confronted and while we confront these, however critically, we cannot be expected to address reflexive issues at the same time. We must go on with the work of recording, describing, and interpreting. Still, "their" practice of reading and ours exist at, or better in, the same time, and that is why the reflections on the current place of reading in anthropological studies of literacy should neither be elevated nor dismissed as "meta"-problems. Deep-seated attitudes and habits inform our practice of studying other practices of reading. It would be sad if future ethnographies of reading would do little more than catalogue conformities and deviations from our own dematerialized conceptions of literacy. Our chances to do more than that will increase to the extent that we "keep listening" to writing, while writing.

NOTES

1. The following is a sweeping review of theoretical developments in anthropological studies of literacy, with no pretensions to completeness. No attempt is made to provide an adequate bibliography. Nevertheless, here are some of the major works I shall be referring to: Gusdorf (1973, pt. 3); Ong (1958); Schousboe and Larsen (1989); Street (1984); Vansina (1961, 1985).

2. Probst makes a similar observation regarding the ways Goody first establishes difference between literate and nonliterate societies and then determines processes of transition from one to the other (1989:478). Notice that this otherwise interesting and critical paper treats of literacy and its conditions and consequences by considering only writing (except for one or two formulaic expressions such as "read and write").

3. A notion generalized by R. Rorty (1980) in his critique of Western philosophy.

4. I want to thank Michael Harbsmeier for calling Schön's study to my attention. Incidentally, the book raises an interesting question regarding the history of anthropology. It is now recognized that one of its origins in the sixteenth century was the so called *ars apodemica* resulting in a vast body of writing on the method of travel (inspired by Ramist philosophy, see Stagl 1980, 1990; a volume in English containing this and other essays of his is forthcoming). A comparable methodologization of reading (documented by Schön) may have had a similar importance for anthropology's ways with "texts" that became the object of ethnographic collecting. The "visualist" bent is common to both, or was, up to the time when the "ethnography of speaking" embarked on the critique of structuralism.

5. I may have exaggerated the absence of concerns with reading in anthropological studies of literacy in order to improve my story—but not much. Notice that in J. Goody's recent summary of his work on literacy throughout human history (1987) "reading" does not even rate an entry in the index.

6. See Boon (1982); Clifford (1988); Clifford and Marcus (1986); Geertz (1988); also Fabian (1900c).

7. Examples for this are the proposal by Mary Louise Pratt (1977) to apply insights from sociolinguistics and speech-act theory to literary discourse, as well as the works written, or edited, by Deborah Tannen (1982 a and b, 1984, 1985). In literary

theory, the writings of M. M. Bakhtin have been influential in ways I cannot even attempt to document bibliographically in this paper (but see Bakhtin 1986 for a first orientation). Both developments may appear as new trends but an entire discipline has existed for some time which has approached "reading" (or "interpretation") as oral and communicative performance. It has produced theoretical treatises, text-books, and even its own historiography (see Bahn and Bahn 1970; Bartine 1989; Thompson et al. 1983, to cite only a few examples for the latter). Aside from the question whether we can learn from it, the fact that it became professionalized should be taken as part of the phenomenon of "literacy."

8. The "Vocabulary of the Town of Elizabethville" (Fabian 1990a), a unique history of the principal town of the mining region in southeastern Zaire—Elisabethville, now Lubumbashi—commissioned by an association of former domestic servants and written by one André Yav: a colonial history written by the colonized for the colonized.

9. Perhaps this is a prejudice; it was nicely confirmed to me, however, by the dismal performance I saw recently of an experimental voice-recognition computer. I imagine that if such a machine should ever work it would have to be because some-one succeeded in binarizing whatever governs writing and reading in the culturally specific and historically contingent ways in which this seems to happen. To my mind such an undertaking is inherently contradictory, which does not mean that it could not reach a low, "practical" level of usefulness.

10. See for example the thoughts on the role of interpreters as interlocutors, with a critical discussion of Owusu's important paper (1978) in Pool 1989.

11. Much of this section is taken from the introduction to Fabian 1990b.

12. Implicit in this observation is yet another set of problems which an ethnography of reading must face: In ways to be determined the strictures and con-straints that are usually ascribed to literacy as *writing* may also be operative in *reading*, even in a literacy which is recent and tenuous and comparatively "uncon-trolled."

13. This is precisely the point made by M. de Certeau when he qualifies read-ing as "poaching" (1984, chap. 12). Margaret Drewal of the Department of Per-formance Studies at Northwestern University brought de Certeau's essay to my attention.

14. I should note that the example for "oralization" required by an ethnographic reading discussed here only covers the very first approach to the *Vocabulaire*, what philologists would call "establishing" the text. How productive it can be to "listen" to a written text is demonstrated on other instances, among them an attempt to re-construct the peculiar composition of this document (see Fabian 1990b: 201ff.).

15. Dell Hymes's seminal statements on the ethnography of speaking (see 1974, chaps. 1, 2) should therefore be read with renewed interest by those who study the ethnography of reading. That similar conclusions regarding the role of cultural knowledge in reading can be reached by a different route—in this case the "per-formance" of school children in reading-ability tests—was shown by C. J. Fillmore and his collaborators (Fillmore 1982). See also Tannen's remarks on reading and writing as "involvement-focused skills" (1985:140).

16. It is also the weakness of arguments that see in silent reading an evolution-ary achievement which necessarily replaces reading aloud. Historically they do not

hold water. Silent reading was practiced, albeit exceptionally, in ancient Greece (see Svenbro 1987, 1988, chap. 9); reading aloud never ceased to be practiced. Theoretically and methodologically such an evolutionary position goes together with "ocular" theories of reading as the mere decoding of signs.

17. Quoted in Schön 1987: 104f.; my translation.

REFERENCES

Bahn, Eugene, and Margaret L. Bahn
  1970   *A History of Oral Interpretation.* Minneapolis: Burgess.
Bakhtin, Mikhail
  1986   *Speech Genres and Other Late Essays.* Austin: University of Texas Press.
Bartine, David E.
  1989   *Early English Reading Theory: Origins and Current Debates.* Columbia: University of South Carolina Press.
Boon, James
  1982   *Other Tribes, Other Scribes: Symbolic Anthropology in the Comparative Study of Cultures, Histories, Religions, and Texts.* Cambridge: Cambridge University Press.
Boyarin, Jonathan
  1991   "Jewish Ethnography and the Question of the Book." *Anthropological Quarterly* 64:14–29.
Certeau, Michel de
  1984   "Reading as Poaching." In *The Practice of Everyday Life*, pp. 165–176. Berkeley: University of California Press.
Clifford, James
  1988   *The Predicament of Culture: Twentieth Century Ethnography, Literature, and Art.* Cambridge, Mass.: Harvard University Press.
Clifford, James, and George Marcus, eds.
  1986   *Writing Culture: The Poetics and Politics of Ethnography.* Berkeley: University of California Press.
Derrida, Jacques
  1976   *Of Grammatology.* Baltimore: Johns Hopkins University Press.
Fabian, Johannes
  1983   *Time and the Other: How Anthropology Makes Its Object.* New York: Columbia University Press.
  1990a   *History From Below. The "Vocabulary of Elisabethville" by André Yav: Texts, Translation, and Interpretive Essay.* Amsterdam and Philadelphia: John Benjamins.
  1990b   *Power and Performance: Ethnographic Explorations through Popular Wisdom and Theater in Shaba (Zaire).* Madison: University of Wisconsin Press.
  1990c   "Presence and Representation: The Other in Anthropological Writing." *Critical Inquiry* 16:753–772.
Fillmore, Charles J.
  1982   "Ideal Readers and Real Readers." In *Spoken and Written Language.* Ed. Deborah Tannen, pp. 248–270. Norwood, N.J.: Ablex.

Geertz, Clifford
    1988   *Works and Lives: The Anthropologist as Author.* Stanford: Stanford University Press.
George, Kenneth M.
    1990   "'Felling a Song with a New Ax': Writing and the Reshaping of Ritual Song Performance in Upland Sulawesi." *Journal of American Folklore* 103 (407):3–23.
Goody, Jack
    1986   *The Logic of Writing and the Organization of Society.* Cambridge: Cambridge University Press.
    1987   *The Interface Between the Oral and the Written.* Cambridge: Cambridge University Press.
Gusdorf, Georges
    1973   *L'avènement des sciences humaines au siècle des lumières.* Paris: Payot.
Harbsmeier, Michael
    1989   "Writing and the Other: Travellers' Literacy, Or Towards an Archeology of Orality." In *Literacy and Society.* Ed. Schousboe and Larsen, pp. 197–228. Copenhagen: Akademisk Forlag.
Hymes, Dell
    1974   *Foundations in Sociolinguistics: An Ethnographic Approach.* Philadelphia: University of Pennsylvania Press.
Larsen, Mogens Trolle
    1987   "The Mesopotamian Lukewarm Mind. Reflections on Science, Divination and Literacy." In *Language, Literature and History: Philological and Historical Studies Presented to Erica Reiner.* Ed. F. Rechberg-Halton, pp. 203–225. Chicago: American Oriental Series 67.
Olson, David, Nancy Torrance, and Angela Hildyard, eds.
    1985   *Literacy, Language, and Learning: The Nature and Consequences of Reading and Writing.* Cambridge: Cambridge University Press.
Ong, Walter J.
    1958   *Ramus: Method and the Decay of Dialogue.* Cambridge, Mass.: Harvard University Press.
Owusu, Maxwell
    1978   "Ethnography of Africa: The Usefulness of the Useless." *American Anthropologist* 80:310–334.
Pool, Robert
    1989   There Must Have Been Something . . . Interpretation of Illness and Misfortune in a Cameroon Village. Ph.D. diss., Department of Cultural Anthropology, University of Amsterdam.
Pratt, Mary Louise
    1977   *Toward a Speech Act Theory of Literary Discourse.* Bloomington: Indiana University Press.
Probst, Peter
    1989   "The Letter and the Spirit: Literacy and Religious Authority in the History of the Aladura Movement in Western Nigeria." *Africa* 59:478–495.

Rorty, Richard
1980   *Philosophy and the Mirror of Nature*. Princeton: Princeton University Press.

Schön, Erich
1987   *Der Verlust der Sinnlichkeit/ oder Die Verwandlungen des Lesers. Mentalitäts-wandel um 1800*. Stuttgart: Klett-Cotta.

Schousboe, Karen, and Mogens Trolle Larsen, eds.
1989   *Literacy and Society*. Copenhagen: Akademisk Forlag.

Stagl, Justin
1980   "Der Wohl Unterwiesene Passagier: Reisekunst und Gesellschafts-beschreibung vom 16. bis zum 18. Jahrhundert." In *Reisen und Reisebeschreibungen im 18. und 19. Jahrhundert als Quellen der Kulturbe-ziehungsforschung*. Ed. B. I. Krasnobaev, Gert Robel, and Herbert Zeman. Berlin: Camen.

1990   "The Methodising of Travel in the 16th Century: A Tale of Three Cities." *History and Anthropology* 4:303–338.

In press   *The History of Travel in the Sixteenth and Seventeenth Centuries* [tentative title]. Reading: Harwood Academic Publishers.

Street, Brian V.
1984   *Literacy in Theory and Practice*. Cambridge: Cambridge University Press.

Svenbro, Jesper
1987   "The 'Voice' of Letters in Ancient Greece. On Silent Reading and the Representation of Speech." *Culture and History* 2:31–47.

1988   *Phrasikleia: Anthropologie de la lecture en Grèce ancienne*. Paris: Editions La Découverte.

Tannen, Deborah, ed.
1982a   *Analyzing Discourse: Text and Talk*. Georgetown University Round Table on Languages and Linguistics 1981. Washington, D.C.: Georgetown University Press.

1982b   *Spoken and Written Language*. Norwood, N.J.: Ablex.

1984   *Coherence in Spoken and Written Discourse*. Norwood, N.J.: Ablex.

1985   "Relative Focus on Involvement in Oral and Written Discourse." In *Literacy, Language, and Learning. The Nature and Consequences of Reading and Writing*. Ed. David Olson et al., pp. 124–147. Cambridge: Cambridge University Press.

Tedlock, Dennis
1983   *The Spoken Word and the Work of Interpretation*. Philadelphia: University of Pennsylvania Press.

Thompson, David W., et al., eds.
1983   *Performance of Literature in Historical Perspective*. Lanham, Md.: University Press of America.

Vansina, Jan
1961   *De la tration orale*. Tenuren: Musée Royale de l'Afrique Centrale.

1985   *Oral Tradition as History*. Madison: University of Wisconsin Press.

SIX

The Presence of the Name:
Reading Scripture in an
Indonesian Village

James N. Baker

The case I am considering here might be thought of as a limiting one for an ethnography of reading. The principal text is the Koran, and those reading from it are people of eastern Indonesia who do not speak or comprehend Arabic, the language in which the Koran is written. We could, of course, choose to distinguish the activity they are engaged in as one of "reciting," rather than "reading." If at base we think of reading as an activity of interpretation that requires from the start some amount of language competence, then we would have to say that the uncomprehending recitation of written texts is something altogether different. But, if we also think of reading as the socially significant practice of taking up a text and going through the process of actualizing the inscribed words in a temporal sequence, expending real time and personal effort in doing so, then we have something essential to the activity of reading without yet concerning ourselves with comprehension and the interpretations that can follow from it. Recitation, in this view, is distinctive only because it requires us to attend to reading more purely as a practice. What I hope becomes evident in the following discussion is that at the level of the social practice, reading involves persuasive forces that do not depend upon the readers' competence to comprehend the text though they influence the subjective evaluations that readers make.

The particular issues I am addressing are ones encountered in the ethnographic study of a village in Tidore in eastern Indonesia. The people living in this village are devoted Muslims who regularly demonstrate their faith through an adherence to adopted Islamic traditions. But they also claim a commitment to their own ancestral traditions. As I will argue, these are brought together as social practices into a common ground of ritually reproduced experience. Thus, Koranic recitation brings Islamic written traditions into a social context that includes the oral traditions of remembering ancestors. The evaluations that are made, according to the potentialities of knowledge that draw upon this ground of experience, display an opposition between orthodoxy and heterodoxy. In discussing this I will make use of Charles Peirce's phenomenological categories to specify the nature of these opposing vectors of knowledge that, we will see, are also found within Islamic traditions themselves in the form of opposing "readings" of scripture given by normative piety and Sufi mysticism. What are found to be pivotal to these different readings, and so also to our understanding of them, are proper names—words that live in the practice of speaking and have a persuasive force undeterred by the foreignness of the language spoken.

ISLAM AND ANCESTRAL TRADITIONS IN TIDORE

Tidore is a small island in the North Moluccas of eastern Indonesia (a region more popularly known to Westerners as the Spice Islands) and the homeland of an ethnic group that I will refer to as the Tidorese. Now the location of a district (*kabupaton*) capital, Tidore was, up to the twentieth century, the seat of one of two influential sultanates in this region.

In the late fifteenth century the first Tidoran ruler converted to Islam, the faith of traders who had already long been buying clove and supplying the court with the foreign wealth that political ascendancy required. Having a firm footing in the Tidoran state, Sufi teachers probably went on to foster ties with lesser nobility in subsidiary centers. Eventually Islam was brought to the village populations throughout much of the realm. Some people in Tidore today tell of how earlier inhabitants of the island had been eager to embrace Islam, seeing it as a source of personal strength and social order. I was told the story of how in one political division of the island Islam came to be adopted after a group of Tidorese men surrounded and captured a foreigner they had spied on their beach performing prayers.

Today, being a Muslim is integral to the ethnic identity of being Tidorese. Most overtly this means that specific devotional practices of the Tidorese unite them with a global community of worshipers; for them and all Muslims there is one confession of faith, one location to face when praying, one lunar month for fasting, and, most importantly for the present discussion, one holy book to read from. The invariance and common focus of these practices signal an acceptance of a universal source of values that, in monotheistic terms, is viewed as an ultimate source of creation and destruction. More subtly, this means that over the centuries diverse elements of Islamic culture have become suffused in Tidorese culture and society.

But the very understanding that Islam came from overseas and was received and embraced by those who had been outside of its pale also sustains the awareness of indigenous origins not shared by other Muslims. The importance of remembering this divergent, non-Islamic past varies among people in Tidore. The more or less "official" myth of the origins of the Moluccan states has it that Jafar Sadik, an Arab Muslim and direct descendant of Mohammad, arrived in the Moluccas and married a local woman. From this union four sons were born who then became the first rulers of the original four Moluccan kingdoms (several generations before Islam is said to have been adopted by rulers of these states).[1] Most people, however, say that the woman was a jin, a local spirit. The coming together of elements of different origins is expressed, then, as a marriage between a foreign man tied by genealogical descent to the source of Islam and a local woman of an invisible spirit realm. In the dualistic form of the traditional state this relationship is expressed as one of continued complementarity. The sultan, whose authority identified him with foreign power and wealth and whose ministers included Islamic religious officials, could be effective as a paramount ruler and military commander only with the received blessings (berkati) of the jins of the island. And such blessings could only be received by way of ritual performed by the paramount mediator between humans and jins. This ritual leader, of an autochthonous descent line that is not represented in the sultan's court by a titled minister (as are other major descent lines), has the indigenous title of *Sowohi Kie*.[2] In Malay this ritual leader is referred to as the Lord of the Land (*Tuan Tanah*). The interdependent relationship between Sultan and Lord of the Land is expressed with the complementary designations Light Lord (*Jou Sita-sita*) and Dark Lord (*Jou Kornono*) respectively.

The idiom of light and dark is used pervasively to convey a distinction between that which is received and that which is original. Knowledge that is foreignly derived and publicly revealed is characterized as "light" (*sita-sita*); knowledge that is locally derived and kept guarded from public view is characterized as "dark" (*kornono*). More often the complementary terms *sareat* (from the Arabic term for "law") and *hakekat* (from the Arabic term for "truth") are used to make this same distinction, especially when speaking of different sources of authority. Whereas matters of *sareat* are the concern of state sanctioned authorities, including Islamic religious specialists and elected village leaders, matters of *hakekat* are the concern of elders and ritual specialists who guard local traditions, especially those that allow for continued communication with jins.

Jins constitute a source of potency and power that is at once removed from the temporal world and interactionally bound to it. I never heard anyone speak of the world of jins as having a location positioned in some way relative to the human world; it is simply spoken of as another world, invisible to humans. But jins do have points of access to the human world at specific named locations scattered throughout Tidore and surrounding islands.

These are regarded as sacred spots. If a person succeeds in establishing communications with a particular jin, the obligation to continue communications persists. A failure to continue in regularly pleasing the jin with offerings could bring ill-health or other forms of bad fortune. The obligation is heritable (patrilineally) and today most of the jins that people propitiate are ones with whom their ancestors first established relations. The more distant the founding ancestor, the more elaborate is the required ceremony and the more potent are the blessings received. The blessings (*berkati*), or "medicine" (*sou*), are said to be necessary for the health and prosperity of ancestrally founded local communities. Jins can be the most valuable, as well as unshakable, form of ancestral property that people hold possession of. More than this, they constitute a motivating force in the continued recollection of ancestral origins (Baker 1988).

How this enters into a reading of scripture will, I hope, become clear below. Here it need only be noted that the transcendental and foreignly-derived authority of Islam and the locally-embedded spirituality of ancestral tradition involve very different orientations for those whose lives are engaged with these sources of knowledge and power.

With this said, there is considerable variability in how people orient themselves with respect to these different sources. The variation by and large reflects economic and political differences that in turn have a decisive influence on occupations and social standings. Among the better educated government employees and officials and religious teachers are those who denounce outright any form of devotion to jins. But, irrespective of the reformist rhetoric that is occasionally used, leadership in Tidore has tended to require signs of piety that display a person's greater knowledge of Islam (history and doctrine) and conscientiousness in the performance of the fundamental Islamic duties (praying, reading from the Koran, etc.) As leadership becomes more removed from the productive activities of farming and fishing and from local social orders so the orientation to local powers usually becomes weaker.

At the other extreme are those whose lives are more wholly grounded in subsistence activities and who see themselves as more tightly committed to remembering ancestors. In the remainder of this paper I will be discussing an inland village, called Kalaodi, whose inhabitants are all swidden horticulturalists. In 1985, when I left Tidore, Kalaodi consisted of seventy-four households clustered in six separate hamlets. Although there are many people from Kalaodi who have received educations beyond grade school, many in Islamic schools, in seeking employment most have had to leave the village. Kalaodi, therefore, ends up having a reputation of being a village left behind, still tightly bound to the "dark" side of ancestral tradition. This is the context to keep in mind when considering their participation as Muslims in Islamic religious traditions, specifically their participation as "readers" of scripture.

RECITATION IN THE VILLAGE

Reciting from the Koran is a basic act of devotion for Muslims. For this reason, the ability to read Arabic script as a coding of sounds to be uttered aloud is regarded as a fairly basic skill. In Tidore the means for learning how to recite (*ngaji*) are readily available to everyone. It is important to begin by stressing the openness of this mode of literacy. Islam is a religion of the Book, and although it is exclusive with respect to other religions of other books, it cannot exclude among its own adherents the promise of what its own scripture reveals. Submission to a single, complete, and unchanging scripture is the bedrock of Islam's radical monotheism. The ability to affirm a faithful commitment to what has been revealed in this one text by reciting the words precisely as they have been written must extend to all Muslims. Koranic recitation, then, is especially noteworthy as a mode of literacy that cuts across all segments of society; it serves to absolutely distinguish believers from nonbelievers without yet distinguishing the more from the less literate.[3]

Not everyone in the village of Kalaodi is able to recite from Arabic script, but among men the vast majority can, and among women the majority in the younger generation can. We could speak of a standard level of proficiency that is generally expected among those who know how to recite. But at the same time there is a keen awareness of variation in the people's ability to recite smoothly and with good tonal control. The skill of recognizing Arabic characters and producing the sounds encoded by them is taught to children as a basic part of their formal education, but it receives more attention than the elementary school curriculum alone gives it. Among the men in the village who are students of outside religious teachers (*jou-guru*) are several who act as tutors to village children. In the evenings, coming out of their houses, can be heard the melodic chanting voices of grade-school age boys and girls simultaneously reciting, over and over again, selected verses from the Koran. They read these verses, by the dim flickering light of a small kerosene torch, from booklets distributed now by the Department of Religion. When a student succeeds in becoming acceptably proficient, the family of the child will often hold a small initiatory ceremony (*tahlil ngaji*) that includes a final testing of the child's skills and formally marks the accomplishment as a change in status.[4]

Before discussing the practice of reading the Koran and the active relationship people of Kalaodi have to scripture, it is helpful to elaborate on two different terms by which scripture is usually identified in Islamic writing, including, most importantly, within the Koran itself: these are *al-Quran* and *al-Kitab*. The former I will speak of as the idea of scripture as a "recitation" (or "the Recitation") and the latter as the idea of scripture as a "book" (or "the Book"). They are interdependent notions, but nevertheless suggest different orienting values.

Al-Quran derives from a root word that can mean "to read," but in an older usage that better reflects the sense it has in scripture, means "to recite," presumably from memory (Watt 1970:136; also see Graham 1985). Identifying scripture as a recitation gives emphasis to the performance of reading rather than to the literal content of what is read. Here the idea of revelation and recitation are closely linked, for it is not enough for Muslims to know that the Koran is a recording of God's words as they were originally received by Mohammad; the revealed word must be continually affirmed and accepted in oral performance. As Hodgson (1974) puts it, the Koran has continued to be "an event, an act, rather than merely a statement of facts and norms" (Hodgson 1974:367). Elaborating on this same character of the Koran, Graham (1985) notes how the sensual oral and aural quality of scripture makes it "a living, active, immediate reality in people's lives" (Graham 1985:28). For the non-Arabic speaking Kalaodi, there is that much less of a question that reading scripture is an oral performance and aural experience that has value independent of any intellectual comprehension of content. What stands out in this is the principal mnemonic function of writing. The invariant manuscript of the Koran serves to assure the verbatim accuracy of what is being recalled aloud in liturgical performance. Indeed, much of what is recited in Arabic is done so from memory. And, even though many of the verses that are regularly uttered aloud are learned from hearing others recite, their invariance across local communities and language boundaries is assured by the one written source against which they could always be checked. In this respect a performance from memory is still a form of reading aloud.

This brings us back to the issue of Islam's monotheism and universalistic appeal which, as we noted, depends upon the affirmation and acceptance of scripture without requiring anything more in the practice of reading scripture than the faithful oral reproduction of what has been written. It is in this way that local communities, regardless of variations in local traditions, can be brought within Islam's universal compass. But, on the other side of this, the written word is also being brought within the compass of local oral traditions. That is, so long as scripture is being affirmed orally, it is also susceptable to the evaluations that are distinctive of oral discourse in local communities. There is, then, no sharp contrast between orality and literacy; the oral recitation of what is written involves an interpenetration of these different modes of communicating knowledge. This becomes important to a discussion of the "full reading" of scripture in Kalaodi, as will be taken up below.

At this point we can simply note how utterances in Arabic become juxta-posed in one way or another with utterances in Tidorese, North Moluccan Malay, and Standard Indonesian. In some cases the situational contexts are kept separate. During worship within the mosque, for example, Arabic is used almost exclusively, with the exception that Standard Indonesian is used for the Friday "sermon" (read from a published book). In other cases there is a more overt joining of Islamic (Arabic) performances to activities in which colloquial or only moderately formal speech is used. For example, the words that begin every sura in the Koran (*bismilla arahman arahim*) are uttered at the beginning of undertakings for which it is appropriate for par-ticipants to demonstrate a submission of their self-will to a higher purpose. Such utterances can serve to frame an occasion within Islamic moral values, as would seem to be the case when village meetings begin and end with Arabic incantations. But other times it is not so clear that such framing is taking place, such as when prayers in Arabic are recited over offerings to jins in ceremonies full of songs, potent invocations and hushed exchanges all in Tidorese and all acknowledged as belonging to non-Islamic traditions.

The other name for scripture, *al-Kitab*, identifies Holy Writ as "the Book." Islamic scholars (see Watt 1970:140–141) have observed that in passages of the Koran attributed to a later period, when a Muslim state was becoming consolidated under Mohammad's political leadership, there is less reference made to "the Recitation" (*al-Quran*) and more to "the Book" (*al-Kitab*). We can find in this change an altered sense of the written word's value. Or, more accurately, we can find in it the addition of the idea of the book to that of the recitation, for what has been said above about the importance of the performance of reading does not change. The mnemonic function of writing that recitation gives emphasis to is strictly a preserva-tion of the accuracy of what is uttered from one performance to the next. What the idea of the book adds is the sense that the writing is a self-containment of knowledge. It is a complete text whose form and content cannot be altered.

Backing away for a moment from considering what this seems to mean for people in Kalaodi, we can see how the idea of the Koran as a book merges universal history with the tenets of monotheistic faith. We could argue that the bounded form of the Book is itself a manifestation of the idea that history decisively began and will just as decisively end, a notion that Hodgson (1974) speaks of as fundamental to Islam's "moral position of monotheism" (Hodgson 1974:373). The reckoning of Judgment day, as it is portended in the Koran, is alluded to as an opening up of the pages of a book, the book being a kind of ledger in which entries for all items of crea-tion and all passing events have been made.[5] The scripture that is in people's hands today is usually not confused with this heavenly book used in final judgment, but reference to scripture as "the Book" no doubt carries these connotations that God's knowledge of history is complete. Watt (1970:141) uses Sura 19 to exemplify the way in which later revelations are concerned with the production of a book (in contrast to an earlier predominant concern with the recitation of God's warnings). We can add to this that Sura 19 illustrates how a vision of history becomes merged with the vision of a singular book. In this sura something is told about the lives of Mary, Abraham, Moses, Ishmael and Idris (among others), and preceding each of these names and stories is God's command to Mohammad, "in the Book mention. . . ." What significance this appears to have for people in Kalaodi who recite verses from the Koran will be considered in the following sections.

It is more immediately apparent, however, that in Kalaodi the self-containment of the Koran as a book is recognized more in form than in such historical content. To begin with, the Koran as a volume is an object of some reverence. The most visible expression of this is the act of holding copies of the Koran in the smoke of burning incense after having read from them in the evenings during Ramadan, the month of fasting. People understandably handle the volumes with care and keep them out of the reach of children. But, the Koran is not an object of reverence in the same way as, for example, some of the ritual artifacts associated with jin propitiation are. Unlike these latter items, which are kept out of immediate sight on special altars and are always handled and transported with ceremony, copies of the Koran are available to anyone who desires to recite.

A person can recite from the Koran at any time as an act of worship, but I have only known it to be done at certain times as a part of regular worship. As a preliminary to the daily prayer (most often the evening prayer) and the congregational Friday prayer, some men will spend a brief period reading aloud from the Koran. It makes no difference what part one reads; any part represents the value of the whole.

The reading that takes place during Ramadan gives much stronger expression to the Koran's bounded unity. Throughout the Muslim world, people join together during the fasting month to read the Koran at least once through in thirty days. In Kalaodi the people of each hamlet share this responsibility and usually set out to read the Koran twice through. Every evening neighbors (men and women) gather at someone's house and sit around a cluster of tables on which are laid several copies of the Koran. The Koran is divided, by small marginal indications, into thirty sections of equal length. These divisions are superimposed arbitrarily over the chapter (sura) divisions of the Koran (which in turn are somewhat arbitrarily arranged by length). Taking turns and correcting each other when mistakes are made, they read each evening two of these one thirtieth part divisions so that in thirty days they will have completed their task of reading the Koran twice.

The serious intent of reading through the Koran without error does not call for somberness. On the contrary, reciting from the Koran is a time to enjoy other people's company. The atmosphere turns more convivial when late in the night, after the reading for that evening is completed, refreshments are served and everyone settles into relaxed conversation before another day of fasting. A village imam, who noted how nowadays youths in coastal villages spend the evenings of Ramadan watching television, said approvingly that in Kalaodi, where there is no television, reading the Koran is "entertainment" (*hiburan*).

I have already mentioned Arabic phrases uttered aloud that, while not read or necessarily even learned from written script, could be considered in the context of the scriptural traditions of Islam. Among the most important forms for collective recitation are those belonging to the mystical Sufi traditions of the *tarekat* (meaning "the path" in Arabic). Although there are some women who study the *tarekat*, the most visible social performances associated with it involve only men. The teachers (*jou-guru*) of the *tarekat* are all fairly wealthy men. They belong to specific descent lines and mostly live in the coastal towns. What they teach their students, in practical terms, is how to lead various kinds of chanting sessions, referred to generically as *ratib*. This means, in the majority of cases at least, little more than having the students perform on their own certain chants with the intent of eventually transferring to these students the authority to publicly lead these chants (*ratib*). This transfer is accomplished by, among other ritual actions, whispering some secret Arabic phrases to the advancing student. The student also receives small handwritten booklets containing the texts to be recited. In Kalaodi there are a number of men who consider themselves to be students of *jou-guru*, although most have not proceeded very far in the *tarekat* and so can only lead, if anything, the lower level *ratib*. All men in the village, however, are able to participate in these chanting sessions.

The reasons for holding a chanting session vary. Most often they are performed as a regular part of extended mortuary ceremonies. But, more broadly than this, *ratib* are performed in conjunction with transitional periods when people have a heightened concern about the likelihood of propitious outcomes. During times of anxious uncertainty it is common for people to make a formal vow to host a *ratib* when conditions turn for the better. The person hosting the *ratib* (the one fulfilling a vow, for example) will invite neighbors to his house to participate. One of the village men having the appropriate knowledge will usually be asked to lead the session. When they arrive, usually in the early evening, all of the men sit in a circle on the floor. In front of the leader is a white cloth laid out on the floor and on which have been placed an incense pot and white porcelain bowl containing water. After first reciting some phrases under his breath, the leader will begin reciting aloud from the handwritten book he has with him. Then, on cue, everyone joins him in the chanting of familiar phrases, most of which are taken from the Koran. After well over an hour of reciting and chanting, the session ends with the recitation of the Confession of Faith and with each participant lightly grasping in turn the hand of every other participant. A meal is served and fairly quickly eaten. After the meal people fall into idle conversation, free to leave whenever they wish.

These different forms of reciting Arabic suggest how the collective responsibilities of public performance can be paramount in giving value to the written words. The reading of the Koran during Ramadan is a particularly clear expression of a relation between demonstrating community responsibility and affirming the unified integrity of the Book. Chanting sessions, which belong to the distinctive Sufi traditions of Islam but make use of the same unvarying phrases, similarly find the persuasive power of the word in public oral performance. At the same time, there is a noticeable openness of the community of readers, the invitation to participate in reciting can be extended to all Muslims. To return to the idioms of light and dark mentioned previously, the public involvement of giving clear and repeated utterance to the revealed word would have the effect of blanketing over any of the rifts and concealments of their more fragmented ancestral traditions. It is an image conveyed well in the identification of Islamic traditions with the quality of light.

We are of course tempted to fit this to our own familiar notion of enlightenment. But, some profound differences cause us to hesitate. For the Kalaodi, the activity of reading remains formal and ritualistic and an enlightened comprehension of what they are reading and affirming remains blocked by the foreignness of the language. What can we say, then, about the content of what they are reading and about the critical evaluations they make? In the remaining sections I will consider this more difficult issue.

READING FOREIGN WORDS

Comprehension can be thought of as an activity by which one takes control of something by way of linguistic competence. That is, when something is comprehended it is taken in, included within a "comprehensive" universe of structured ideas, explored operationally, and reworked under the forces of predication (wedding generalized meanings to particular references) to emerge as recognizably the same thing, though transformed. When sense is "made" out of some uttered statement, then something different can be said about it. The demonstration of an ability to verbally transform what is given is usually taken to be a test of one's comprehension ("Let me see if I understand what you are saying: . . .". No longer resigned to reiterate, the one who comprehends something has the transcendent means to operate upon what has been given. Implicit in such a willingness and ability to take something and reoffer it in one's own terms is the power of conceptual thought and analysis that we tend to attribute to language use generally but find especially accentuated in literacy (see Ong 1967; Olson 1977).

For Kalaodi scriptural reading we are faced with literacy in the absence of comprehension. But, rather than requiring us to abandon the significance of these notions altogether, the situation only requires us to push the issues back to a different level. Comprehension does not belong to the situated *practice* of reading, as an activity occurring in real time, but to a seemingly timeless and private process of reasoning through what has been written. We are still left with the problem of dealing with, in explicit terms, the practice of reading—the real time spent engaged in the process of actualizing what has been preserved in writing. After all, comprehension, as an abstractive exercise, only occurs insofar as the conditions for its possibility are reproduced in practice. At this level there is no reason to radically distinguish what the Kalaodi are doing from what others are doing when they read Arabic.

Having introduced the notion of comprehension as an activity in which one has subjective transformational control over that which has been offered, I will distinguish the notion of *apprehension* as an activity, inherent in the practice of communicating—and thus also in reading—, in which one confronts and takes hold of what there is to know and remember. In comprehending something one makes use of the verbs of predication to, as Ong (1967) puts it, bring "an *accusation* to bear against a subject" (Ong 1967:157). In apprehending something one is involved in the less self-assured and more socially engaged process of coming to grips with what there is to know without necessarily knowing how to subject it to predications, that is, how to adequately comprehend it. As a first approximation of this, apprehension has more to do with substantive nouns than with verbs. And it has more to do with the give and take of words that one feels belong to things substantially (as a child does in learning a language) than with the creative competence to use words with conventional meanings to talk about things in one's own terms. The link between writing and mnemonics, which indicates a primary concern for presenting things in the right order, should direct our attention to reading as, first of all, the active apprehension of things.

It is clear, in any event, that in Islam much depends upon the real interaction and commitment people have to the written word of scripture, not first as a matter of abstract conceptual thought or doctrinal belief, but as a matter of regular practice. Recitations for the Kalaodi are part of regularly occurring social performances that reproduce the sensible qualities and patterns of what we might call (following Bourdieu 1977) a deeply felt Muslim "habitus." At this level of prereflective experience, of what is given and re-produced in faithful practice, the words of the Book retain a structured pres-ence in the social life of Kalaodi independently of anything more that the people of Kalaodi, or anyone, might have to say about their significance. We can go on to consider reading, then, as an apprehending activity that belongs to a substratum of social practices generating the experiences that different understandings draw upon.

Within Islamic tradition, we can identify two different vectors of knowl-edge or understanding: one is a path of what Woodward (1989) calls "normative piety," the other is the mystical path of Sufism. Using the ter-minology introduced above, we can say that the former leads in the direc-tion of increased comprehension. That is, normative piety gives value to the ability to comprehend the literal meaning of what is written and the ability to rationally elaborate on the historical and moral significance of what is said in scripture. It draws adherents toward institutionalized education and seeks the authority of literal interpretations. The latter, Sufism, leads in the opposite direction toward an effacement of all literal meanings and seeks in-timate, personal contact with the unity of God. Rather than leading from apprehension to comprehension, it strives for a loss of oneself and a move-ment back to the substance of original unity. That is, it ultimately strives to dissolve even the interactional nature of apprehension (as will become clearer below). In Tidore, Sufi mystical traditions are in the hands of the *jou-guru.*

It is already clear that these vectors of knowledge are aligned with dis-tinctive forms of authority. As Islam continues to be thought of as a religion introduced from abroad, so religious authority continues to be marked by signs of foreignness. "Speaking Arabic" is one such sign. Those who are re-ligiously learned usually have a reputation of knowing how to speak Arabic, even though this may mean only that they are able to talk about religious doctrine with more informed use of Arabic terminology. Foreign descent can also serve as a sign of religious authority. The *jou-guru* are of descent lines that people identify as Arabic in their origins. In the realm of norma-tive piety, it is affiliations with centrally organized institutions of learning and reform that count. Those who carry the voice of authority in speaking of doctrine, history and moral behavior are qualified by a formal education that imports knowledge from decidedly nonlocal sources. The greater use made of Standard Indonesian, a register marked as being written and for-eign (in the sense of nonlocal), also indicates an orientation toward outside sources of knowledge. Insofar as there is an acceptance of these vectors of knowledge, those who are fully immersed in the practices, but who lack the means of attaining more rational comprehension or more substantial mystical union, find themselves at a loss. Taking part in the reading and apprehension of words, but not coming very close to the achievement of these ends, they remain dependent on others who are able to come closer to the valued ends.

We cannot rightly characterize Kalaodi as homogeneous in this respect. But there is a tendency in Tidore to identify the village as a whole as one lacking in the attainments of these higher levels of learning and awareness. Thus, one *jou-guru* explained to me that villagers in a place like Kalaodi take part in recitations and help complete their performance, but, like a person moving an ashtray from here to there upon command without knowing what an ashtray is, they do not understand what they are doing. More cruelly, accentuating even more so the unthinking bodily involvement of performers, another *jou-guru* put it that most villagers are just interested in the food that is served afterward. And so too, though usually in the course of advocating economic progress or religious reform, educated government employees speak of the villagers' lack of understanding and mistaken notions.

But of greater interest is the way that most people in Kalaodi would, often with noticeable self-mockery, profess their own ignorance. They had little to say about the meaning of what they did and what they recited, and acknowledged that others were in a position to better comprehend and talk about these things. How are we to take such statements? The irony contained in a profession of one's own ignorance, since it is a knowing self-mockery, is a sure indication that there is something more. They cannot be in any abject state of lacking knowledge if they so confidently formulate such an opinion about their ignorance. We are forced to consider, then, the source of this understanding.

To see what other kinds of understanding can bear upon a substratum of experience, we can continue to look at the practice of reading as an activity of apprehending what there is to know. What is blocked from the Kalaodi by the foreignness of the language is semantic meaning. This without question blocks comprehension. But, the foreignness of the language does not impede the apprehension of words as names—in particular, words recognized as proper names. As I will go on to argue in much of what follows, for the Kalaodi the revelation of the Word in scripture is most importantly a revelation of names.

Not understanding Arabic myself, I can attest from listening to recitations that proper names flash out as recognizable entities in a stream of pleasingly lyrical but uncomprehended utterances. In the chanting sessions, some of these names are contained in the refrains that everyone recites together. More are in the lines that the leader of the session alone reads out of the small book in front of him. Many of the names are ringingly familiar if only because they belong to the inventory of Arabic names the Tidorese use. But they are names contained within a recited text now. In characterizing the activity of chanting, people in Kalaodi would sometimes refer explicitly to the reciting of names; as they put it, they "receive names" (*tero ronga*) by these chants. Being more specific, they would identify the different chants by the names received. Thus, for example, in many of the chanting sessions, and in the friday prayers, there is a chant that they refer to as one in which they receive the names of "the four imams"; the words recited are the names of the four schools of law in Sunni Islam—Hanafi, Hanbali, Maliki, and Shafii (named after their respective founders). The name of Ali is often received in chants, as are the names of other saints. In the same way they would refer to the often chanted formulae that contain the name of God or the name of the Prophet Mohammad (such as the Confession of Faith) as ways by which these names were received. On one occasion I asked a man who was listening with me, and who was pointing out to me the names that were being received, who the named people are. He said, with a noticeable air of reverence, that they are people in Arab history. He immediately added that he himself had never studied history.

What was said above about the idea of recitation being conjoined with the idea of the Book takes on new significance. The completeness of the Book for the Kalaodi was seen, up to now, as an affirmation of its form only (as a volume with various divisions). In their receiving of names, the Kalaodi are apprehending and affirming something of its content. I have already indicated that the idea of history's completeness, which is the idea that all that passes from beginning to end is known, is conveyed by the image of a book as a complete collection of records. In the sura used to show how the idea of a book in this sense can, at least figuratively, be applied to scripture, God commands Mohammad to "mention in the book" particular people and their stories (Sura 19). What we can see now is that the Kalaodi, who as Muslims are committed to the Book and are a part of the universal history it proclaims, receive in their recitations names belonging to this history.

We can go on to ask, then, what it means for people in Kalaodi to apprehend proper names in the absence of much of a comprehensible context for these names (the syntax of the language and the sequenced events of the stories). It is helpful to first give some attention to the significance of proper names.

THE APPREHENSION OF NAMES

Proper names are words that are foreign to any language. They are without question linguistic elements, for they find their place in strings of utterances and are subject to grammatical and (to a somewhat lesser extent) phonological constraints. But, despite the possibility that words used as names might be semantically meaningful in a particular language, as names they have a value no longer constrained by the internal sense relations of any language. That names do not primarily convey semantic meanings is perhaps evident enough, but that for this reason they exist as foreign words, presentable in any language but belonging to none, can escape our attention, especially if we are intent on seeing languages only as discretely separated systems of meaning.[6] Language philosophers, who have struggled with the recalcitrance of proper names to the internal logic of language (as the vast and still growing literature on the subject attests), have not by and large emphasized this "otherness" of names that says less about how the world is comprehended through the interdependent concepts of language than about how it is encountered and apprehended interactively in the practice of speaking and, more importantly here, reading.

On the face of it, we do not necessarily expect proper names to present a problem to a self-assured and abstractive use of language. Our image of two kinds of books working in tandem—a dictionary containing words of a language and an encyclopedia containing the names of things—can obviate the dynamics and indeterminacy that is involved in conjoining language and knowledge. The names taken from a compendium of factual knowledge can simply be inserted as referring expressions in our statements and thereby be brought in line with semantic conventions to say something true or false about the world. But looking at this closer we find a lack of certainty, or an indefiniteness, about what knowledge is being brought in by a particular name. A proper name does not have a definition but only alludes to contingently associated ideas, so the task of determining the truth or falsity of what is "literally" said, or whether anything is really referred to at all, is undermined. Some attempts to deal with this "referential opacity" (Quine 1960:141) have involved turning names into something else—into definite descriptions and demonstratives (Russell 1956:200–201), or into predicates of bound variables (Quine 1960:176–180). But this only serves to bypass the problems they pose.[7] In more recent literature, questions about the significance of proper names have led to a deeper questioning of basic premises in our understanding of language and knowledge (see especially Kripke 1980; Schwartz 1977; Rorty 1982).

We will find it useful here to consider names as motivated signs, using Saussure's and Benveniste's conceptions, and as indexical signs, using Peirce's conceptions.

As is well known, Saussure (1959) attached fundamental importance to the arbitrary nature of the linguistic sign. It is what protects a language's own solidarity from fortuitous changes of history. Because the sign is arbitrary, with nothing either reasonable or natural about its signifying role, there will be no competing outside claims upon it to steer its meanings away from those established strictly by convention. In other words, the sign must give itself over to the necessary relations within a language, severing contingent motivational ties that extend outside of the synchronic conventions of language. Most of Saussure's concern is for motivation and arbitrariness in the relation between the sounds of the utterance and the ideas they invoke. Proper names are clearly arbitrary at this juncture; a name does not resemble any of its associated ideas. But motivation can operate through other junctures as well, and according to Benveniste's reappraisal of this issue it is really the arbitrary relation between the utterance and any object of reference that is important to Saussure's theory. If this is so, we are concerned not only with the fact that the word "ox" does not resemble an actual ox, but also that the word does not belong to—is not taken to be a part of—an actual ox. It belongs to the semantic structure of a language. Proper names are on this second count motivated signs because they do belong to "substances" that are outside of the solidarity of a language. To say this does not mean we have to be able to specify what the substantial things are (the question of our ability to ever finally do this is a major source of debate among language philosophers). It means simply that in using a name the speaker is forcing a search for attributes outside of the semantic conventions of a synchronically structured language.

Thus, "a bachelor" is not the name of something that happens to be a man and unmarried. Rather, the expression denotes these attributes necessarily, independently of how it is used in referring to someone. If it were a name, and therefore bound to something outside of the semantic conventions, the freedom and control of comprehension would be lost. Not only would we always be uncertain about whether or not we apprehended things correctly (is what we call "a bachelor" really unmarried?), but we would also need to keep track of the changes that take place (was "a bachelor" something different than this in the past?) Semantic knowledge is freed from this contingency, for what is meant by an expression is accepted by synchronic convention. But proper names are not secured in this way; they are inherently diachronic, directing us to the contingencies of history out of which our synthetic knowledge of the world is constructed.

There are ways of attempting to secure names in the synthetic knowledge that is socially shared, and logical (and therefore synchronic) principles can be used in doing this. Names can be brought under, if not sometimes replaced by, standardized positional designations that are rationally meaningful because they constitute a set of terms in an operational (i.e., structural) space. Such procedures of designating named things positionally include dating and chronological ordering, the assigning of spatial coordinates, genealogical reckoning, the determining of rank by title, and even alphabetizing. In all of these cases named things are secured in some kind of relational order. But at the same time, the names themselves remain as something existing apart from the designations. Positional designations can, after all, make use of only selected attributes, leaving other attributes, of no set number, to be reckoned with differently and perhaps in ways that would overthrow the rule of any standard designations.[8]

There are two points that can be made to emphasize that names do not directly constitute an established order of things that are known determinately, as an encyclopedic image of knowledge might suggest: 1) the use of names has an affinity to the use of figures of speech in symbolic modes of meaning; 2) although they are singular referring expressions, names do not contain in themselves a delimitation of what belongs to their singularity. Both of these become more apparent when we recognize that names are significant to us not because they refer to things present before our eyes (demonstratives can do as much), but because they allow us to do the work of consolidating a potentially unlimited range of facts and impressions that cannot be made empirically present all at once. In individual and collective memories, they are loci around which associated attributes and connecting events, gathered through time from diverse sources, cohere. Thus, even when a name is uttered with reference to some small bit of evidence relevant at the moment, any new knowledge must be made to fit with whatever knowlege associated with that name has already been gathered. That names are likened to figures of speech in the symbolic use of language only follows from their status as motivated signs. Lacking an encoded semantic meaning and not thoroughly secured in a logical order of designations, names act in a figurative (i.e., nonliteral) fashion to direct attention outwardly to the substantial things to which they are felt to belong (see Todorov 1982:241). They involve the language user in real communicative interaction that produces new meanings with the importation of new associations. We can speak again of a certain loss of comprehensional control in this mode of referring to things through substantial connections. Just as a person who speaks too figuratively might be thought to be awash in contingent associations, so a person who uses proper names for ordinary things in his or her surroundings might be thought to be enjoying an exceptionally enchanted world, if not thought to be neurotically obsessed.

The second point mentioned, that nothing in the name delimits the range of its singularity, is but another aspect of its figurative, or nonliteral, status. This is what prevents names from being meaningful, even as reference terms, in logical statements: the particulars to which they would directly refer cannot be brought under quantification. Having the image of knowledge as primarily encyclopedic, and therefore determinate and relatively secured, we can easily lose sight of how far the individuality of a named "particular" can extend—that is, how much can be subsumed under any one name. Bertrand Russell, who perhaps more than any other analytic philosopher struggled with the issue of proper names, fully recognized this aspect of the recalcitrance of names to logical procedures of reasoning. In his *Philosophy of Logical Atomism*, after first saying that "you cannot ever talk about a particular particular except by means of a proper name" (Russell 1956:200), Russell goes on to say that "each particular that there is in the world does not in any way logically depend upon any other particular. Each one might happen to be the whole universe" (Russell 1956:202). His own solution for reining them in is to keep to empirical facts and to replace names that can accrue boundless associations with demonstratives that refer us to things with which we are actually acquainted and that can be made present before us. But of course demonstratives ("this" and "that") are not names, and, as pointed out, people use names as a way of holding on to things removed from their direct acquaintance.

The extensions and transformations of named things, that one is committed to tracking simply by virtue of keeping (remembering) the names, can lead imperceptibly into myth. To philosophers not committed to an analytic tradition, this is what is most characteristic of names in the first place.[9] We can add that it is freedom from semantic content (as a kind of reversal of the freedom from substance in semantics) that gives names over to the diachrony of myth and history. For example, when "The Moral Majority" is used as a name, it makes no difference whether that which goes by this name is really moral or really a majority. If this did make a difference, we would no longer be regarding the expression for its function as a name, but for its function as a definite description or possibly a formal designation. Once it is a name, it is freed from semantic constraints and free to take on new contingent associations as synthetic knowledge of the world forms and changes.

So long as we keep with Saussure's formulation we are at a disadvantage if we want to attribute a fundamental importance to names and naming. In giving priority to the synchronic system, he has little to say about names, or motivated signs generally, except to dismiss them as elements in these systems. Peirce's theory of the sign is more inclusive and involves, at every point, a relation to what he calls a "dynamic object." In a very concise statement of his theory, that connects his triad of signs with his triad of phenomenological categories, Peirce (1958) speaks of the Symbol as Saussure would speak of the arbitrary linguistic sign: "I define a Symbol as a sign which is determined by its dynamic object only in the sense that it will be so interpreted. It thus depends either upon a convention, a habit, or a natural disposition of its interpretant..." (Peirce 1958:391). In Saussure's diadic thinking, this leaves motivated signs; but in Peirce's triadic thinking it leaves two other kinds of signs, the Icon and the Index. In discussing the significance of names, we are most immediately interested in the Index, which Peirce defines as "a sign determined by its Dynamic object by virtue of being in *a real relation to it*. Such is a Proper Name...; such is the occurrence of a symptom of a disease" (Peirce 1958:391, my emphasis). Whereas the symbol belongs to the category of Thirdness, which always contains a "mental element" (Peirce 1958:388), the index belongs to the category of Secondness, which contains "the experience of effort" and "brute action" (Peirce 1958:384–385). The Icon, which Peirce defines as "a sign which is determined by its dynamic object by virtue of its own internal nature" (Peirce 1958:391), is important in this discussion insofar as that which lies behind the name, such as a face or fragrance or any other sense of something whole, can be desired as an icon (even if it remains hidden). The category of Firstness that the icon belongs to is characterized by "qualities of feeling" and unity (Peirce 1958:383).

Combining Saussure's dichotomies with Peirce's categories we can first of all avoid the error of confusing the issue of what words mean in their abstract generality and according to synchronic rules (in Peirce's third category) with the issue of how they can be used as referring expressions in the practice of saying something with them (in Peirce's second category). This is not a trade off, but two different levels in which signs of language participate.[10] But when an expression is regularly used as a name, which is how it takes on the status of being a proper name, it is freed from its participation in a language's synchronic semantic relations as other expressions are not; we do not look first for its conventional sense. In this way, a proper name, not belonging to any particular language, only participates at the level of discourse practice (as a category of Secondness) and thus is only valued insofar as it functions to indexically refer to something. Although we can compare this to the referring function of, for example, the demonstratives "this" and "that," there is the important difference that these are expressions belonging to the English language and that they do have semantic content (albeit not very much). Thus, instead of bringing something in with them, they point outwardly toward something. "This" and "that" and personal pronouns, unlike proper names, do not carry with them the history of their use because they are not indexically attached to anything substantial, even though they are, like names, particularly instrumental at the level of discourse practice where referencing occurs.

Another important distinction can be made between a word as an arbitrary sign whose meaning emerges from the interdependencies of sense relations of a language system and a word as a motivated sign whose value is bound to a dynamic object, again emphasizing the practice and "brute action" that is manifested at this level. A word when it means something to someone as a name can withstand the practice of that person repeating it over and over. Indeed, in order to bring out its value, which is to bring to mind its dynamic object, the person might deliberately go through the practice of repeating the name, for example, when he or she wants to bring to mind the face of a lover. Now a word, insofar as it is valued as an arbitrary sign, depends on its context, which includes its syntactic contact with other words. If it is repeated over and over, by itself, it will lose its denotative sense. A person is left then experiencing a foreign word. What has been lost is the value of a word in comprehending things; what can be gained is a new regard for it in its foreign state as a name by which something is apprehended. In this way the fundamental character of the name, as a word having a real relation to its dynamic object, can be had by any word when it is brought into a regimen of practice. Freud, who attached great significance to the way proper names (and foreign words) are forgotten, also noted how repetition can be part of the "work of remembering" (Freud 1914:153). We can understand what Freud thought was its obsessional quality when we recognize that the practice of repeating leads to an evacuation of semantic meaning, and thus a loss of one's comprehensional control. It turns speaking into naming.

Peirce's notion of the index, as a sign valued in action and therefore directly linked to experience rather than mental activity, is helpful in our understanding of the "otherness" of names. If we are satisfied that we know what something is definitely, we do not use a name for it but simply speak of it in definite terms. It is only when we recognize something as having its own being, its own "character," and when we are never satisfied that we have finally come to terms with this character, that we will call that "something" by name. We not only expect that what has a name will change in the future, but also that our knowledge of what it was in the past will change. As Kenneth Burke (1950) would put it, there is in our use of names, as opposed to definite terms, a "courtship" going on.[11] With an encyclopedic frame of mind, that sees all names as being already accountable in a global order, we might not see such a notion of courtship as anything more than an added romanticism. We are usually confident that what is named will never really escape its positional designations and the assured facts that hold them to these designations. There is a hedging of any direct indexical action between name and thing. But, when designations do not constrain what is named, then the indexical value of the name, connecting it to something no less real in memory, can make the name dangerous to use. There is much in the anthropological literature about the use of names that suggest it to be in certain situations an unacceptable or dangerous kind of courtship. Levy-Bruhl, for example, says about certain North American Indians, "alluding to a name is the same thing as laying hands on the very person or being that bears the name. It is making an attack upon him, outraging his individuality, or again, it is invoking his presence and forcing him to appear, a proceeding which may be fraught with very great danger" (Levy-Bruhl 1985:51). We could not dispute the charge that there is nothing reasonable in this; but, using names, wherever it occurs, is never at base a matter of reason and comprehension, but of action and apprehension.[12]

THE FULL READING

On different occasions when I was asking in Kalaodi about some aspect of Tidore's history, geography or political order, I was struck by the way the person I was talking to would stop normal conversation to recite a series of names. This happened, for example, when I asked about the village territory; a perimeter would be traced by a rote naming of landmarks—the names of hills, streams, springs, cliffs, and boulders. Or when asking about Kalaodi's or some other village's position in the political order of the traditional state, I would usually be given at some point an ordered list of the names of the state's formal political divisions, each preceded by the title of that division's minister in the sultan's court. They were, of course, telling me something about the state of things in telling me these names. But it was not something to be comprehended conceptually, for there was nothing that could be put in other words. Indeed, in the span of their recitation there was even limited need for me to know the Tidorese language. What they were telling me was the order of things as it was to be apprehended directly by knowing what things are called. And this knowledge, rather than being settled in an internalized awareness, was evocatively enlivened in the experience of saying and hearing the names. The pleasure of the performance appeared to be as much of a motivating factor as any intent to be informative.[13] This would make such recitations similar to the more obviously pleasurable activity of singing or reciting poetic verses, many of which begin with the mentioning of local place names (in a rhyming scheme, if not always a pertinent geographical or historical scheme). Also, we can note that all of these activities are compellingly valued as *public* performances. Part of the pleasure in reciting aloud is derived from having others hear and respond with recognition, or at least with some preliminary intrigue. Even if not profoundly so, there is a sense that the uttering aloud of these words is revelatory, having the effect of not only evoking memories, but also of impressing upon a collective memory an accepted order of things. We could say that the vision of order that is being recreated in such public performance is an orthodox one.

It is in this context that I am also considering scriptural reading in Tidore. This is not to say that reciting from the Koran is the same thing as reciting lists of names or reciting poetic verse, or that Koranic reading could not be approached from other very different perspectives. It is simply a choice on my part to begin with what is common to such activities. Specifically, they are activities for which we are forced to give considerable attention to what is happening at a level of practice. We are struck by the way people engage themselves with the world not by speaking about it through the novel use of abstract concepts, but by affirming a particular recollection of it by more simply reciting what there is to know. It is, in other words, an apprehension more than a comprehension of things. I am using Peirce's category of Secondness to isolate the salient features of recitation as a practice and referring to this category as a ground of prereflective (neither analyzed nor unified) experience. The attention that is drawn to proper names follows from the indexical character of sign relations at this level of experience. The "brute action" and "struggle" that Peirce attributes to Secondness is, when we consider the recitation of names, the "all or nothing" effect of recalling what there is. Words that are valued as names are fated by the efforts people put into remembering or forgetting them; they have no logical sense relations keeping them in place independently of these efforts. Conversely, the rational freedom of paraphrase and translation, that allows us to work with concepts and meanings independently of words that strictly name things, is absent here. In Freud's thinking, the practice of simply naming what there is would belong to the obsessional work of remembering.

More specifically here, our concern is for Koranic "reading" as a practice by which the Kalaodi bring the revealed word into their own experience. Through this practice they remain engaged with the world as Muslims everywhere recognize and "remember" it. Thus, the Koran is full of indexical significance, even if for the Kalaodi it lacks literal significance. But, recognizing this much does not get around the question of what significance, or value, this revelation has for people in Kalaodi. The ignorance that is often professed in Kalaodi, as I mentioned earlier, is not an indication of an utter lack of knowledge on their part, or lack of significance on the part of what they recite. On the contrary, to the extent that it is a knowing evaluation, it indicates that there is something more. Indeed, the very notion that the recited words have value, to whomever, requires us to look for differentials and therefore to specify what more there is that the experience of reciting would lead toward. There must be, in other words, potentialities of knowledge that extend beyond realizations at the level of practice and experience.

I have already mentioned the two different vectors of knowledge that Islamic traditions employ, and I will expand upon these below. But, more importantly now as we consider the "full reading" of scripture in Kalaodi, we need to include the potentialities of knowledge that local oral traditions employ. In doing this we are not forcing together the otherwise separable oral traditions of Tidore and written traditions of Islam. The (prereflective) ground of experience that I have chosen to start with is also a meeting ground for written and oral traditions, for as the written word of scripture is actualized in its oral presentation, so it meets with and joins the utterances that are more obviously a part of oral knowledge and evaluations. I have begun by focusing on the recitation of names and have suggested that the public performance of "revealing" names constructs an orthodox vision of what there is to know. As I will go on to argue, the full reading brings in the inherent heterodoxy of oral tradition that looks for the truth in what is unspoken and concealed from public view, thus leaving room for the significance of names that remain unrevealed.

Continuing to invoke Peirce's categories, the realm of experience is a middle ground also in the sense that, belonging to the category of Secondness, it is bounded by the other categories of an irreducible triad. These correspond to the different vectors of knowledge, or understanding, that I have alluded to above. To put it somewhat differently now, we could say that whatever is presented in experience is of suspended value in our knowledge about the world because it leads to, and supposedly connects with, something that is not immediately consumed by the fleeting present.[14] (Peirce does in fact identify Secondness with the present.) Limiting our attention to the names that are presented in recitation, we can identify one direction as leading toward the more generalizable features that place the plurality of names in an analyzable order: what are the generalized principles that account for the positioning of elements within a lawful order and that, in the end, would allow for the passing of informed judgment? This is asking about the category of Thirdness (identified with the always anticipated future). The other direction is a more particularizing one: what is the substantial reality or truth, impressed as a feeling or image of original unity, with which, by uttering a name, we would attempt to achieve real contact? This is asking about the category of Firstness (identified with the never fully recoverable past).

To fill this out with respect to scriptural reading, we can note how these two different directions are suggested in the two ways of identifying scripture, as these were mentioned above. The idea of scripture as the Book (*al-Kitab*) emphasizes the compilation of historical knowledge and, by implication, all knowledge that can be used in final judgment. The idea of scripture as the Recitation (*al-Quran*) emphasizes the pure performance of reading and would lead to an unquestioned feeling of the unity of its truth (what is referred to in Arabic as *tawhid*).

But it is more fruitful to approach this as a distinction drawn between the historical vision and moral aims of normative piety on the one hand, and the meditative and mystical aims of Sufi piety on the other.[15] Normative piety, as Woodward (1989) discusses it, is that aspect of faith that emphasizes obedience and submission to the Law (*sharia*) of Islam. I am connecting it here to the idea of "the book," not only as it is conveyed archetypically in the reading of the Koran (the Book), but as it extends to the perceived value of books generally. The path of normative piety is one that leads by way of institutional education to a comprehension of the knowledge contained in books and to the ability to make more informed judgments. There is in Kalaodi a respect for this kind of book learning, even if most people freely admit that they themselves have attained very little of it. Their lack, however, is a relative one along a continuum of knowledge that allows, in principle, for movement. As the Kalaodi speak of education, it is open to anyone who might have the ambition and intelligence to pursue it. There is no categorical separation between the unlearned and the learned, although the more educated and powerful might in fact attempt to construct barriers (by barring advancement in education or secluding books). As the Kalaodi speak about books, it is their quality of being public (published) that is most decisive in characterizing the knowledge they contain. There are no essential hidden mysteries, no special states of communion required between the knower and the known, and no restrictions on the passage of knowledge from one person to another. With the idea of the book comes the notion that knowledge of the world can be made explicit: "all is in a clear book" (Koran 11.6). The blanketing authority of the Law and the open disclosure of knowledge in books are brought together in Tidore by the idiom of "light." The term *sareat*, derived from the Arabic word for "law," is also used to convey the notion of public exposure.[16]

In literature on the subject, the mystical path (*tarekat*) of Sufism is generally described as a path leading in the opposite direction. It refers to the devotional methods that followers use in their search to personally know and love God. Theirs is a struggle to get beyond the veils that separate the human from the divine and to experience what is the central mystery of Islam, that God is One. As Sufi traditions arose in reaction to an over-intellectualizing "lawful mindedness," so it continued to be a skeptical response to those who regarded their spiritual progress as a moral advancement that could be made by reading books for their informational content. Thus, Schimmel in her study of Sufism states: "True gnosis, namely the gnosis of the One, is not attained through books, and many a legend tells how a Sufi who had reached, or thought he had reached, his goal threw away his books" (Schimmel 1975:17). So long as recitation is at the heart of Koranic reading, there is always to some extent this pulling back from ever regarding the revealed word intellectually as if it were about God and His creation and not constitutive of a personal relationship to God as the Creator. There is in this also a tendency, as we might expect, to give prominence to names—in particular names that would lead to God as a source of all creation. "The connecting thread of the Koran is not the stories of the prophets, the legal injunctions, the threats of punishment and promises of reward, or the descriptions of nature and the cosmos, but the Most Beautiful Names, which are mentioned singly, often in pairs, and sometimes in groups throughout the text. Most of Islamic theological thinking revolves around the names revealed in the Koran" (Chittick 1989:33). Sufism, however, with its more deliberate aims to achieve a union with God, is that much more committed to reading from the Koran the names that call upon the reality lying behind them, rather than the words that call upon conventional meanings. All of the words used as attributes of God and His creation can be read as Divine Names. This is according to the well known and influential thirteenth-century mystic, Ibn al-Arabi, who speaks in his writings of the many faces of God one would encounter through these many names, and of the One Essence, arrived at through the Name of names, hidden behind them all (see Chittick 1989).

Words become names in the act of repeating them. A form of chanting that specifically works through the Divine Names and is performed throughout much of the Islamic world, including in Kalaodi, is called *dhikr*, which in Arabic means "remembrance." In chanting the *dhikr*, one's thoughts are cleared so that the remembrances invoked by the words, now as names, appeal directly to one's feelings. It is, of course, a remembrance of God that the Sufi is after, and as a sought after communion it is variously spoken of as, for example, a longing return to home and a desirous uniting of lovers. To cite Schimmel: "*Dhikr* is the first step in the way of love; for when somebody loves someone, he likes to repeat his name and constantly remember him" (Schimmel 1975:168). The ultimate aim of remembrance is to get beyond the names to a state where "recollecting subject, and recollected object become again one, as they were before the Day of *Alast* [when the primordial covenant between God and humanity was created]" (Schimmel 1975:172). But the mystery of this unity is never dispelled so long as there continues to be a longing effort to attain it. Schimmel (1975) goes on to say, "the last mystery of recollection is complete silence" (Schimmel 1975:172). If what is reached by way of uttered words is something ineffable, then one invites paradoxes in speaking about it. Thus Sufi teachers can say that God's name, that above all others needs to be remembered, is beyond recollection (Schimmel 1975:81), and that "true *dhikr* is that you forget your *dhikr*" (Schimmel 1975:172). We can add that besides the poetic mystery of recollection there is the more prosaic uncertainty of knowing who, if anyone, has ever really been able to attain such a state of gnosis.

I mention this much about Sufism as it is generally understood for two reasons. First of all, I found no indication that people in Kalaodi, who so frequently took part in the chanting performances, considered the aims of the *tarekat* in this manner. Second, some of these same pulling values of mystery, substantial unions, and ultimate sources of origins appear in the regard they give their own locally preserved and guarded ancestral traditions.

As for the first point, it was already mentioned above that the Kalaodi speak of "receiving names" in their recitations. But these are names of historical figures. The more complete historical (and doctrinal) knowledge they profess to lack belongs to the realm of normative piety. It would lead them not to mystical union, but to greater literacy through formal education. Some other explanations were also given to me about recitations, but allusions were usually made to the respect it showed for the dead (most chanting is done in conjunction with mortuary ceremony) or to the need to fulfill vows. Again, these are behavioral and contractual concerns of normative piety. For those who pursue the *tarekat*, rather than just participate in it, there is the expressed purpose of gaining greater self-control. But the value of the *tarekat* in cultivating self-control is associated most directly with the ideal qualities of strong leadership. We can add to this by noting that Sufism to the Kalaodi is by and large viewed as being closed to them in a way that normative Islamic and local traditional knowledge are not. The *jou-guru* outside the village have a firm grip on Sufi traditions, for despite the claim sometimes made that anyone who has the personal strength and purity of heart to follow the *tarekat* far enough can become in turn a *jou-guru*. The "title" of *jou-guru* has long been transferred exclusively within a few descent lines. The secrets that the *jou-guru* hold, and that are used in authorizing students to lead chanting sessions, are not felt by the Kalaodi to be significantly absent, or removed, from their normal discourse and therefore to be necessary in the end to the coherent sense of all that is present to them. They are secrets of instrumental value to those who choose to become students of the *tarekat*.[17]

To go on to the second point, that Sufi traditions and Kalaodi ancestral traditions have similarities, whereas I never heard people in Kalaodi speak of recitation as a way of remembering, the idiom of remembrance (*sonyinga* in Tidorese) is a key one in referring to the ritual practices of local tradition. More specifically, the rituals involved in propitiating local spirits, or *jins*, are generally referred to as ways of remembering. What is it that they are remembering? If they use a direct object with this verb, they usually put it that they are remembering their ancestors. But we can be misled by this answer if we primarily think of ancestors as quasi-historical figures positioned in genealogical space, as if the knowledge of ancestors was of an encyclopedic sort. Without denying the importance of genealogical connectedness to the *idea* that the order of ancestors is a given one, we need to recognize the mystery that is central to the unwritten knowledge of ancestry and that bears more on ritual practice and faith in original order than on intellectual thought and factual knowledge about this order. A comparison can be made to the mystery confronting the Sufi, for the intent of the Kalaodi when they remember their ancestors is also to renew contact with something that belongs to an originating past but that is not so evidently and freely named in the present.

Knowledge of ancestors, then, always points back beyond whatever names might be apprehended in an interconnected series of names, just as the knowledge of God to a Sufi points back beyond the names that are presented in writing and recited aloud. In both cases, the mystery does not begin with a deliberate hiding of something that would otherwise be known definitely alongside of other things known and named. It is better described as a feeling that something of an originating value, and therefore of a more unifying order, lies behind and gives purpose to the regularities of ritual practices that people of a community say they are committed to performing. The intent in ritually remembering something is to interactionally maintain real, sensual contact with the full character of what is beyond naming, at least in any self-assured discursive sense. To the Kalaodi there are always hidden names of a deeper past corresponding to a "darker" and more essential truth (*hakekat*) of the original relations established between ancestors and locally embedded spiritual powers (jins and sacred spots).

Whatever formal similarities there are between Sufism and local tradition, substantially they stand in contrast (and from a reformed Islamic point of view they are of course in real conflict). The material with which the Kalaodi and the Sufi mystic work in their "reading," as a way of remembering, differ significantly. In Sufism it is still the written word of scripture that holds the promise of leading one to a felt source of origins. Normative piety and Sufism, then, are united in that they begin and end with the experience of reciting the words of a book whose authority is similarly unquestioned, even though they take their readings in different directions—outwardly toward an intelligible world on the one hand, inwardly toward a felt source of creation on the other. Among learned Muslims these are sometimes regarded as complementary approaches to scripture.[18]

In the Kalaodi reading, the ground of manifest experience, of what is revealed in repetitive enactments, is an expanded one, not limited to the recitation of scripture. The complementarity is formulated now in such a way that recited scripture opens up possibilities separate from those opened up in the performance of ritual belonging to ancestral traditions. The Kalaodi use the idioms of light and dark to make this distinction. As Islamic traditions in general are associated with "light," so all that is revealed (named) in the reciting of scripture becomes strongly associated with the possibilities of a normative reading that upholds a sense of orthodoxy (the publicly accepted historical and moral order). This leaves, however, the "dark" side of knowledge containing the secrets (unrevealed names) of that which has been ancestrally "inscribed" in present-day ritual experiences of propitiating jins. The historical and moral authority associated with all that is revealed in the recitation of scripture remains. But a feeling of real contact with sources of primordial origins is not drawn out of Islamic scriptural traditions so much as it is drawn out of the practices of these local ancestral traditions.

The vector of knowledge that begins with participation in the rituals for honoring jins and points back to ancestral origins is unlike the "straight path" of Islam. Being only vaguely grounded in scriptural tradition (jins are mentioned in the Koran), having no liturgical basis, and working with a plurality of unseen ancestors and spirits, the knowledge and practices lead through a tangle of implications that can only be heterodoxic in their effect. Most importantly for the argument I am making here, it is knowledge characterized by a reluctance to utter significant names publicly rather than a compulsion to pronounce and repeat them. The continual deferral of finally and outwardly naming whatever it is that would ultimately substantiate people's lives in a primordial past motivates interests and desires along this vector of knowledge. This deferral of naming not only contrasts with knowledge drawn more exclusively out of a reading of scripture, for which names are visibly laid out from the start, but also figures into the written word's full reading.

As I have already pointed out, health and prosperity in the present is said to depend upon remembering the ancestral past. But, "remembering" (*sonyinga*) in this sense is not the same thing as "knowing" (*waro*).[19] The Kalaodi say that in fulfilling the ritual obligations they have inherited, especially those of propitiating jins, they are remembering their ancestors. This notion of remembering can also be used in a more general way to refer to the preservation of signs of an ancestral past (e.g., large trees that mark patrilineal land claims) or to mean that they continue to do things as they were done in the past (sometimes to make a contrast with others who strive to be "progressive"). Though this range of usage, "remembering" alludes primarily to a compulsion people have to conform to established patterns and not to a need they have to possess explicit communicable knowledge about the past. At least those who are actively involved in remembering the past do not need to let on that they have much explicit knowledge about it, whatever common understanding there might actually be. The knowledge of names, in particular the names of ancestors, is more deliberately separated from the generalized practice of remembering. Those who faithfully remember can freely deny that they have this knowledge. Nevertheless, there is the conviction that certain people do know about the past, and therefore are able, if not always willing, to truthfully tell about it. More importantly, they are the ones who know the "secrets," which include the uncirculated real names of originating sources (ancestors and places). Retaining this uncommon knowledge, not with everyone but with someone, is in the end also held to be of critical significance to the remembrance of the past. Whoever knows the names of the past knows the essential summational truth about it and therefore about the way things should be ordered and practiced in the present.

Pragmatically this means there is no finality in outwardly coming to grips with the past that is so essential to remember. Convictions about secrets and uncirculated names act to perpetuate a state of uncertainty about the ultimate correctness of people's devotional actions and about the validity of any established social patterns and statuses, including purported ancestral entitlements. Thus, despite there being a fairly standardized version of how descent lines are interrelated and how settlements were founded, hints are often given in private conversation that the true ordering is different. There is no limit to how far back these doubts can extend nor to how revolutionary the required corrections would be. The truth that certain descent lines have originating ties to the most important jins of the village, and of the island, can be brought into question, as can the truth that Islam originated in the Middle East. Always the implication is that the true origins are closer to home and lead back through the speaker's own ancestry, namely, through his or her own ritual remembrances. But it is the real names of ancestors and places, said to be kept as "secrets" and therefore out of circulation, that are essential to have if one is to actually *know* the truth.

Insofar as these secrets represent a faith that the deeper truth is hidden, there are again similarities with Sufi mysticism. The truth (as if it were a full image to behold) only recedes behind more veils with any attempt to finally grasp it or to make it explicit. Because it is knowledge that is not itself revealed (belonging to the category of "dark"), anything that *is* revealed necessarily leaves behind it something else of a deeper truth still not disclosed. It was inevitable that my own efforts to uncover knowledge about the past, and to put this in writing, would be met by frustration. Though there was a strong conviction that the truth was there to be found, I was forever told to go elsewhere and to speak to others if I wanted to find it. Anything that was offered was subject to doubt or devaluation; either it was a lie or it was common knowledge that did not extend very far ("high") into the past. Those who spoke too openly exposed themselves to the harsh criticism of being called liars and of being ostracized for dangerously playing with knowledge of the past. But many who denied knowing very much, and whom I believed to be sincere, were also said to be lying, though for the understandable and acceptable reason of protecting what they know.

For me it seemed to come down to an inescapable paradox: whatever is said to be true cannot ultimately be true because it is said. No one in Kalaodi ever identified a state of knowledge in this way. But then, they were not involved in deliberate and systematic efforts to compile information for the purpose of writing about a state of knowledge. The premise that writing achieves accuracy in recording what is known has difficulty overriding another premise that the speech of individuals, from which information is obtained, is inherently untrustworthy. We do not need to go so far as to assume general deceptiveness. We only need to recognize that knowledge of the world (which assumes truth, since false knowledge is no knowledge at all) cannot ultimately rest on what fallible individuals have to say about it with the use of words that, in their signifying nature, always admit the possibility of lying.[20]

To put this differently, we are concerned about the relationship the Kalaodi have to the past as the conditioning source of their present lives. How they come to know it is directly tied to how they come to meet responsibilities inherited from it. In this responsive relationship, there can be no finality in their present grasp of the past (how they purport to know it) any more than there can be finality in their dealings with jins. Like the past from which they are inherited, jins remain separate and invisible though they enter into present affairs through signs and partial manifestations. There is a perpetuation of a sense of mystery in this, but alluding to an unrevealed truth is not at the outset a mystification of anything. It follows from the simple and sound conviction that the past must always be something other than what people make of it in the present. So long as the past is valued for what it is, as a conditioning source, a present statement of objective conditions could never be accepted as final. Conversely, hidden knowledge of the past always poses the potential for overthrowing what presently serves to represent the past.

Much of this can be brought within the scope of our understanding of orality. Ong (1982) argues that because knowledge in an oral culture is participatory and empathetic, "embedded in the human lifeworld," it remains situated in a "context of struggle" (Ong 1982:44). By this I take him to mean that the close empathetic and communal identification that the knower has with the known precludes the settling of a pacified state of evident knowledge that can exist independently of the more tumultuous and less evident states of personal interests and desires that influence social exchanges. But we could argue that it is not so much a lack of separation between knower and known (which would mean that there is nothing to know that is not present in experience) as it is an inwardly directed separation for which moral responsibility and longing recovery are the compelling motives for maintaining communicative interaction. In Kalaodi, breaking relations with ancestors, jins, or more generally, the past, invites disaster. These are focal elements of what we would refer to as their oral traditions and they all direct attention from the regularities of outwardly performed practices to guarded knowledge and interminably kept secrets. For the Kalaodi, as for the Sufi mystic, the idiom of "remembrance" conveys this sense that a submission to the regularities of devotional practices keeps people in touch with that which is unifying and originating for their present conditions. The essential knowledge that lies beyond public awareness is not valued objectively, as something to be grasped outside of oneself, but empathetically, as something at the heart of one's own health and well being.

Orality is, of course, being contrasted with literacy in specifying these characteristics of knowledge. As Ong (1982) discusses it, "writing separates the knower from the known and thus sets up conditions for objectivity" (Ong 1982:46). In arriving at this, he touches on the issue that is being highlighted here—that of reciting names: "A chirographic (writing) and even more a typographic (print) culture can denature even the human, itemizing such things as the names of leaders and political divisions in an abstract, neutral list entirely devoid of a human action context" (Ong 1982:42). In considering how different forms of knowledge are valued in Kalaodi, there does seem to be something to this. But we need to be discerning in our reference to types of culture based upon the presence or absence of writing, especially if there is any suggestion that orality must be free of the written word or that objective awareness can generally be attributed to the influence of writing. In Islamic cultures, the devotional act of reciting scripture allows the printed word of the Koran to lead as readily to an empathetic oral understanding as it does (for those who understand Arabic at least) to a more objective literal one. And the Sufi mystic who accentuates the oral potentials of scripture is certainly not innocently unaware of the more objective and literal readings that are possible. In this same vein, it would be artificial to suppose that the oral culture of the Kalaodi persists at the exclusion of any regard for writing and print. This would obscure the question of how the inward directedness and inherent "struggle" of orality bears upon the written word. Again, we need to start with the middle ground of experience and interaction where the activity of reading is evaluated as an activity of speaking. In this context, the issue of how proper names are handled seems especially important.

Belonging to Peirce's category of Secondness, proper names are indexical signs. That is, a proper name is a word held to be a causally connected, substantial part of a "dynamic object" it serves to signify. We do not fall to naive realism in admitting this much, for a name does not stand for something that can be known determinately; no amount of definite descriptions can stand in the place of the dynamic object to which the name belongs. In remembering a name, we are tracing contingencies and attributing them to a particular, the true character of which we are always in the process of coming to know. Names are thus motivated signs, significant outside of conventional structures of meaning, bringing in new associations ("meanings" in a loose sense) as rapidly as contingent knowledge of the world changes. If we keep in mind that names have essentially evocative meanings rather than denotative (semantic) ones, that as markers of contingencies they can proliferate without respect to logical necessities, and that they can accumulate significant associations and persist in memory and speech with little supporting factual evidence, we cannot help but appreciate how the element of struggle Peirce attributes to Secondness is especially applicable to the use of names. I would argue that the notion of struggle in Ong's

(1982) characterization of orality overlaps with this. People are invested in the uncertain career of names—how they are invoked, remembered and forgotten—in a way they could not be invested in the systemically protected, less perturbable significance of other referring or designating expressions (e.g., kinship terms and titles). The closer face-to-face social interactions and greater empathy between knower and known that is associated with orality seems to also mean that there is a more pronounced sense of caution and responsibility in the use of names.

This at least seems to be the case in Kalaodi. As I mentioned above, ancestral traditions are such that the more significant names, of a deeper past, tend to be withheld from public circulation. Some names are deliberately guarded, as parts of secrets that would reveal the most essential truth of origins. The supposed nondisclosure of others is probably as much a matter of faith that origins are still known as it is an actual retention of names. But there is more to this, as I also indicated above, than deliberate mystification, either on the part of those who hide knowledge or those who suppose the knowledge is somewhere hidden. What is more crucially involved begins, I think, with a deeply felt sense of moral responsibility and a reluctance to betray oneself (or others) by exposing to common and always fallible public opinion names that belong to one's own origins. The hiding of names begins with feelings of insecurity more than with ulterior intentions. Thus, even names of fairly recent ancestors, that many people know anyway, would often not be uttered, or uttered with noticeable discomfort. Some would justify their refusal by claiming that it is taboo to say these names. But elders told me that it is not really a taboo. It is only that saying these names gives people a bad feeling inside (indicating the lower chest). Remembering ancestors by fulfilling obligations is one thing; naming their names is something else. The latter is fraught with uneasy suspicion and uncertainty, and outside of tightly constraining ritual contexts or private settings, it incites harsh feelings and conflicts. We can understand the value given in Kalaodi to circumspection and the avoidance of names when matters of the past, and therefore of social identities, are broached.[21]

What is striking about this is how much can in fact be known by most everyone without their knowing the most essential names. This too seems characteristic of orality. Goody (1987), for example, says of the teaching of ritual secrets in LoDagaa society that probably ". . . little is imparted on these occasions that is not already known to the neophytes, having been acquired, less formally, in the give and take of ordinary life." And when the ultimate secrets are finally given, they are ". . . almost nonsense from the semantic point of view" (Goody 1987:151). Similarly, a secret that a man of Kalaodi descent finally entrusted to me (after my having talked to him on several occasions about the history of Tidore) consisted of only a few names and cryptic phrases that added nothing to my comprehension. What he had to say prior to revealing the secret was full of meaning, not only to me, but also to some others who listened in but did not receive the secrets.

Without their affecting comprehension, unrevealed essential names have the real effect of holding purported knowledge, knowledge held at present, in suspension. It cannot be final without the names that belong to origins. Thus, hidden names, for all their lack of positive content, are potent in their effect of engendering differences (there remains something other than what is revealed) and keeping dramatic tensions high.

This is an important turning point in the contrast we make between orality and literacy. As Ong (1982) suggests in the passage quoted above, writing (and more so print) "denatures" what is human in names by providing the socially neutral medium in which they can be itemized and presented. We can elaborate on this by tying it to our understanding now of the significance of proper names. As motivated signs and markers of contingencies, words as names can never fall into any kind of necessary ordering. Whatever accepted positionings they have is attained through persuasive force. The regularity of their being presented (and therefore acknowledged) in a certain way, and the authority behind any such regular presentation, does not make this something other than persuasion and thus does not do away with the element of struggle characteristic of Secondness. The very notion that proper names are "proper," as if they have by lawful decree a deserving status, is actually an indication that rhetorical forces are at work in literate culture; we are persuaded to accept the names that are itemized (as entries of an encyclopedia, for example) as properly belonging to an indexical list. Although the evidence (printed books) is overwhelming that names listed are the ones truly worth knowing, it is nevertheless by persuasion, rather than reasoning, that we come to accept them.

But we are not implicating the written (or printed) word categorically in saying this, even if the persuasive means it makes available for securing such orders are exceedingly powerful. Here we depart from Ong's argument about a radical distinction between oral and written cultures. In giving emphasis to the always temporal and socially situated *practice* of reading, rather than to the existence of written sources, and in expanding this notion of reading to include recitation, we lose any fundamental basis for making this distinction. The oral and the written, in other words, are brought together at this level. More to the issue at hand, in Kalaodi we find in their activity of recitation the persuasive efforts of putting names (with the compendious knowledge that attaches to them) into "practiced" orders. And we can in this respect compare the reciting of scripture with the reciting of local place names and landmarks. The manner in which they bring contingent knowledge to light and affirm its public acceptance is similar. They are ways of making available frameworks of historical and geographical knowledge in which names are secured and in reference to which people can more freely communicate and join their experiences. We can further-more speak of this as a construction of a realm of orthodoxy insofar as the general acceptance of what is established and affirmed in practice pushes back the threat of hidden names; namely, the disruptive remembrance of contingent associations not secured and affirmed in the orthodox order.

If names are thereby "denatured" (and we should probably be careful not to exaggerate this), it is because, there being little to hide by them, there is less personal responsibility required in guarding them. Without implying that the affective feeling for names is altogether lost (recalling the enjoyment of reciting names), we could argue that so long as names are regularly disclosed and kept in place by externally evident means there will be less of a feeling of betrayal in uttering them. Thus, in Kalaodi there was never shame or hesitation in saying place names that belong to public discourse anyway. More importantly, I did not find that their reluctance to utter ancestors' names was matched in any way by a similar reluctance to utter the most important names that are mentioned in scripture. I was, in fact, struck by their freedom to joke on occasions about the words and names that they regularly chanted.

In contrast to the inwardly directed knowledge of orality, that points to-ward undisclosed names that lie beyond what is made evident in present experience, the enlightened knowledge of literacy works with the articula-tion of names that are publicly affirmed. But as I have argued here, these are not alternatives for different types of cultures, one replacing the other, but movements along different vectors of knowledge. Although they are oppositional, the ground of experience can be the same for both. Thus, Sufi mysticism and normative piety entail different readings, taking off in differ-ent directions, of the same scripture. And even if their oppositional relation is expressed as a complementary one (which is an ideal way of putting it), it nevertheless preserves conditions for a dialectical struggle, for each has a basis for criticizing the other. So it is in considering recitation in Kalaodi, only now it is the joining together of Islamic scriptural traditions and local ancestral ones. I have also referred to these as existing in complementarity, alluding especially to the idiom of light and dark that the Kalaodi some-times use. But there is dialectical opposition in this as well, for each side can pride itself on being in a position to undo the other. This is especially evident when we express the relation as an opposition of heterodoxy to orthodoxy.[22] Islamic reformists, who aspire toward greater orthodoxy and the elimination of any form of devotion toward jins, have had a voice in Kalaodi, but a relatively weak one, not wholeheartedly taken up by any of the permanent residents of the village. We find ourselves, then, giving greater attention to the other side of the opposition—the undoing of a literal and lawful minded reading by the imposition on the same ground of experience of the values that motivate a continued devotion to ancestors, jins, and local origins. In other words, the values, or potentials, of orality are not displaced by the written word, but are still employed in the reading of scripture.

Most simply put, it is a matter of holding the value of "darkness" over that of "light." This amounts to giving priority to what is hidden but essential (*hakekat*) in relation to what is publicly revealed and lawful (*sareat*). With reference to proper names, this means that names that are recited aloud cannot be the most essential names, for they would not be disclosed if they were. It is a variation, as I have pointed out, on the Sufi mystic's insistence that finding the truth involves coming to know, through one's devotional practices, what is hidden from public view and can thereby be valued for its closeness and authenticity. The range of relevant practices, however, is broadened to include the rituals by which people in Kalaodi remember their own ancestors and thus includes the signifying potential of names of local import that could never be revealed with certainty.

CONCLUSION

In one rather cryptic conversation about history that I had with a man from Kalaodi, mention was made of "the four imams" whose names are contained in a familiar chant. When I returned home, read books, and talked to people more knowledgeable than I was about Islamic history, I was able to learn more about these names that were being recited in Tidore. Hanafi, Hanbali, Maliki, and Shafii are the four schools of Sunni Islamic law, each named after its founder. Had I thought to, I could have asked a *jou-guru* or any of a number of educated Tidorese about these names and, I feel certain, would have received information that agreed with what I later read. Even the Kalaodi man I was talking to, who was an advanced student of the *tarekat*, probably could have told me something that fit in with this broadly held historical knowledge. But on this occasion when he brought up these names he was leading me to believe that there was something different and more essential to know about them, something that was not available to common knowledge and could not be elaborated upon with book learning. These names, that everyone devoted time to chanting aloud, were indeed significant to a shared past, but as he explained to me, they were not the real names, they were merely the publicly disclosed ones. Only with access to the uncirculated names could one know the deeper truth lying behind the devotional practice of reciting these and other names. The hushed tone of voice and furtive gestures he used in telling me this I recognized to be the same as those used by people when they talk about the ancestral past. The hidden names were ones for which personal responsibility must be taken. He never told me what the real names were, and I am not even sure that he was confident that he knew them, but the implications were that the four Moluccan states and the four imam became joined in these hidden names and that by knowing them one would know that origins of a global order are bound to local origins.

Here, then, were two opposed readings of the same bit of text—one objective and literal minded, the other empathetically attuned and mystical minded; one orthodox, the other heterodox; one publicly confirmable, the other frought with personal uncertainty. What I hope to have shown in the above discussion is that proper names, which are the linguistic entities upon which these different readings turn, invite the reordering of a heterodox reading as much as they demand the affirmations of an orthodox one. There is no way of refuting the *possibility* that the names recalled leave others of greater significance behind, or that the knowledge associated with any remembered names is incomplete or wrong. As logicians and analytic philosophers are aware, proper names are always opaque linguistic elements better done away with if assured clarity and precision are sought. But then, knowledge without names is inconceivable; and people do put considerable stock into the names they remember. In admitting this we are admitting that the claims we might make of knowing about (comprehending) things by way of generalizing principles can never be divorced from the persuasive efforts, at a social interactional level, of acknowledging (apprehending) what particulars there are worth knowing and remembering.

We do not want to conclude, then, that the Kalaodi *believe* the world to be a certain way and that their view simply differs from an orthodox one. This would be to lose sight of the fact that they live with the orthodox view, most of the time giving support to it and always eyeing with some suspicion those who would offer their alternative visions. The heterodoxy of their local traditions is in responsive interaction with the orthodoxy of Islam, not as a replacement of one revelation for another, but as a questioning of the truth that is made evident in any public revelation. As the past is removed from the present, so the truth that belongs to origins cannot be mistaken for anything that is made altogether present in public experience. Heterodoxy persists with orthodoxy as the opening of different possibilities. Taking off, not from a point of logical reasoning, but from a point of persuasion— namely, the persuasion involved in receiving and offering names—the heterodoxic responses in Kalaodi to normative piety's orthodoxy seem to be driven by a sense of irony. Thus, it is with detectable pride and a knowing air that people in Kalaodi profess their ignorance of history. We might say that it is the force of irony, always putting into question the presented order of things, that makes their reading of the written word an essentially oral one. But, more broadly than this, we would want to say that, so long as we attend to reading as a social practice and therefore regard it within the context of real interaction and struggle, there can be no claim that the rhetorical potentials most apparent to us in oral discourse are ever really displaced by the written word to begin with.

NOTES

This essay is based on research conducted in Indonesia between October 1983 and July 1985. I would like to express again my deep gratitude for the hospitality of people in Tidore. The research was funded by a Fulbright Hays fellowship, a National Institute of Mental Health fellowship, and a grant from the National Science Foundation. The essay was written during the tenure of a National Institute of Mental Health fellowship at the University of North Carolina at Chapel Hill. I would like to thank John Bowen and participants of the "Ethnography of Reading" panal at the AAA meetings for their helpful responses to the paper that led to this essay. For their insightful comments on later drafts, I would like to thank James Peacock, Jonathan Boyarin, and Bruce Lawrence.

1. Jafar al-Sadiq is the name of the sixth Shiite Imam. He was a prominant mystic and founder of the dominant Shiite school of law. From a genealogy diagramed by one of the Tidorese court officials, I know that Jafar Sadik, the man identified as the founder of the Moluccan sultanates, is this same person. However, I never heard stories in Tidore that connected these histories together. Although I will not be elaborating on this particular case, it will be clear that the issue of Jafar Sadik's identity is relevant to the discussion of proper names that is taken up in this essay.

2. "*Kie*," which is used possessively here to mean "of the island," distinguishes this the paramount *sowohi* from lesser ones of other descent lines. As the use of the present tense indicates, the position of *Sowohi Kie* (unlike that of Sultan) has continued to be filled.

3. Hodgson (1974) makes this point when he speaks of the self-image of Muslims as the exclusive defenders of the faith of Abraham: "The same exclusivity was expressed in the overwhelmingly central role played by the *Quran* in Muslim piety— by that *Quran* which was in some measure, at least, on everyone's lips, and which no educated or specially trained elite could monopolize" (Hodgson 1974:366).

4. There is little gender discrimination made in this early and most basic religious education.

5. "We have left out nothing in Our Book. They shall all be gathered before their Lord" (Koran 6:38).

6. "In a number of linguistic situations, the behavior of proper names is so unlike that of other linguistic categories that it involuntarily suggests the idea that we have before us *some other, differently constructed language incorporated into the midst of natural language*" (Lotman and Uspenskij 1977:236, emphasis mine).

7. Quine (1953), finding names to be inadequate referring expressions, claims that "whatever we say with the help of names can be said in a language which shuns names altogether" (Quine 1953:13).

8. Note how Rudolf Carnap, taking an extreme logical positivistic position, contrasts proper names and positional designations: "The method of designation by proper names is the primitive one; that of positional designation corresponds to a more advanced stage of science, and has considerable methodological advantages over the former" (quoted in Russell 1948:74).

The point I have tried to make is that designations do not replace proper names and that, in the end, there is no guarantee that the significance of that which continues to be called by name will not (charismatically) alter or escape any designated positions. A genealogy, for example, might be thought of as a designative grid keeping ancestors' names in place. But, as is well known from anthropological literature, the memory of particular ancestors who have "big" names can be strong enough to alter the designations. Beyond a few generations we would have to suspect that the memory of the "names" takes control.

9. See especially Lotman and Uspenskij (1977) and Cassirer (1946).

10. This also means that a word as a name and a word as a lexical item are not two different categories of expressions so much as two different ways any expression can be valued. A word, of course, is being valued as a name when we look for its etymology. Conversely, a word more often used as a proper name can also be valued as a lexical item. In an odd way, "John Smith" is used as a common noun, like "plumber," in the sentence, "I know a John Smith in New York." It is odd because it can only be defined tautologically as, "a person with the name John Smith" (see Jakobson 1971).

11. "There is the 'mystery' of courtship when 'different kinds of beings' communicate with each other" (Burke 1950:208).

12. This is at odds with what Lévi-Strauss says about proper names in *The Savage Mind*. In arguing that proper names do in fact have meaning, and are to be understood as structural elements in synchronic systems of differences, he explicitly (if offhandedly) rejects Peirce's notion that a proper name is an index. Without going into a counterargument, I will only say here that we can agree with Lévi-Strauss that proper names "form the fringe of a general system of classification" (Lévi-Strauss 1966:215), and represent a threshold of meaning, without agreeing that the use of names is to be accounted for by the intellectual operations that make use of logical classifications. We cannot lose sight of the persuasive forces at work in securing names in systems of classification and the threat that names pose in escaping or overthrowing these systems. To say that names represent the *possibility* of classification is not to say that there really is any finally accepted classification in place.

13. See Basso (1984) for a discussion of place names among Western Apache. When the author asked why they pronounced names of places, usually repeatedly, they would respond with: "'Because we like to,' or 'Because those names are good to say.'" (Basso 1984:27)

14. Whereas Peirce speaks of Secondness (encompassing notions of experience and indexicality) as immediacy, he speaks of both Firstness and Thirdness as possibility and potentiality (see Peirce 1940). We can stress here also that the triad is irreducible and relational; the separate attention we might give to prereflective experience and indices in our own analyses does not mean that there are things that actually belong to a separable realm or that a quality of immediacy could be absolutely attributed to anything.

15. The distinction Hodgson (1974) makes in this way is between *kerygmatic* and *mystical* components of personal piety. For the former, "ultimacy is sought in irrevocable datable events, in history with its positive moral commitments." For the latter "ultimacy is sought in subjective inward awareness" (Hodgson 1974:363–364).

16. For example, when a ceremonial performance is done in public, for anyone to see, it is said that the performer "goes out into the *sareat*" (*fugo to ma sareat*).

17. Much has been written of Sufism's corruptibility. One *jou-guru* in Tidore told me how this kind of instrumentality was a corruption of what Sufism should be and that most of the *jou-guru* today in Tidore are not really acting as gurus (teachers) at all.

18. It is interesting that these complementary orientations within Islam are sometimes expressed with the same idiom of "light" and "dark" that people in Tidore use to distinguish Islamic and local traditions. The unveiled source of all light that the mystic seeks is referred to as being invisible, or "black" (see Schimmel 1975:280–281). In both cases, that which is found inwardly ends up being characterized as "dark" and thus contrasted with all that is enlightened and outwardly known. This would add to the argument that Sufi traditions and local ancestral traditions are in some sense analogous in their oppositional relation to normative social practices.

19. The distinction conforms closely to one Ryle (1949) makes between "knowing how" and "knowing that" and which could also be put as a distinction between "remembering how" and "remembering that." Knowing (remembering) how to ride a bike is not the same kind of thing as knowing (remembering) that Trenton is the capital of New Jersey. In the Tidorese usage that I am discussing, remembering corresponds to the notion of remembering or knowing how to do something; knowing corresponds to the notion of knowing or remembering that something is *in fact* the case.

20. "Every time there is a lie there is signification. Every time there is signification there is the possibility of using it in order to lie" (Eco 1976:59).

21. The situation is similar to what Michelle Rosaldo (1980) notes about Ilongot oral traditions: "Knowledgeable speech is, of necessity, indirect," always showing a respect "that avoids calling things by name." Especially avoided, she goes on to say, is the affront of saying the "true or 'big' names" (Rosaldo 1980: 197–198).

22. What Bourdieu (1977) says about orthodoxy and heterodoxy applies to the argument I am making: "Orthodoxy, straight, or rather *straightened*, opinion . . . exists only in the objective relationship which opposes it to heterodoxy, that is, by reference to the choice—*hairesis*, heresy—made possible by the existence of *competing possibles* and to the explicit critique of the sum total of the alternatives not chosen that the established order implies" (Bourdieu 1977:169). His notion of doxa corresponds to what I am referring to as a prereflective ground of experience.

REFERENCES

Baker, James N.
    1988   *Descent and Community in Tidore*. Ann Arbor: University of Michigan. Microfilm.
Basso, Keith H.
    1984   "Stalking with Stories: Names, Places, and Moral Narratives Among the Western Apache." In *Text, Play and Story: The Construction and Reconstruction of Self and Society*. Ed. Edward Bruner, pp. 19–55. Washington, D.C.: American Ethnological Society.

Benveniste, Emile
1971   "The Nature of the Linguistic Sign." In *Problems in General Linguistics*, pp. 43–48. Coral Gables: University of Miami Press.
Bourdieu, Pierre
1977   *Outline of a Theory of Practice*. Trans. Richard Nice. Cambridge: Cambridge University Press.
Burke, Kenneth
1950   *A Rhetoric of Motives*. Berkeley: University of California Press.
Cassirer, Ernst
1946   *Language and Myth*. Trans. Susanne Langer. New York: Dover.
Chittick, William C.
1989   *The Sufi Path of Knowledge: Ibn al-'Arabi's Metaphysics of Imagination*. Albany: State University of New York Press.
Eco, Umberto
1976   *A Theory of Semiotics*. Bloomington: Indiana University Press.
Freud, Sigmund
1914   "Remembering, Repeating and Working Through." In *Standard Edition of the Complete Psychological Works*. Vol. 12. Ed. James Strachey, pp. 147–156. London: Hogarth.
Goody, Jack
1987   *The Interface Between the Written and the Oral*. Cambridge: Cambridge University Press.
Graham, William A.
1985   "Qur'an as Spoken Word: An Islamic Contribution to the Understanding of Scripture." In *Approaches to Islam in Religious Studies*. Ed. Richard C. Martin, pp. 23–40. Tucson: University of Arizona Press.
Hodgson, Marshall
1974   *The Venture of Islam*. Vol. 1. Chicago: University of Chicago Press.
Jakobson, Roman
1971   "Shifters, Verbal Categories, and the Russian Verb." In *Selected Writings*. Vol 2, pp. 130–136. The Hague: Mouton.
Kripke, Saul A.
1980   *Naming and Necessity*. Cambridge, Mass.: Harvard University Press.
Levy-Bruhl, Lucien
1926   *How Natives Think*. Trans. Lilian Clare. Princeton, N.J.: Princeton University Press.
Lévi-Strauss, Claude
1966   *The Savage Mind*. Chicago: University of Chicago Press.
Lotman, Ju. M., and B. A. Uspenskij
1977   "Myth-Name-Culture." In *Soviet Semiotics: An Anthology*. Ed. Daniel P. Lucid, pp. 233–252. Baltimore: Johns Hopkins University Press.
Olson, David R.
1877   *From Utterance to Text: The Bias of Language in Speech and Writing*. Harvard Educational Review 47(3):257–281.
Ong, Walter J.
1967   *The Presence of the Word*. New Haven: Yale University Press.

1982   *Orality and Literacy: The Technologizing of the Word.* London and New York: Methuen.

Peirce, Charles S.
1940   "The Principles of Phenomenology." In *Philosophical Writings of Peirce.* Ed. Justus Buchler, pp. 74–97. New York: Dover.
1958   "Letters to Lady Welby (1903–1911)." In *Charles S. Peirce: Selected Writings.* Ed. Philip Wiener, pp. 380–432. New York: Dover.

Quine, Willard Van Orman
1953   "On What There Is." In *From a Logical Point of View*, pp. 1–19. Cambridge, Mass.: Harvard University Press.
1960   *Word and Object.* Cambridge: M.I.T. Press.

Rorty, Richard
1982   "Is There a Problem about Fictional Discourse?" In *Consequences of Pragmatism*, pp. 110–138. Minneapolis: University of Minnesota Press.

Rosaldo, Michelle
1980   *Knowledge and Passion: Ilongot Notions of Self and Social Life.* Cambridge: Cambridge University Press.

Russell, Bertrand
1948   *Human Knowledge: Its Scope and Limits.* New York: Simon and Schuster.
1956   "The Philosophy of Logical Atomism." In *Logic and Knowledge.* Ed. R. C. Marsh, pp. 177–281. London: G. Allen & Unwin.

Ryle, Gilbert
1949   *The Concept of Mind.* Chicago: University of Chicago Press.

Saussure, Ferdinand de
1959   *Course in General Linguistics.* New York: McGraw-Hill.

Schimmel, Annemarie
1975   *Mystical Dimensions of Islam.* Chapel Hill: University of North Carolina Press.

Schwartz, Stephen P., ed.
1977   *Naming, Necessity, and Natural Kinds.* Ithaca, N.Y.: Cornell University Press.

Todorov, Tzvetan
1982   *Theories of the Symbol.* Trans. C. Porter. Ithaca, N.Y.: Cornell University Press.

Watt, W. Montgomery
1970   *Bell's Introduction to the Qur'an.* Edinburgh: Edinburgh University Press.

Woodward, Mark R.
1989   *Islam in Java: Normative Piety and Mysticism in the Sultanate of Yogyakarta.* Tucson: University of Arizona Press.

SEVEN

Literacy, Orality, and Ritual Practice in Highland Colombia

Diana Digges and Joanne Rappaport

INTRODUCTION

In the native highland community of Cumbal, Colombia, leaders of the ethnic-rights movement use oral and written evidence in their construction of a communal history that is incorporated into their political demands and rhetoric. The nature of the themes that they draw upon from the documentary record is determined in great part by their historical relationship with the Colombian state, especially as that relationship is filtered through Indian legislation. Their historical interpretations are presented to the public in narrative form. Nevertheless, their selection of specific pieces of evidence from the written record is governed by nontextual criteria, in particular, by ritual and practical activities in the present. This paper will explore the relationship between the oral and the written worlds in Cumbal as they are mediated by nontextual forms of understanding and changing reality.

THEORETICAL FRAMEWORK

The ethnography of reading cannot be examined independently of the ethnography of writing and of ritual practice. In the case of Cumbal, as in many "paraliterate" societies (Street 1984), many of the "readers" of historical documents and of legislation are themselves illiterate; they are therefore forced to depend upon readings by other individuals, frequently disseminated in the form of contemporary legal documents. In addition, the texts they choose to examine are often no more than a prompt for oral elaboration, and the meaning of these texts only emerges in the course of such performative acts as ritual. Thus, the meaning that the Cumbales "retrieve or construct" from legislation and historical papers is mediated not only by the written word, but also by what Paul Connerton (1989:4) calls "incorporating practices": the storage and transmission of cultural information using the body in ritual performance. The written word, argues Connerton, has been overly emphasized by literate scholars at the exclusion of understanding "practices of a non-inscribed kind (1989:4)."[1] Such practices, as we shall see, have been central to the Cumbales' experience; they are part of the previously acquired knowledge brought to bear on reading and writing the texts in question.

THE COMMUNITY OF CUMBAL

Cumbal lies along the Colombia-Ecuador border. Composed of four communities, Cumbal, Chiles, Mayasquer, and Panán, the sixteen thousand indigenous agriculturalists who live there till the high mountain slopes, raising dairy cattle and potatoes for the regional market, and other Andean tubers, maize, and wheat for their own subsistence. The four communities are *resguardos*, communally owned territories administered by semiautonomous political authorities (*cabildos*).[2] Under Colombian Indian legislation, resguardo lands are legitimized by eighteenth-century titles granted by the King of Spain (Colombia 1983); notwithstanding this appeal to colonial authority, many of the lands encompassed by such documents have fallen into the hands of local non-Indian landlords, so that Indians generally inhabit the mountain slopes, surrounded by *mestizo*-owned cattle ranches located in the valley bottoms; many resguardo members are forced to seek their livelihoods as day workers on haciendas or as domestic employees in nearby cities.

While the land base controlled by the cabildo has diminished considerably since the colonial period, the native population has grown, forcing land-poor communities to pursue a variety of legal and extralegal methods for reclaiming their lands. Repeated failures to regain territory through the courts led cabildos of the early 1970s to embark upon a militant program of land claims that has included the peaceful occupation of those ranches that lie within resguardo boundaries, as well as the revitalization of native culture and historical consciousness (Rappaport 1988a; 1992). This newfound militancy has caused the Cumbales to reread their colonial resguardo titles of which they acquired certified copies in the 1940s. Our story opens shortly after these documents were discovered at mid-century.

CONFLICTING DISCOURSES

The following letter was written in 1950 by the cabildo of Cumbal in defense of its sulphur deposits on Mount Cumbal, which were in danger of being leased by the Colombian Ministry of Mines and Petroleum:

REFERENCIA: Parcialidad de Cumbal por sus yacimientos de azufre cuya explotación-extracción y beneficio del mineral data desde la REAL AUDIEN-CIA DE SAN FRANCISCO DE QUITO 9 de junio: 1758 52 años antes del grito de INDEPENDENCIA del 20 de JULIO: 1810.

————Los derechos adquiridos con observancia de las leyes del rey de ESPA-ÑA fueron declarados por la PRIMERA CONSTITUCION de la REPUB-LICA que serían reconocidos, protegidos y de ninguna manera vulnerados por las nuevas AUTORIDADES.

————Y por una y otra vez el Capitán de Infantería Española, y Alcalde de JUSTICIA MAYOR DE LOS PASTOS, Don MAURICIO Muñoz de Ayala en comisión de la REAL AUDIENCIA DE SAN FRANCISCO DE QUITO refrendó la posesión, la hizo buena, y otro tanto hizo bueno el dominio a los cuatro caciques *TAPIES* del globo de tierras en cuyo centro vino a destacarse como una pirámide el volcán de nombre EL CUMBAL. DURANTE ocho días el Capitán de Infantería tuvo que identificar uno por uno de los linderos naturales con los que quedó circunscrito el globo de las tierras concedidas a las indiadas en la cabeza de sus caciques. HECHO lo cual pacientemente de la linderación a que fueron llamados los demás pueblos, el Capitán de Infan-tería Española se puso de rodilla en la pampa, y luego ciñándose la corona de oro de su rey, su señor natural, en alta voz hizo entrega de la tierra en su tenencia, en su posesión, en su mismo dominio a los caciques, representantes genuinos de sus pueblos de CUMBAL. Y a la vez quedaba el descrito globo de tierras limpio de negros, de españoles y de todo advenedizo. ENTONCES como hoy sigue lo accesorio a lo principal· era la tierra de importancia máx-ima, sin igual, ya que élla le daba a la indiada de comer aunque con su traba-jo, y a sus ganados los pastos de cada día les proporcionaba espontáneamente y en abundancia.

————ASI es como se adquirió la tenencia, posesión y propiedad, frente a todas las gentes con ayuda del Rey, su REAL AUDIENCIA DE SAN FRAN-CISCO de QUITO sus Capitanes de Infantería y sus Alcaldes Mayores de Justicia.

. . .

————EN la Notaría Nro. lo de Pasto, a 9 de junio de 1908 han sido protoco-lizados los títulos de que hacemos mérito, y valen para nosotros como la tabla de SALVACION. SOMOS de la raza que necesita a gritos un nuevo redem-tor, a la grandeza de SIMON BOLIVAR.[3]

REFERENCE: Community of Cumbal regarding its sulphur deposits whose exploitation-extraction and mining of the mineral date from the ROYAL COURT OF SAN FRANCISCO DE QUITO—9th June, 1758—52 years before the call for INDEPENDENCE of July 20: 1810.

————The rights acquired through the observance of the laws of the king of SPAIN were declared by the FIRST CONSTITUTION of the REPUBLIC, to be recognized, protected, and by no means violated by the new AUTHOR-ITIES.

————And one and another time, the Spanish Infantry Captain and Magis-trate of HIGH JUSTICE OF THE PASTS, don MAURICIO muñoz de

Ayala—by commission of the ROYAL COURT OF SAN FRANCISCO DE QUITO—legalized the possession, he made it good, and he also made good the dominion of the four hereditary chiefs—TAPIES—over the expanse of land in whose center the volcano named CUMBAL stood out like a pyramid. For a week the Infantry Captain had to identify, one by one, the natural boundaries within which the expanse of land granted to the Indian masses, with their chiefs at their head, was encompassed by boundary-markers. ACCOMPLISHED the patient tracing of boundaries, to which chiefs from other towns were invited, the Spanish Infantry Captain knelt on the plain, and then, assuming the gold crown of his king, his natural lord, handed over in a loud voice, the land in its tenancy, its possession, and its very dominion, to the chiefs, the genuine representatives of the peoples of CUMBAL. And at the same time, the expanse of land was cleansed of Blacks, of Spaniards, and of all interlopers.[4] THEN as now, came the accessory to the principal: the land was of maximal importance, without equal, given that from it the Indian masses were given their sustenance, albeit with their own work, and the daily pastures provided for their cattle were spontaneously theirs and in abundance.

————THIS is how tenancy, possession, and ownership was acquired, in front of all the people, in the presence of the King, his ROYAL COURT OF SAN FRANCISCO DE QUITO, his Infantry Captains and his Magistrates of High Justice.

. . .

————In the office of the First Notary of Pasto, on June 9, 1908, the titles we use to distinguish ourselves were registered, and they are worth as much to us as a LIFESAVER. WE are the race that dearly requires a new redeemer, of the stature of SIMON BOLIVAR.

The government's attorney responded with the following note:

> Aviso a ustedes recibo de su memorial del 2 de junio en curso, para el señor Ministro de Minas y Petróleos.
>
> En atención a que se trata de una comunidad de Indígenas que, acaso no conozcan las leyes y decretos sobre concesiones mineras, debo decirles que si ustedes estiman que con la concesión solicitada se menoscaban legítimos derechos de la parcialidad de Indígenas de cuyo Cabildo son ustedes miembros, deben presentar ante el Gobernador del Departamento su memorial de oposición a la celebración del referido contrato, junto con los documentos que comprueben sus derechos. El Gobernador remitirá la documentación a este Ministerio y aquí se estudiará esa oposición y, si se encontrare formalmente presentada, se ordenará pasar para su decisión al Tribunal Superior de Pasto.
>
> Mientras no se formule la oposición legalmente, nada puede hacer este Despacho en relación con su memorial referido.
>
> Soy de usted atento y seguro servidor.[5]

Please be advised I am in receipt of your petition of June 2 of this year addressed to the Minister of Mines and Petroleum.

In view of the fact that this is a matter concerning a community of indige-nous people who, perhaps, are not familiar with the laws and decrees con-cerning mining concessions, I am obliged to inform you that if you consider the requested concession to be an infringement of legitimate rights of the in-digenous community of whose Council you are yourselves members, you must present your written objections to the Governor of the Department at the time the proposed contract is considered—along with the documents that verify your rights. The Governor will forward the documentation to this Ministry, which will take the matter into consideration and, if the objection is formally presented, it will be sent to the Superior Court of Pasto for a ruling.

Inasmuch as the objection is not formulated legally, this Office can do nothing regarding the above-referenced petition.

I am at your service.

THE ISSUES AT HAND

Here we have a written exchange involving two completely different types of discourse. The issue is simple: indigenous control of mineral resources on Indian lands. The authors of the petition could simply have made reference to specific legal precedents granting Indians control over the territory. Instead, they do something quite different.

The first letter begins, as shrewd minority discourses often do, with an implicit acknowledgment of the majority form of the codification of power: in this case, the law. The first paragraph refers to colonial legislation grant-ing Cumbal the right to exploit its mineral beds; the second paragraph refers to the continuation (and protection) of that right under Republican law, a theme returned to in the last paragraph, with the reference to Simón Bolívar, father of Colombian independence.[6] Although the Cumbales were later to make strategic and successful use of law in their campaign to re-claim their lands, here the two paragraphs are really only a passing nod at legal codes as the dominant discourse of Colombian society. It is the third paragraph that erupts into something quite different: an apparently irrelevant but detailed description of a ceremony granting the community possession to its lands, one that is vaguely anchored in time, witnessed by local and neighboring chiefs, and repeated at unknown intervals. Why is such information included and what can it tell us about indigenous repre-sentations of meaning in Cumbal?

First, let us turn to the sources that the reservation council used to con-struct its petition. In order to be recognized as an indigenous community, the Cumbales were required to register copies of their colonial land titles in state notary offices. Copies of these colonial titles are retained in the council archives and although they are rarely consulted, they have been read by some community historians.[7] However, these eighteenth-century titles are frequently confused, by nonhistorians who have not read them, with an entirely different text, Law 89 of 1890, the centerpiece of Colombian Indian legislation (Colombia 1983:58). Law 89 is frequently glossed as "history" by people in Cumbal and thus conflated with the resguardo title; in neighboring Mayasquer, history books kept in the reservation archive are also called "titles" or "Law 89." Thus, several written sources, separated by a century or by a century and a half, are collapsed into one for present-day purposes.

In addition, colonial titles have symbolic importance much like reclaimed lands and other symbols of political power, such as the staffs of office carried by council members. These symbols are all commonly referred to by the Cumbales as the "Royal Crown," constituting a core of key images that lie at the heart of Cumbal Indian identity and whose colonial origins lie very much on the surface of Cumbal ethnic consciousness (Rappaport 1988a). This constellation of symbols is articulated almost weekly in the possession ceremony by which the cabildo grants usufruct rights to communal lands to resguardo members. The modern possession ceremony faithfully reproduces similar Spanish rituals that are described in detail in colonial land titles. Thus, it is no accident that the 1950 letter to the Minister of Mines focuses on the possession ceremony by which Mauricio Muñoz de Ayala granted the eighteenth-century hereditary chiefs of Cumbal rights to their lands. The possession ceremony operates as a conceptual filter through which colonial titles are remembered and reinterpreted. Although the colonial chiefs won their right to the lands only after a protracted struggle documented in the title, their claims were only validated through the possession ceremony that is still relived, week after week, by resguardo members.

Here we have a complex weave of orality, literacy, and ritual practice that runs counter to the evolutionary approaches to the development of literacy that have been popular in the anthropological and philosophical literature (Goody 1977; Ong 1982).[8] On the one hand, the contemporary Cumbales are obliged by Colombian law to define their identity as native people by virtue of written documents. But on the other hand, they read their titles in culturally specific ways dictated by contemporary political practice, extracting from the documents only those features of colonial ritual that *they* recognize as bestowing legitimacy upon modern reservation members: walking the boundaries, kneeling on the land, calling together eyewitnesses, declaring possession.[9] Those who do not have access to the titles, or who have not consulted them in a long time, remember and recount their contents in oral form, focusing in particular upon the possession ceremony of Mauricio Muñóz de Ayala.[10] It becomes difficult, indeed, to determine which element, literacy, orality or action, is anterior to the other two.

LAYERINGS OF LITERACY AND OF LAW

If we travel back in time to the colonial period, we discover yet further layerings of literacy, orality, and practice. Although the Spanish colonial administration was fueled by a fetishization of the written word, its laws and statutes were validated, enacted, and experienced by most people through ritual practice (Phelan 1967; Vidal 1985).[11] And although these rituals are encoded in written form in legal titles and other documents, their description is more properly a product of oral, than of written communication: they do not demonstrate the economy of expression that characterizes literacy, but duplicate in written form, repetitively, the words spoken at these ceremonies.[12] This orality was expressed in written form by colonial scribes whose task was to revalidate for posterity those claims already sanctioned through ritual practice. It is taken up, repeatedly, by twentieth-century readers who perceive such repetition as inherently meaningful, even when it was not initially meant to be understood this way: "And one and another time, the Spanish Infantry Captain . . . legalized the possession, he made it good. . . ."

Colonial documentation is intertextual in its very construction. The legal papers with which we are concerned are amalgams of a number of documents hailing from a variety of time periods:

> The notion of "title" in the colonial Spanish world went beyond the concept of a simple deed. Full title—whether to land, territory, or jurisdiction—involved not only an original grant or sale, but also an investigation on the spot to consult third parties and see if the situation was as described, and finally formal acts of giving and taking possession. Only then did the grant or sale, until that point merely virtual or hypothetical, enter into force. A Spanish notary would keep a running record of the whole proceeding, repeatedly signed by officials and witnesses; this record, appended to the original grant, order, or the like, constituted the title. (Lockhart 1982: 371)

Cumbal's titles contain a variety of records spanning some forty-six years, from 1712 to 1758, including multiple testimonies of local chiefs and with non-Indians residing in the area; written records of ceremonies granting land rights to any of a number of parties to the dispute; documentation of the numerous requests for testimony, judicial consideration or investigation that kept the lawsuit going for more than four decades; copies—and occasional originals—of earlier documents, especially royal decrees, granting Indians territorial autonomy in the seventeenth century. Thus, the titles exhibit a considerable layering of documentation, a unique sort of intertextuality which it is not at all clear that colonial, nineteenth-century, or even modern Indians could comprehend. A correct reading of these briefs presupposes a competence that includes an understanding of the arrangement of varied forms of documentation within a single record[13]; that the titles were produced by multiple authors over several centuries is frequently obscured by the fact that they were commonly copied into the record by a small number of scribes, and hence are written by only one or two distinguishable hands.[14]

The documents themselves prove confusing to their twentieth-century indigenous readers, generally men with extensive political experience and a deep knowledge of community oral tradition, but with only two to four years of formal schooling. Let us take, for example, Panán historian Don Nazario Cuásquer's understanding of his community's title:

> Y entonces hicieron un quejatorio. Se vinieron las parcialidades que eran de Muellamués, de Cumbal, de Carlosama, Guachucal, Panán, Mayasquer, Chiles y se echaron el quejatorio a la Audiencia Real de Quito. Y la Audiencia Real de Quito entonces les dijo el informe. Principalmente fue el quejatorio a las Antillas, a Turman, a Conde, y entonces al Rey Corona. Ordenó, dice, que pase una comisión de la Audiencia Real de Quito, hacerle respetar esas tierras.
>
> And then they lodged a complaint. The communities of Muellamués, Cumbal, Carlosama, Guachucal, Panán, Mayasquer, Chiles, came, and they made the complaint to the Royal Court of Quito. The Royal Court of Quito then sent their brief, principally the complaint, to the Antilles, to Turman, to Count, and in turn, to everyone, and in the end, to the Spanish King Crown. Then the King Crown ordered, it says, that a commission from the Royal Court of Quito go there to force them to respect these lands.

Don Nazario's reading is essentially a mis-reading of the multiple titles of the Spanish King that open all royal decrees, in which he lists the King's titles as though they were distinct individuals to whom the complaint was sent. This is apparent when we compare his account to the following excerpt from one of the decrees included in the title to Cumbal:

> Don Felipe por la gracia de Dios, Rey de Castilla, de Leon, de Aragon, de las dos Sicilias, de Jerusalem, de Navarra, de Granada, de Toledo, de Valencia, de Galicia, de Mallorca, de Sevilla, de Sardiña, de Cordoba, de Murcia, de Jaen, de los Algares y Algeria, de Gibraltar, de las de Canarias, de las Indias Orientales y Occidentales y las de Tierra Firme del Mar Oceano, Archiduque de la Siria, Duque de Borgoña, Conde de Napoles, de Flandes, Tirol, de Barcelona, Señor de Viscaya y de Molina, etc., etc.[15]
>
> Don Felipe, by the grace of God, King of Castile, of Leon, of Aragon, of the two Sicilies, of Jerusalem, of Navarro, of Granada, of Toledo, of Valencia, of Galicia, of Mallorca, of Seville, of Sardinia, of Cordoba, of Murcia, of Jaen, of the Algares and Algeria, of Gibraltar, of the Canary Islands, of the East and West Indies and of the Main Land of the Ocean, Archduke of Syria, Duke of Burgundy, Count of Naples, of Flanders, of Tirol, of Barcelona, Lord of Viscaya and of Molina, etc., etc.

Similar errors are inherent in the letter to the Minister of Mines, demonstrating that the nature of the titles was not all that transparent to the 1950 letter writers. For example, we note a jumbled chronology in the last paragraph of the letter:

———In the office of the First Notary of Pasto, on June 9, 1908, the titles we use to distinguish ourselves were registered, and they are worth as much to us as a LIFESAVER. WE are the race that dearly requires a new redeemer, of the stature of SIMON BOLIVAR.

Here, the Indians date their title to the 1908 registry of the colonial copy, instead of pointing to its eighteenth-century origin which is, ultimately, what validates the document. In another instance, they create their own layering by jumping from the colonial period to the early nineteenth century, presumably seeking validation of their claim by associating the title with Simón Bolívar:

REFERENCE: Community of Cumbal regarding its sulphur deposits whose exploitation-extraction and mining of the mineral date from the ROYAL COURT OF SAN FRANCISCO DE QUITO—9th June, 1785—52 years before the call for INDEPENDENCE of July 20: 1810.

Finally, their insistence that Don Mauricio Muñóz de Ayala granted possession "one and another time," is a clear indication of the fact that instead of perceiving the title as an amalgam of documents produced at different times by different individuals, many of which include descriptions of the same possession ceremony, they read it as a collection of repeated identical images that, moreover, are significant only so far as they legitimize current practices.

This leads us to consider a second type of layering inherent in the reading of these documents. Although the titles contain multiple references to ceremonies outwardly similar to those performed today, the rituals have undergone slight alterations in content over time, given that they have been played out in widely divergent social contexts. Twentieth-century Indians reinterpret modern typescript transcriptions of the titles through the filter of these rituals and transmit this knowledge in oral form to other community members. The memory of the existence of the colonial document has thus principally been maintained through oral means, as well as through reference to symbols, such as the "Royal Crown," that coalesce such disparate items as lands, markers of political authority, and even written documents around a common metaphor (Rappaport 1988a). In the end, we are confronted with a written interpretation, most probably prepared by individuals who never read the document in question.

Let us note an example of this, using, once again, Don Nazario Cuásquer's reading of the Panán title:

Entonces a donde el Capitán les cogió las manos a ellos, y los sometió a la posesión, a los cuatro caciques, al llegar, a Sebastián Tarapuéz, Hilario Nazate, Gabriel Nazate, Bernardo Tarapuéz, y los sometió a esa posesión en nombre de la República de Colombia, por la autoridad de la ley, rueden. Entonces rodaron, después pajearon pajas, terrones, en verdadera posesión. Terminó ese auto y les advirtió a los que estaban oyendo de los otros, les dijo que cuidado vayan a engañar a los indígenas en contra, que el que se someta a eso, con una multa de cien patacones.

Then the Captain took their hands and gave them possession, the four hereditary chiefs who arrived, Sebastián Tarapuéz, Hilario Nazate, Gabriel Nazate, Bernardo Tarapuéz. And they were given possession in the name of the Republic of Colombia, under authority of the law, they should roll. So they rolled. Then they threw grass, sod, [symbolizing] true possession. The decree ended and those others there listening were told to take care not to fool the Indians, that whoever did would be fined a hundred *patacones*.

Don Nazario's references to the Republic of Colombia are, clearly, a product of the post-Independence period, despite the fact that he concerns himself with colonial-era chiefs. The colonial chiefs, although they understood Spanish, were also competent in the Pasto language, which was lost some time in the early nineteenth century. Thus, their linguistic understanding of the ceremony and the way in which they shared their impressions with their subjects contrasts with that of post-Independence cabildos. Second, in the colonial example, we are dealing with hereditary chiefs, recognized as such by the Spanish administration and permitted certain trappings of nobility, such as the title "Don." Nowadays, cabildos are elected for a year's term, and individuals hold no permanent claim to political authority. Finally, during the nineteenth-century consolidation of the Colombian republic, cabildos lost much of their authority, transformed from semiautonomous political leaders to intermediaries between state and citizen (Rappaport 1990). Within this context, the text of the possession ceremony, while similar, bears a highly different meaning.

Finally, we must consider a third layering that characterizes any contemporary reading of these documents. The cabildo's understanding of the contents of the titles is conditioned by the development of the Colombian legal system. The competence necessary to read or produce these documents, even in the colonial period, was conditioned more by a familiarity with the legal idiom, than with an expertise in alphabetic literacy. It could be argued, for example, that recourse to the written word fostered an exclusivity and an individualization of the indigenous subject. But this was not so much due to any supposed linearity of the written word, as much as to a restructuring of the legal subject under Spanish law.[16] Those who read the titles today operate simultaneously under multiple legal systems: the colonial, the Republican, and the contemporary legal codes, each of which builds upon the others but can only be comprehended within its social and historical context.[17] So for example, the indigenous letter writers must refer, in one breath, to colonial, independence, and contemporary legislation in a highly confusing juxtaposition of dates and legal codes, in order to establish their claim to the sulphur beds of Mount Cumbal. Similarly, they frequently confuse their colonial title with late-nineteenth-century national Indian legislation because they employ eighteenth-century documents within the context of a twentieth-century land struggle. Indigenous politics in Nariño was spurred in part by the expansion of agribusiness and in part by the growth of ethnic rights movements throughout the country. It is led by contemporary cabildos, whose powers have been redefined by post-Independence legislation.

While it is true that the Cumbal readers of colonial documents are employing the same technology of writing common to other regions, the nature of their reading of the Spanish language is conditioned by other factors. There is no linear "fixity of text" that literacy supposedly promises, but instead a circular and constant movement between literacy and orality, between orality and ritual practice, between ritual practice and literacy. This movement cannot be simplified into an oral/literate dichotomy. Moreover, it cannot be generalized across political, historical, and cultural situations.[18] Ultimately, the lack of "fixity of text" proved to be all too confusing to the Colombian authorities who read the council's petition.

AN INTERRUPTION OF CONSENSUS

Let us look again at the bureaucrat's response. Not surprisingly, he ignores the centerpiece of the letter—the description of the possession ceremony—and reasserts the legalistic, written appropriation of the past as the only legitimate one. He advises the petitioners of the proper procedure to be followed, informs them that they have not adhered to it, and extricates himself from the uncomfortable position in which the Indians have placed him, saying that ". . . inasmuch as the objection is not formulated legally, this Office can do nothing regarding the abovereferenced petition." In short, he acts like a bureaucrat in the service of the state, reasserting the dominant discourse and simultaneously informing the petitioners that they are *outside* of it: a classic case of the construction of power by excluding certain kinds of information.

Although his response makes clear the political nature of this exchange between the petitioner and the state, what is of interest to us is how that third paragraph describing the possession ceremony functions as an interruption of consensus, a reassertion of a way of appropriating the past that is distinct from the legal, written one.[19] We know that the possession ceremony was Spanish in origin, but so was the written law. What is it about the ceremony that makes it more accommodating, more malleable than the law? Is it hospitable to other ways of knowing and expressing? Is it generative of other images? Does it introduce evidence excluded by the dominant discourse and thereby interrupt the apparent consensus of what constitutes ownership of land and resources?

The sign which lives on in collective memory is always the superior, meaningful one (Clanchy 1979). For the Cumbales, the possession ceremony, with its multivocal, pluridimensional aspects, allows for the enactment and transfer of memories from one social group to another. Social memory, Connerton (1989:43) points out, is manifested in commemorative ceremonies involving ritual performance with a purpose not to remind participants of events or knowledge, but to *re-present* them. It is in the re-presentation that the community is both constructed and reminded of its constitution (Ibid.:59). Walking the boundaries, kneeling on the land, assembling eyewitnesses, are all incorporating practices which, like the inscribing practices of writing, transfer to (topographic) space a line of thought in the mind.

Clearly, the possession ceremony is a richer vehicle than written law for encoding the past and ratifying ownership: there is room in it for the reenactment of Andean categories of meaning as well as Spanish ones. For example, the possession ceremony validates land use within a particularly Andean context, in which the community is divided into a series of sections that follow a strict hierarchical order (Rappaport 1988a, 1988b). This formal ordering of space is alluded to in the references to the expanse of land surrounding the central volcano of Cumbal and the patient outlining of the boundaries.

Just as essential to the interruption of consensus are the Indians' symbols of dominion (which have no meaning in twentieth-century discourse): the presence of the four local chiefs, the people's "genuine representatives"; the eyewitnesses, chiefs from neighboring towns; and finally, the oral declaration of dominion. Words, acts, and images all come together here to form a signifying system; they cannot simply be translated into the dominant discourse of written law. They are mediated by political power that is itself ceremonially, historically, and geographically validated. It is the unity of words, acts, and images in a particular context or event that gives them meaning.

WORD-AS-EVENT AND WORD-AS-THING

Here, Walter Ong's contrastive notions of "word-as-event" and "word-as-thing" might be helpful (Ong 1982). In oral communication, speaker and hearer are held together in an interaction characterized by physical nearness and the immediacy of fleeting sound: what he calls "word-as-event."

Such an interaction is susceptible to immediate revision, clarification, inter-pretation, or elaboration, depending upon the needs of the participants. It is, potentially, a rich exchange using a variety of senses.

According to Ong, written discourse, on the other hand, is distinguished by distance between the participants, who are often, in fact, unknown to each other. All that connects them are visual marks on a page. It is thus a thing or an object—letter, book, manuscript—that embodies their com-munication rather than a context or event. This reification of the word—in Ong's phrase, "word-as-thing"—has its own set of rules for successful dis-course that are quite distinct from those governing oral communicative events.

The possession ceremony is certainly closer to word-as-event than word-as-thing because in it, participants re-present historical knowledge as per-formative act. Ong's distinction is thus challenged and clarified by the sig-nifying unity of word, act, and image. They are inseparably woven together in an event that has retained central meaning for the Indians, despite the existence of written documents that preceded and later ratified the decision embodied in the possession ceremony. This intertwining of word, act, and image is so complete that each becomes the repository for the others: the words granting ownership to the Indians are embedded in the image of the Spanish king's representative kneeling on the plain. His image is in turn embedded in the legal documents ratifying ownership. The law, then, if it is to be effective, does not merely ratify the property relations made explicit by the possession ceremony, but describes the words, acts, and images that were part of that ceremony. In short, to be meaningful, the law must recre-ate, as much as possible, the word-as-event. Mere recitation of the law is not sufficient: it must incorporate the acts and images that were part of the original event. The fact that at "one and another time" the Spanish infantry captain identified the natural boundaries of Indian lands, that his actions were witnessed by neighboring chiefs, that he knelt on the plains wearing the symbol of his king, and declared the lands to belong to the Indians, is all irrelevant in a written discourse with a national bureaucrat. The mean-ing of the event—control over communal resources—is codified in numer-ous laws, to which the petitioners could have made reference. Clearly, however, the written law is merely word-as-thing and must be fleshed out, given meaning, given life, by creating the original word-as-event. This is how Cumbal's council read their title, and it is from this perspective that we should interpret their communications with the Colombian state.

NOTES

This article is based upon field and archival research conducted in the municipality of Cumbal, Nariño, Colombia and in local and regional archives from September,

1986 to August, 1987, and sponsored by the Council for the International Exchange of Scholars (American Republics Program), the National Science Foundation (grant no. BNS–8602910) and the Social Science Research Council. Research was conducted under the supervision of the Cabildo Indígena del Gran Cumbal and with the assistance of Luz Angélica Mamián Guzmán and Jesús Iván Villota Bravo of Pasto and Gilberto Helí Valenzuela Mites of Cumbal. Analysis of the data was made possible through the support of the University of Maryland Graduate School at Baltimore. Jonathan Boyarin offered valuable comments and criticisms on a previous draft of the article.

1. An emphasis on literacy has prompted a parallel focus on its absence, leading to the construction of an unhelpful dichotomy between oral and literate modes of communication (see, for example, Goody 1977, 1987; and Ong 1982). Street (1984), among others, has addressed this problem by focusing instead on the mix of oral and literate modes. However, following Connerton (1989), we would go further to suggest that greater attention be paid to the unity of a range of signifying practices, beyond simply verbal modes of communication.

2. The resguardo system was established during the early colonial period as a means of containing indigenous tributaries in a delimited territory closed to non-Indians (González 1979). The institution was later adopted by post-Independence authorities and is widespread among highland ethnic groups (see, for example, Rappaport 1990 on nineteenth-century resguardos among the Páez).

3. Archivo del Cabildo Indígena del Gran Cumbal, Nariño (ACIGC/N), "Borradores de cartas del Cabildo al Ministerio de Minas, sobre los yacimientos de azufre del Cerro de Cumbal," Fondo Asuntos Varios, ff. 4r–v, 1950.

4. Common to colonial-era titles, this clause refers to the ethnic isolation that the Crown imposed upon resguardo Indians.

5. Ibid., f. 10r.

6. The petitioners state that they are awaiting a "second Bolívar." They might be referring here to the fact that their first post-Independence title was granted by Bolívar. But they may also be alluding to the assistance that Bolívar Córdoba, an employee in the Ipiales regional office of the Office of Indigenous Affairs, was giving them at the time.

7. Notaría Primera de Ipiales (NP/I), "Expediente sobre los linderos del resguardo del Gran Cumbal," escritura 997, 1906 [1712–58]. The copy consulted was made in 1944 and is kept in the cabildo archives (ACIGC/N).

8. Goody's later work is a departure from the technological determinism that characterized his earlier writing (Goody 1987).

9. In spite of the fact that the possession ceremony is Spanish-colonial in origin, and hence widely disseminated in the past throughout the Americas, the form in which it is interpreted today by the Cumbales is unique to the department of Nariño, and has disappeared from other Colombian Indian communities.

10. During the course of an intercommunity dispute, the reservation council of Panán asked Rappaport to study a photocopy of their colonial title. As she summarized the contents of the document, the council members requested that she read aloud certain selected portions. Significantly, they were most interested in the descriptions of colonial possession ceremonies. Cabildo permission to conduct field research in Cumbal was granted with the understanding that Rappaport would share

her data with the community through meetings and discussion groups, making available copies of historical documentation, the preparation of written oral history anthologies, and the sharing of her analyses in written form in Spanish or in taped translation. On multiple occasions, written documents were given to the cabildo. To give two further brief examples: Supreme Court decisions relating to a mid-nineteenth-century dispute over lands were deposited in the cabildo archive, were read to the community, and were frequently referred to later at meetings. Her historical analyses of the nature of colonial-period territorial organization (Rappaport 1988b) were shared with the community and consulted by mediators in the course of some intercommunity land disputes.

11. A similar mix of literacy and ritual practice is described for medieval England by M. T. Clanchy (1979).

12. A good example is the encoding in documents of the public proclamation that accompanied legal processes. If a decision was announced thirty times in public, it was written out thirty times in the document arising out of the case (see Cummins and Rappaport 1990).

13. Street (1984) has examined the spatial component of literacy in his study of how Iranian villagers understand the placement of paragraphs on the written page.

14. The layered nature of the legal brief was mimicked in the eighteenth century by Nahuatl-speaking scribes in Mexico, who fabricated their own titles, adopting the layered form that characterized the original documents to which they did not have access (Gruzinski 1988; Lockhart 1982). But although the indigenous authors were able to mimic the layered effect of the legal record, it is not clear that they fully understood why so many documents had been juxtaposed.

15. NP/I, 1906, p. 8.

16. For an excellent discussion of the impact of legal conventions upon Andean peoples, see Stern (1982).

17. See, for example, Sally Falk Moore's studies of the relationship between customary law and governmental law in Africa (Moore 1986, 1989).

18. This is especially clear when we compare this analysis of Cumbal to Boyarin's study of readers of the Hebrew Bible and the Talmud (this volume). In the Jewish example, mastery of the text is more complete; writing is not an imposed form of meaning construction as it is in Cumbal.

19. See, for example, other forms of interruption typical of minority discourse: José María Arguedas's eruptions into Quechua in *Los ríos profundos* (Arguedas 1971) or Joan de Santacruz Pachacuti Yamqui and Felipe Guaman Poma de Ayala's use of pictorial representation and of Quechua quotations in their Spanish-language texts (Pachacuti Yamqui 1968; Guaman Poma 1980). See also analyses of these indigenous texts (Adorno 1986; Salomon 1982).

REFERENCES

Adorno, Rolena
    1986   *Guaman Poma: Writing and Resistance in Colonial Peru.* Austin: University of Texas Press.

Arguedas, José María
    1971   *Los ríos profundos.* Buenos Aires: Losada.
Clanchy, M. T.
    1979   *From Memory to Written Record: England, 1066–1307.* Cambridge,
                Mass.: Harvard University Press.
Colombia, República de (Ministerio de Gobierno)
    1983   *Fuero indígena: disposiciones legales del orden nacional, departamental y
                comisarial—jurisprudencia y conceptos.* Bogotá: Presencia.
Connerton, Paul
    1989   *How Societies Remember.* Cambridge: Cambridge University Press.
Cummins, Thomas, and Joanne Rappaport
    1990   "Literacy and Power in Colonial Latin America." Paper presented
                at the World Archaeological Congress 2, Barquisimeto, Venezuela,
                September, 1990.
González, Margarita
    1979   *El resguardo en el Nuevo Reino de Granada.* Bogotá: La Carreta.
Goody, Jack
    1977   *The Domestication of the Savage Mind.* Cambridge: Cambridge Uni-
                versity Press.
    1987   *The Interface between the Written and the Oral.* Cambridge: Cambridge
                University Press.
Gruzinski, Serge
    1988   *La colonisation de l'imaginaire: sociétés indigènes et occidentalisation dans le
                Mexique espagnol, XVIe—XVIIIe siécle.* Paris: Gallimard.
Guaman Poma de Ayala, Felipe
    1980   *El primer nueva corónica y buen gobierno.* Ed. John Murra and Rolena
    [1615]   Adorno. Mexico City: Siglo XXI.
Lockhart, James
    1982   "Views of Corporate Self and History in Some Valley of Mexico
                Towns: Late Seventeenth and Eighteenth Centuries." In *The Inca and
                Aztec States, 1400–1800: Anthropology and History.* Ed. G. A. Collier,
                R. I. Rosaldo, and J. D. Wirth, pp. 367–393. New York: Academic
                Press.
Moore, Sally Falk
    1986   *Social Facts and Fabrications: "Customary" Law on Kilimanjaro, 1880–
                1980.* Cambridge: Cambridge University Press.
    1989   "History and the Redefinition of Custom on Kilimanjaro." In *History
                and Power in the Study of Law.* Ed. J. Starr and J. F. Collins, pp. 277–
                301. Ithaca: Cornell University Press.
Ong, Walter J.
    1982   *Orality and Literacy: The Technologizing of the Word.* London and New
                York: Methuen.
Pachacuti Yamqui Salcamaygua, Joan de Santacruz
    1968   "Relación de antigüedades deste reyo del Pirú." In *Crónicas peruanas
    [1613]   de interés indígena.* Ed. Francisco Esteve Barba. Madrid: Biblioteca de
                Autores Españoles.

Phelan, John L.
  1967   *The Kingdom of Quito in the Seventeenth Century.* Madison: University of
               Wisconsin Press.
Rappaport, Joanne
  1988a   "History and Everyday Life in the Colombian Andes." *Man* 23:718–
               739.
  1988b   "La organización socio-territorial de los pastos: una hipótesis de tra-
               bajo." *Revista de Antropología* 4(2):71–103.
  1990   *The Politics of Memory: Native Historical Interpretation in the Colombian
               Andes.* Cambridge: Cambridge University Press.
  1992   "Reinvented Traditions: The Heraldry of Ethnic Militancy in the
               Colombian Andes." In *Andean Cosmologies through Time: Persistence
               and Emergence.* Ed. Robert Dover, Katherine Seibold, and John
               McDowell, pp. 202–208. Bloomington: Indiana University Press.
Salomon, Frank
  1982   "Chronicles of the Impossible: Notes on Three Peruvian Indigenous
               Historians." In *From Oral to Written Expression: Native Andean Chroni-
               cles of the Early Colonial Period.* Ed. Rolena Adorno, pp. 9–39. Syra-
               cuse: Maxwell School of Citizenship and Public Affairs.
Stern, Steve
  1982   *Peru's Indian Peoples and the Challenge of Spanish Conquest.* Madison:
               University of Wisconsin Press.
Street, Brian V.
  1984   *Literacy in Theory and Practice.* Cambridge: Cambridge University
               Press.
Vidal, Hernán
  1985   *Socio historia de la literatura colonial hispanoamericana: tres lecturas orgáni-
               cas.* Minneapolis: Institute for the Study of Ideologies and Litera-
               tures.

EIGHT

Japanese Spirit and Chinese Learning: Scribes and Storytellers in Pre-modern Japan

H. Mack Horton

Ever since the disappearance of the land bridges that linked Japan to the Asian mainland in the Pleistocene epoch, the history of the archipelago has been animated at a profound level by the interaction between native traditions and foreign importations. Nowhere is that dynamic more apparent than in the literary history of the country.

I would like to review briefly here the history of reading in Japan by exploring the dynamic between orality and orthography that developed as the Japanese gradually learned both to manipulate the Chinese language and its writing system and to devise ways to adapt Chinese orthography to their own very different native language and its rich corpus of oral literature.[1] I will then explore a few of the implications of that dynamic for strategies of reader reception of pre-modern Japanese texts.

The interaction between the written and oral Japanese traditions is demonstrated in microcosm by the etymological development of the word "to read" itself, *yomu*. In its earliest sense, *yomu* means "to count." This meaning survives in modern Japanese phrases like *saba o yomu*, "to count mackerel," meaning, to inflate one's count or cheat at counting. A second early meaning of *yomu* is "to chant." And the word also came to mean "to compose poetry," possibly deriving from the fact that Japanese poetry is based on syllabic meter and hence is both composed and chanted on the basis of "counting" syllables.

Those meanings for the word *yomu* focus on oral counting and oral telling, an etymological phenomenon that has numerous Western parallels. In Old English, for example, the verb *tellan* means both "to count" (as in to "tell" one's rosary) and "to narrate" (to "tell" a "tale"). Likewise in French, *compter*, "to count" and *conter*, "to tell a story," both derive from the same Latin root *computare* and are reflected in the English similarity be-

tween "count" or "compute" and "give an account," or "recount a story."
And Hebrew seems to possess a very similar bivalence in the word *hāgāh*,
which in Psalm 1 means "to murmur [prayers]" (the King James Version
translates it to "meditate day and night" but the word more accurately involves orality). In Psalm 2, however, the word means "to count" (Dahood
1965:1, 3).

Considerable correspondence appears to exist, therefore, between the
Japanese word *yomu* and Western concepts of counting and chanting and
tale telling. But none of these meanings of the word *yomu* directly relates to
what we mean by "to read" in modern English, or for that matter, in modern Japanese. The application of the verb *yomu* to the apprehension and recitation of a written passage could have occurred *ipso facto* only after Japan
acquired a writing system. That began to occur in the first centuries of the
common era, when Chinese orthography was gradually introduced from the
Asian continent. The very word for "civilization" in Chinese, *wen²ming²*
文明, is based on the concept of literacy, being rendered by the characters
for "writing" and "clarity" or "understanding."

It was then that the great bifurcation occurred in Japan between oral
and written apprehension. Where *yomu* continued to mean "to count" and
"to chant," it also acquired the meanings of "to decipher written Chinese,"
"to read written Chinese" (either silently or aloud), and "to render Chinese
into Japanese." The word *yomu* at this point can variously mean to read
silently, read aloud, or to compose; the person performing *yomu* can thus
either be a "reader" or an "author."

According to a legend recorded in Japan's oldest extant book, the *Record
of Ancient Matters* (*Kojiki* 古事記, 712), Chinese writing was first introduced
into Japan by an immigrant from the Korean kingdom of Paekche (J:
Kudara) during the time of Emperor Ōjin, whose reign is traditionally
dated from 270 to 310 c.e. The account runs as follows:

> Emperor Ōjin addressed the King of Paekche thus: "Present to me a wise
> man." In accordance with this command, the King sent in tribute Wani Ki-
> shi 和邇吉師, together with the *Confucian Analects* in ten volumes and the
> *Thousand-Character Classic* in one volume, for a total of eleven volumes. (Tsu-
> gita, 1980:2:224)

Archaeological evidence, however, demonstrates that the Japanese,
known as the Wa people by the Chinese of the Han Dynasty (206 b.c.e.–
200 c.e.), were introduced to Chinese writing far earlier than the purported
date of the legendary account. The oldest extant material evidence of that
transmission is a seal thought to have been presented to a Japanese king
by the Chinese emperor Guangwu 光武 in 57 c.e. The seal, which reads,
"King of Na in Wa, [Vassal of] Han," is believed to be that mentioned in
the earliest known account of contact between a Japanese kingdom and the

Chinese mainland, the "Chronicle of Wa" (C: *Wo zhuan*, J: *Waden* 倭伝) in the *History of the Later Han Dynasty* (C: *Hou Han shu*, J: *Gokanjo* 後漢書):

> In [57 c.e.], the Land of Na in Wa offered up tribute and congratulations to the Emperor. The envoys from Na styled themselves ministers. Their land is in the southernmost region of Wa. A seal of state was bestowed on them by Emperor Guangwu.[2]

Swords bearing Chinese inscriptions on their blades have also been unearthed from second- and third-century Japanese sites. The extent to which contemporary Japanese could actually decipher those inscriptions, however, is unknown. Malformed characters on bronze mirrors manufactured in Japan in the same period suggest that Chinese characters were initially applied with more symbolic than semantic intent (Fujii 1985:160). It is likely that Chinese characters were valued first as potent magical signs, and only later as a means of linguistic communication. But by the fifth century Chinese was being employed by the central government for record keeping, and scribes had been assigned to each province.[3] It is probable that those scribes were either immigrants or the descendants of immigrants from the continent.

The adoption of the Chinese writing system was but one reflection of the pervasive influence of Chinese culture on early Japan. Buddhism was introduced from the continent in the mid-sixth century, bringing with it an immense pantheon, sophisticated philosophy, and awe-inspiring temple architecture. A century later the Taika Reforms of 646 and then the Taihō Codes of 701 instituted a wholesale restructuring of the Japanese state after the Chinese model. The Japanese adopted, with modification, the Chinese legal system and its policy of land tenure, and Japanese courtiers assumed Chinese-style offices, ranks, and costumes. In 710 the court moved to the new Heijō Capital in Nara, which was laid out on the model of the Tang capital of Changan. The city eventually included numerous Buddhist temple complexes and a massive palace compound of several hundred buildings. The main hall of the largest temple, Tōdaiji, is still today the largest wooden building on earth, though only two-thirds its eighth-century size. Envoys and scholars were frequently sent to the continent, and Japanese aristocrats became familiar with Persian glass and goods from central Asia imported via the Silk Road. Though the Japanese provinces remained far less sinified, the Nara capital was doubtless compatible with the expectations of continental emissaries and traders who walked along its broad thoroughfares.

China also exerted a far-ranging influence on the literature of those centuries. The Japanese court subscribed to the Chinese concept that poetry was a mirror of character and an aid to government, and the first extant Japanese poetic anthology was of Chinese, not Japanese verse. The first surviving anthology of Japanese verse, the *Man'yōshū* (c. 760), was to some extent a memorial to a tradition already in decline, as hundreds of its verses show the heavy influence of the Chinese poetry of the Six Dynasties (222–589). It was Chinese verse that dominated the court for the next hundred years, so much so that the period from 750 to 850 is known in Japanese literary history as "the dark age of Japanese poetry."

The pervasive nature of Chinese influence is already apparent in the oldest nonepigraphical example of writing that remains, the *Seventeen Article Constitution* (*Jūshichijō no kenpō* 十七条憲法), reputed to have been composed by Prince Shōtoku 聖徳 (574–c.622) in 604. Selections from its first several articles demonstrate the extent to which Confucian principles of harmony and social order, together with veneration for the Buddhist Law, were being actively imported from the continent together with the Chinese writing system:

1. Harmony is to be valued. . . . [W]hen those above are harmonious and those below are friendly, and there is concord in the discussion of business, right views of things spontaneously gain acceptance.
2. Sincerely reverence the three treasures. The three treasures, viz. Buddha, the Law, and the Monastic orders . . . are the supreme objects of faith in all countries.
3. When you receive the imperial commands, fail not scrupulously to obey them. The lord is Heaven, the vassal is Earth. Heaven overspreads, and Earth upbears.
4. The ministers and functionaries should make decorous behavior their leading principle. (Tsunoda, et al., 1969:48)[4]

By the eighth century, the aristocracy and clergy were probably nearly all literate.[5] Indeed, courtiers of this and succeeding centuries prided themselves on, and in a sense defined themselves in terms of, their mastery of reading and writing and of the concomitant literary tradition. Even after actual political power had passed from the civil bureaucracy into the hands of the Minamoto and then the Ashikaga warrior governments in the medieval period (thirteenth through sixteenth centuries), courtiers in the capital still commanded immense respect for their role as living repositories of the exalted cultural traditions of the past. And as warriors rose to positions of wealth and responsibility, they too often devoted considerable energy to literary pursuits, for such activities marked them as civilized and helped legitimize before the world their newly acquired political and economic power. Some military potentates patronized literary gatherings in the capital and invited courtiers to their provincial domains to serve as tutors in the literary arts.[6]

But the far-reaching appropriation of the Chinese episteme that began in the sixth century took place against an ancient and well-developed native tradition of oral myth and song preserved and transmitted by lineage groups that specialized in oral recitation. This is reflected in part by the formulaic coda of certain of the songs handed down in *The Record of Ancient Matters* and other early sources. The coda, which reads, "This was transmitted/ By word of mouth" (*Koto no katarigoto mo/ ko o ba*), indicates that the song had been aurally apprehended by the scribe rather than copied from an earlier written source. Much of this prehistoric material was religious in nature, a characteristic that led Origuchi Shinobu to assert that Japanese literature began with incantations to the gods (Origuchi 1954:124 ff.).[7] While Chinese literature was cultured and sophisticated, Japanese was divine, its very words pregnant with spiritual power, called "word-mana" (*kotodama*). Words orally pronounced in the form of spells (*kotoage*) were thought to effect magical results (Fujii 1985:33–37).[8]

Even after the introduction of Chinese writing and the development of a technique for using Chinese orthography for Japanese words, oral delivery of the native vocabulary was believed to be essential if the word-mana of songs and incantations was to be effective. The names of gods too had to be given correct oral pronunciation if prayers addressed to them were to receive a divine hearing, and *The Record of Ancient Matters* therefore included notes on the proper reading of godly names in the long divine genealogies (Mōri 1985:171).

The introduction of Chinese characters and their gradual application to the transcription of the Japanese language inevitably meant a gradual weakening of the belief that the word-mana could only be activated through the human voice. Oral traditions, however, were so deeply ingrained by the time the Chinese writing system was introduced that they never entirely disappeared. But before discussing the influence of Japanese oral and Chinese orthographic principles on the subsequent history of Japanese literature, it is necessary to review in somewhat more detail the process through which Chinese characters where introduced into Japan and the mechanics through which they were eventually applied to the transcription of native Japanese.

The importation of Chinese characters, known in Japanese as *kanji* 漢字 (C: *hanzi*, lit. "Han characters" after the Chinese Han Dynasty) and Chinese writing (*kanbun* 漢文) did not originally mean the appropriation of just the Chinese writing system but of the entire Chinese literary episteme. When the Japanese needed to commit something to paper, silk, or wood, they first did so not in their own language but in Chinese. Moreover, they read Chinese books in the Chinese language. This approach of course parallels the process of literary acquisition in northern Europe, where previously illiterate cultures learned to read and write Latin and to pronounce the writings in Latin as well, as a matter of course. But in Japan the process was made far more complex by the logographic nature of the Chinese writing system. To be sure, most Chinese characters contain some phonetic hints, but meaning and pronunciation remain largely separate; the pronunciation is not built into the word as it is in most Western languages.[9] Arabic numerals have of course functioned exactly the same way in the West. Just as the numeral "1" can be read "one" in English or "un" in French, or "eins" in German, or understood visually without being pronounced at all, Chinese characters can be recognized by sight, and then pronounced in any language. Initially, therefore, there was a total divorce in Japan between the spoken and written languages. The subsequent history of Japanese reading is one of the adaptation of the Chinese writing system to Japanese needs.[10]

The dynamic between Japanese orality and Chinese orthography is illustrated early on by the circumstances behind the composition of Japan's oldest extant book, *The Record of Ancient Matters*. Its preface records that an imperial scribe, Ō no Yasumaro 太安万侶, was commanded to edit and record (*senroku* 撰録) material "recited" by Hieda no Are 稗田阿礼 (Tsugita 1986, 1:30). The account is written in Chinese, of course, and the character for "recited" is 誦 (C: song,[4] J: *zu, shō, tonaeru, yomu*, etc.). In Chinese the word represented by the graph means to read aloud, to explicate, to recite from memory, or to read to a rhythm. No one knows, therefore, whether the passage means that Hieda no Are recited the orally transmitted body of national myths or whether he (or she) had memorized the correct way to read aloud earlier texts written in quirky, uncertain orthography so that Yasumaro could transcribe them in a more regular and up-to-date orthographic style. The process probably involved both written and oral aspects (Konishi 1984:161–162).

The problem of recording the oral Japanese myths centered not on the stories themselves, which were relatively easy to translate into Chinese, but on the names of Japanese gods, place names, and other native proper nouns for which there were no Chinese equivalents. The solution the Japanese reached was borrowed from one the Chinese themselves had used for transcribing Sanskrit and other foreign terms. The process involved ignoring the semantic value of each character and using it only for its phonetic element. Characters used this way constituted a phonetic syllabary, albeit one of extreme complexity and inefficiency. When faced with the Sanskrit term *asura*, "titan king," for example, the Chinese transliterated it using three characters (nearly forty written strokes) meaning "hook-shape hill" (阿 Ancient Chinese *a*; Modern Chinese *a*[1]), "to put in order" (修 Ancient Chinese *siəu*; Modern Chinese *xiu*[1]), and "net" (羅 Ancient Chinese *la*; Modern Chinese *luo*[2]) and read them "a-siəu-la" ("Ancient Chinese" refers to the language of the Sui [581–618] and Tang Dynasties [618–907]; Chinese phonological reconstructions are after Tōdō [1984]).

The Japanese appropriated this system, learning to use these and other

Chinese characters to represent their native sounds /a/, /su/, and /ra/.[11] The process became extremely complex in Japan, however, for several reasons. First, there was no initial limit on the number of Chinese characters that could be chosen to represent any one Japanese syllable. 天 (Ancient Chinese *t'en*, "heaven"), 帝 (*tei*, "thearch"), 亭 (*deŋ*, "belvedere"), 轉 (*ţıuɛn*, "turn"), 傳 (*ḍıuɛn*, "transmit") and other characters, for example, could all be used to represent the Japanese sound /te/. "Playful writing" (*gisho* 戲書) appeared as well, where, for example, the two characters meaning "bee sound" (蜂音) could be used to stand for the one syllable /bu/. Second, while appropriating many Chinese characters for their phonetic values alone, the Japanese also continued to use them for their semantic values, often in the same sentence. Where, for example, the character for "heaven" 天 might be used simply for the sound /te/ in one place, it might actually represent the word *ten*, "heaven," in another context.

Adapting the Chinese writing system to Japanese was further complicated by the fact that Chinese and Japanese are phonologically and structurally as different as any two languages on earth; Chinese has an SVO word order while Japanese is SOV. Chinese is a monosyllabic language and now a tonal one, while Japanese is polysyllabic, agglutinative, and atonal (though it has pitch accents). It was perhaps unfortunate from an orthographic point of view that Japan was closer to China than to Rome, for the Latin alphabet would have been far better suited to their purposes.

After the introduction of Chinese, Japanese also began adopting thousands of loan words from Chinese and inserting them into native Japanese sentences, while pronouncing them in imitation of the way they were pronounced in Chinese. This is to some extent analogous to the English practice of borrowing words from Latin and French, inserting them into native sentence structures, and pronouncing them with an English accent. In Japan, those borrowed pronunciations became the so-called Sino-Japanese or *on* 音 readings. For example, the two Chinese characters for "years and months" or "time," *nian²yue⁴* (Ancient Chinese *nenŋıuʌt* 年月), went into Japanese as the phonetically similar *nengetsu*. But the two characters could also be read according to the preexisting native words for "years" and "months," *toshitsuki*. These became known in contradistinction as native Japanese or *kun* 訓 readings. This is much like English borrowing the word "journal" from French via Latin, but gradually coming to pronounce it somewhat differently from the French *journal*, all the while retaining the native "daybook."

To illustrate the literary ramifications of this linguistic bifurcation, let us consider a couplet of five-character phrases (*gāthās*) from the *Lotus Sutra* (Skt. *Saddharma-pundarīka-sūtra*; J. *Myōhōrengekyō* 妙法華蓮経 , abbrev. *Hokekyō* 法華経). The sūtra was translated from Sanskrit into Chinese, and it later made its way to Japan, where it continued to be "read," as it were, directly from the Chinese text, but in various ways.

The phrase in question is, in Japanese, *shoashuratō kozai daikaihen*
諸阿修羅等，居在大海辺，which translates as "the various asuras and the
rest dwell by the great sea (Sakamoto and Iwamoto 1977, 3:96)."[12] Asuras
again are "titan kings," Hindu and then Buddhist deities variously con-
ceived of as benevolent beings or as enemies of Indra (Taishakuten 帝釈天
in Japanese). The Japanese reader could approach this line in several ways.
He (or, rarely, she) might read it in Chinese, with the Chinese pronunciations of all the words, more or less as it would have been read by a Chinese
(see table 1). As time went on, however, and Japan's contact with the continent lessened, fewer and fewer Japanese could acquire that mastery of
Chinese. But they *could* read the characters in their Sino-Japanese (*on*)
pronunciations. The phrase could be read off in the same word order as
Chinese, simply changing the Chinese pronunciations to Sino-Japanese
ones: "Shoashuratō, kozai daikaihen." That style of reading is known
variously as "plain reading" (*hakudoku* 白読), "unadulterated reading"
(*sodoku* 素読), or "straight reading" (*bōyomi* 棒読).

The practice was complicated, though, by the fact that Japanese has no
tones and fewer sounds to distinguish syllables than Chinese does, with the
result that this phrase is nearly unintelligible orally when read in Sino-
Japanese plain reading, one must be able to *see* the characters to understand them. Plain reading, therefore, enables reading comprehension by
sight, but not necessarily reading comprehension by *sound*.

A method was accordingly developed to read Chinese in Japanese word
order, while concurrently changing some of the Sino-Japanese *on* readings

Table 1

諸	阿	修	羅	等	
tʃɪo	a	siəu	la	təŋ	Ancient Chinese (Sui-Tang)
sho	a	shu	ra	tō	Sino-Japanese (*on* readings in *sodoku*)
moromoro	a	shu	ra	nado	Japanese (*kun* readings, except "ashura")
moromoro (no) ashura nado					Japanese *kundoku*

居	在	大	海	辺
kɪo	dzəi	da	həi	pen
ko	zai	dai	kai	hen
[sumai]		ō	umi	hotori
ōumi (no) hotori (ni) sumai (shite)				

to native *kun* readings. The phrase in question eventually came to be read "moromoro no ashura nado no ōumi no hotori ni sumai shite." This is called *kundoku* 訓読, "reading according to the *kun* readings," or as *yomiku-dashi* 読下, 訓下, "reading down" or as *kakikudashi* 書下, "writing down" or "writing out." Thus another meaning for *yomu* becomes "to read out Chinese in Japanese" or even "translate into Japanese."

But this style, though verbally intelligible, is translationese; no Japanese then or now would ever confuse it with a normal native utterance. And it was of course useless for reproducing Japanese oral ritual prayers, Japanese oral poetry, and Japanese vernacular conversation.

The situation was remedied by the development in the ninth century of two Japanese phonetic syllabaries, *hiragana* 平仮名 and *katakana* 片仮名. Both were derived from Chinese characters used for their phonetic values, but now written in simple cursive script rather than in their complete and highly complex forms. The sound /a/, for example, could now be written in *hiragana* as あ (taken from the more cumbersome 安), and in *katakana* as ア (taken from 阿). The system was quite irregular, with several cursive forms being available for each sound.[13] The development of the two *kana* syllabaries finally made it possible to read and write Japanese quickly and effectively. It is not surprising that the greatest literature of Japan's classical period was composed not in Chinese, which after all was a foreign language, but in the native vernacular after the advent of *kana*. In these works, the most important being *The Tale of Genji* (*Genji monogatari* 源氏物語, c. 1010), the gap between the written and the oral came close to disappearing. Modern Japanese is still written in a combination of standardized *hiragana* and Chinese characters. *Katakana* is today, by and large, reserved for words of foreign origin and some onomatopoeia.

The rise of Japanese native literature corresponds with a general re-crudescence of native taste after centuries of wholesale adoption of continental customs. This began to occur in the last decades of the ninth century, when the Tang empire was in its final stages of collapse. The new inward-looking quality of the Japanese court, now located in the Heian capital, is demonstrated in diplomatic history by the cessation of missions to the mainland, and in literary history by an imperial order to compile a new anthology of Japanese verse. The *waka* poems in the resultant anthology, the *Kokinshū* (*Ancient and Modern Collection*, 905) came to be viewed as the template of basic *waka* style, and the format of the anthology became the model for twenty subsequent imperial collections that appeared over the next six centuries. The decision by the *Kokinshū* compilers to reject the *Man'yōshū* practice of transliterating Japanese with Chinese characters used mostly phonetically and instead to adopt the newly developed *hiragana* syllabary is believed to reflect a conscious decision on the part of the compilers to turn to native sources of inspiration (Konishi 1986:142).

The next century, the eleventh, was the apogee of the Heian Period (794–1185), Japan's classical age. The era is represented most memorably in literature by *The Tale of Genji*, which has been called the world's first novel.[14] Its author, Murasaki Shikibu 紫式部 (b. c. 978), was only one of several highly talented literary ladies-in-waiting then serving at court, and their creations, which also include *The Pillow Book* of Sei Shōnagon and the first historical tale in Japanese (*rekishi monogatari*), *A Tale of Flowering Fortunes*, represent the early maturation of native literary prose.[15]

The court society for which those women were writing was small, highly sophisticated, and aesthetically sensitive.[16] The reputation of a courtier or a lady-in-waiting depended in large part upon his or her dress, choice of fragrance, and particularly poetic skill and elegant calligraphy. The "rule of taste" that dominated court life was nowhere seen to more advantage than at poetry competitions, where teams of left and right matched verses for fame and prizes. Some competitions were of such scale and magnificence they were recorded in detail in diaries, such as that added to the record of the *Tentoku Waka Competition* of 960:

> Four page-girls carried in the centerpiece [suhama]. They were wearing blue under lined willow-green robes that perfectly matched their hair in length. The embroidered centerpiece cover was dyed a deeper blue around the hem. The centerpiece rested on a cushion of pale blue gauze. The upper parts of the centerpiece were made of dark aloeswood wrapped in silver wire. The poems, written on fine paper, were presented as follows: waka on blossoms were tied to silver- or gold-blossoming branches, depending on their poetic topic. Poems on burning love were placed in the brazier of a miniature cormorant boat. Those on late spring were piled in the boat. Poems on the warbler were held in miniature warblers' beaks.[17]

Literary accomplishment and aesthetic sensibility were also linked to political power. Murasaki Shikibu's patroness, Empress Shōshi, was only one of two empresses and numerous other aristocratic consorts in the harem of Emperor Ichijō. Shōshi's success at wooing the Emperor away from his other ladies would be in part related to the brilliance of her salon, and her father accordingly took pains assembling it. *A Tale of Flowering Fortunes* records the process:

> Shōshi . . . entered the Palace on the First of the Eleventh Month [999], some time after the Tenth, accompanied by forty ladies-in-waiting, six young girls, and six servants. Her attendants had been selected with the utmost discrimination. It was not considered sufficient for a candidate to be personable and even-tempered: even if her father held the Fourth of Fifth Rank, there was no hope for her if she was socially inept or lacking in the niceties of deportment, for only the most polished and elegant were accepted. (McCullough and McCullough 1980:218)

The restricted and self-contained nature of court society also meant that taste was to a large extent uniform. The writer of poetry or prose could assume that all his or her readers would have read and assimilated certain basic canonical Japanese and Chinese works. The expectation of a shared code in turn gave rise to a highly elliptical and allusive literature that cannot be read today without a commensurate appreciation of the cultural milieu in which the works were originally composed.

But the burgeoning of the native literary genius at court did not signal the complete abandonment of Chinese. Such was the prestige of the Chinese tradition that male courtiers often continued to write in that language and read it according to the rules of Japanese *kundoku* well after the Japanese syllabaries had come into common use. Male diaries were usually kept in Chinese (*kanbun*), though the grammar became progressively naturalized to the point that it might be opaque to a Chinese native. Hence the paradoxical situation where many Japanese continued to write in a language that sounded ungainly to them and could not necessarily be comprehended by Chinese either. But *kanbun* diaries continued to be written until relatively recent times.

And Chinese, when read aloud in *kundoku*, could indeed sound grand and impressive, rather like a Victorian speech larded with Latin locutions. Japanese with learning and perhaps some pretension thus began writing native Japanese according to many of the rules of *kanbun kundoku*. This resulted in a somewhat stilted yet learned *kanbun kundoku chō* 漢文訓読調 style that sounded as though it was read directly from a line of Chinese *kanbun*, though it had been written from the first in Japanese with the Japanese phonetic syllabary interspersed among the Chinese characters.

But Chinese-style Japanese, whether written completely in Chinese characters or mimicked in a combination of Chinese characters and Japanese syllabary, remained essentially a *written* language meant more for visual than oral apprehension. It could be reproduced orally as we have seen, but at best it retained a touch of the inkhorn, and at worst it was orally unintelligible.

Chinese-style Japanese required other adjustments, therefore, before it could be assimilated in an oral context. Let us return to the Asuras again. The passage was adopted into the greatest of Japanese war tales, *The Tale of the Heike* (*Heike monogatari* 平家物語).[18] *The Tale of the Heike* was in its heyday essentially vocal literature; the text was memorized and then recited by blind priests who accompanied themselves on *biwa* lutes.[19] The line in question was recited as follows:

諸阿修羅等, 居在大海辺とて, 修羅の三悪四趣は, 深山大海のほとりにありと, 仏の解きをき給ひたれば

Shoashuratō, kozai daikaihen to te, shura no san'aku shishu wa, shinzan daikai no hotori ni ari to, Hotoke no tokiokitamaitareba. . . . (Ichiko 1973, 29:229)

Since the Buddha taught that "Shoashuratō kozai daikaihen," that is, that the three evil worlds and the four [evil] spheres of the Ashuras are by the deep mountains and the great ocean. . . .

When the written sutra lines are delivered in an oral context, the sutra must be verbally explained; what reads as a tautology in written Japanese is required repetition for oral comprehension. This "running commentary" approach to narration was one technique that oral storytellers used to put written, Chinese-style Japanese into an oral vernacular context.

As was pointed out earlier, the Japanese eventually developed two very adequate phonetic syllabaries to reproduce the Japanese vernacular in written form. But just as Sino-Japanese remained a written style even when delivered orally, vernacular Japanese often retained a sense of the oral even when committed to paper. Just as one "reads" Sino-Japanese as a written language, one often tends to "read" vernacular Japanese as intrinsically oral. To be sure, this effect is more apparent in some Japanese genres than in others. But this phenomenon of reception is particularly well demonstrated in Japanese poetry and in vernacular tale literature (*monogatari*).

Even after the introduction of the Chinese writing system, Japanese poetry retained a great deal of its oral quality. It will be recalled that *yomu* means at once "to compose" and "to chant Japanese poetry aloud." The continuing oral nature of poetry was directly linked to the lingering and widespread belief in the mana of words, the *kotodama*, whose power was unlocked through the medium of the human voice. The prescription is given its most memorable expression in the *Kana Preface* to the first imperial anthology of Japanese poetry, the *Kokinshū*:

Japanese poetry has the human heart as seed and myriads of words as leaves. It comes into being when men use the seen and the heard *to give voice* [*iidaseru*] to feelings aroused by the innumerable events in their lives. The song of the warbler among the blossoms, the voice of the frog dwelling in the water—these teach us that every living creature sings. *It is song that moves heaven and earth without effort, stirs emotions in the invisible spirits and gods, brings harmony to the relations between men and women, and calms the hearts of fierce warriors.*

Our poetry appeared at the dawn of creation. (McCullough 1985:4, emphasis mine)

Moreover, those orally pronounced words had to be pure Japanese words (*Yamatokotoba*), not Sino-Japanese loans, as the word-mana existed only in traditional Japanese speech. The dynamic and often problematic relationship between native "Japanese spirit" (*wakon*) and imported technology or "Chinese learning" (*kansai*) that has characterized the whole of Japanese history to the present day is clearly intimated in Japanese poetic history.

Despite the fact that the Japanese poetic tradition became a largely written one in and after the tenth century, numerous poetic treatises continued thereafter to counsel poets to pay ample attention to the sound (*shirabe*) of their compositions and to avoid locutions difficult to comprehend by ear. Even in private, the Japanese poem was best apprehended by softly chanting it to oneself, as indicated by the practice of the great medieval poet Fujiwara Shunzei 藤原俊成 (1114–1204), described here by his son:

> Very late at night he would sit by his bed in front of an oil lamp so dim that it was difficult to tell whether it was burning or not, and with a court robe black with age thrown over his shoulders and an old court cap pulled down to his ears, he would lean on an arm-rest, hugging a wooden brazier for warmth, while he recited verse to himself in an undertone. Deep into the night when everyone else was asleep he would sit there bent over, weeping softly.[20]

The thirty-one syllable *waka* poem is still today chanted in formal situations in five separate parts. Linked verse (*renga*, an outgrowth of *waka* in which seventeen- and fourteen-syllable verses are combined into hundred-link sequences) was also primarily composed and apprehended aurally. Each verse was composed mentally and submitted by voice alone for the delectation of the assembled poets and the critical judgment of the scribe, who again chanted it; only when accepted by the scribe and the linked-verse master was the verse written down and then chanted again. The linked-verse master Kensai 兼載 (1452–1510) counseled a three-breath chant for three-unit (seventeen-syllable) verses and two breaths for those of two units (fourteen syllables).[21] The chanted delivery no doubt helped give rise to the convention that prohibits beginning any of the five segments with a connective grammatical particle. That in turn contributed to each of the five segments a basic *aural* quality of self-containment. The fundamental oral quality of the genre, therefore, exerted a strong influence on the final written form of the verses.

In the case of the vernacular tale (*monogatari*) as well, the rhetorical stance is predominantly oral, one of a narrator speaking to an audience. The earliest extant collection of Japanese poetry, the *Man'yōshū*, includes this pair of verses (MYS 3: 236–237 [Kojima et al., 1971:199–200]) that demonstrates that much tale literature remained oral even after it was possible to write it down.

A verse bestowed upon the old woman Shii by the Empress:

It has been so long   ina to iedo
since I had to listen to   shiuru Shii no ga

those uninvited tales	shiikatari
old Shii would force upon me	kono koro kikazute
that now I find I miss them!	are koinikeri

A response presented by old woman Shii:

I would rather not,	ina to iedo
but because of your command	katare katare to
to "tell one! tell one!"	norase koso
Shii will tell one of those	Shii iwamōse
tales you call uninvited.	shiikatari to iu

In the same fashion that the English "tale" derives from the verb "to tell," so does the name for the tale genre in Japanese, *monogatari*, derive from the verb "to tell," *kataru*, plus "thing," *mono*. Even after tales came to be composed from the start with brush and paper, they retained elements of their oral beginnings. Thus even when the greatest of the *monogatari*, *The Tale of Genji*, was composed centuries later, the author appears to have adopted a layered narrative framework to give the impression that the written story was being orally delivered. That framework was first posited by Tamagami Takuya, who labeled it the "oral reading theory" or "oral performance theory" (*ondokuron*)(Tamagami 1966a).[22]

The complete narrative construct he posited is as follows:

1. The events in the story are witnessed by various ladies-in-waiting.
2. Years later in their old age, they *tell* the story to another lady-in-waiting while adding their own occasional comments.
3. That second lady, the scribe and editor, writes down those accounts and edits them, while also adding the occasional comment or addition of her own.
4. This written account is then read aloud by yet another lady-in-waiting to an audience, with more occasional asides.

Tamagami's theory holds that one must therefore read with an awareness of not one but several levels of narrators and characterized readers. Current English translations of *The Tale of Genji* do not reflect the multilayered program, perhaps out of consideration for western narrative conventions. For example, one English translation of the tale gives the following two paragraphs from "The Wormwood Patch" chapter (*Omogiu*), which clearly shows a narrated passage and then a characterized narrator making an appearance:

> The princess [Suetsumuhana] stayed there for two years, after which [Genji] moved her to the east lodge at Nijō. Now he could visit her in the course of ordinary business. It could no longer be said that he treated her badly.

Though no one has asked me to do so, I should like to describe the surprise of the assistant viceroy's wife at this turn of events, and Jijū's pleasure and guilt. But it would be a bother and my head is aching; and perhaps— these things do happen, they say—something will someday remind me to continue the story. (Seidensticker 1985, 2:302)

The end of the second paragraph could also be translated: ". . . but my head is aching and I don't feel up to it. Perhaps there will another time when I can offer you the rest, *she said* (*to zo*)."[23] The first English translation above gives the impression that we are dealing from the first with a written medium, and that the author, like Jane Austen, was writing a story with one narrator who addresses a silently reading audience. But the underlying oral construct of the work suggests that the different reading indicated in the second English translation may be the more accurate. The structure of the passage may imply that it is actually being narrated by an old lady-in-waiting who then steps out of her role as a narrator and orally gives an aside about her reasons for not continuing. And finally a *second* lady-in-waiting records the oral remarks in written form, adding the final quotative particles *to zo*.

The second lady, the scribe and editor, is thus to some extent both reader and author, at least where she adds the quotation. In other passages the scribe comments at greater length on the testimony of the older witness. The question of the nature of the characterized and implied readers therefore becomes considerably more complex in the context of the *monogatari* tale.

The construct also affected point of view. If the tale were to be ostensibly based on the commentary of witnesses, complete narratorial omniscience regarding the minds of the principal characters became impossible. This narratorial formulation at once complicated the authorial task and made the resultant discourse more vague, conjectural, and in a sense truer to the reader's own limited experience than a completely omniscient text could have been. There are passages, however, where the author could not maintain her reportorial pose and entered directly into the minds of main characters (Stinchecum 1980:375–376).

Now, of course, this was only the narrative construct; Murasaki Shikibu was a single individual producing a *written* work, not an oral one. A rhetorical strategy that posited actual eyewitness accounts authenticated the tale and lent it credibility.

In addition, the oral construct of the narrative elegantly reflected the predominantly oral form in which the tales were initially received at court. *The Tale of Genji* and many other *monogatari* of the time were not originally composed as preconceived totalities then disseminated in written form. They were instead written as serials, with each chapter composed then read aloud to the highborn literary patron or patroness for whom they were first intended. If the work proved popular, a sequel would be added, then another sequel, with the larger world of the story taking shape only gradually. Later the entire work might be copied and disseminated in written form, and even then it would as likely as not be read aloud to a group of listeners.

It was one of the tasks of ladies-in-waiting to make copies of popular stories for a larger court readership. Murasaki Shikibu attested to this practice in her diary:

> We now learned that the Consort [Shōshi] was preparing to have us copy a book for the royal collection. . . . We selected writing paper in several shades, arranged them, matched each booklet of the *monogatari* with an appropriate amount of paper, and sent them off to other quarters with notes requesting those ladies' participation. This was labor enough; but once the copying was completed, I worked day and night assembling and binding the booklets.[24]

Serial production and corporate copying meant that each chapter was separately bound, a practice that inevitably gave rise to variations in chapter order. Fascicles of *Sarashina nikki*, for example, were later bound in the wrong order and continued to be read that way until 1924, when rigorous textual criticism unequivocally demonstrated the errors that had caused earlier scholars to dismiss the work as "a vague, rambling account" (Morris 1971a:30–34). Serial production also meant that an author was free to go back and add earlier chapters to flesh out a good story. Most scholars agree that some of the fifty-four chapters of *The Tale of Genji* were not written in their present order (Gatten 1981).

Konishi Jin'ichi has even suggested that stylistic changes in some *monogatari* may have been the result of a change in patronage as the writing continued (Konishi 1986:274). The first duty of the author was, after all, to her highborn mistress, who provided the copyists and the extremely expensive paper for the project. A change in audience could very likely bring about a change in authorial approach.

The original oral delivery could also constitute a critical baptism of fire for the work, and the author was free to rewrite the story after seeing in person the effects of her work on the group of listeners. There are numerous manuscript variants of Sei Shōnagon's *The Pillow Book*, some of which may represent later emendations by the author herself (Konishi 1986:385).

Fittingly, a passage in *The Tale of Genji* itself makes specific reference to the contemporary oral mode of *monogatari* reception, in which the tale, after being written down, was read aloud by a lady-in-waiting to her highborn mistress, who listened while looking at painted illustrations. The passage reads, "[Nakanokimi] had pictures and such brought out, and [she and

Ukifune] looked at them while Ukon read the texts."[25] The twelfth-century *The Tale of Genji Scroll* (*Genji monogatari emaki* 源氏物語絵巻) contains an illustration of the scene (that illustration is reproduced here).[26] The full narratorial schema, then, that Murasaki Shikibu seems to have had in mind for reader reception of *The Tale of Genji* is as follows:

The "Oral Performance Theory" of *monogatari*

1. Fictional world of the characters
2. Recollections of aged witnesses, with comments
3. Scribe/Editor's transcription, with comments
4. Reader of the transcription in the text, with comments
5. Actual reader/reciter of text
6. Highborn audience

Though the tale was certainly often read in private, diary evidence shows that *The Tale of Genji* continued for centuries to be read aloud to groups of listeners. *Saga no kayoi* 嵯峨の通ひ (*Visiting Saga*) by the medieval courtier Asukai Masaari 飛鳥井雅有 (1241–1301) chronicles a two-month period in 1269 in which the work was read aloud to a group of court literati by the wife of Fujiwara Tameie 藤原為家 (1198–1275), the master of the house and head of the main poetic school of the period. Masaari's entry for the seventeenth of the ninth month, 1269, reads in part as follows:

> Seventeenth. I called about noon. They began *The Tale of Genji* and asked the mistress of the house to read and comment on the text. She read from behind the blinds. It was fascinating, far better than when read [*yomu*] by the usual sort of person. It would seem the *Genji* traditions of her house have been transmitted to her. We read to the "Lavender" chapter.
>
> When evening came we drank sake poured by two ladies summoned by the master of the house [Tameie]. The mistress called me over to her curtain and said, ". . . Few are the times in the past that poets have met at this acclaimed house at Ogurayama and refreshed their spirits with elegant conversation about tale literature [*monogatari*]. I thought there were none left, but I find that you indeed are like the men of old." She favored me with these and other elegant remarks. The host was a kind man well on in years, and when in his cups, his tears overflowed. We parted at dawn. (Tanaka 1985:61–62)[27]

The "mistress of the house" herself was a well-known literata; after the death of her famous husband she took Buddhist orders and as "The Nun Abutsu" 阿仏尼 (d. 1283?) went on to write *The Diary of the Waning Moon* (*Izayoi nikki* 十六夜日記), a classic of the medieval travel diary genre. Her oral delivery plus commentary on *The Tale of Genji* was necessary in part because that was the way the tale had often been traditionally apprehended, and in part because the vernacular in which the text was originally composed had in the intervening centuries already begun its development into a

"[Nakanokimi] had pictures and such brought out, and [she and Ukifune] looked at them while Ukon read the texts." *The Tale of Genji Scroll* (*Genji monogatari emaki,* twelfth century). Courtesy of the Tokugawa Reimeikai.

written, classical style, increasingly divorced from colloquial speech and current customs.

The most famous of the "war tales" (*gunki monogatari*), *The Tale of the Heike*, likewise demonstrates the essential orality of the *monogatari* form. It will be recalled that though the vulgate version of the text was written down, its primary form of reception throughout the medieval period was through vocal performances by blind lute players who chanted segments of the memorized text to their own lute accompaniment. Kenneth Butler has proposed that the textual history of *The Tale of the Heike* is one of reoralization, wherein an original *kanbun* text was gradually reworked into chantable form (Butler 1966a, 1966b). Like *The Tale of Genji*, then, the predominant form of reception of this most famous of war tales was oral, delivered via a written text, though here not read but memorized.

Once the great *monogatari* were written down, their language was necessarily fixed in time. But spoken language is never stable, and as the centuries passed the old vernacular tales became increasingly difficult to comprehend aurally. By the early modern (kinsei) period (1600–1868), *The Tale of Genji* was normally read in book form in conjunction with commentaries. The style of the Heian-period *monogatari*, which had originally been very close to the spoken vernacular, therefore became a written, literary form, imperfectly understood without recourse to scholarly annotations. Indeed, by the early modern period Japan boasted a literary history of more than a thousand years, and most writers worked in literary styles more or less influenced by earlier classical forms divorced from current oral speech. It would not be until the late nineteenth century and the Western-influenced advent of the *genbun'itchi* 言文一致 movement to unify speech and writing that the gap between spoken Japanese and the language of high literature would again come as close to disappearing as it had in *The Tale of Genji* of nearly a millennium before.[28]

NOTES

This is a revised and expanded version of a paper presented at a colloquium titled "Is Reading a Universal?" with Brian Stock (University of Toronto) and Daniel Boyarin (University of California, Berkeley) at the Townsend Center for the Humanities, University of California, Berkeley, November 13, 1990. I would like to thank Professors Terry Kleeman, William McCullough, and Marian Ury for helpful suggestions made during the preparation of this study. Japanese names throughout this article appear in Japanese order, with given name following surname.

1. For an introduction to the Chinese language, see Ramsey (1987) and Norman (1988); for Japanese, see Miller (1967), Martin (1988), and Shibatani (1990).

2. Adapted from Konishi (1984:81). For a translation of the entire account, see Tsunoda 1951:1–6.

3. The first mention of this practice occurs in the *Nihon shoki* 日本書紀 (720), fourth year of the reign of Emperor Richū, whose traditional dates are 319–409 C.E. (Sakamoto et al. 1965–1967, 1:426).

4. Together with these Confucian and Buddhist concepts, the Seventeen Article Constitution also incorporated Chinese Taoist and Legalist concepts. The original version of the work does not survive; we know it through a copy preserved in the *Nihon shoki* (Sakamoto et al. 1965–1967, 2:180–187).

5. The presence of graffiti on the walls of eighth-century structures suggests that a broad section of the nonaristocratic population had also acquired a degree of literacy by this period.

6. For more on the cultural activities of provincial warriors, see Horton (1986).

7. On the religious and political uses of early song, see Ebersole (1989).

8. The early Japanese terms for "word" and "thing" (*koto*) were identical. I use for convenience the modern Hepburn romanization for ancient as well as modern Japanese. The phonology of the language of the eighth century (to say nothing of even earlier forms) was considerably different from that of modern Japanese. See Lange (1973).

9. Most graphs do, however, contain a phonetic hint as to their pronunciation. Bernard Karlgren holds that fully 90 percent of Chinese characters include a "signific" and a "phonetic" element. See Karlgren (1924:4).

10. For more on this process, see Miller (1967) and Kōno (1969).

11. 修 is, however, not usually used as a cursive model for /su/.

12. The passage appears in the *Hosshi kudokuhon* 法師功徳品 chapter. Hurvitz (1976:266) translates the phrase, "The asuras,/ Dwelling by the edge of the great sea."

13. The orthographic system was not regularized until after Meiji Restoration of 1868 when Japan emerged from its more than two centuries of seclusion. It was at that time that one *hiragana* character and one *katakana* character were chosen to represent each of the forty-eight separate syllables in the language. The system was further refined to its current two sets of forty-six symbols after World War II.

14. See Bowring (1988) and Shirane (1987).

15. All three works are available in English translation; see Waley (1960), Seidensticker (1985), Morris (1967), and McCullough and McCullough (1980). For more on the literature of ladies-in-waiting, see Horton (1993).

16. For more on the culture of Japanese society in the Heian period, see Sansom (1984) and Morris (1969).

17. Adapted from Konishi (1986:378).

18. For an English translation, see McCullough (1988).

19. There were also versions of the tale meant purely for reading. See Butler (1966a and 1966b) and Ruch (1991). My use of "vocal literature" is based on Barbara Ruch's distinction between "oral literature," which "is a product of and flourishes in a world of illiteracy," and "vocal literature," which "has . . . firm ties to the written language . . . [and] was usually based upon written texts." See Ruch (1977).

20. The reminiscence was handed down by the linked-verse poet Shinkei 心敬 (1406–1475). See Ijichi et al. (1973:136). The translation is adapted from Brower and Miner (1961:257).

21. Kensai 兼載, *Shuhitsu no omomuki* 執筆之趣 (*The Duties of the Scribe*) (Kaneko 1987:128).

22. For an examination of the implications of Tamagami's work, see Nakano (1971).

23. The passage in the original reads:

Futatose bakari kono furumiya ni nagametamaite, Higashi no in to iu tokoro ni namu, nochi wa watashitatematsuritamaikeru. Taimen shitamau koto nado wa, ito katakeredo, chikaki shime no hodo ni te, ōkata ni mo wataritamau ni, sashinozoki nado shitamaitoutou, ito anazurawashige ni motenashi kikoetamawazu.

Kano Daini no Kitanokata, noborite odorokiomoeru sama, Jijū ga, ureshiki mono no, ima shibashi machikikoezarikeru kokoroasasa o hazukashū omoeru hodo nado, ima sukoshi towazugatari mo semahoshikeredo, ito kashira itō, urusaku monoukereba, ima mata mo tsuide aramu ori ni, omoiidete namu *kikoyu* beki, *to zo*. (Tamagami 1966b, 3:156)

24. Adapted from Konishi (1986:273). For a translation of *Murasaki Shikibu Diary* (*Murasaki Shikibu nikki*), see Bowring (1982).

25. The passage appears in "The Eastern Cottage" (*Azumaya*) chapter (cf. Seidensticker 2:958). The original reads: *E nado toriidesasete, Ukon ni kotoba yomasete mitamau ni. . . .* (Tamagami 1966b, 9:167).

26. For a reproduction and discussion of the picture scroll, see Morris (1971b).

27. It will be noted that the lady of the house did not simply read the text, but she also provided a running commentary. "It would seem the *Genji* traditions of her house have been transmitted to her" is the editor's interpretation of the problematic *narai abekameri*, literally "it seems there must be a custom."

28. For an introduction to the *genbun'itchi* movement, see Twine (1978 and 1988).

REFERENCES

Bowring, Richard, trans.

1982   *Murasaki Shikibu: Her Diary and Poetic Memoirs*. With study. Princeton: Princeton University Press.

1988   *Murasaki Shikibu: The Tale of Genji*. Cambridge: Cambridge University Press.

Brower, Robert, and Earl Miner

1961   *Japanese Court Poetry*. Stanford: Stanford University Press.

Butler, Kenneth

1966a   "The Textual Evolution of the Heike Monogatari." *Harvard Journal of Asiatic Studies* 26:5–51.

1966b   "The Heike Monogatari and Theories of Oral Epic Literature." *Bulletin of the Faculty of Letters, The Seikei University* 2:37–54.

Dahood, Mitchell, ed.

1965   Psalms I (1–50). The Anchor Bible. Vol. 16. Garden City, N.Y.: Doubleday.

Ebersole, Gary L.

1989   *Ritual Poetry and the Politics of Death in Early Japan*. Princeton: Princeton University Press.

Fujii, Sadakazu 藤井貞和

1985   "Bungaku izen" 文学以前. In *Nihon bungaku shinshi* 日本文学新史, vol. 1. Ed. Nakanishi Susumu 中西進, pp. 26–47. Tōkyō: Shibundō.

Gatten, Aileen

1981   "The Order of the Early Chapters in the Genji Monogatari." *Harvard Journal of Asiatic Studies* 41:5–46.

Horton, H. Mack

1986   "Saiokuken Sōchō and the Linked-Verse Business." *The Transactions of the Asiatic Society of Japan*. 4th ser., vol. 1:45–78.

1993   "They Also Serve: Ladies-in-Waiting in *The Tale of Genji*." In *Approaches to Teaching Murasaki Shikibu's The Tale of Genji*. Ed. Edward Kamens. New York: The Modern Language Association of America.

Hurvitz, Leon, trans.

1976   *Scripture of the Lotus Blossom of the Fine Dharma*. New York: Columbia University Press.

Ichiko, Teiji 市古貞次, ed.

1973   *Heike monogatari: Nihon koten bungaku zenshū*. Vols. 29, 30. Tōkyō: Shōgakukan.

Ijichi, Tetsuo 伊地知鐵男, ed.

1973   *Sasamegoto* ささめごと. In *Rengaronshū, nōgakuronshū, haironshū*. Ed. Ijichi Tetsuo, Omote Akira 表章, and Kuriyama Riichi 栗山理一, pp. 63–160. Tōkyō: Shōgakukan.

Kaneko, Kinjirō 金子金治郎,

1987   *Renga sôron* 連歌総論. Tōkyō: Ōfūsha.

Karlgren, Bernard
  1974.   *Analytic Dictionary of Chinese and Sino-Japanese.* New York: Dover
               Publications.
Kojima, Noriyuki 小島憲之, Kinoshita Masatoshi 木下正俊, and Satake Akihiro
佐竹昭広, eds.
  1971   *Man'yōshū* 万葉集. Vol. 1. Tōkyō: Shōgakukan.
Konishi, Jin'ichi 小西甚一
  1984   *A History of Japanese Literature.* Vol. 1. Trans. Aileen Gatten and
               Nicholas Teele, ed. Earl Miner. Princeton: Princeton University
               Press.
  1986   *A History of Japanese Literature.* Vol. 2. Trans. Aileen Gatten, ed. Earl
               Miner. Princeton: Princeton University Press.
Kōno, Rokurō
  1969   "The Chinese Writing and Its Influences on the Scripts of the
               Neighbouring Peoples." In *Memoirs of the Research Department of the
               Toyo Bunko* 27:83–140.
Lange, Roland
  1973   *The Phonology of Eighth-Century Japanese: A Reconstruction Based upon
               Written Records.* Tōkyō: Sophia University.
McCullough, Helen Craig, trans.
  1985   *Kokin Wakashū.* With annotations by the translator. Stanford: Stan-
               ford University Press.
  1988   *The Tale of the Heike.* With an introduction by the translator. Stan-
               ford: Stanford University Press.
McCullough, William H., and Helen Craig McCullough, trans.
  1980   *A Tale of Flowering Fortunes. Annals of Japanese Aristocratic Life in the
               Heian Period.* With an introduction and notes by the translators. 2
               vols. Stanford: Stanford University Press.
Martin, Samuel E.
  1988   *The Japanese Language Through Time.* New Haven: Yale University
               Press.
Miller, Roy Andrew
  1967   *The Japanese Language.* Chicago: University of Chicago Press.
Mōri, Masamori 毛利正守
  1985   "Moji ni yoru bungaku" 文字による文学. In *Nihon bungaku shinshi*
               日本文学新史, vol. 1. Ed. Nakanishi Susumu 中西進, pp. 26–47.
               Tōkyō: Shibundō.
Morris, Ivan
  1969   *The World of the Shining Prince.* Baltimore, Maryland: Penguin Books.
Morris, Ivan, trans.
  1967   *The Pillow Book of Sei Shōnagon.* 2 vols. New York: Columbia Uni-
               versity Press.
  1971a   *As I Crossed A Bridge of Dreams: Recollections of a Woman in Eleventh-
               Century Japan.* New York: The Dial Press.
  1971b   *The Tale of Genji Scroll.* Introduction by Tokugawa Yoshinobu.
               Tōkyō and Palo Alto: Kōdansha International.

Norman, Jerry
    1988   *Chinese*. Cambridge: Cambridge University Press.
Nakano, Kōichi 中野幸一
    1971   "Genji monogatari no sōshiji to monogatari ondokuron" 源氏物語
                の草子地と物語音読論. In *Genji monogatari*, vol. 1. Ed. Nihon Bun-
                gaku Kenkyū Shiryō Sōsho, pp. 203–212. Tōkyō: Yūseidō.
Origuchi, Shinobu 折口信夫
    1954   *Origuchi Shinobu zenshū*. Vol. 1. Tōkyō: Chūōkōronsha.
Ramsey, S. Robert
    1987   *The Languages of China*. Princeton: Princeton University Press.
Ruch, Barbara
    1977   "Medieval Jongleurs and the Making of a National Literature." In
                Japan in the Muromachi Age. Ed. John Hall and Toyoda Takeshi,
                pp. 279–309. Berkeley, Los Angeles, and London: University of
                California Press.
    1991   "Akashi no Kakuichi." *Journal of the Association of Teachers of Japanese*
                24(1):35–47.
Sakamoto, Tarō 坂本太郎, Ienaga Saburō 家永三郎, Inoue Mitsusada 井上光貞,
and Ōno Susumu 大野晋
    1965–67   *Nihon shoki* 日本書紀. 2 vols. Nihon koten bungaku taikei, vols. 67,
                68. Tōkyō: Iwanami Shoten.
Sakamoto, Yukio 坂本幸男 and Iwamoto Yutaka 岩本裕, eds.
    1977   *Hokekyō* 法華経. 3 vols. Tōkō: Iwanami Shoten.
Sansom, George
    1984   "The Rule of Taste." In *A History of Japan*, vol. 3, pp. 178–196.
                Tōkyō and Rutland, Vt.: Charles E. Tuttle Co.
Seidensticker, Edward G., trans.
    1985   *The Tale of Genji*. 2 vols. Tōkyō and Rutland, Vt.: Charles E. Tuttle
                Co.
Shibatani, Masayoshi
    1990   *The Languages of Japan*. Cambridge: Cambridge University Press.
Shirane, Haruo
    1987   *The Bridge of Dreams: A Poetics of "The Tale of Genji."* Stanford: Stan-
                ford University Press.
Stinchecum, Amanda Mayer
    1980   "Who Tells the Tale? 'Ukifune': A Study in Narrative Voice." In
                Monumenta Nipponica 35(4):375–403.
Tamagami, Takuya 玉上琢弥
    1966a   "Monogatari ondokuron josetsu" 物語音読論序説 and "Genji
                monogatari no dokusha" 源氏物語の読者. In *Genji monogatari ken-
                kyū*, supplemental vol. (*bekkan*) 1 of *Genji monogatari hyōshaku*, pp. 143–
                155, 247–265. Tōkyō: Kadokawa Shoten.
Tamagami, Takuya, ed.
    1966b   *Genji monogatari*. 10 vols. Tōkyō: Kadokawa Shoten.
Tanaka, Norio 田中祝夫, ed.
    1985   *Asukai Masaari nikki zenshaku* 飛鳥井雅有日記全釈. Tōkyō: Kazama
                Shobō.

Tōdō, Akiyasu 藤堂明保
1984   *Gakken kanwa daijiten* 学研漢和大字典. Tōkyō: Gakushū Kenkyūsha.
Tsugita, Masaki 次田真幸, ed.
1986   *Kojiki* 古事記. 3 vols. Tōkyō: Kōdansha Ltd.
Tsunoda, Ryusaku
1951   *Japan in the Chinese Dynastic Histories: Later Han Through Ming Dynasties*. South Pasadena, Calif.: P.D. and Ione Perkins.
Tsunoda, Ryusaku, Wm. Theodore de Bary, and Donald Keene, eds.
1969   *Sources of Japanese Tradition.* Vol. 1. New York and London: Columbia University Press.
Twine, Nanette
1978   "The Genbun'itchi Movement: Its Origin, Development, and Conclusion." *Monumenta Nipponica* 33(3):333–356.
1988   "Standardizing Written Japanese: A Factor in Modernization." *Monumenta Nipponica* 43(4):429–454.
Waley, Arthur, trans.
1960   *The Tale of Genji.* New York: Random House.

NINE

Textual Interpretation as Collective Action

Elizabeth Long

In her provocative book, *Academic Writing as Social Practice*, Linda Brodkey explores and assails what she calls the image of "the writer who writes alone." As she says,

> When we picture writing we see a solitary writer. We may see the writer alone in a cold garret, working into the small hours of the morning by thin candle-light. The shutters are closed. Or perhaps we see the writer alone in a well-appointed study, seated at a desk, fingers poised over the keys of a typewriter (or microcomputer). The drapes are drawn. . . . Whether the scene of writing is poetic or prosaic . . . it is the same picture—the writer writes alone. . . . And because such a picture prevails as the reigning trope for writing, we find it difficult to remember that the solitary scribbler tells only one story about writers and writing. In this story, writers are sentenced to solitary confinement, imprisoned by language. . . . We know this story well, for there are moments when the solitude overwhelms us, when we do not understand the words we are writing, and when we cannot recall our reasons for doing so. (1987:54–55)

Brodkey claims that the image of the solitary scribbler is "taken from the album of modernism," and that it presents a hegemonic vision of writing by reifying only one moment of the writing process—the timeless freeze-frame of isolation and alienation. This "official story," according to her account, is replicated both in modern formalist literary criticism, which construes the autonomous and self-referential text as a "homologue of the alienated artist," and in academic studies of "composition," as a purely individualistic and cognitive affair (1987:57–70). I would contend that modernism provides just one permutation of the ideology of the "writer-who-writes-alone," one that puts the spin of romantically alienated genius on a far older story. Nonetheless, I agree with Brodkey that the image of the solitary scribbler is an ideological synecdoche that truncates our understanding of writing by overprivileging the moment of isolation. It also suppresses the social aspects of writing: reading other writers, discussing ideas with other people, and writing to and for others in a language whose very grammar, genres, and figures of speech encode collectivity. As Raymond Williams puts it in "The Tenses of the Imagination":

> I am in fact physically alone when I am writing, and I do not believe, taking it all in all, that my work has been less individual, in that defining and valuing sense, than that of others. Yet whenever I write I am aware of a society and of a language which I know are vastly larger than myself: not simply "out there," in a world of others, but here, in what I am engaged in doing: composing and relating. (1983:261)

Our understanding of reading is, I argue, governed by a similarly powerful and similarly partial picture of the solitary reader. In reader response theory, this isolated individual appears in several guises: the phenomenological reader of Poulet and Iser, the subjective or psychoanalytic reader of Bleich and Holland, the "ideal reader" spun out of textual strategies imputed by the academic analyst, even, to a certain degree the "resisting reader" who is a women, although there at least the individual reader brings a social identity to her encounter with the text (Bleich 1975, 1987; Fetterley 1978; Holland 1968, 1975; Iser 1974, 1978) .

The solitary reader also has a complex iconographic history, and I would like to summon it up briefly as indicative of some of the lenses through which we have envisioned reading as a cultural practice—lenses that have not always clarified the object of inquiry. The first set of images represents a tradition that begins in early Christian art and continues through the nineteenth century. Here the reader, like the writer who writes alone, is withdrawn from the world, and suspended from human community and human action. He is a scholar, surrounded by the symbolic attributes of serious research. Or he considers the book and his own mortality—whose grim aspect can be transcended through the word, which links each reader to another man in a genealogy of immortal ideas, and, in its most serious and sacred aspect, harks back to that original author, the transcendent patriarchal God who was, in the beginning, the word. These images represent the sacral aura of reading in a period of severely limited and, among Christians, mostly clerical literacy. The boundaries between reading and writing are blurred because both are privileges of scriptural authority, but such authority exacts its price: the scholar-anchorite is allowed at most a distant view of the sensuous delights of earthly intercourse. These images not only oppose reading to sociability and the vita activa, but also privilege a certain kind of reading: erudite, ideational, analytic, and as morally and intellectually weighty as the tomes that inhabit these cells and are inhabited by their solitary readers. This is the visual topos of the serious reader, and, however diluted his lineage has been by secularization, mass education, democracy, and affirmative action, as academics we are all his heirs.[1]

The initial perturbations of these vast social transformations—which brought literacy to new constituencies of class and gender—were recorded in late medieval images of the Virgin Mary and the Magdalen reading, illustrations that began to appear in the psalters and books of hours destined for aristocratic and often female readers. As the secular and private sphere of leisure expanded, images of women reading proliferated. Seventeenth-century Holland, whose commercial expansion fueled an iconographic revolution that elevated the bourgeois interior as subject and what one might call "domestic realism" as genre, was a particularly fruitful site for early modern representations of the figure of the female reader. In such pictures, the solitary woman reads, encompassed by an interior that is no less timeless than the scholarly study, but profoundly domestic. Her reading is inscribed within the family circle, and, as in the painting by Metsu, her "serious" reading is interruptible. Usually, in fact, she reads a note, so her reading is ephemeral, and circumscribed by the personal ties of affective relationships. If the scholar transcends the world, she is firmly positioned in the mundane. In Vermeer's painting, the map of the world pulls us toward the distant horizon of Dutch mercantile adventures, while the woman preserves the heart of the home. But the letter seems to mediate between the two, bringing the outer world inside, and enabling the woman to go beyond a purely interior life through her reading.

By the eighteenth and nineteenth centuries, many images of women reading alone complement those of the serious male reader/writer. Domesticity continues to frame these readers, but now it is less serene than sensuous, frilled, frivolous. The pictures celebrate the sheen and softness of the feminine sphere; they are as decorative as the women, and the books—grown tiny now—serve as the cultural decorations of a literacy at once leisurely and trivialized. The women themselves are less contemplative than langorous, narcissistically absorbed in imaginative literature that helps them while away the hours. Although upper class or solidly bourgeois, these readers provide the iconographic ancestry for our modern conceptualizations of escapist readers of mass market genres (Radway 1984).[2] Such women do not read to write, but passively consume . . . what? Perhaps the novels whose moral effects were so debated one hundred and fifty years ago. When these women do write, it is not books, but letters, as is so delicately portrayed in a picture by Marie Cassatt. Thus the solitary woman reader/writer finds her ideological place in a binary opposition that associates authoritative men with the production and dissemination of serious or high culture, and even privileged women with the consumption and "creation" of ephemeral or questionable culture.[3]

Antonella Da Messina, *St. Jerome in His Study*. Reproduced by courtesy of the Trustees, The National Gallery, London.

Johannes Vermeer, *The Astronomer*. The Louvre. Copyright Photo R.M.N.

Important distortions of either pole of real literacy are wrought by this gender dichotomization of icons of reading—the solitary male representing a simplistic image of even high cultural literacy, the image of the self-absorbed female delimiting women even as it trivializes the notion of culture as soft and inconsequential. Moreover, their very iconographic absence shows that certain class and racial groups' access to representations of reading has been even more circumscribed than their access to literacy itself. But rather than exploring such issues, I would like to concentrate instead on some consequences of construing textual interpretation as a funda-

Edgar Degas, *Edmond Duranty in His Study*. Private collection, Washington, D.C.

mentally solitary practice. All involve suppression of the collective nature of reading. Most of the essay will focus on one sociocultural form—the group of readers—that has been rendered all but invisible to academic analysis, so I will briefly point out some other theoretical and empirical repressions that are accomplished by the cultural hegemony of "the solitary reader."

Theoretically, this trope locates reading securely in the realm of private life. This is problematic because of pervasive assumptions in social science

Vittore Carpaccio, *The Virgin Reading*. National Gallery of Art, Washington. Samuel H. Kress Collection.

Gabriel Metsu, *The Letter.* Courtesy of The Putnam Foundation, Timkin Museum of Art, San Diego, California.

that there exists a strict and exclusive dichotomy between public and private life, and that significant social development and change occur only within the public realm. Such views privilege the level of large formal institutions and macrosocial processes, whose development has, it is assumed, characterized the emerging contours of the modern world and similarly shaped the contours of social identity. Further, the most important locus of social change is also presumed to be large and organized aggregates of people, so here, too, the public realm is held to be paramount. If practices such as reading, and other forms of cultural consumption, are fit into this procrustean dichotomy, they tend to fall analytically into the "private" sphere of solitary activity, which leads theorists to see them as epiphenomenal, mar-

Johannes Vermeer, *Woman in Blue Reading a Letter*. Courtesy of the Rijksmuseum, Amsterdam.

Jean Honore Fragonard, *A Young Girl Reading*. National Gallery of Art, Washington. Gift of Mrs. Mellon Bruce in memory of her father, Andrew W. Mellon.

Jean Baptiste Camille Corot, *The Magdalen Reading*. The Louvre. Copyright Photo R.M.N.

ginal, or inconsequential: constituted by "macro" processes rather than, at least in part, constitutive of social identity and the sociocultural order. See Anthony Giddens's work for one overview of this tradition, and an attempt to destabilize this categorial framework (1979, 1984). Jürgen Habermas has outlined a more interesting relationship between public and private spheres than the traditional dichotomy, although feminist critics take him to task for not pushing his critique far enough (Fraser 1989; Habermas 1989). There is an important self-alienated irony here, since as intellectuals most of us are moved to write not only by instrumental imperatives, but by the conviction that our ideas may have effects on those who read them, a conviction that calls into question at least some of the above distinctions and assumptions.

The theoretical location of reading in the private sphere or, most extremely, in the heads of isolated individuals (and obviously, like Brodkey, I do not mean to deny the immensely private aspects of reading, but only their reification as the whole story) neglects two crucial aspects of its collective nature. The first I will discuss is the social *infrastructure* that is necessary, at the most concrete level, for enabling and sustaining literacy and sustained reading itself.

By the "social infrastructure of reading" I mean two things. Foundationally, that reading must be taught, and that socialization into reading always takes place within specific social relationships. Early images show mothers teaching children how to read, which substitutes a relational maternal lineage of literacy for the abstract paternal genealogy of books and ideas that assumes both adulthood and prior reading competence. Familial reading is both a form of cultural capital, and one of the most important determinants of adherence to reading in later life.

Classrooms provide a more formal, public context for teaching reading, and one that varies immensely depending on who the parties to the relationship are, partially explaining why reading rarely "takes" among certain groups of students. As Daniel and Lauren Resnick explain in their essay on "Varieties of Literacy," books and reading can be profoundly transformed in the school setting: "A test, as in school literature courses, for example, can change the context for even the best of literary texts from pleasure-giving literacy to functional literacy" (1989:188). At its best, this social relationship can open up new ways of reading (symbols, structure, attention to intertextuality), while at its worst, it can produce "the deadly serious word," and a sense of thralldom to a deadening educational process. This can so alienate poor students that they never feel the pleasure of the text, and leads even good students to invent ways of reclaiming the autonomy of their reading from scholastic authority—by, for example, reading ahead so as not to read "for class."

Even beyond formal socialization into reading, the habit of reading is profoundly social. As mid-century American empirical studies of adult reading show, social isolation depresses readership, and social involvement encourages it. Most readers need the support of talk with other readers, the participation in a social milieu in which books are "in the air" (Berelson 1949; Ennis 1965; Mathews 1973; McElroy 1968a, 1968b; Yankelovich 1978).

Reading thus requires, in the second sense of the term, an infrastructure as *social base*, in much the same way as modern transportation requires a physical infrastructure of highways, airports, and fuel supplies. Robert Darnton's multifaceted study of the Enlightenment in France represents perhaps the best example of what it means to take seriously the social infrastructure of a literary movement—one that has been remembered as a constellation of philosophical giants which, through abstracted processes of dissemination, set in motion the avalanche of social revolution and cultural modernity. In a series of books and articles, Darnton anatomizes the complex web of commerce, law, literary patronage, and ideosyncratically responsive readers who in fact constituted the literary culture of the Enlightenment. In his analysis, mercenary Swiss typesetters and monopolistic Parisian publishers, corrupt censors, ill-paid peddlars, and cunning book smugglers working provincial byways and local fairs were the circulatory system that gave life to the Enlightenment.

More subtly, he argues that the content of the Enlightenment itself was much more complex and closely linked to popular forms and audiences than its representation in the twentieth century academy indicates. Would-be philosophes, literary hacks, and readers who ordered erotica or scurrilous, crudely antiauthoritarian political pamphlets much more commonly than Diderot or Rousseau, or who, if they ordered Rousseau, read him as a manual for how to raise their children, such people—the bastards of literacy—created the political ferment and shift in moral sensibility whose development we have enshrined in a legitimate genealogy of great thinkers and the intellectual heirs who read them. Understanding the social infrastructure of reading, then, demands reconsideration not just of reading itself, but of the ways we conceptualize culture and its impact on social change (Darnton 1974, 1979, 1982, 1984).

The hegemonic picture of reading as a solitary activity also suppresses the ways in which reading is *socially framed*. By this I mean that collective and institutional processes shape reading practices by authoritatively defining what is worth reading and how to read it. In turn, this authoritative framing has effects on what kinds of books are published, reviewed, and kept in circulation in libraries, classrooms and the marketplace, while legitimating, as well, certain kinds of literary values and correlative modes of reading. Academics tend to repress consideration of variety in reading practices due to our assumptions that everyone reads (or ought to) as we do professionally, privileging the cognitive, ideational, and analytic mode. Further, recognizing the importance of the collective activity that determines the availability of books, privileges certain modes of reading, and valorizes certain books, inevitably brings into view both the commercial underside of literature and the scholar's position of authority within the world of reading. Both raise questions of the politics of culture, including the role of the academy itself. This may partially explain resistance to scholarship that discusses issues of literary value in relation to historically contingent social relationships within the academy and questions of power and authority among the various elites and constituencies that make up the world of literacy.

For example, Fish's work on "interpretive communities," however contentious and nonsociological, demonstrates conclusively that textual interpretion among those Bourdieu calls "professional valuers" is dependent on shifting conventions or paradigms within a hierarchized academic community (1980). It has aroused opposition that seems only partially explicable by his "bad boy" relativism (Bloom 1987; Hirsch 1987). Similarly, another crucial strand of this research into reading has investigated the social relationships among publishers, booksellers, popular and authoritative readers, and aestheticians that determine the fortunes of books by way of the literary canon (Davidson 1986, 1989; Eagleton 1983, 1984; Ohmann 1976, 1987; Smith 1988; Tompkins 1985). Again, the scholarly outcry that has greeted this work seems to a certain degree symptomatic of a desire to return literary debates to the realm of "pure" aesthetics unsullied by commerce or other sociocultural interests.

The ideology of the solitary reader, then, suppresses recognition of the infrastructure of literacy and the social or institutional determinants of what's available to read, what is "worth reading," and how to read it. But perhaps most importantly, it has helped to frame our understanding of the cultural world so that the importance—historically and in the present—of groups of readers and their modes of textual appropriation has been invisible to scholarship. This lacuna also seems related to the prevailing analytic dichotomization of "culture" and "society" and to the related tendency to seek the sources of change either in an idealist conception of "great men of ideas" (the writer who writes alone), or in a materialist frame that locates innovation in abstracted forces of technological determinism.

The empirical and conceptual repression accomplished by the ideology of the solitary reader is most obvious when one begins to examine the relationship of groups of readers to those broad transformations of moral sensibility and social structure that have molded Western culture. Such work is being carried forward by a new generation of cultural historians, whose work promises to undermine some of the constraining conceptual frames mentioned above. Darnton's scholarship exemplifies this orientation. Equally important are Natalie Davis's contributions. For instance, in her important essay on "Printing and the People" in sixteenth century France, she discusses the ways that groups of readers made newly available printed material their own, in so doing becoming not merely vehicles for cultural dissemination but agents of cultural change, sometimes by becoming not just readers but writers as well. At the bottom of the social hierarchy, rural *veillées*, evening gatherings within village communities, began to feature readings from *Le Roman de la Rose* (which brought new ideas about women and love), and perhaps more radically, from the vernacular Bible. Craftsmen, too, read in groups—often instructional books as well as the Bible— and especially if they were printers, occasionally built up reputations as scholars and authors themselves. The most innovative reading groups were probably the secret Protestant assemblies, because, among other reasons, "they brought together men and women who were not necessarily in the same family or craft or even neighborhood" (1975:214).

These groups, which Brian Stock calls "textual communities" (Stock 1983), not only empowered their members, but also helped to create community, sustain collective memory, and challenge tradition.[4] Reading in such contexts, can, in Davis's words, "provide people with new ways to re-

late their doings to authority, new and old" (1975: 214). Groups of readers
clearly gave sixteenth century French women a new sense of their own competence, for Davis's work traces women authors, writing in some numbers
on subjects from poetry to midwifery (this entry into print a bold contesta-
tion of received and often nonempirical medical authority), to participation
in humanist circles that nurtured text-based disputation and conversation.
Attention to such groups of readers enables the analyst to generate a much
more complex and gender-balanced picture of the cultural currents contributing to the moral shifts of early modernity than does acceptance of
the image of the solitary reader.

Reading in groups not only offers occasions for explicitly collective textual interpretation, but encourages new forms of association, and nurtures
new ideas that are developed in conversation with other people as well as
with the books. Reading groups often form because of a subtext of shared
values, and the text itself is often a pretext (though an invaluable one) for
the conversation through which members engage not only with the authorial "other" but with each other as well. In such groups, reading becomes
more communal than our image of the scholar-anchorite would have it, and
more active than the picture of reading as a leisured feminine pastime.
I have claimed elsewhere that they occupy a social space that calls our
received distinction between public and private into question, and offer
forums for critical reflection that have been crucial in negotiating the moral
and ideological dimensions of social identity (Long 1986, 1988).

Two other historical examples demonstrate that the social and intellectual empowerment engendered by this form of cultural association has had
consequences in the realm of social action as well as ideas and indeed constitute a *de facto* demand to reframe the action/idea dichotomy by paying
attention to culture less as a group of static and abstracted values than as
ideas or beliefs articulated and sustained within concrete social practices.
The first, and more familiar, is E. P. Thompson's account of Chartism and
working-class radicalism. In *The Making of the English Working Class*, he
shows that artisanal study groups and correspondence societies played a
crucial role not only in the ideological ferment of reformism, but in stitching
together isolated groups of working men into a powerful social movement
(1964).

Somewhat closer to home, and contributing to a reform movement of
more ambiguous meaning, are the progressive era women's literary societies
and study groups. (Note the changing inflection of gender and class.) In
studies by Karen Blair, Andrea Martin, and Megan Seaholm, it becomes
clear that middle-class women formed reading groups at first for "self-
culture," namely, becoming in today's phrase "culturally literate" (Blair
1980; Martin 1987; Seaholm 1988). But the groups had unexpected consequences. Meeting to discuss Browning or English history brought these

Washburn House Reading Club, 1886. Photo by Notman Photo Co., Boston, Smith College Archives, Smith College.

women out of the home (often despite resistance from husbands and pastors). Deciding on proper procedures gave them a sense of how to organize. Giving reports on the books they read brought them out of genteel silence. They discovered the eloquence of their voices and the strength of their convictions, and very quickly their study circles began addressing more public (although still appropriately womanly) issues of progressive reform: pure food and drug laws, protective legislation for women and children and the establishment of public schools and libraries, parks, and healthy water supplies, to mention a few of their urgent concerns. The Houston Public Library was founded by one such group of women readers, who solicited funds from Andrew Carnegie and persuaded the city government to donate land and budget annual operating expenses (Hatch 1965). And an early twentieth-century reading group of back women in Dallas played a progressive role in developing their community as well, as the historian J. Mason Brewer acknowledged by dedicating his 1935 book on *Negro Legislators of Texas and Their Descendants* to the Ladies Reading Circle of Dallas:

Because of their faithfulness and foresightedness in fostering a cultural program for the older women of their racial group, and because of the inspiration they have given the younger women of their community to read, study, and acquire culture. (Brewer 1935)

My own work, of which this historical discussion is one component, centers on an ethnographic-like investigation of contemporary reading groups, male and mixed-sex as well as female, in Houston, Texas. Already, this scholarship has revealed a far more extensive, varied, and active population of book discussion groups than anyone might have (or has) predicted—at the most elementary level illuminating and unsettling preconceptions about cultural practices that have been shaped by the ideology of the solitary reader. At the beginning of the project, no one—myself included—thought there would be more than six to ten groups in all Houston.[5] A year later, after outreach efforts through contacts among known reading groups, a letter circulated to Rice faculty and staff, and calls to local bookstores and churches, approximately sixty groups were located. By now, I know of between seventy-five and eighty groups, and in order to generate a complete "census" of reading groups in Houston, outreach continues through organizations (e.g., service groups, universities and their alumni groups, special interest groups), churches, and bookstores, with a special emphasis on finding groups that are not like the "typical" reading group—white, upper-middle class, and female—and thus may be more difficult to locate.

Groups meet in libraries, bookstores, cafes, and—most commonly—members' homes, and observing them covers the territory of middle- and upper-class literary culture in Houston. I have driven to settings ranging from a mystery book store, the library in LaPorte (a small community by the water that draws science fiction afficionados from a twenty-mile radius), neo-Georgian mansions in the ever-more gentrified West University neighborhood, and older mansions in the River Oaks and Memorial areas, to condominiums in inner-city Montrose (deemed by conservative Houstonians to be a den of homosexuals, artists, and left-wingers), and suburban apartments in the FM 1960 area, under the pines north of Houston, that bear the signs of transience in their rented furniture and folding bookshelves. I have visited over thirty groups, some for several months. Typically this involves recording or taking notes on book discussions, often supplementing those observations with interviews of some or all of the members. For every group contacted, I generate an "inventory" of information about social composition, literary selection, and group procedures. The individual members of a smaller number of groups are also requested to complete a short survey about group participation, other leisure and organizational involvements, and demographic data, as well as a more open-ended question sheet about individual feelings regarding the group's literary choices, book discussions, and interpersonal dynamics.

This research has established the ways group participation constitutes social identity and solidarity, illuminated the moral and cultural dimensions of this process, and indicated the kinds of innovative positions people take up regarding the literary institution and their own experience—cases of personal insight and collective cultural or critical reflection. It is less easy to establish whether these processes give rise to important social effects because of two epistemologically significant constraints that implicate both positionality and its discursive framing. The first involves temporality. How can analysis give contemporary groups the analytic prestige that comes from linking their activities to broader social transformations or macro-social developments, without knowing what the crucial and determining developments of our era are? Such questions raise the more general historiographical problem that human activity has tended to be valorized only if it *is* related to public policy or the sphere of public action, so at issue is not just where we stand in history, but what constitutes history or, indeed, social action.

Similarly, the study is grounded within reading groups and their activities. Most members see such activity as primarily "cultural," placing it analytically (much as would most social theorists) on one side of a categorial divide that demarcates culture from "society" and "politics." Examining this kind of cultural group and its uses of literature as a set of social practices (as this study does), constitutes one kind of effort to rework this distinction. So does questioning members about their social and political involvement beyond their reading groups. Such research strategies engage the issue of how to blur the boundaries between modes of activity whose separation (practical and theoretical) is one of the hallmarks of modernity. Thus, the study as a whole points to the need to remap analytically the definitional territory of "culture," "politics," and "society," and establish a suggestive point of departure for that larger program. Examining the cultural practices of reading groups in relationship to critical thinking and transformational personal or group insight is not only an attempt to destabilize a familiar field of analytic distinctions, but also an implicit claim that a predominantly female and heretofore analytically devalued arena of human behavior that links cultural consumption to moral reflection is important for understanding sociocultural identity among the middle classes.

It is clear, for example, that the act of joining a reading group and deciding what its program will be proves an occasion for people to define who they are culturally and socially and to seek solidarity with like-minded peers. For many, joining a reading group represents in itself a form of critical reflection on society—or one's place within it—because it demands taking a stance toward a felt lacuna in everyday life and moving toward addressing that gap. This action, in turn, reveals both to participants and to the analyst some of the ways in which contemporary society fails to meet its members' needs, needs that correspond in patterned ways to their social situations.

Housewives with young children and technically oriented professionals provide stark examples of this process. Many women join reading groups during the time when they find themselves isolated in the suburbs with young children. They talk about their reading groups as providing a "life-line" out of their housebound existence into a world of adult sociability and intellectual conversation. One such woman told of standing in line in a bank with her boisterous toddler and confessing to the woman ahead of her that she was at the end of her rope: no subtantive talk; hadn't read a book for months. . . . The other woman recruited her for a reading group. Technical workers like engineers find, conversely, that their workdays are filled with purely specialized information. An Exxon engineer who had led a reading group for three years said, "You may not believe that engineers read, but we do," and told me about his coworkers' thirst for general and intellectually challenging reading. The group continued until corporate transfers dispersed the members.

Joining a group also demonstrates members' recognition of their own, often critical, position toward literary or social values. Sometimes this positioning is explicit from the group's inception, as was the case with one feminist group that began by advertising meetings through the Unitarian Church (a local center of progressive social activity), and the Women's Community Newspaper, a publication that targets the feminist and lesbian communities. A science fiction group, contesting by its very existence the general devaluation of that genre, is similarly explicit about its literary values; it advertizes in science fiction bookstores and in the programs for local and statewide "Cons."

Sometimes, on the other hand, the process of self-definition is more complex, as was the case for a group of by now avowedly "traditional" women. Three members started a reading group without an explicit social or literary program, but as the group grew in size, the members gradually recognized both that they were using the group to explore literature about women, in the main, and also that discussing such books revealed how much they shared certain deeply held convictions about womanhood. As one woman said, "We're all married to our first husbands, and we really believe in that. . . . Everyone cared for her own children when they were young, and there's an open commitment to that. And an open wonderment at people who live differently—at people who have children and then leave them in other people's care, or who think they should leave their husband

to find someone 'better.'"... We're fighting to hold the tide back" (Mac-
Bride 1988).

The interpersonal dynamics and modes of textual appropriation at work
in many reading group meetings also make them occasions for engendering
a particular kind of critical reflection that has transformative potential
either for individuals or for the group as a whole. (They can, in other
words, be sites for cultural innovation, although this raises a set of questions about the conditions that enable these innovations to take root in
people's lives—either personally or collectively—beyond the compass of
the group.)

Reflection usually takes place through the lens of character, a category
that links texts to individual members' lives. On the one hand, the cen-
trality and ontological status accorded to literary characters in book
discussions—they are the focus of most analysis, and are often analyzed as
if they were real people—serves as an indication that the group uses books
and their interpretation primarily as "equipment for living" rather than as
occasions, for example, of expert display or professional advancement. On
the other hand, the social composition of most groups, in which members
will typically have one or two close friends, but feel "comfortable" ac-
quaintanceship with the others, permits empathy and self-disclosure without the responsibility of deep involvement. Both factors allow members
to reflect on life choices and orientations, using the books as a lens into
the lives of the other group members, similarly using other members' personally associative interpretations of the literary characters as a lens into
the books, and taking as much or as little from the discussions for their
own personal insight as they are moved to do.

Such processes of self-definition through identification with "characters"
are often relatively complex. For example, one can feel close to but also dis-
approve of a character. One reader said in a discussion about the three
heroines (or three aspects of one heroine) of a Latin American novel *The
Girl in the Photograph,* "I found myself closest to the one who wanted to listen
to music, yet I found her despicable. Of the three, she was the one I could
most change places with." It later became clear that she despised this character because of political apathy, but her self-recognition in the mirror of
the character enabled her to question whether she should become more
politically involved: a reflective process implicating social action (My Book
Group, April 5, 1983).

Probably the most powerful example of this process was provided by a
group I encountered before I had begun systematic research on this topic.
The founders were women who had all been in the same sorority at the
University of Texas, and who all were then at home raising children. In the
1970s they decided that one of the social/literary movements "in the air"—

a phenomenon they felt they should understand—was the women's movement. So they began to read "feminist novels" such as Jong's *Fear of Flying*
or French's *The Women's Room*. Discussing these books, members would
often isolate certain traits from fictional characters—as people do in reflecting on other people's character and choices—for fascinated examination.
That examination, which also included examining other members' emotional responses to those traits, helped each individual expand and clarify
her own aspirations. For instance, several members hated Erica Jong's
heroine for her "narcissism and superficiality," but were intrigued with
her idea that women might want a "Zipless Fuck" (sex without emotional
involvement), and admired her search for "selfhood." Similarly, many
members of the group took Marilyn French to task for excessive anger
and simplistic negative stereotyping of the husband in *The Women's Room*,
yet felt inspired by the heroine's decision to return to school and forge a demanding and creative career for herself. In fact, one by one, the group
members used these books and the insights and support of their group discussions to negotiate a passage for themselves out of a house-bound existence and back into the world of professional employment (University of
Texas Group, November, 1980).

The process of "living" other stories than one's own may be crucial for
confronting times of individual or social change, in part because it is then
that such "equipment for living" is especially needed. Julie Cruikshank
makes this point in her discussion of modern Native American Yukon
women's refusal to abandon traditional storytelling during a time of irrevocable cultural change (Cruikshank 1984). Carolyn Heilbrun's discussion
of reading about other women's lives in *Writing a Woman's Life* makes it
clear that contemporary uses of literature among other women can be similarly motivated (1988).

In fact, gender is an occasion for much of this reflection—being arguably
the dimension of social and personal change that has most deeply affected
the American middle classes in recent years. It is certainly the issue that
has challenged groups to engage in the most innovative working through of
values and beliefs. A discussion of Ntozake Shange's *Cypress, Sassafras and
Indigo* among a group of white women is one example of this process.

Despite reservations about the book's "hostility" toward whites and
about individual characters' erotic choices—one tolerated battering from
a lover, another became a lesbian—all endorsed the author enthusiastically
for having created "powerful," "nurturing," "creative," and "sensuous"
women. As one member said, "Being female was truly celebrated without
any of the 'be carefuls.'" The book describes in visionary terms rituals to
mark women's menarche; the group responded by describing their own
unhappy experiences of their first periods and expressing a desire to experiment with some of the "earthy" potions and a magnolia bath Shange

detailed. One member suggested "maybe we can have a female purification ritual next time," and others excitedly seconded the idea with "a menses celebration!" and "a celebration of the womb!" This theme surfaced again and again throughout a three-hour meeting (My Book Group June 4, 1984). Though unlike academic critical discourse, this discussion articulated the distressing consequences of our society's denigration of female sexuality, and affirmed practices that might revalorize female embodiment and challenge the traditional dichotomy between spirituality and the (female) flesh.

This example encompasses only one meeting, and indeed the group never acted *as a group* on these insights. A more extended process of cultural innovation related to gender occurred in a book group of single people that was meeting at a classical music cafe when I observed them, and that still recruits new members through *Leisure Learning Unlimited* (a local compendium of noncredit courses in everything from canoeing to cooking). The members were highly educated but proud of being very catholic in their tastes; one of the Great Books groups called them "the group that reads trash." They chose books by vote, and one of the more persuasive women in the group generally pushed for books about modern women's issues.

Resentment among the men about books they perceived as hostile to their sex finally came to a head when she "sponsored" a discussion of Lisa Alther's *Other Women*, a book about a woman who is deeply depressed, gets little pleasure out of men, and finds happiness through therapy and a lesbian relationship. Deeply offended by this "take" on gender relations, the men began teasing her every time she suggested another book: "Is this another book about women in pain?" This tactic silenced her for a while. But gradually she began to renegotiate her participation in the group by accepting "women in pain" as her literary genre of choice, saying, for example, "I know I'm always suggesting 'women in pain' books, but this is much more interesting than most of them." By reformulating their derision as a literary category, she worked herself back into the group's conversation.

Then the men decided that women had no monopoly on pain, and began a search for "men in pain" books that could serve as a moral equivalent to "women in pain" so they would not be marginalized or silenced in turn. By now, both categories are a routine part of the group's generic mapping of modern literature. And, although "women in pain" is a recognizable, although trivializing, label for women's literature from the nineteenth century on, in order to work themselves back into the group's conversation the men had publicly to articulate something new about modern literature, modern life, and their own emotional makeup. By negotiating through their deeply felt differences about how each sex views the other to a common ground they agree on, the men and women in the group invented new cultural categories that articulate a new framework for literary and social experience (Bookpeople, Fall, 1986 through Spring, 1988).

What I want to stress here is neither the profundity nor scope of these discursive categories, but the dynamic and collective nature of their constitution. A socially negotiated process of cultural reflection makes these groups—when functioning well—sites for insight and innovation in the arena of identity, values, and meanings. Further, it is already possible to indicate several aspects of group organization and processes that are important determinants of reflectiveness within these groups.

First, the kinds of constituencies a group brings together affect both the reading choices and the nature of discussion. The degree to which the group must (and is willing to) "work" to adjudicate differences has seemed especially salient in ensuring open-minded discussion. The singles group, for instance, assembles a rather diverse group of people—more so than is the case for many neighborhood- or organization-based groups—so the task of finding common ground may involve more innovative cultural "moves" than would be the case for a more homogeneous group. But the group is not pure diversity; it is a heterosexual singles group, and thus is willing to accede to both women's and men's refusal to be marginalized. The category "men in pain" might fare very differently in a lesbian group. Moreover, both men and women are willing to choose and discuss books about gender, since it is a category centrally implicated in the very constitution of the group itself. So, at play in each reflexive book discussion is a dynamic between differences and commonality—a dynamic that is also of necessity predicated on people's desire to continue meeting as a group, since that desire motivates people either to tolerate or to "handle" the difficulties of heterogeneity.

One must also consider the prior values that people bring to their groups. A feminist group with strong connections to the lesbian community provides the clearest example of how sociopolitical allegiances condition engagement with books. A sense of deep concern about feminist theory and praxis informs all the group's book choices, from Gerda Lerner's *The Creation of Patriarchy* to Margaret Atwood's *Cat's Eye*, and makes book discussions among the most focussed and "academic" of any group in Houston. Even the informal talk about films, concerts, and other cultural events that takes place after the book discussions is suffused with a sophisticated awareness of the politics of culture, and judgments are rarely cast in a purely aesthetic mode. (I found the atmosphere of the group bracing—a slightly intimidating but exhilarating reminder that America's materialism and truncated politics is not a universal condition of the human species.)

Related to more *literary* values is the question of how reading groups gear into literary authority and the established hierarchy of taste. Local reading groups, for instance, often welcome visits from professors at nearby universities, eagerly soliciting their opinions on classics and new fiction or non-fiction. They also use course reading lists from their college-age children as authoritative sources on developments in literature. Personal booksellers are important as opinion-leaders as well, often working with reading groups to set up an entire year's program of reading.

Even Cliff notes can provide discussion questions, and thereby shape modes of textual appropriation. The ironic comments these notes often excite, however, shows a refreshing distance from authority. For example, in one coed group discussion of *Huckleberry Finn*, a Cliff note question about the symbolism of the river precipitated gales of laughter and a hilarious discussion about nature symbolism in college literature courses and everyone's favorite trick for getting 'A's. As one person said, "My favorite symbol was the ocean. It could mean death, sex, rebirth—you could do *anything* with the ocean" (Bookpeople, February, 1987).

More generally, reading groups all operate within a commonly recognized hierarchy of taste that enshrines literary classics and "serious" modern books, while denigrating genre books and other "trash."[6] Groups do establish differing relationships to this hierarchy, but all recognize it— the historical sediment of the kinds of activities the new literary scholarship has begun to investigate under the rubric of cultural studies.

Equally interesting is the fact that the reading choices and value judgments of these same readers also demonstrate the limits of scholastic authority when it conflicts with the values that they hold dear because of their social location in the world beyond textual circulation. For example, many groups show irritation with some aspects of literary modernism, preferring a clear narrative structure and recognizably "realistic" characters over textual experimentation. Others refuse to entertain the literary merit of books that deal with certain subjects (one group will not read about incest) or that embody a "realism" that they do not find morally elevating. Nabokov's *Lolita* and William Kennedy's *Ironweed*, for example, came in for harsh criticism by such criteria.

This stance seems only partially explained by the familiar category of "middle-brow," for the category is drawn from the domain of aesthetics or taste, while what is interesting about such readers' cultural behavior is precisely the limits of authoritative aesthetics vis à vis nonaesthetic systems of value. A Bourdieuian analysis of class fractions and cultural capital can account for some aspects of this phenomenon: many of the readers have a strong sense of cultural entitlement that derives from their own position of educational and social privilege, so they can eschew with ease the pronouncements of the academy, which is to them just another fraction of the sociocultural elite.[7]

The complexity of groups' relationship to a literary authority that is itself both a "carrier" of critical discourse and a legitimating force for sociocultural distinction has ramifications for the analysis of their ability to be "critical." Deference to the academy can encourage confrontation with difficult texts and disturbing ideas. Yet that same deference can shade into smugness, giving groups a warrant to indulge in self-congratulation about their authoritatively ratified taste. Similarly, rebellion against cultural authority can give rise to a critical iconoclasm that questions deeply held assumptions about criteria for literary worth, or can encourage an attitude of facile know-nothingism.

Conditioning which of these responses to cultural authority will be enacted are the actual practices of selection and discussion. Many groups select by an informal process of suggestion and consensus that seems to give weight to those members who are either especially vocal or have established themselves as authoritative readers within the group by virtue of training, heavy reading, or the (usually informal) position as leader or "core" member. Other voices can be obscured in this process, which is the harder to criticize because of its very informality.[8] Choosing by formulating a program of several months reading, however, usually involves a more self-conscious process of self-definition and more explicit mechanisms for ensuring democratic discussion about choice. Voting as a group on book selections or following a policy of strict individual choice appear to challenge groups' informal reading boundaries most deeply. A reading group in the FM 1960 area felt that a policy of individual choice had significantly expanded their range of selection. They cited mysticism, the black experience, and science fiction as subjects and genres they would never have "taken on" otherwise (FM 1960, March 24, 1982). Similarly, the singles group mentioned above found itself committed to reading science fiction and "women in pain" books because they voted as a group—and at meetings when new recruits joined the established group—rather than allowing the authority of the more "literary" core members to prevail.

Finally, the general quality of the group dynamics can encourage an atmosphere of trust which seems crucial for the sometimes tentative and exploratory openness—toward new ideas, about one's own feelings—that characterizes critical reflection in reading groups.[9] On the other hand, informal processes of social control can be extremely effective in silencing or stigmatizing members so as to enforce conformity. Joking and a lack of responsiveness appear to be most often used "enforcement mechanisms." For example, one member of my original book group was greeted with total silence when she proposed discussing a book by Shirley MacLaine; her suggestion simply vanished from consideration (My Book Group, June 4, 1984). The humorously derogatory label of "women in pain" was intended to be another such silencing mechanism.

Both examples show groups falling short of attaining the "ideal speech situation" described by Jürgen Habermas, in which an egalitarian group process enables people to mobilize communicative rationality in order critically to reflect on the presuppositions undergirding the instrumental reason that, in his view, has deformed the life world. Indeed most groups do not approach that ideal most of the time because of power relations both within the groups and within the discursive world that frames their activities—for example, most are middle to upper-middle class, and share the partialities of their social group. Also, most accept distinctions between the spheres of literature, society, and politics that inhibit some varieties of critical thinking, although those same distinctions underwrite the existence of reading groups as sites of cultural reflectiveness. However, an almost Habermasian Enlightenment ideal is at play in most groups' understanding of what makes a "good discussion," and those good discussions are remarkable for the ways they mobilize texts in the service of multileveled and often creative reflection. This reflection bridges the world of books and the world of social experience, which may be taken as a text for purposes of analysis, but presents possibilities for action that cannot be reduced to either reading or writing.[10]

In conclusion . . . a return to the image of the isolated reader. Unseating the ideology of reading as essentially and only a solitary activity challenges the hegemony of an associated model of how culture works, a conception I call the "trickle down" model of cultural dissemination. It holds that innovative ideas and values originate with transcendent high cultural figures and are delivered by abstracted processes—and in diluted form—to the lower (and in this model, relatively passive) levels of the sociocultural hierarchy.

Understanding that this model, like the image of the solitary reader, is at best a partial one, in turn opens up for scholarly exploration the immense variety of ways that reading practices—like other kinds of cultural "usage"—contribute to the formation of sociocultural identity. The groups discussed in this essay are at the same time one aspect of this kind of negotiation, in which people figure both as products and producers of culture—and, I would contend, are emblematic of the general process of cultural dissemination or invention itself.

NOTES

I would like to thank Michele Farrell, Dorinne Kondo, and Sharon Traweek for their comments on many stages of this paper's evolution, and Jane Gregory for her help with the archival research on Houston's early groups. The Rice University Center for Cultural Studies made it possible for me to begin this work and provided me with an audience for its first presentation. The National Endowment for the

Humanities made it possible for me to complete not only this paper but also much of the research and writing for the book of which this work is one component. I am very grateful for their support.

1. Such images do not intentionally portray "the solitary reader"; they are portraits of individuals, saints, or writers of the gospels, surrounded by the symbolic attributes of serious reading and writing. I am interpreting them as *representing* a certain understanding of reading, an ideology if you will, much as the sex-differentiated pictures of boys and girls playing with toys on commercial packaging can be construed as representing a certain, unintended, construction of gender in the late twentieth century.

2. The cover art of Radway's *Reading the Romance* is an ironic comment on this point.

3. Feminist literary theorists have already traced many implications of the dichotomy between male and female authorship, and serious or high culture versus ephemeral or questionable culture in their considerations of women writers. The parallels between female readership and female authorship are striking. See *Writing and Sexual Difference*, edited by Elizabeth Abel (1982), and note *that* cover for a representation of that, related, iconographic dichotomy.

4. This process clearly brought cultural capital and social distinction, but its importance does not seem exhausted by the Bourdieuian notion of cultural usage.

5. The book-page editor of *The Houston Post*, in fact, refused to consider running an article about book groups because of that assumption. Ironically, he eventually did run a story on reading groups after I discussed some findings from my project—including the large population of groups—with a book discussion group that included a *Post* reporter.

6. "Trash" is not a fixed category, but rather a contested boundary-marker for dividing the upper levels of literary value from those books not worth discussing; depending on the specific reading group, it may or may not include, for instance, bestsellers or bestselling authors like Michener or Uris, and some science fiction or mysteries. Shakespeare is never trash.

7. However, their behavior also implicates the link between cultural consumption, social experience, and social action, which has been undertheorized in the study of audience behavior as well as the study of social change, each field's problematic being rooted in one side of the familiar culture/society dichotomy.

8. Although most groups seem happy to give authority, and responsibility, to certain members. For instance, one woman told me she didn't have the time to "read around and think about what the group might enjoy."

9. The discourse of academic critical thinking presupposes participants' immersion in certain debates and familiarity with a process of hammering out one's views in agonistic or even polemical encounters; it is structured, in other words, in very particular ways. I would contend that nonacademics can be critically aware without being immersed in the same debates or comfortable with the same styles of thinking; critical questions may be both framed and expressed differently, although to be "critical," such nonacademic discourse must also challenge assumptions and taken-for-granted views.

10. Indeed, the link between cultural consumption and social action, seems relatively clearly established by historical evidence about reading groups. How it

operates in the present, and how it might best be theorized, is a question addressed by several orientations in cultural studies. Bourdieu, for example, has presented an extremely systematic study of cultural consumption and social distinction that adumbrates issues of individual mobility and collective repositioning within the sociocultural hierarchy, the latter offering at least the possibility of substantive change of the hierarchy itself. However, his survey research tends not to focus on actual groups or collectivities, and he is less attuned to popular forms than to hegemonic processes. Perhaps more importantly, processes of insight, identity-formation through identification, and other ways by which people forge themselves through culture seem less interesting to him than the strategic acquisition and deployment of taste, so the very category of "action" seems somewhat truncated in his analysis (Bourdieu 1984).

Perhaps more promising are those initiatives under the loose rubric of "Birmingham School of Cultural Studies" that also understand cultural consumption as social practice, but focus on popular forms through historical and ethnographic research (Davidoff 1987; Hall 1980; McRobbie 1984, 1991; Radway 1984). This work, my own study, and "process-oriented" studies of sociocultural change like those of Lynn Hunt and George Lipsitz, which begin with everyday life and thereby integrate culture, memory, and social action a priori, have begun to offer insights into the way people use culture to define themselves, and thereby remake both themselves and their social world (Hunt 1984; Lipsitz 1988, 1990).

REFERENCES

Abel, Elizabeth
    1982   *Writing and Sexual Difference.* Chicago: University of Chicago Press.
Berelson, Bernard, with L. Asheim
    1949   *The Library's Public: A Report of the Public Library Inquiry.* New York: Columbia University Press.
Blair, Karen J.
    1980   *The Clubwoman as Feminist: True Womanhood Redefined, 1868–1914.* New York: Holmes & Meier Publishers.
Bleich, David
    1975   *Readings and Feelings: An Introduction to Subjective Criticism.* Urbana, Ill.: National Council of Teachers of English.
    1987   *Subjective Criticism.* Baltimore: Johns Hopkins University Press.
    1988   *The Double Perspective: Language, Literacy, and Social Relations.* New York: Oxford University Press.
Bloom, Allan David
    1987   *The Closing of the American Mind: How Higher Education Has Failed Democracy and Impoverished the Souls of Today's Students.* New York: Simon and Schuster.
Bookpeople
    1986   (Fall)
    1987   (February)

Bourdieu, Pierre
    1984   *Distinction: A Social Critique of the Judgment of Taste.* Cambridge,
                Mass.: Harvard University Press.
Brewer, J. Mason
    1935   Negro Legislators of Texas and Their Descendants. Dallas: Mathis
                Publishing Co.
Brodkey, Linda
    1987   *Academic Writing as Social Practice.* Philadelphia: Temple University
                Press.
Cruikshank, Julie
    1984   "Life Lived Like a Story: Women's Lives in Athapaskan Narrative."
                Paper presented at the Canadian Ethnology Society Annual Meet-
                ing, May, Montreal.
Darnton, Robert
    1974   "Trade in the Taboo: The Life of a Clandestine Book Dealer in Pre-
                revolutionary France." In *The Widening Circle: Essays on the Circulation
                of Literature in Eighteenth-Century Europe.* Ed. Paul J. Korshin. Phil-
                adelphia: University of Pennsylvania Press.
    1979   *The Business of Enlightenment: A Publishing History of the Encyclopedie,
                1775–1800.* Cambridge, Mass.: Harvard University Press.
    1982   *The Literary Underground of the Old Regime.* Cambridge, Mass: Harvard
                University Press.
    1984   *The Great Cat Massacre and Other Episodes in French Cultural History.*
                New York: Basic Books.
Davidoff, Leonore, and Catherine Hall
    1987   *Family Fortunes: Men and Women of the English Middle Class, 1780–1850.*
                Chicago: University of Chicago Press.
Davidson, Cathy N.
    1986   *Revolution and the Word: The Rise of the Novel in America.* New York:
                Oxford University Press.
    1989   *Reading in America: Literature and Social History.* Baltimore: Johns Hop-
                kins University Press.
Davis, Natalie Ann Zemon
    1975   *Society and Culture in Early Modern France: Eight Essays.* Stanford: Stan-
                ford University Press.
Eagleton, Terry
    1983   *Literary Theory: An Introduction.* Minneapolis: University of Minnesota
                Press.
    1984   *The Function of Criticism: From The Spectator to Post-Structuralism.* Lon-
                don: Verso.
    1990   *The Significance of Theory.* Oxford: Blackwell.
Ennis, P. H.
    1965   *Adult Book Reading in the United States: A Preliminary Report.* National
                Opinion Research Center Report No. 105. Chicago: National Opin-
                ion Research Center.

Fetterley, Judith
1978   *The Resisting Reader: A Feminist Approach to American Fiction.* Blooming-
            ton: Indiana University Press.
Fish, Stanley
1980   *Is There a Text in This Class? The Authority of Interpretive Communities.*
            Cambridge, Mass: Harvard University Press.
FM 1960
1982   (March 24)
Fraser, Nancy
1989   *Unruly Practices: Power, Discourse, and Gender in Contemporary Social
            Theory.* Minneapolis: University of Minnesota Press.
Giddens, Anthony
1979   *Central Problems in Social Theory: Action, Structure and Contradiction in
            Social Analysis.* Berkeley: University of California Press.
1984   *The Constitution of Society: Outline of the Theory of Structuration.* Berkeley
            and Los Angeles: University of California Press.
Habermas, Jürgen
1989   *The Structural Transformation of the Public Sphere: An Inquiry into a Categ-
[1962]   ory of Bourgeois Society.* Reprint of German edition. Cambridge,
            Mass.: The MIT Press.
Hall, Stuart et al.
1980   *Culture, Media, Language: Working Papers in Cultural Studies, 1972–1979.*
            London: Hutchinson.
Hatch, Orin Walker
1965   *Lyceum to Library: A Chapter in The Cultural History Of Houston.* Pub-
            lication Series vol. 9, no. 1. Texas Gulf Coast Historical Association.
Heilbrun, Carolyn G.
1988   *Writing a Woman's Life.* New York: Norton.
Hirsch, Eric Donald, Jr.
1987   *Cultural Literacy: What Every American Needs to Know.* Boston: Hough-
            ton Mifflin.
Holland, Norman N.
1968   *The Dynamics of Literary Response.* New York: Oxford University Press.
1975   *5 Readers Reading.* New Haven: Yale University Press.
Hunt, Lynn Avery
1984   *Politics, Culture, and Class in the French Revolution.* Berkeley and Los
            Angeles: University of California Press.
Iser, Wolfgang
1974   *The Implied Reader: Patterns of Communication in Prose Fiction from
            Bunyan to Beckett.* Baltimore: Johns Hopkins University Press.
1978   *The Act of Reading: A Theory of Aesthetic Response.* Baltimore: Johns
            Hopkins University Press.
Lipsitz, George
1981   *Class and Culture in Cold War America: A Rainbow at Midnight.* New
            York: Praeger.

1988　　　　*A Life in the Struggle: Ivory Perry and the Culture of Opposition.* Philadelphia: Temple University Press.

1990　　　　*Time Passages: Collective Memory and American Popular Culture.* Minneapolis: University of Minnesota Press.

Long, Elizabeth

1985　　　　*The American Dream and the Popular Novel.* Boston: Routledge & Kegan Paul.

1986　　　　"Women, Reading, and Cultural Authority: Some Implications of the Audience Perspective in Cultural Studies." *American Quarterly* 38, no. 4 (Fall):591–612.

1988　　　　"Reading at the Grassroots: Local Book Discussion Groups, Social Interaction, and Cultural Change." Unpublished ms., Rice University.

MacBride, Elizabeth

1988　　　　(Summer) Personal communication.

McElroy, E. W.

1968a　　　"Subject Variety in Adult Reading: I. Factors Related to Variety in Reading." *Library Quarterly* 38 (1, April):164–166.

1968b　　　"Subject Variety in Adult Reading: II. Characteristics of Readers of Ten Categories of Books." *Library Quarterly* 38 (2, July):261–269.

McRobbie, Angela

1991　　　　*Feminism and Youth Culture: From 'Jackie' to 'Just Seventeen.'* Basingstoke: Macmillan.

McRobbie, Angela, and Mica Nava

1984　　　　*Gender and Generation.* London: Macmillan.

Martin, Theodora Penny

1987　　　　*The Sound of Our Own Voices: Women's Study Clubs, 1860–1910.* Boston: Beacon Press.

Mathews, V. H.

1973　　　　"Adult Reading Studies: Their Implications for Private, Professional, and Public Policy." *Library Trends* 22 (2, October):149–176.

My Book Group

1983　　　　(April 5)

My Book Group

1984　　　　(June 4)

Ohmann, Richard M.

1976　　　　*English in America: A Radical View of the Profession.* New York: Oxford University Press.

1987　　　　*Politics of Letters.* Middletown, Conn.: Wesleyan University Press.

Radway, Janice A.

1984　　　　*Reading the Romance: Women, Patriarchy, and Popular Literature.* Chapel Hill: University of North Carolina Press.

Resnick, Daniel P., and Lauren B. Resnick

1989　　　　"Varieties of Literacy." In *Social History and Issues in Human Consciousness: Some Interdisciplinary Connections.* Ed. Andrew E. Barnes and Peter N. Stearns. New York and London: New York University Press.

Seaholm, Megan
  1988   "Earnest Women: The White Woman's Club Movement in Progressive Era Texas." Ph.D. diss., Rice University.
Smith, Barbara Herrnstein
  1988   *Contingencies of Value: Alternative Perspectives for Critical Theory*. Cambridge, Mass.: Harvard University Press.
Stock, Brian
  1983   *The Implications of Literacy: Written Language and Models of Interpretation in the Eleventh and Twelfth Centuries*. Princeton: Princeton University Press.
Thompson, E. P.
  1964   *The Making of the English Working Class*. New York: Pantheon Books.
Tompkins, Jane P.
  1985   *Sensational Designs: The Cultural Work of American Fiction*. New York: Oxford University Press.
University of Texas Group
  1980   (November) Interview.
Williams, Raymond
  1983   *Writing in Society*. London: Verso Editions.
Yankelovich, Skelly & White, Inc.
  1978   *Consumer Research Study on Reading and Book Purchasing. BISG Report No. 6* (October). Book Industry Study Group.

TEN

Voices Around the Text: The Ethnography of Reading at Mesivta Tifereth Jerusalem

Jonathan Boyarin

We always stand outside the given object, whereas we are situated inside the literary text . . . instead of a subject-object relationship, there is a moving viewpoint, which travels along inside that which it has to apprehend.

—WOLFGANG ISER,
THE ART OF READING

It was true that I could hear only my own voice, but my own voice was the voice of the dead, for the dead had contrived to leave textual traces of themselves, and those traces make themselves heard in the voice of the living.

—STEPHEN A. GREENBLATT,
SHAKESPEAREAN NEGOTIATIONS

The title of this article was inspired by a piece called "Voices in the Text" by my brother Daniel Boyarin (1986). His article is a close analysis of a brief example of midrash, the early genre of rabbinic literature which records the sages' expansions on the Bible. His title pointed to the multivocality of the founding rabbinic texts, whose primary character is that of represented dialogue. My "voices around the text" are those of myself, my fellow students, and teachers in an informal class that has been meeting for several years at a yeshiva on the Lower East Side of New York City.

The quotes from Greenblatt and Iser suggest that, despite the apparent gap in time, the voices "in" and "around" these texts are mutually dependent and coexistent. Without the text, we who constitute the class would have no basis for dialogue among ourselves. Without us, the rabbis' inscribed words would remain only potential.[1] The intersubjectivism Iser identifies as inherent in any literary reading opens into a vast (though bounded) number of relational possibilities when several voices together read several voices. The dialogism *between* reader and text identified in these quotes should not blind us to the social process *among* groups of readers collectively constructing given texts. Therefore this article aims to address three primary issues:

- The ways people mark themselves as distinct groups through unique recombinations of various cultural genres.
- The convergence between the concerns of anthropology and those of literary theory in the study of textual practices.
- The anthropological understanding of Judaism, insofar as founding texts are critical to the perpetual recreation of Jewish identity.

The first two points are familiar. The third has fairly recently begun to receive the attention it deserves both from literary scholars concerned with the history of reading and interpretation, and from ethnographers of Jewish life (Goldberg 1987; Heilman 1983).

Through my emphasis on the continued, creative role of texts in Jewish life, I hope to call into question a lingering antitextual bias among practitioners of cultural anthropology. This bias sometimes appears in the guise of a critique of what has been accurately called "the myth of the Judaeo-Christian tradition" (Cohen 1969). It has been suggested that the phrase "Judaeo-Christian" eradicates the specificity and autonomy of Jews in much the same way that the phrase "mankind" eradicates the specificity and autonomy of women.[2] This is a highly ideological and power-laden reduction. It is similar to the presumption of a monolithic (and alienated) "Western" culture which, in the discourse of critical scholars, usually suffers by comparison to the rich variety of indigenous cultures threatened by imperialism.

In this way, critiques aimed at the dominant Christian ethos effectively denigrate the Jewish voice. An example of this is found at the beginning and end of Dennis Tedlock's masterful *The Spoken Word and the Work of Interpretation.* Tedlock's distortion is particularly distressing and revealing because his book otherwise constitutes an eloquent and daring exploration of dialogic oral cultures which are both threatened and precious:

> Neither Zuni nor Quiche begins the world from nothing, and neither traces it to the Intention of a single Author, that monologue artist who is so obviously alphabetically literate: "I am the Alpha and the Omega." Instead, Zuni and Quiche gods need spoken dialogue just as much as humans do. (Tedlock 1983:18)

> [In California Indian myths of "creation by will"] there is no solitary male nude saying, "Let there be this and that." (Tedlock 1983:338)

Talk about Alpha and Omega, first and last! It is precisely in a *book* like Tedlock's that the beginning and the end are made to bear the greatest illocutionary force, and these "offhand comments" are hardly accidental. It is hard not to hear a sneer in the words "alphabetically literate," though it is not obvious after all why that is a condemnation of anything or anyone. In any case, nowhere in what Jews call the Bible does God refer to himself by an alphabetical metaphor. Nor does God refer to himself by an anthropomorphic metaphor, preferring to say *"ehiye ma she ehiye"* (usually, though problematically, glossed as "I am what I am"). Tedlock's burlesque of the "Judaeo-Christian concept of God" as a male nude refers back, in the first instance, to his discussion of Lévi-Strauss's figure of *l'homme nu*, who (as the figure of revealed Universal Man) Tedlock identifies in a confused way with the Christian biblical logos. Unfortunately again for Tedlock's thesis, in contrast to the foregoing sequence of "Let there be"s, when God is ready to create humanity the utterance is "Let us make man." The midrash interprets this as an indication of God's dialogue with the angels.[3]

This midrashic claim is simultaneously a constative and a performative speech act (cf. Austin 1962). That is, it both grounds the rabbis' implicit claim of the right to coproduce scriptural meaning (as the angels coproduced humanity), and at the same time exercises that right. Thus, drawing on imperatives inherent in the biblical text, as it were, generations living in radically changed circumstances over thousands of years have understood continuing interpretation as intrinsic to the Bible's divine character.[4] To paraphrase von Rad (1965:119), part of the task faced by each Jewish generation is in "first becoming Israel"—reliving the collective acceptance of the Torah at Mount Sinai. Interpretation is a dynamic tool enabling mediation between the realities of everyday circumstance and culture, and the impossible demands of *imitatio dei*. The range of acceptable interpretations of biblical texts is determined by the tension between the collectivizing force of the search to establish a shared identity, and the desire to identify one's unique individuality with the essence of Judaism.[5]

A recent article by Thomas Csordas on Catholic Pentecostalism addresses issues very similar to those here. Csordas calls for a scholarly effort to define empirically "the conditions under which particular genres might serve traditional authority or liberation" (1987:463). I would counter that affirmation of traditional authority and the service of liberation are not necessarily antithetical. There can be no objective or "empirical" way to identify the service of liberation, since liberation is an autonomous, intersubjective effort. Similarly, "traditional authority" is not a monolith (as the standard and still pervasive binary distinction between "traditional" and "modern" would suggest), but is as various as the groups that express loyalty to multiple sources of authority. In particular, there is no reason to assume a priori that forms of authority grounded in an interaction between text and speech are any more repressive than those which are exclusively based in orality.

Csordas also argues that

in their ignorance of social conditions for creativity, what participants necessarily misapprehend is that, through ritual language in performance, they
have created a new reality. (1987:463)

I believe, however, that far from being mutually exclusive, participation
and critical awareness can and sometimes must be linked in the search for
identity. This is so for any individual to the extent that she or he is dissat-
isfied with the founding of "modernist and post-modernist consciousness
. . . on separation, on self-difference" (Docherty 1987:207). "Alienation"
cannot be overcome by denying our deeply ingrained heritage of doubt. I
believe, in fact, that all of the participants in my class at the yeshiva, and
probably Catholic Pentecostals as well, are to varying degrees aware of the
social conditions—and know that one of those conditions is a good deal of
public discretion regarding the social conditions.[6] (If the converse of Csordas's claim were true, and those who are aware of the social conditions
could not be participants, then the notion of participant observation truly
would be bankrupt.)

Before proceeding to my discussion of the class's reading strategies
proper, I will briefly discuss the neighborhood setting of the yeshiva, and
the individuals who have participated in the class. This information is
basic to understanding how these readers read. Also, it should imply what
cannot be analyzed more explicitly here: that the strategies employed in
reading are part of the general strategies of personhood in a world of multiple and conflicting cultural demands.

SETTING

Neither the Jewish population of the contemporary Lower East Side, nor
the yeshiva that is located there, would at first seem to be likely places to
look for cultural innovation. True, there are a number of young male rab-
binical students at the yeshiva. But as one of them related to me, the
mashgiach (dean) understands what tourists see at the yeshiva: "Old books,
old benches, and old rabbis." And it is undeniable that the yeshiva and
the neighborhood have been in decline for years.

Yet even in decline, Mesivta Tifereth Jerusalem (MTJ) is still very much
a streetwise, down-to-earth neighborhood yeshiva. The teachers and
students range from Modern Orthodox to Hasidic in affiliation. There are
also a number of unclassifiable individuals—"characters" in New York
parlance—who contribute greatly to MTJ's consciousness of its offbeat and
authentic Jewish style.

The range of styles of Jewish identity that coexist on the Lower East Side
is different and in some ways more dramatic than in the flourishing Orthodox population centers in the outer boroughs and the suburbs. In a certain

sense Reb Moshe Feinstein, the revered former head of the yeshiva, institutionalized this tradition of tolerance. He insisted that all Jewish boys, regardless of their family background, could attend his yeshiva, and defended that policy by arguing that traditionally Orthodox Jews would be challenged and stimulated by the presence of non-Orthodox children.

Reb Moshe's approach can be contrasted to two others that are prevalent in the Orthodox and Hasidic world today. Some communities attempt to isolate themselves as much as possible not only from Gentile influences, but from contact with Jews whom they believe to be too involved with the Gentile world (Poll 1973 [1962]; Rubin 1972). Other communities take an opposed approach, reaching out to anyone of Jewish birth and attempting to influence her or him to follow that community's particular style of observance (Harris 1985).

Whatever may be the case at other yeshivas, MTJ certainly does not constitute a "closed society" (Helmreich 1982:x). What is remarkable about MTJ is, on the contrary, precisely the high degree to which it permits worldly discourse and simultaneously remains essentially within the standards of Orthodox values. That at least some of the participants at MTJ are aware of this synthesis was indicated by a young man who pointed out that his winter coat could be buttoned either left over right—as is the European secular male convention, followed by many Orthodox Jews as well—or right over left, as is the custom among Hasidim, following the biblical precept of maintaining distinctive differences of clothing between Jews and non-Jews. His comment—"I'm a double agent"—made explicit his awareness of his ability to fit into either social sphere.

It probably requires less social energy[7] for Orthodox East Siders to be "double agents" than it would to exclude the non-Jewish or non-Orthodox world from their consciousness. Jews are a minority on the Lower East Side now; in particular, more and more of what was formerly "Jewish territory" is occupied by East Asians. Maintaining a sense of the Lower East Side as Jewish therefore entails creatively reimagining the place. The heteroglossia freely employed in this task, examples of which I will present in the following paragraphs, will also serve as a foretaste of the strategies of textual intercourse that are my main focus here.

The yeshiva is located on the fringe of the intact center of Jewish residence, on East Broadway, a commercial street where virtually all of the businesses are now Chinese. One day, during the portion of the class in which we study the weekly Bible reading, our Bible teacher arrived at a phrase which he pronounced *shawm sawm loy* ("there he placed [gave] him," Exodus 15:25). One of my classmates immediately made a pun: "*Shawm sawm loy*—that's the Chinese store across the street, no?" His "interpretation" of the phrase was a parody of the phrase-by-phrase reading and translation process that is the method of traditional Jewish study, but its humor came from a twofold juxtaposition: first, between the teacher's traditional European Jewish style of Hebrew pronunciation, and the contemporary pronunciation this particular student learned in Israel; and second, between the supposed sanctity, the "otherness" of Torah study and the actual proximity of an alien culture whose names are completely opaque to our interpretation, hence "all sound alike" to us. He was making a comment about the change of the neighborhood, but also staking a claim to the territory by borrowing this apt-sounding phrase from our class to ironically "re-Judaize" the neighborhood.

Another example relating to the neighborhood illustrates heteroglossia as a strategy for stretching the limits of "decent" discourse within the class, in this case by permitting an attitude of intimate familiarity toward the patriarchs that balances on the line between affection and disrespect, as one might with a parent. The text that sparked this brief exchange, Exodus 19:3, reads in the translation of the Jewish Publication Society: "And Moses went up unto God, and the Lord called unto him out of the mountain, saying: 'Thus shalt thou say to the house of Jacob, and tell the children of Israel. . . .'" Our teacher explained that, by the principle of nonredundancy in the biblical text, "children of Israel" (literally *bney*, which can also mean "sons") must mean the men, and "house of Jacob" (*beys yakov*) must mean the women. For this reason, the chain of Orthodox girls' schools is known as *Beys Yakov*. There is such a school on the East Side. When the phrase was mentioned, one of the newer members of the class asked incidentally, "Where is the Beys Yakov?"

To which our teacher replied matter-of-factly: "Broome [Street] and Ridge [Street]." (This location is a few blocks up from the yeshiva.)

> I quipped: "Yeah, that's why it says he 'went up.'"
> A third participant: "Yeah, he went up to the Ridge."
> Me: "Riding on a. . . . Well, never mind. Forget I said it."
> Third participant: "You've been watching 'Bewitched' too much!"

I guess you had to be there. The point is the way the biblical text was actualized through its juxtaposition with images from popular culture on one hand (television, Halloween witches), and with the geography of the Lower East Side on the other. Moses is domesticated; a reference to popular culture, "underground" in the context of the yeshiva, is briefly shared, thus reinforcing our class's distinctiveness within the yeshiva; simultaneously, the prosaic neighborhood takes on biblical dimensions.[8]

THE CLASS

The two young rabbis who teach the class, who are described below, decided to start what they originally thought of as a *baal teshuva* ("penitent" or "returnee") class in 1983. They never publicized the class widely and its membership has remained constant at between two and four students. Recruitment is by word of mouth. When I first attended the class in 1984, my fellow students were a jazz guitarist, an avant-garde composer, and a sculptor. During the past year of study (1987–1988), the class included a painter, a former painter turned futures trader, and a young man who had built up his own bottled seltzer delivery business, but who had formerly traveled in Asia and earned his living importing Asian handicrafts. Since the class meets during working hours, participation in the class demands a flexible schedule—an occupation outside the *balebatish* (normal, conventional, bourgeois) mainstream. At the same time, since we are not full-time students, and we neither pay tuition nor receive stipends, we do not fit as members of the *kollel*—the body of young adult males, usually married, who continue to study full time.

For reasons related to my own position as observer and participant, I have chosen not to *commit* the formal interviews that would afford the data for a comparison of the participants' respective motivations and internal rationalizations. In addition to my own self-understanding, the only information I have relevant to this question is available because one of the current members of the class, whom I will call Andrew, chose to open himself to me privately—perhaps sensing that I had already dealt with some of the dilemmas he was confronting in adopting aspects of Orthodox belief and practice.

Andrew's mother was Jewish, his father was not. He was raised with a minimal consciousness of Judaism and was not given a Jewish name as a child. Years ago, he was active in socialist movements. At a certain point, a friend of his who was a political scientist wrote a series of articles concluding that the reason for the failure of political socialism was that it did not acknowledge the existence of God. Upon reading this, Andrew decided that the argument rang true, and that, as the son of a Jewish mother, the logical conclusion was for Andrew to acknowledge the claim of Judaism on him. He began concentrating on biblical themes in his art and started attending synagogue. Eventually, he felt the need to gain competence in the Bible and Talmud, which he explains now by saying that if he was going to depict biblical scenes in his work, he needed to know "how they really happened" in detail. He has begun observing the Sabbath and would like to keep his head covered in accordance with Orthodox standards. However, his wife, who was born to two Jewish parents and raised with considerable Jewish cultural awareness, resents and resists his turn toward Orthodoxy, basing her criticisms especially on the subordinate position of women in Orthodox Judaism.

The last point in particular—a disparity between the opportunities for involvement and the enthusiasm of men in the class, and coolness combined with exclusion experienced by their wives—is a tension several participants have felt. It seems likely, in fact, that part of the reason this particular group devotes so much social energy to mediating between liberal social standards and the tenets of Orthodox loyalty is because they are married to women who are unwilling to submit to Orthodox standards of female comportment. The one member of the present class who is not married is the most severe and uncompromising *baal teshuva* among us, and has also on occasion railed against "liberals." Referring to the strict and logically arbitrary rules laid down in a certain section of the Bible, he declared: "This is a *parshe* [section] that'll separate the liberals from the *yidn*." Though he transposed the usual terms in his paraphrase, wasn't he also suggesting it was a *parshe* that would separate the men from the boys?

I burned and kept my mouth shut at this. I felt he had transgressed the unwritten ground rules of tolerance in the class, and could think of no reply that would be within my own conception of them; apparently, he understood the ground rules differently. Furthermore, his comment reminded me of the sometimes awkward fact that I am indeed an anthropologist, a liberal and a dyed-in-the-wool cultural relativist. Which raises a further issue: it is altogether to the credit of the class that they tolerate the presence of an anthropologist, but it is not obvious why they do so. There are several answers to this question.

First, although I introduced myself as an anthropology student when I first joined the class, I did not adopt the ethnographer's attitude until almost three years later. My involvement in the class stemmed initially from my felt need to work through, slowly and consciously, a passage from academic study toward internalized participation in religious Judaism (J. Boyarin 1988). Only when I had agreed to present a paper about the yeshiva at an academic conference did I begin keeping notes during the class. Other members of the class occasionally took notes as well, which mitigated what I had feared would be an obtrusively "clinical" effect of my recording. This did not prevent my note taking from being immediately commented on:

One day, as we were beginning a new Talmudic tractate, our Talmud teacher explained that what the rabbis were doing in the debate recorded by the text was "trying to knock each other's arguments out, like the T.V. show in the sixties—rock 'em, sock 'em robots. Remember that?"

To which one of the members immediately followed: "Rock 'em, sock 'em rabbis!"

I took out a scrap of paper to record this witticism, and our teacher laughed: "He's an anthropologist—he's gonna write about us!" The good humor of his acknowledgment reflected his own practice at observing and remarking on the distinctive, offbeat character of the Jewish Lower East Side in general, and of MTJ in particular.[9]

Our Bible teacher's acceptance was somewhat more resigned and skeptical: One day I asked his forgiveness for making him wait while I take notes. Thinking I was simply recording the lesson itself, he said that he didn't mind, because it was the only way I'd remember the Torah. I explained that I was taking notes about MTJ as well. He replied, "*Nu*—if somebody else came in, he'd write that there's a *meshugener* [madman] standing in the corner and yelling and screaming." In other words, he was willing to accept my *also* being an outsider because at least I was listening to voices, and not merely hearing cacophony.

Inherent in my own stance is a paradox between primary identification with Judaism, and an equally ingrained doctrine of cultural relativism. Given the anthropological truism that, so to speak, every language has the same word for "human being" and "member of our group [often specifically male],"[10] the only way any anthropologist could avoid this paradox is through claiming the dubious privilege of nonadherence to any particular culture.[11] Ironically, that claim actually rationalizes solid faith in academic postulates and in the rewards of observing them.

Incidents of radical discrepancy between my views (especially on the Israeli-Palestinian conflict [D. Boyarin and J. Boyarin 1989]) and the opinions of others in the class are occasional and extrinsic to the ongoing business of study. The most immediate, ongoing threat to empathy for me in the class—one which I both suppress and mediate in my own cognition—is between the principle of *toyre lemoyshe misinay* (that the Torah was given to Moses at Mt. Sinai) and the record of critical, secular biblical research. Of course this looks like a particular form of the usual tension between the "native view" and the "scientific," but there is more to be said, not least because I am a native.

The strategy that I (and perhaps other members of the class) adopt at points in the biblical reading where the seams of redaction seem particularly unavoidable is suggested by Meir Sternberg. His comments are also pertinent to the dilemmas of intercultural interpretation:

> And as long as we adhere to the text's self-definition as religious literature with such and such singularities, we need not even submit to the dictate of identifying ourselves as religious or secular readers. Those who play by the Bible's rules of communication to the best of their ability can keep their opinions to themselves; only those who make up their own rules may be required to lay their ideological cards on the table. (1985:37)

Sternberg also identifies essentially what those rules are:

> The ubiquity of gaps about character and plot [and, by extension, apparent redundancies, contradictions, et cetera] exposes to us our own ignorance: history unrolls as a continuum of discontinuities, a sequence of non sequiturs, which challenge us to repair the omissions [and other "flaws"] by our native wit. (1985:47)

Finally, and relevant to the point I just made about the culturally marked character of all academic analysis, Sternberg makes a cogent claim against all pretensions to purely "positive" source criticism of the Bible:

> Source-oriented critics often imply that they deal in hard facts and consign "aesthetic" analysis to its fate at the none too reliable hands of the literary coterie. If seriously entertained, this is a delusion, bearing the name of positivism with none of its excuses and facilities. There is simply nothing here to be positive about—no, or almost no, facts concerning the sources of the Bible apart from those we ourselves make by inference from the Bible as source. The movement from text to reality cannot but pass through interpretation. (1985:16)

These are, in essence, very convincing solutions to the problems of my position as participant and analyst in the class, helping me to explain how someone with a secular academic background can participate in a Bible study class on traditional terms; to define what those terms are; and to reveal the cultural specificity of the "secular academic" approach. However, it is worth asking what is *lost* as well as gained in "keeping one's opinions to oneself," because Sternberg's prescription implies the kind of suppression of subjectivity referred to in the introduction to this article. I do indeed "keep my opinion to myself" when I am tempted to explain a textual difficulty with reference to source criticism, yet I am rewarded for pointing out the difficulty and even more so if I can propose or solicit a resolution in accordance with rabbinic hermeneutics.

Thus my own opinions are mixed and often conflicted. As Strathern suggests, "the tension must be kept going, there can be no relief in substituting the one for the other" (1987:286). I find this tension bearable largely thanks to the tolerance exemplified by our Bible teacher's repetition of the dictum that one's students should be considered one's children. He implicitly expanded on this idea in explaining that *urkhats*, the apparently superfluous ritual washing that is part of the Passover seder, is included to arouse the children's curiosity and induce them to ask questions, so that we can relate the Passover story to them. "Now," he continued, "our closest relations in the world are our children—and isn't it sad that *sometimes* we have to relate to them?" In other words, the most important people to relate stories to are one's relatives; and by implication, one becomes related to those with whom one shares stories. In this way, the shared experience of reading fosters a nonauthoritarian intimacy that many who contrast literacy and orality (e.g., Goody 1982) implicitly deny.

THE GROUP READING

The most important story about the class is the one we invent together, in collective dialogue with the biblical and Talmud texts around which we arrange ourselves. Or to put it in more academic terms, the core of this article is an analysis of discourse focused on texts that are themselves records of discourse. My situation at MTJ offers an opportunity not only for the application of literary theory to ethnography, but for an interrogation of social/literary theory by ethnography. As the literary theorist David Bleich complained recently:

> There has been considerable *speculation* about how people read, but the actual work done by Fish, Iser, Culler, and others has been textual analysis . . . the various models and concepts of "reader-text interaction" proceed on a highly polarized and impoverished sense of human social life: there is the individual reading experience, and there is the general collection of "others." (1986:402, 419)

Bleich argues instead for a critical practice focused not only on the text as a record of dialogue (à la Bakhtin), but even more so as an *occasion* for dialogue—in "the family, the classroom, the academic meeting" (1986:418).

Bleich's critique is forceful, but he stops short of acknowledging that the ideas of those he criticizes concerning dialogue *in* the text are indispensable for understanding dialogue *around* the text. This is especially true of Bakhtin, who, reacting against the inadequacy of the traditional narrow concept of "stylistics" in analyses of novelistic discourse, created tools for understanding discourse that are equally applicable to text and speech. Two of these tools that are critical to my making scholarly sense of my experience in the class, and that have already been referred to in this essay, are those of the constant interplay of centripetal and centrifugal (integrative and disintegrative) forces in language, and of the resulting situation of heteroglossia, intended to describe the full range of contexts which determine the meanings that a particular use of a word within a given utterance may have (Bakhtin 1981).[12] These dynamics were exploited to the utmost by the rabbis, dialogic readers par excellence (sometimes, Meir Sternberg complains, past the point of fidelity to the text [1985:50]).

The motivation of intersubjective readers such as the members of the class at MTJ to swim through the sea of meanings is suggested by Caryl Emerson, one of Bakhtin's translators: "It is the lack, the absence at the center, that keeps the outer word and our inner speech in permanent dialogue" (1983, quoted in Varenne 1984:296). It might be more to the point to speak about the *desire* for a center, or for an "identity"—a term that has already been used to mean many different things in the course of this essay, but which I will provisionally define as a sense of collective belonging without loss of individual consciousness. Perhaps in Judaism, the lack and the desire, along with the conviction that there is or can be a center, motivate the diverse phenomenon scholars call Messianism. Perhaps as well it is this lack and desire by which the past exercises its claim on "our *weak* Messianic power" and which ensure that the "secret agreement between past generations and the present one" (Benjamin 1969:264) is fulfilled in study. Such motivations are not unique to Jews, of course. Michael Holquist notes that the elderly Bakhtin was centrally

> concerned with continuity in time, that "great time" in which all utterances are linked to all others, both those from the primordial past and those in the furthest reach of the future. (1986:xxi)

Another implication of the role played by centrifugal and centripetal forces in biblical reading is suggested in the course of Johannes Fabian's discussion of the production and internal criticism of sacred texts in a new West African religion. Fabian points out that sanctified texts both "open avenues toward understanding" and place "constraining demands" through their "rhetoric power" (1979:173). On one hand, this dual aspect of simultaneous creativity and repression cannot be denied. On the other hand, it is precisely the "rhetoric power" that also opens "avenues toward understanding."[13] Particularly in the case of an ancient, rich, and hermeneutically elaborated interpretive tradition, one in which the constraints are almost invariably enforced by the implicit threat of social marginalization rather than by the coercive force of state power, it would be both misleading and invasive to suppose that the two aspects can be clearly separated. Rather, the collective task of our class, and of all Jewish intersubjective readers, is to accept upon ourselves the constraining demands as that which makes possible avenues toward understanding. We want to be both inspired and strengthened; we need to find our common ground without losing ourselves.

In particular, because everyone in the class—including our teachers, who have been strictly observant Jews throughout their lives—has grown up with American mass culture, we collectively employ the strategy of managing and drawing on our multiculturalism, rather than denying it. Again, we are "double agents." We irreverently tease the yeshiva's pretensions to be a "closed society," yet always ultimately subordinate our "external" references (to television shows, classical music, and the like) to the unifying message of the continued binding and life-giving relevance of the holy texts.

This attitude toward American mass culture amplifies the remarks about different Jewish neighborhoods made in the "Setting" portion of this article. The strategy of simultaneous appropriation and ironic distancing is characteristic not only of our class, but of the East Side as a whole. It may be contrasted, as above, both to the studious avoidance of secular culture by some Hasidic groups, and to others' tactic of militant exploitation of American mass-marketing and public relations techniques in recruiting Jews for a uniformitarian Orthodoxy. Nor does it require a professional anthropologist to note this contrast. Our Talmud teacher, whose ethnographic bent has already been referred to, once cited approvingly the great pains taken by one of the Hasidic groups to distance themselves from America: "We have to create our own *midber* [desert]"—implying that only when we are free from extraneous influences can we properly receive the Torah. He thus offered a countervoice to the repeated allusion to secular culture that he himself relishes and puts to great rhetorical effect. The combination of distancing and appropriation is not unique; I suppose every ethnic enclave both avoids and coopts capitalist mass culture at various times. As Fernandez (1988) warns, we should beware of exaggerating contrasts between places, especially when those contrasts flatter our own favorite places. Nevertheless, the variety of cultural registers in our class and the techniques and resources used in negotiating among them, are in any case richer than the stereotype would suggest.

The distinctive intonation patterns of oral Talmudic argument are one such resource. One day, for example, while guiding us through the record of a particular dispute, our Talmud teacher indicated that the text had reached a definitive conclusion by saying, "El Exigente approves [intonation up; pause], and the people rejoice [intonation down]." Several purposes were served by this. The daunting foreignness of Talmudic language was overcome with an immediately recognizable expression. The power of yeshiva culture to encompass and incorporate mass culture was demonstrated. Most important, since the reference to El Exigente was immediately accessible to everyone in the class, but clearly not part of the standard yeshiva oral repertoire, this idiom simultaneously enriched the repertoire of study, and marked out (as in a Venn diagram) the distinct combination of cultural competencies possessed by the class—an important form of reinforcement for adult beginners with professional ambitions and credentials in their own various fields.

Another technique is to undercut petrified standard translations through new forms of linkage. Thus, the standard English translation of the biblical verb *vayolinu*, used in regard to the Israelites' complaining against Moses in the desert, is that they "murmured" against him—a verb that has no obvious connotation of complaint in contemporary American usage. Following the example of the great commentator Rashi, who defends his interpretations of biblical words with examples of other contexts in which the word has the same connotation, our teacher[14] cited Rodgers and Hammerstein: "In 'Cinderella,' it says, 'Ten minutes ago I met you, and we murmured our "how do you dos."' So that word doesn't quite fit here." Again, the lessons are several. First, that at least some of Rashi's techniques are altogether applicable to our own work of translation and interpretation. Second, to demonstrate the possibility of his own exposure to secular culture (and, a fortiori, that of those who were not raised within Orthodoxy at all) enhancing his grasp of Judaism. Third, to show that the work of translation is neither exhaustively nor satisfactorily contained in existing scholarship, but needs to be constantly taken up and renewed.

Such references are measured and counterbalanced by both teachers with comments about how "wholesome" entertainment was when we were children. Nostalgia for a protected, more innocent golden age of entertainment confirms the valorization of the past at the expense of the present—a deeply ingrained Jewish habit. This was made explicit when our Bible teacher proposed holding a *melave malke*—a "going away party" for the Sabbath on Saturday night—and showing an old East Side Kids movie. He would consider such entertainment—free of the violence, open sexuality and other flaws of mass media today, and furthermore reinforcing the distinctiveness of the Lower East Side—suitable for the enhancement of religious conviviality.

Because of the generally tolerant atmosphere at MTJ, it is possible for such "insider" codes of piety and belonging as do exist to be revealed as such through creative misappropriation. One member of the class—the futures trader—has made a special good-humored effort to acquire by imitation various catch phrases, characteristic Yiddish gestures and intonation patterns. Several times he heard someone say to a friend who had just rendered a small favor (such as finding change for a dollar bill), *tizke lemitzves*—"may you merit fulfillment of religious commandments." The futures trader finally spoke up: "What's he saying—'fistful o' mitzvahs?'" This was received as a *bon mot* rather than a *faux pas* by everyone who heard it. The cogent implication of his mishearing is that *they*, the world outside, go for the "fistful o' dollars" that served as the title of a famous Clint Eastwood movie, while *we* want to grab the merit and pleasure of fulfilling God's will. But the hermetic pretensions of the code phrase *tizke lemitzves* (as a substitute for a simple "thank you") are undercut by the simultaneous implication that mitzvahs are the object of "our" acquisitive instinct just as dollars are the object of "theirs."[15]

The interpretation of religious and popular culture is not the only axis of dialogic contrast in our class. Of course, the texts themselves are highly dialogic, but my topic here is not "the texts themselves." It is worth mentioning, however, that insofar as both Bible and Talmud are studied with constant reference to Rashi's commentary, printed on the same page, the printed page is "multivocal." Furthermore, there is a distinctive contrast between the modes of grounding of textual authority, and hence of the implicit or explicit rules for reading, vis-à-vis (*voix-à-voix?*) the Bible and the Talmud.

In the Talmud, where opinions are ascribed to particular, named rabbis or to "the sages" as a collective, every represented voice is an authoritative voice (though of course not all carry the day). It is the logical flow of their debate that demands correct understanding—though even at that level, students' or commentators' interpretations may legitimately vary. In the Bible, as discussed above, every nuance (including orthography), every apparent redundancy, gap, contradiction is conventionally regarded as divinely intended, hence demanding of human interpretation. In Talmud, the halachic (legal) debates inspire more discussion and dialogue; in Bible, the narrative portions are more compelling. The Yiddish expression *a kashye af a mayse*—[what's the point of asking] a logical question about a story—applies to those who mistakenly interrogate narrative in the Talmud, not to those who appropriately interrogate biblical narrative. These differences help to shape a structural arrangement of the class—first hour Bible, second hour Talmud, the texts varying in mode of study and the teachers varying in personal style.

Without exaggerating the contrast, the kinds of story-creation stimulated by Talmud and Bible study may be illustrated with "the grapefruit" and "the *shtreimel* [Hasidic fur hat, worn only on Sabbath and holidays]." Herewith "the grapefruit":

Two advanced young scholars sat and studied for some time quite near to our class. Once one of them, a rabbi in between pulpits, was peeling a grapefruit. A member of our class, sitting with his back to the rabbi, said "Someone's eating a grapefruit."

The rabbi responded, "Just because you smell a grapefruit near me, it doesn't mean I'm eating a grapefruit. It so happens I'm *peeling* a grapefruit. You don't have the Talmudic training to grasp such subtle distinctions, but that'll come with time."

As we finished our class, he finished his grapefruit. Then I resumed: "Would we be entitled to conclude from the fact that you formerly were peeling the grapefruit, the smell of grapefruit has disappeared and there's a pile of peels on the table next to you, that you *now* have eaten the grapefruit?"

Our Talmud teacher had an answer ready: "No, we couldn't conclude that, because even if you see someone chasing someone else with a knife, and they both turn the corner, and then you see the second person bleeding and the first holding the bloody knife, he can't incur the death penalty." (In other words, according to Jewish law, there can be no death sentence based on circumstantial evidence.)

The rabbi who had peeled the grapefruit pointed to his study partner, who was bent over his book so still that he looked like he'd been drugged, and concluded, "You guys are ignoring one thing: the grapefruit was poisoned!"

No doubt this sort of banter is ubiquitous in yeshivas, but here it reinforces the ambience of tolerance, of welcome to Torah, which is part of Reb Moshe Feinstein's legacy at Tifereth Jerusalem. An assertion is made about a trivial matter. It is disputed in an equally trivial fashion. The person who disputes the original assertion announces that he is engaging in sophisticated Talmudic logic, and clearly undercuts what is on the surface a put-down by simultaneously implying that Talmud students may sometimes admit the triviality of the issues to which that logic is seriously applied. Then, one of the "beginners" resumes the dialogue with a display of his ability to frame an appropriate question. Another credentialed participant validates the beginner's question by citing the Talmudic ruling on an analogous situation, and the contrast between the life-and-death seriousness of that analogy and the inconsequentiality of the present issue heightens the game. Finally everything is drawn together, and the joke is on everyone: on the rabbi with the grapefruit, who "confesses to a crime"; on his regular study partner, whose intense concentration is likened to rigor mortis; on the rest of us, who "fail to see the real truth" because we are uninitiated; and ultimately on the Talmud itself. which is entirely capable of considering a grapefruit as a murder weapon. This verbal play bears a message that may be expressed thus: "We are all insiders. We share the same idiom. It is worthwhile for the pleasure we derive from exercising that idiom, if for no other reason. And that idiom permits us to laugh at ourselves without fear."

And now "the shtreimel":

One day Andrew, the painter in our class, announced to our Bible teacher: "I want you to know that your shtreimel [which he had seen our teacher wearing in the synagogue] inspired me. In my new painting, Boaz is wearing a shtreimel when he goes out to meet Ruth in the field."

I noticed a discrepancy based on the fact that the shtreimel is only worn on holy days, which I wanted to point out without causing embarrassment: "Well, it certainly wasn't *Shabbes* [the Sabbath] or a holiday, because why would Ruth have been in the fields on those days? Boaz must have known he was going out to meet his bride, and he honored her by putting on his holiday clothes."

Then our teacher said: "I'll tell you a story that brings to mind. It concerns the Arugas Habosem,[16] who was from the part of Hungary called Oberland. The Jews in Oberland didn't wear shtreimlekh and long coats like the Hasidim. They dressed like Western European Jews. But the Arugas Habosem became a Hasid of the Belzer Rebe. When he went to Belz, he was the only one who wore a top hat instead of a shtreimel, but in his home, all the rabbis wore top hats. He wanted to wear a shtreimel, but he knew if he did his wife would hit the roof. So he went to the Belzer Rebe and asked for advice. The rebe told him the following: 'Next Wednesday, put on the shtreimel. Your wife will get angry. To calm her down, tell her you'll compromise with her—you'll only wear it on Shabbes!'"

Andrew had the last word: "I'm in an exactly analogous situation! I want to wear a yarmulke now, but my wife said that's the last straw—if I start wearing a yarmulke, I'm on my way out! So maybe if I tell her I'll wear it only on Shabbes. . . ."

This exchange does not require much comment, inasmuch as it is basically a catalogue of all the dialogic techniques documented throughout this essay. There is the depiction in a contemporary art form of a biblical scene—a religious expression in a secular medium. The potential embarrassment of the artist's apparent ignorance of the fact that a shtreimel is only worn on holidays is avoided by an interpretation saving him from contradiction, just the way the biblical text is routinely "saved" from apparent contradiction through enriching narrative resolution. This, in turn, affords an opportunity for the extension of oral storytelling about ancestors, reinforcing the identification of the biblical heroes Boaz and Ruth with illustrious ancestors placed in our relatively recent history.[17] Finally, the story about ancestors at least suggests a resolution to a current practical dilemma faced by a member of the class. As Fishbane says (n. 4), we are "extending divine authority into historical time"; but at the same time we are, so to speak, locating ourselves in God's time as well.

CONCLUSIONS

Three programmatic claims about tradition, text, and time in Jewish culture grow out of my participation and analysis of the class at the yeshiva.

1. *Tradition is not a thing but a process.* As Hans-Georg Gadamer understands, there is a false dogmatism involved in "asserting an opposition and separation between the ongoing, natural 'tradition' and the reflective appropriation of it" (1976:28).[18] That observation is made as part of a critique of objectivist assumptions on the part of historians, stressing correctly that their perspectives are always culturally and historically determined. Yet Gadamer's unreflective use of the word "natural" suggests that he may not be aware of an implicit corollary which is centrally relevant here: *the means of appropriation of the ongoing tradition is reflective.* Until Gadamer's thesis is turned inside out in this fashion, it is possible for scholars to follow him through a valid self-critique without confronting their own reification of "tradition" as something exotic or innocent "out there," either unmarked by change and inquiry, or alternatively, succumbing to the irresistible disenchantment of Western capitalist sign systems. Treating tradition in a way suggested by the Oxford Etymological Dictionary's second definition of the word—"delivery, transmission"—would be more productive, and perhaps even yield more dynamic comparisons between cultures than we have achieved until now. In the light of this approach, tradition would be evaluated not as the relative completeness of some presumed primary stock of cultural traits, but as the relative possession by a group of people of the means (symbolic and institutional) to interpret their lifeworld in a way that

satisfies their desire for personal integrity, their sense of belonging to the group, their connection to past and future, and their place in the world. Of course, this is a culturally determined definition. How could it not be?[19]

According to this definition, Jewish sacred literature, beginning with the Bible, is a central means of dynamic tradition, not a "fixed text" to be "merely repeated" (as Csordas implies 1987:462). Questioning—interrogation of the authoritative text—is the essential pattern of Jewish study, along with reflection on the interaction between text and everyday life. It is *traditional* constantly to dispute and recreate what Judaism is; the loss of that capacity reflects in turn a weakening of Jewish tradition.

I am not arguing that the differences between my evaluation and Csordas's are simply differences between Judaism and Christianity. I know at least enough of Christianity to realize that the schematic contrast of the two traditions in this fashion is unenlightening. Of course, as a committed Jew and a partisan of dialogue I am flattered by Julian Hartt's claim that

> Somewhere along the line [the transition from Jewish to Christian theology] a shift is made from the "dialogical" relation of God and man to a unilaterally determined ontological relation. The Old Testament is dialogical . . . [whereas in] High Christian Orthodoxy . . . God transcends time absolutely. (1986:186)

Yet its very convenience makes me suspicious of this sweeping judgment; at any rate, Hartt is comparing the expression of theology in texts, not their reception and interpretation by readers. Judaism and Christianity should not be treated as monoliths, but rather as interacting traditions which also contain internal debate (see D. Boyarin 1990). Otherwise, a critique like Tedlock's, with which I began, reduces the dialogism inherent in Jewish textuality and reinforces the Pauline canard that "the letter killeth." In response I offer my second conclusion, to wit:

2. *Text and speech are of equal priority in Jewish study.* As Swearingen notes, "texts used in formally defined oral situations are complex mixtures of 'literate' and 'oral'" (1986:139). In the class at the yeshiva, it is bootless to attempt to specify whether the situation itself is "textual" or "oral." The voices around the text are the voices in the text; that is the point of the epigraph from Iser at the beginning of this essay. The texts not only are read as simultaneously oral and literate, but *arose* as that "complex mixture." In regards to the Bible, whether we view it as a redaction of oral traditions, or it is regarded as *toyre lemoshe misinay*—either way it is both book and speech. As to the Talmud, of course, there is no argument between religious and secular scholarship: it is a written record of dialogue.[20]

This existing rich complexity offers the trace of an opportunity for the creation of an ethnographic text that is genuinely "related" (as both story-telling and family-building). In the service of communication that tradition engages in a constant process of reverbalization and reinscription, and ethnography should be able to become part of that process. Which seems to lead straight to the third conclusion:

3. *The task of Jewish study is to create community among Jews through time via language.*[21] A specific sense of that loaded term "community" is intended here. It is certainly not that impoverished sense in which the appellation ("the American Jewish community," "the financial community," "an adult community in southern New Jersey") is used to impute a more profound empathy to those specified as belonging to any given interest or affinity group. Nor yet does it refer to the American definition of voluntaristic community as "people joining together to create societies according to the principles they jointly produce" (Varenne 1986:211), since in Judaism, both adherence to the group and the principles of the group are almost always prior to any individual's consciousness. Rather, there is an implicit Jewish ideal of community as that which is attained in the course of the shared (so far, generally male) task of rearticulating how to be Jewish.

The normative male Jewish view of Paradise—at least for the past few centuries of European Judaism—sees a great reward in the opportunity to study with the great scholars of previous generations. One day our Bible teacher, expounding on the multiplicity of valid understandings, cited Rabbi Akiba Eger's vision of the messianic age, when all the righteous will sit and study together in a circle. The point of the image is equidistance and equal view of one another: I can see your truth and you can see my truth. A related image is that of the Tablets of the Law, which, the midrash asserts, were legible from all sides: truth can be seen from every perspective. Thus, much as the Sabbath is viewed as a foretaste of messianic peace, the conduct of our class is imperfectly guided by a polyvocal ideal, which revives voices in the past, creates a voice for the present, and seeks faithfully to await a liberated, tradition-filled future.

NOTES

This chapter first appeared as an article in *Cultural Anthropology*, vol. 4, no. 4 (November 1989). My thanks to Elissa Sampson for her usual editing, encouragement, and general support; to Barbara Kirshenblatt-Gimblett, Deborah Dash Moore, and the anonymous readers of *Cultural Anthropology* for specific editorial comments; and to Shmuel Deitel, Sholem Drucker, Richard McBee, Yosi Rosenbaum, and others for reading with me at the yeshiva.

1. Edmond Jabès writes: "You are silent: I was. You speak: I am" (1976:29), virtually compelling the reader to speak in the name of the one who is written.

2. See the preface to Daniel Boyarin's *Intertextuality and the Reading of Midrash* (1990), where he cites Julia Kristeva as the inspiration for this formulation. For an example of the way the idea of the text is almost always already understood as the Christian Bible, see Barbara Christian, attacking the jargonistic emphasis on "text"

in contemporary literary theory: "Because I went to a Catholic Mission school in the West Indies... the word 'text' immediately brings back agonizing memories of Biblical exegesis" (1987:55). "Bible" in this passage means, of course, the Christian Bible, not the Jewish.

3. Stephen Tyler's essay "On Being Out of Words" is a more blatant example of the totalizing, anti-"Western" bias Tedlock displays. Although he is specifically criticizing fossilized traditions of ethnographic writing, the entire "Western" tradition is implicitly attacked, and Jewish textuality once again subsumed: "Orality makes us think of many voices telling many tales in many tongues in contrast to *the inherent monologism of texts*" (1986:136; emphasis mine).

His analysis: "Our recovery of rhetoric and poetry, those writings marked by the presence of speech, signifies our discontent with plain style, with a form of writing defined by the absence of voice and the pretense of an absence of interest" (1986:135).

I beg to differ: We are indeed discontented with "the pretense of an absence of interest," but that pretense has usually been couched in scientistic, not plain style. The answer is not obscure language (Tyler's idea of rhetoric and poetry here seems to consist of Francophile language tricks, such as his neologism "origin-alienation"). Part of the answer is to move beyond addressing a privileged coterie, whether of scientists or deconstructive adepts.

Tyler's prognosis is that eventually there will come about a "new writing [which] ...must first be disconnected not only from the voice, but from the eye as well. It must break the whole spell of representation and project a world of pure arbitrariness without representation. It must be disconnected from any world that is not built into its own circuitry and programs" (1986:137).

But a nonrepresentational language (written or oral) seems to be utterly inconceivable. If I am correct in this, then Tyler's demand for an inconceivable "nonrepresentational language" (recourse to the evidence of "nonrepresentational art" won't help, since what such art does is throw back onto linguistic conceptualization the task of creating meaning) "represents" nothing but a desperate crisis in professional cultural anthropology. This despair is expressed by Tyler as a desire to overcome difference (blamed on writing). But living with difference—living with language—is being human, and even Derrida, upon whom Tyler leans heavily, takes care to point out that writing "does not *befall* an innocent language" (1976:37).

I suppose my alternative suggestion is that we explore how writing (in its many forms) is at work around us, and how we can use it as a communicative tool in a less alienated way, without longing for the kind of "death and transfiguration" expressed in Tyler's bizarre mystic vision. I've tried to do that here.

4. This has been well formulated by Geoffrey Hartman: "The accented, promissory narration we call Scripture is composed of tokens that demand the continuous and precarious intervention of successive generations of interpreters, who must keep the words as well as the faith" (1986:17). Or again, by Michael Fishbane: "a root feature and the paradoxical task of inner biblical (as well as later Jewish) exegesis [is] to extend the divine voice into historical time while reasserting and reestablishing its hierarchical preeminence over all other cultural voices" (1986:25).

Note, however an important difference in tone: Hartman emphasizes the "demands" of the text, while Fishbane seems to view the challenge to the exegete as prior to any impulses stemming from "the text itself." This is consistent with Fishbane's concern with the redactive process analyzed by biblical source criticism, a point which will be alluded to further in this article.

5. The idea that the range of interpretations is an open issue is related to Lyotard's identification of the range of acceptable questions and explanations as the stakes of the game in science (1984). This notion, along with my use of the term "heteroglossia," is also suggested by Bakhtin's discussion of the dynamics of language; more on this below. The rage for Bakhtin in the past few years seems to be an indication of the degree of loneliness suffered in the process of standard scholarly writing.

6. Csordas skirts the ways in which authority is also used by Catholic Pentecostals in a mystifying or exploitative way. Despite my point about the exclusion of women below, this essay perhaps suffers from a similar lack. In any case, as Fabian (1979:174) points out, critical statements from within the group are difficult to document.

7. This term is borrowed from Greenblatt, who writes:

> We identify *energia* only indirectly, by its effects: it is manifested in the capacity of certain verbal, aural, and visual traces to produce, shape, and organize collective physical and mental experiences. Hence it is associated with repeatable forms of pleasure and interest, with the capacity to arouse disquiet, pain, fear, the beating of the heart, pity, laughter, tension, relief, wonder. (1988:6)

Bearing in mind that we are thinking of a concept that can only be observed indirectly, it seems useful to speak of "social energy" also as that which makes possible creative mediation among different or competing cultural worlds, as here.

8. Before focusing further in the following sections on the class and its discourse, I must make explicit what has probably been assumed even by those readers who have never heard of a yeshiva: no girls or women study at MTJ. This—along with lesser repressions, such as expressed contempt for non-Orthodox Jewish denominations—must be emphasized, since it discourages both discursive community and the scope of the critical issues addressed to the tradition, and thus limits severely my entire thesis about the creative tolerance of tradition at MTJ. This point deserves more attention than I can give it here.

9. For an example of his acute ethnographic observation, see J. Boyarin (1989).

10. As a translator, I have often faced the dilemma of whether to translate *a yid* as "a Jew" or "a man." Perhaps another way to say this is that Yiddish is a Jewish language precisely *because* the two concepts can be expressed by the same word. Whatever connotations "Jew" may have in English (and it has many), it never means "man."

11. Boon (1982) purports to expand on the thesis of the mutual culturalism of the ethnographic encounter. But he shows this most graphically and persuasively when discussing the representations created out of early European encounters with the non-Eurasian world. Those Europeans seem blatantly riddled with cultural bias to us. Yet when Boon reaches Max Weber, he rehearses Weber's theories, apparently in support of his own thesis, rather than focusing on how Weber is culturally marked; he gets lost among the trees, and loses sight of the forest of theoretical symbols. Fischer (1986) offers a suggestive reading of the ethnographic content of

"ethnic writing," which is helpful in breaking down the dichotomy between professional ethnography and interested cultural representations, but this of course is not the same thing as the cultural situatedness of ethnographers. Radhakrishnan (1987) is directly relevant to this issue, though the critical force of that essay is almost totally reburied in jargon.

12. These meanings may then be "unpacked" in a manner very similar to the close analysis of poetry (albeit always in a contingent way; cf. Friedrich [1986] on indeterminacy in both poetry and linguistics). Were it not for the danger of reinforcing the stereotype of the "wandering Jew," I would be tempted to explore the metaphor of Jewish writing and reading as the repeated packing and unpacking of our cultural baggage.

13. Anthropologists, literary critics, and other scholars are exploring the paradox that lies between these two hands (which we may imagine as outstretched, palms up, attached to two shrugging shoulders, linked by a head tilted to one side, topped by a pair of raised eyebrows), saved from a pure and hence sterile cultural relativism by the idea that in different social situations, access to dialogue (hence to creativity and the opportunity to set the defining terms) is differentially distributed.

14. Remember, this is a young man who has a long black beard, *peyes* (sidelocks), and a long dark coat. The visual presentation that goes along with these cultural juxtapositions heightens the impression of audacity and creativity.

15. A peculiar hermeneutic bind may be noted here. I'm trying to suggest both an extension and a corrective to Foucault's general thesis about the incorporation of subversion into social control. If, in analyzing a particular cultural instance, I first mention the subversion and then the way it validates the general cultural assumptions, I imply (following sequential logic) that the latter point is "what counts." If I reverse the order, as here, the opposite implication is made. In this case, I would argue that the deflation of incipient sanctimoniousness "cleanses" and invigorates the overall value system rather than threatening it. But it seems worth repeating almost *ad nauseum* that while these meanings are analyzed as discrete and sequential, they are produced as unified and simultaneous.

16. "Scented furrow," a biblical allusion. From the later Middle Ages until the early modern period, it was common for rabbinic authors to be referred to by the titles of their books: they named their books, and their books named them.

17. The apparent anachronism of a biblical character in Hasidic garb is quite consistent with the Jewish cultural pattern Max Weinreich aptly calls "panchrony." He cites the example of depictions of King David eating gefilte fish (Weinreich 1980:280).

18. An unfortunate insistence on the separation between the socially determined mythification characterizing Jewish collective memory and the critical, alienated consciousness of the Jewish historian mars Yerushalmi's otherwise erudite and ground-breaking *Zakhor: Jewish Memory and Jewish History* (1982).

19. Dell Hymes anticipates the general point of this paragraph by writing, "Let us consider the notion [of the traditional] not simply as naming objects, traditions, but also, and more fundamentally, as naming a process . . . intact tradition is not so much a matter of preservation, as it is a matter of re-creation" (1975:353–355).

20. An anonymous reader of an earlier draft of this article complained that my "conclusions concerning text and dialogue do not seem to give recognition to the

priority of value bestowed on the text within the oral-textual 'encounter' of the text in Judaism." Indeed: I am explicitly *denying* that "priority of value," though I do not consider the issue closed by any means. Issues relevant to this question include the emphasis on public oral reading of the Torah in the synagogue; the difference (*differance?*) between the way a number of words are written in the Torah and their indicated pronunciation; the frequent interpretive technique of suggesting alternate vocalizations to imply new meanings; and Rabbi Nachman bar Yitzchak's statement that in the world to come, unlike this world, the pronunciation and spelling of the divine Name will be identical (Babylonian Talmud, Tractate Pesachim, Folio 50:a).

21. Jewish culture has failed at this task precisely to the extent that opportunities for study have been denied to women and the poor.

REFERENCES

Austin, J. L.
    1962   *How to Do Things With Words*. Cambridge, Mass.: Harvard University Press.
Bakhtin, Mikhail
    1981   *The Dialogic Imagination*. Ed. Michael Holquist. Austin: University of Texas Press.
Benjamin, Walter
    1969   *Illuminations*. New York: Schocken Books.
Bleich, David
    1986   *Intersubjective Reading*. New Literary History 18:401–422.
Boon, James
    1982   *Other Tribes, Other Scribes. Symbolic Anthropology in the Comparative Study of Cultures, Histories, Religions, and Texts*. Cambridge: Cambridge University Press.
Boyarin, Daniel
    1986   "Voices in the Text." *Revue Biblique* 93:581–597.
    1990   *Intertextuality and the Reading of Midrash: A Study in the Mekilta*. Bloomington: Indiana University Press.
Boyarin, Daniel, and Jonathan Boyarin
    1989   "Toward a Dialogue with Edward Said." *Critical Inquiry* 15:626–633.
Boyarin, Jonathan
    1988   "Waiting for a Jew: Marginal Redemption at the Eighth Street Shul." In *Between Two Worlds: Ethnographic Essays on American Jews*, pp. 52–76. Ithaca: Cornell University Press.
    1989   "Un Lieu de l'oubli: Le Lower East Side des Juifs." *Communications* 49.
Christian, Barbara
    1987   "The Race for Theory." *Cultural Critique* 7:51–63.
Cohen, Arthur A.
    1969   *The Myth of the Judaeo-Christian Tradition*. New York: Harper & Row.

Csordas, Thomas
1987   "Genre, Motive and Metaphor: Conditions for Creativity in Ritual Language." *Cultural Anthropology* 2:445–469.
Derrida, Jacques
1976   *Of Grammatology*. Baltimore: Johns Hopkins University Press.
Docherty, Thomas
1987   "Theory, Enlightenment and Violence: Postmodern Hermeneutics as a Comedy of Errors." *Textual Practice* 1:192–216.
Emerson, Caryl
1983   "The Outer Word and Inner Speech: Bakhtin, Vygotsky and the Internalization of Language." *Critical Inquiry* 10:245–264.
Fabian, Johannes
1979   "Text as Terror: Second Thoughts About Charisma." *Social Research* 46:166–203.
Fernandez, James
1988   "Andalusia on Our Minds." *Cultural Anthropology* 3(1):21–35.
Fischer, Michael
1986   "Ethnicity and the Post-Modern Arts of Memory." In *Writing Culture*. Ed. James Clifford and George E. Marcus, pp. 194–233. Berkeley: University of California Press.
Fishbane, Michael
1986   "Inner Biblical Exegesis: Types and Strategies of Interpretation in Ancient Israel." In *Midrash and Literature*. Ed. Geoffrey H. Hartman and Sanford Budick, pp. 19–37. New Haven: Yale University Press.
Friedrich, Paul
1986   *The Language Parallax*. Austin: University of Texas Press.
Gadamer, Hans-Georg
1976   *Philosophical Hermeneutics*. Berkeley: University of California Press.
Goldberg, Harvey, ed.
1987   *Judaism Viewed from Within and from Without*. Albany: State University of New York Press.
Goody, Jack
1982   "Alternative Paths to Knowledge in Oral and Written Cultures." In *Spoken and Written Language: Exploring Orality and Literacy*. Ed. Deborah Tannen, pp. 201–215. Norwood, N.J.: Ablex.
Greenblatt, Stephen
1988   *Shakespearean Negotiations*. Berkeley: University of California Press.
Harris, Liz
1985   *Holy Days: The World of a Hasidic Family*. New York: Summit Books.
Hartman, Geoffrey H.
1986   "The Struggle for the Text." In *Midrash and Literature*. Ed. Geoffrey H. Hartman and Sanford Budick, pp. 3–18. New Haven: Yale University Press.
Hartt, Julian N.
1986   "Theology as a Hermeneutic Salvaging of History." *New Literary History* 17:183–194.

Heilman, Samuel
    1983   *People of the Book*. Chicago: University of Chicago Press.
Helmreich, William
    1982   *The World of the Yeshiva*. New Haven: Yale University Press.
Holquist, Michael
    1986   "Introduction." In *Speech Genres and Other Late Essays*. M. M. Bakhtin, pp. ix–xxii. Austin: University of Texas Press.
Hymes, Dell
    1975   "Folkloric Nature and the Sun's Myth." *Journal of American Folklore* 88:345–369.
Iser, Wolfgang
    1979   *The Act of Reading*. Baltimore: Johns Hopkins University Press.
Jabès, Edmond
    1976   *The Book of Questions*. Middletown, Conn.: Wesleyan University Press.
Lyotard, Jean-François
    1984   *The Postmodern Condition: A Report on Knowledge*. Minneapolis: University of Minnesota Press.
Poll, Solomon
    1973[1962]   *The Hasidic Community of Williamsburg*. New York: Schocken.
Radhakrishnan, R
    1987   "Ethnic Identity and Post-Structuralist Difference." *Cultural Critique* 6:199–220.
Rubin, Israel
    1972   *Satmar: An Island in the City*. Chicago: Quadrangle Books.
Sternberg, Meir
    1985   *The Poetics of Biblical Narrative: Ideological Literature and the Drama of Reading*. Bloomington: University of Indiana Press.
Strathern, Marilyn
    1987   "An Awkward Relationship: The Case of Feminism and Anthropology." *Signs* 12:276–292.
Swearingen, C. Jan
    1986   "Oral Hermeneutics During the Transition to Literacy: The Contemporary Debate." *Cultural Anthropology* 1:138–156.
Tedlock, Dennis
    1983   *The Spoken Word and the Work of Interpretation*. Philadelphia: University of Pennsylvania Press.
Tyler, Stephen A.
    1986   "On Being Out of Words." *Cultural Anthropology* 1:131–138.
Varenne, Hervé
    1984   "Collective Representations in American Anthropological Conversations About Culture: Culture and the Individual." *American Anthropologist* 25:281–300.
    1986   "'Drop in Anytime.' Community and Authenticity in American Life." In *Symbolizing America*. Ed. Hervé Varenne, pp. 209–228. Lincoln: University of Nebraska Press.

von Rad, Gerhard
   1965   *Old Testament Theology*. Vol. 1. New York: Harper & Row.
Weinreich, Max
   1980   *The History of the Yiddish Language*. Chicago: University of Chicago Press.
Yerushalmi, Yosef Haim
   1982   *Zakhor: Jewish Memory and Jewish History*. Seattle: University of Washington Press.

ELEVEN

Keeping Slug Woman Alive: The Challenge of Reading in a Reservation Classroom

Greg Sarris

STORIES AND STRATEGIES

About four years ago a strange thing happened to my cousin. He was with his older brother and they were on their way home to the Kashaya Pomo Reservation, driving along Tin Barn Road. It was early evening and they had just turned off Highway 1, the coastal route. There is a steep grade and then the road levels along the mountain ridge. Somewhere there, where the road levels, my cousin began looking over his shoulder. His older brother, who was driving, asked what the matter was.

"I thought someone was following," my cousin said.

His brother checked in the rearview mirror and saw nothing. But all the way home my cousin kept turning, looking. His brother said that once he jumped clear around and looked, as if someone were sitting in the back seat.

My cousin went to bed when he got home. He complained that after a long and discouraging baseball game in Santa Rosa he felt tired. "That's why you acted so weird in the car," his brother said to him. But in the days ahead my cousin began to wander. He would walk out the front door and keep on. Once he was found five miles down the road in a redwood grove. Another time his father found him sitting on a river bank, staring blankly into the waters of Gualala River.

My cousin didn't know what was happening to him. At night he was afraid and couldn't sleep. He didn't know anything except the urge to walk, and once he was out of the house, once he was out walking, he had no sense of place or time, or where he was headed. Each morning his father or older brother escorted him to the school bus. Twice the high school principal called and asked that his parents pick him up. In the middle of class, he got out of his seat and began shuffling aimlessly up and down the halls.

His brother recalled the strange occurrence along Tin Barn Road. My aunt suspected Indian poison, that is, the work of some harmful spirit or of some evil person using such a spirit. She was raised around the old people on the reservation. She is, as she puts it, "well-versed" in Indian ways. "I've heard and I've seen; I've seen and I've heard," she says. But by this time, because of requests from the high school counselor, my aunt had taken her son to medical doctors in Santa Rosa. It was possible that my athletic cousin had suffered a blow to the head in a game. The other possibility, one that the counselor suggested, was that the fifteen-year-old had taken some drug. "You know," the counselor said, "so many of those Indian kids drink and take drugs."

After a brain scan and countless other tests, which took place over three weeks, nothing out of the ordinary showed up. The doctors, like the high school counselor, suspected my cousin had taken drugs. But my cousin, at fifteen, had never tried even a cigarette. He was obsessed with sports and played on several teams. His mother and father and brothers and sister watched him compete. They drove him back and forth to town. Because of this, he was always close to the family. The doctors told my aunt that perhaps she didn't know as much about her son as she thought she knew.

My aunt called an Indian doctor, a woman from a nearby reservation. The woman prayed and sang over my cousin. After she left, he had his first good night's sleep. Before going to bed, he said, "I feel I can go to school tomorrow." But in the morning, after he left the house, he started for the woods, in the opposite direction of the school bus. He walked with the same lolling gait, the way we had seen him walking for the past six weeks. My aunt then called Mabel McKay, the last Maru (Dreamer) and sucking doctor. Mabel prayed and sang one full night. My cousin slept peacefully. But in the morning, Mabel announced that the young man would rest only as long as she was present "This young man, something got him on that road [Tin Barn Road] out there," she said. "Something is singing in him yet, calling him to it, chasing him. I can only calm it. I can't get it out."

As a last-ditch effort Mabel suggested my aunt take her son to a doctor woman who lived two hundred and fifty miles away. "She might be able to trick it [the disease] and get it out," Mabel said. Mabel had known the woman many years before and guaranteed the woman was a fine doctor. So my aunt and her husband drove their son the great distance to find this woman. And it was worth it. In a trance, the medicine woman confirmed Mabel's diagnosis, saying that something had met the young man along the road and followed him home. The medicine woman spoke through an interpreter who said in English: "You have many harmful things along that road: a little girl in a pink gingham dress with the face of a monkey; a sheep with eyes that leave its head and follow its victim; bearpeople trails; and a place where that small, ancient woman walks, that woman you call Slug Woman, the one who carries an empty baby cradle in front of her, as if she is begging."

The doctor began to massage my cousin's head, and, they say, she lifted something invisible from his brow, just above his eyes, something that had planted itself there, and she held it cupped in her hands before she cast it away. It was the voice of a woman singing. My aunt said she thought it sounded like the woman in Healdsburg who disagreed with her in a local Indian election.

My cousin was well after that. For six months, while he regained confidence in his well-being, a home tutor helped him with his schoolwork. Then he returned to school. For a long time the family discussed the incident along Tin Barn Road and all that had happened as a result. My aunts told stories about taboo places and people suspected as poisoners. They speculated about the neighbor whose voice my aunt heard singing in the medicine woman's hands.

I listened. I recalled stories I had heard from my Kashaya Pomo elders. I thought of the stories about an old woman from a Pomo tribe in Lake County, some eighty miles east of our reservation. At the time my aunts were talking, this woman was over one hundred years old. I had heard before that she was lethal. At funerals she massaged the faces of the dead to take from the bodies whatever diseases she could so that she might use them against enemies. People claim to have seen this. They said she possessed ancient songs and could take the form of a newt, a dog, or even the feared Slug Woman. She couldn't die, they said, until she passed on to another person whatever poisons she carried. That was the term of her contract with the poisons.

One night, shortly after my cousin was well, one of my aunts said she remembered hearing from somebody that the woman under suspicion, the woman whose voice rose from the healer's hands and was cast away, was seen coming out of a creekbed with this old poison woman. "She's training her," my aunt said. "Remember, this woman is her niece."

Last year in an attempt to foster cultural pride in the classroom on the Kashaya Pomo Reservation the teacher Mollie Bishop introduced written, translated Kashaya stories to the students. One of the four Kashaya school-board members suggested in a meeting with Bishop that it was important that the students get "Indian values" in the classroom. Bishop had been teaching the twenty-six K–8 children in the one-room schoolhouse for approximately three months. She needed to hear from the board what they wanted for the students, and she took the suggestion regarding the teaching of "Indian values" seriously. She felt it was important to integrate the curriculum with materials that the students "could relate to" so they might in turn become more interested in classroom activity. She figured if the students saw Kashaya cultural materials used in the classroom and could feel proud about their backgrounds they might not only be more interested in school, but might, at least, be more attentive. "I wanted the students to feel they could be who they are here at school," Bishop said. "I thought maybe that would help things. Something they had in common. So one day, instead of pulling out our readers, I gave them the story about Slug Woman."[1]

Things, in fact, were not so good. The older children were two to four grades behind in their reading. Two fifth graders read at a first grade level. As Bishop said, "those two were basically non-readers." The students were behind in math also. A sixth grader could not multiply or divide. And there were significant behavior problems. One day, after Bishop had been teaching for about two months, I visited the classroom and witnessed what Bishop later referred to as "a typical infraction." Bishop and members of the Kashaya schoolboard, two of whom were my relatives, wanted any suggestions I might have after observing the class for improving the dismal state of affairs. Bishop had asked an eight-year-old to put away his crayons so that he would stop drawing and pay attention to the math she was putting on the blackboard. A straightforward request. The student lifted his head, looked Bishop in the face and said, "Fuck you, you white bitch." Bishop informed the student that he was immediately suspended and she began filling out a form letter that he was to take home with him. "You better put that away, bitch," he warned her, "or I'm gonna hire someone and they're gonna find your dead ass on the side of the road someplace."

I was jolted, but not surprised. A few weeks before a substitute teacher closed the school after she had been there one hour and wrote the school district that she feared for her life.

This typical infraction occurred shortly after the class had finished telling Bishop and me what "they wanted to be when they grow up." They wanted to be doctors and nurses and businessmen and firemen and teachers. The eight-year-old wanted to be a lawyer. They all wanted to be rich like the people they saw on T.V. But the chasm between their wants and reality, like the chasm between their lives and those seen on television, would prove, for the overwhelming majority of them, too wide to cross. Eighty percent of California Indian school children drop out by ninth grade. Less than 8 percent graduate from high school. At Kashaya the statistics are no better than the state averages.

Bishop's idea, following the ideas of many teachers working in culturally complex classrooms, was to use "culturally relevant" materials, in this case the Kashaya story, to bridge the gap between the students' lives, or their lived experience, and those of others represented elsewhere, particularly in their readers. In that way, it was hoped, reading would become significant, meaningful, and eventually students would be able to engage critically other texts and stories. They would be able to read and at the same time have a cultural base—their own—from which to work. The students would get "Indian values," as the schoolboard member suggested, and they would be able to use them.

But Bishop's idea proved futile. "Most of the students hated the story," Bishop reported. "We couldn't even discuss it." "There's no such thing as Slug Woman," one student proclaimed. "That's all devil worship," another said. The scurrilous eight-year-old shouted, "I don't want to read about no savages." The few students who didn't protest were seemingly unimpressed. "It's just like a cartoon. Not real. Something like *Peanuts*," said one girl. Another student, a sixth grader, mentioned she had heard different versions of the story from her mother. She was going to ask her mother to talk more about Slug Woman. But, according to Bishop, the girl never said another word about the subject in front of her classmates. Bishop went back to the standard reader.

How might the students' reactions be understood? Was the story unreal for the students, not connected to anything in their lives, and therefore uninteresting? For my aunts and me the story about Slug Woman would have significance. For us Slug Woman is alive in certain ways. She is seen and talked about in the stories we tell to understand the events of our lives. In the story I told she is associated with a neighbor. Certainly we will be cautious, suspicious, reminded of that which may be harmful. The students are two and sometimes three generations removed from my aunts, and at least one from me. Still, all of them admitted they had heard of Slug Woman. Might she not also be alive for some of them, in which case their relationship to what they read was deferred or hidden in their responses? Might the context of their reading, that is, the classroom environment governed and determined by a non-Indian unfamiliar with the community, affect their verbal responses? What about the particular practice of reading in the classroom?

In this paper I want to explore these questions as a means of understanding, or beginning to understand, the dismal classroom situation and establishing criteria for positive change. This way Bishop and the Kashaya schoolboard might have a way to think about ideas and suggestions for change. I will center my discussion upon the students' reading of the Slug Woman text. Yet to discuss the students' reading, I must consider their cultural and historical community, the classroom environment, their particular practice of reading, and the ways in which these facets of their encounter and response to the text interrelate. A response such as "There's no such thing as Slug Woman" might not only be seen beyond its stated or surface meaning through contextualization, but it can, subsequently, illuminate relations and patterns of relations students have with texts and school in general that cause disinterest and alienation.

In examining the various facets of the students' reading, my work becomes what Jonathan Boyarin calls an ethnography of reading where there is "a convergence between the concerns of anthropology and those of literary theory in the study of textual practices" (this volume: 213). As an ethnographer, I am positioned as both participant and observer (and the observed) of certain cultural practices among my people. The story I tell at the beginning of this paper indicates to large extent the reflexive stance I take as a reader and writer of the Kashaya students' practice of reading. The details I use and the manner in which I tell the story as well as my comments regarding how I feel about Slug Woman reveal biases that necessarily influence my observations and conclusions. But, at the same time, my telling of the story becomes a way for me to continue its life as I come to use and understand it in the context of writing this paper. My sense of Slug Woman affects the experience of observing and reflecting on the students' reading, but the experience also enables me to see and create Slug Woman anew. Story mingles with ethnography which mingles with story. This paper tracks the intermingling.

In an earlier paper, I discussed how certain kinds of pedagogies maintain chasms between home life, or lived experience, and school life.[2] Such chasms make genuine critical involvement with texts impossible. Here, as I explore the Kashaya students' reading of the Slug Woman story, I am able to expose cultural conflicts and associated psychological tensions that play an integral role in the formation of chasms leading to student dissatisfaction and alienation. While my discussions and stories are concerned with one particular community, I hope they can provide a means for thinking about issues of student reading and response elsewhere.

KASHAYA: PEOPLE, CLASSROOM, READING PRACTICE(S)

It's genealogy—where we come from, who we are—that's happening right this moment, just as I'm talking to you. It's our stories.
—VIOLET CHAPPELL, KASHAYA POMO TRIBAL HISTORIAN

Pomo is the name given by ethnographers to several tribes of north central California natives, speaking different but related languages, and residing in Lake, Mendocino, and Sonoma counties. The Kashaya Pomo, or southwestern Pomo, speak a distinct language somewhat intelligible to central Pomo immediately north and to southern Pomo immediately east. To the Pomo beyond these two tribes, Kashaya is unintelligible. There are today at least one thousand people known to be of Kashaya Pomo ancestry, about one hundred and ten of whom live permanently on the Kashaya Reservation located five miles inland from Stewart's Point, a one store/gas station town on the northern California coast in Sonoma County. (Local Indians often refer to the Kashaya Reservation as Stewart's Point; the Kashaya Indians are referred to as being from Stewart's Point.) The total number of Kashaya Pomo today probably exceeds what it was at the time of European contact. Estimates of the number of Kashaya at the time of contact range from about four hundred to one thousand.[3]

Today the overwhelming majority of people identified as Kashaya Pomo are of mixed heritage. Intermarriage with Indians from neighboring tribes (i.e., central Pomo, southern Pomo, Coast Miwok) and with Mexicans, Filipinos, and many European groups, particularly Spanish and Portuguese, is common. The forty-acre reservation, given to the Kashaya in 1914 by the State of California, is located on a ridgetop in the northern part of a thirty-five to forty mile strip of coastal land the Kashaya once claimed as their own. The mouth of the Russian River marked the southern boundary between the Kashaya and Coast Miwok, while the mouth of the Gualala River marked the northern boundary between the Kashaya and central Pomo. It was understood by the Kashaya and the inland tribes of central and southern Pomo, those tribes living in the valleys east of the coastal mountains, that Kashaya territory extended roughly ten miles inland.

The climate is generally cool along the coast, foggy during the summer and damp and rainy during the winter. Inland, where the reservation is located, the weather is much fairer, with warm, sunny days most of the summer. Winters are wet with forty to fifty inches of rain. Yet seldom does it freeze. The landscape is typical of northern California: a series of coastal shelves and steep mountain cliffs line the ocean; inland, along the mountain ridges, are redwood and pine forests. Since the immense redwood forests were logged at least once, sometimes twice, in this region, the trees today are second or third growth.

The Kashaya once had small permanent and semipermanent settlements throughout their territory. All features of the landscape were named and stories were associated with each of them. People moved from place to place during the summer months, fishing and gathering mussels, clams, abalone, and seaweed along the coast and hunting small game and gathering acorns and edible bulbs, berries, and the like inland. In the winter, they returned to permanent settlements.

The principle permanent settlement was Métini, located on a coastal shelf in the heart of Kashaya territory. It was also where the Russians landed in 1812 and founded Fort Ross, the Russian Colony that is a noted historical landmark today. Like their European counterparts, the Russians came to colonize the land and its people. They virtually enslaved the Kashaya, forcing them to work the land growing crops that the Russians in turn sent to their Alaskan colony. They hunted sea otter for the pelts and in 1842, when the otter had become extinct in the region, they abandoned the fort. They sold their possessions to John A. Sutter, who moved all the Russian farm animals and equipment to his ranch in Sacramento. Mexican and American settlers then began to invade Kashaya territory. They laid claim to the land, on which a few of them established "rancherias" where they allowed small groups of Kashaya to live in exchange for their labor. During this time disease, kidnapping (Indian men and women were sold into slavery first by the Mexicans and then by the European and Euroamerican invaders), and starvation reduced the Kashaya population so drastically that by the latter part of the nineteenth century less than a hundred Kashaya survived.[4]

Kashaya resistance was particularly significant, however. Because the Russians, out of self-interest, protected the Kashaya from the Spanish and Mexicans, the Kashaya were never subjected to the mission system. They were able, under the Russians, to maintain their religious beliefs and practices. Though there was considerable contact with the Mexican and American invaders after the Russians left, there never was any major attempt to convert the Kashaya to Christianity, which was not the case for the valley Pomo tribes to the east. Then, in connection with the revivalistic Bole Maru (Dream Dance) movement, which spread through all the Pomo tribes in the late nineteenth century, the Kashaya produced exceptionally strong leaders, locally referred to as Dreamers. Annie Jarvis, as religious head, or Dreamer, from 1912 to 1943, continued the Bole Maru doctrine of Indian nationalism and isolationism even as its influence faded within the neighboring groups of Pomo and Coast Miwok. She outlawed intermarriage with non-Indians, forbade gambling and drinking, halted attempts by government officials to take Indian children to boarding schools, and demanded the Kashaya restrict their interactions with whites to work related situations. Essie Parrish, the last Bole Maru Dreamer among the Kashaya, held sway from 1943 until her death in 1979. While she insisted that the Kashaya maintain Kashaya beliefs and participate in ceremonials, she favored open relations with non-Indian communities. She was particularly interested in education and felt schooling could help the Kashaya defend and further their interests.

Linguist Robert Oswalt says "Kashaya is derived from the native term [kàhšá·ya], which probably contains [kàhša] 'agile, nimble'" (1964:8). He notes that other tribes refer to the Kashaya as "light (weight)" and "expert gamblers" (1964:8). According to tribal historian Violet Chappell, the Kashaya always referred to themselves as [wina·má·bake ya] "people who belong to the land."

Today how people think of themselves as Kashaya with a distinct history varies. In the mid-fifties Mormons made the first inroad on Kashaya religion. Ten years later the community split into two factions, those who were Mormon and those who were not. Family turned against family, sister against sister, in conflicts that were ugly and at times violent. Essie Parrish's dream flags which flew above the ceremonial Roundhouse were ripped down and then soaked in human excrement and placed on her porch step. Fistfights erupted between members of rivaling families. Annual community picnics were set on the same date so that friends of the community had to choose sides visibly. It was during this period, particularly the late fifties and early sixties, that a number of ethnographers and linguists concerned themselves with the Kashaya community where they found what they considered vestiges of "the last true Pomo culture," where language and religion were still, as one ethnographer said, "intact." The University of California in association with various faculty members and the Department of Anthropology made over a dozen films of Essie performing "traditional activities"—making acorn mush, dancing, doctoring. She also served as principal informant for Robert Oswalt as he assembled *Kashaya Texts* during this time.

After Essie Parrish's death a group of individuals within the Mormon faction built a new ceremonial Roundhouse where they revived various Kashaya religious songs and dances. The activity of this group angers those faithful to Essie's rules. According to Bole Maru doctrine, dances and songs brought about by the Dreamer must end with her death. Prayer songs given by the Dreamer to particular individuals for protection and health may continue after the Dreamer's death only if she has given explicit permission. Everything else associated with the Dreamer stops. (The old Roundhouse was locked after Essie Parrish's death.) New or revived ceremonies must come only with a new tribally recognized prophet. There is no consensus today as to who is or is not a Dreamer.

The Kashaya continue to splinter. Currently, among the one hundred and ten permanent residents, there is a faction faithful to Essie Parrish, a faction of Mormons, a faction once associated with the Mormons reviving Kashaya religious activities, and a faction of Pentecostals preaching fire and brimstone at nightly revival meetings. Shouts of "Hallelujah" and "Praise the Lord" hang in the air with Kashaya dance songs. But this is not necessarily a convivial intermingling. Perplexed children pray earnestly for relatives condemned to hell for not accepting the Lord. Family members abandon one another because of conflicting beliefs. None of the factions has stemmed the widespread use of alcohol and drugs. None has affected the student drop-out rate.

The younger generations are not learning the language; few, if any, people under the age of fifty speak Kashaya fluently. While acorn mush, seaweed, abalone, mussels, and certain kinds of "wild meat" such as venison are still served occasionally, usually at family picnics, the younger generations show little interest in learning how to gather and prepare these foods. In the families where Kashaya singing and dancing is maintained few young people participate. Only three households on the reservation have telephones, but many of them have televisions and stereo systems. Though T.V. and radio reception is limited, young people watch popular T.V. shows and listen to Top 40 radio stations. The *Cosby Show* and soap operas, such as *Dynasty* and *Knotts Landing*, and Rock and Roll and Rap are known by young people in every household. They talk more openly about products of popular culture than just about anything else; indeed, popular culture appears to unite them as a group.

Many of the children in the school have lived off the reservation, mostly in the nearby towns of Healdsburg, Santa Rosa, and Sebastopol, and attended public schools in the respective vicinities. Some families come and go, often following seasonal work in the canneries and agriculture. Children must adjust and readjust to the one room K–8 school on the reservation. Many families are broken; children sometimes are raised by single parents, aunts and uncles, and grandparents. So Kashaya cultural history and oftentimes complicated, unstable living circumstances position students in ways within the community, certainly with the teacher and with one another in the classroom, that make interaction of any kind complex.

It is impossible to isolate any one feature of a given student's experience as a Kashaya Pomo that influences how he or she reads and responds to a text. So far I have talked about cultural history and family life at Kashaya. Interrelated with and influencing cultural activity and family dynamics are many other issues, including the predominantly lower-class status of Kashaya residents, that affect students as readers. Few parents or guardians read regularly; of necessity making a living takes precedence over the students' schooling and school related activities, such as reading. Most parents have had unfavorable experiences as students and few believe their childrens' school life will be any different. My point, though, is that the notion of culture, as it might be applied to the Kashaya Pomo, as something fixed, homogeneous, and uniformly shared becomes not only obsolete and naive but also, as a result, impedes sensitive working relations with the community. As Renato Rosaldo discovered in his study of the Ilongot, this "classic concept of culture [cannot] readily apply to flux, improvisation, and heterogeneity" (1989:208). To isolate one feature of the Kashaya culture, say that of so-called traditional learning styles, and determine how that influences the way children might read and respond to a given text and then develop a certain supposedly sensitive pedagogy, is to overlook how those learning styles are associated in meaningful ways to other elements of culture and how they may or may not be a part of every child's experience as a Kashaya Pomo.

The ethnographers who swarmed the reservation during the late fifties

and early sixties sought Essie Parrish as an informant undoubtedly because
they thought that as a "traditional" Bole Maru Dreamer she might give
them "pure products" (Clifford 1988). It was Essie Parrish who converted
and led the tribe into the Mormon Church. Her husband, Sidney Parrish,
was chief of the Kashaya for over twenty years and yet he was from another
tribe, the Manchester-Point Arena band of central Pomo, and spoke a different language. This does not mean the Kashaya have no culture. To say
the Kashaya have no culture is to say they are "like everybody else," like
mainstream culture, and therefore culturally invisible. It enables mainstream others to claim the authority and knowledge to measure or assess
the Kashaya in mainstream terms, particularly with regard to certain competencies such as reading and writing, because the Kashaya are assumed to
be no different. Granted, the Kashaya might be poorer and uneducated, in
which case they are viewed in terms of what they don't have, what they
need, rather than in terms of what they have. To assume the Kashaya have
no culture is to overlook the ways in which the Kashaya accommodate and
resist other cultural influences in given social and political contexts. What,
for example, might have been the cultural, political, and personal terms of
Essie Parrish's acceptance and eventual rejection of Mormonism? Kashaya
culture must be seen as emergent. It is heterogeneous and pluralistic and
always present in a dynamic manner. What is pure or authentic is that
which is complex and dynamic in the moment it is experienced. This is so,
albeit in different ways, for insiders as well as outsiders associated with the
community.

A Kashaya individual's ethnicity, or the individual's sense of identity as
a Kashaya Pomo Indian, then, is dependent on how the individual in situations both personal and social, conscious and unconscious, negotiates and
mediates a range of cultural and intercultural phenomena to establish and
maintain a sense of self. A Pentecostal Kashaya might internalize her
mother's or grandmother's stories about poisoning and so forth as Other in
order that she see herself as Christian. Indeed, that part of her Kashaya experience, and hence that part of her self as a Kashaya Indian, becomes
Other. Likewise, those people reviving Kashaya singing and dancing may
bury their association with the Mormon religion, or, they may, as I have
heard, assimilate Mormon doctrine to new Roundhouse activities. The
twelve apostles become the twelve roof beams of the Roundhouse. Kashaya
ethnic identity cannot be seen as uniform among the Kashaya. The individuals who make and remake the culture are complex and different; they
make and remake the culture as they negotiate and mediate a range of
cultural and intercultural phenomena in a variety of ways to fashion a sense
of identity, a sense of self.

Tradition is often considered as that which is fixed in a culture, that which is canonical and governs, or at least influences in significant ways, peoples' lives. It is in this way understood, like commonly accepted notions of culture and ethnicity, as a thing, complete, still. Accordingly, that which is *traditional* is that which is of, or representative of, the tradition. Seen in the context of Kashaya culture, tradition is not fixed, but an ongoing process.[5] That which is viewed as tradition or traditional is subjective, dependent on the viewer. Mollie Bishop, for example, found that in the Kashaya classroom her sense of what was traditional, that is, the story of Slug Woman, was at odds with the students' sense of what was traditional. Yet the students' responses might have masked something other than mere rejection of the story as tradition, or as a relevant part of their lives as Kashaya Indians. My brief discussion of Kashaya cultural history may begin to suggest as much. Yet, at this point, more can be said of Bishop's reading of the Kashaya students and their community than can be said of the Kashaya students' reading of the Slug Woman story. Bishop read the students and the Kashaya community as homogeneous, fixed in time and place, where the Slug Woman story would be familiar, part of "tradition," "something they had in common," uniformly read and understood. The students may have had the story in common, but they necessarily did not understand it commonly. Bishop's unfamiliarity with the community at that time obscured any challenge to her presuppositions about culture, ethnicity, and tradition that knowledge of the community might have afforded. The schoolboard member who suggested that Bishop incorporate "Indian values" in the classroom was not, as Bishop supposed, representative of the entire community.

My discussion of Kashaya cultural history and diversity thus far indicates little more than the trajectory of Kashaya experience. If there was no chance that the students in their verbal responses hid or occulted their relationships to the text, I could start a matchmaking game, matching students' responses with points on an (invented) Kashaya cultural continuum. The purpose here, however, is not to unmask, or read, precisely each student's response, which is, I believe, impossible. Rather, it is, as I stated at the start, to look at the responses in terms of what they might suggest about relations and patterns of relations with the text in the classroom that foster a breakdown in communication about the text between students and teacher and students themselves. So, again, as I stated earlier, I must also consider the classroom environment and the practice of reading in that classroom. But before I go any further, I must present the text, what the students were given to read, so that it is known what the students were responding to in the classroom and what I am using as a focal point simultaneously in my ethnography of the students' reading and my understanding, as the subjective ethnographer, of the story itself.

A Description of Slug Woman

They say she is a woman with long hair. She is not a big woman; she is small and short.

Above the knees she wears clothes of cloth or skin or something else. From there down, her legs are bare.

She carries around a baby basket covered all over with abalone shell ornaments. She does not pack this basket on her back. She carries it in front of her. When she walks you can hear abalone ornaments jingling.

Nobody knows if there is a real baby lying in the basket.

This is all that is told about the Slug Woman. Maybe somebody else knows more about her but I have never heard it.

This is the end of the description of the Slug Woman.

A Story About the Slug Woman

There were some people living at Timber's Edge. From there they used to go to hunt deer.

One time a youth married a woman. They lived alone, not with his mother as was the custom. His mother lived close by.

The young wife had a baby. When that happened the husband's mother came to their house and admonished him.

She said, "Don't go around in the wilderness. Don't hunt deer. Don't fish. Don't even go for slugs or things like that. If you do, you will be punished."

She reminded him of the ancient Indian law that says the father of a newborn baby must not go outside until after the fourth dawn. He can't hunt deer for one month. He must not collect shore food or gather slugs. If these laws are broken the father of the baby will be punished.

The son said, "It won't happen that way to me. I don't believe that, Mother. I'm going anyway. I'm going to gather slugs." Then he set out.

When he reached the woods, he searched for slugs. He gathered a lot of them and carried them by stringing them on broken-off hazel twigs.

It began to get dark. He looked around in the forest for a place to spend the night. He walked toward a big upright tree. The tree had a hollow base. He prepared his bed there. He hung the slugs up to dry in the hollow tree. Then he lay down to sleep.

At midnight he heard something moving outside. He sat up and listened. It sounded like abalone shell ornaments tinkling along.

A short woman with long hair sat down in his living place. She carried a basket that tinkled when it moved.

After he had sat for a while the woman set the basket on the young man's knee. She said, "Hold this baby."

"Alright," he said. He clasped the basket to himself.

He began to wonder about the strange woman. Suddenly he became frightened. He didn't know what to do. He decided to leave the woman and go home.

"Here, hold this," he said. "I'm dying of thirst. I'm going for a drink of water."

He leaped outside of the hollow tree and started to run away. He ran for a long time.

He looked back and saw the woman carrying her tinkling baby basket. She was running along after him. He ran quick as a deer but she kept pace right behind him. He ran toward home but she started to catch up to him.

When he reached home, he stumbled through the doorway into the house. "Something is chasing me!" he shouted.

His mother said, "That is what I was warning you about. This is why we tell our children; so they will not be punished for breaking the law."

Slug Woman arrived right behind the man. She was clasping her baby basket covered with abalone shell ornaments.

Slug Woman said that she would not let the young man stay in the house. She would lead him back with her. "I want him!" she said. "He has become mine."

"No, save me!" cried the young man. "Make her leave me behind."

Slug Woman grabbed him and dragged him away. She led him into the hollow tree where he had been before.

The young man couldn't think much. He was already sickening. He sat on the ground. His body became weak. He couldn't run anymore. He couldn't even stand up. He became so weak he could hardly sit up.

"What's the matter with you?" Slug Woman asked. She gave him the baby to hold, but he couldn't hold it.

She said, "Is this what you wanted to see? Did you want to see what would happen to you? These are the things you were told about when your baby appeared on this earth."

The youth sat still, unable to answer.

Suddenly, a supernatural event began happening right before his eyes. He was on fire inside.

"When you don't believe," said Slug Woman, "these things happen to you. This is why you can't go home. You'll be staying with me, hereafter."

Three or four dawns later, the young man died.

After his death, Slug Woman left. Having burned up the young father she vanished.

The young man's baby was a boy. While growing up, he overheard some people talk about his father. He often asked his mother if he had a father, but she didn't tell him anything for a long, long time.

Finally she said, "You had a father."

"Where did he go?" asked the boy.

His mother didn't answer.

One day he set off into the wilderness to look for traces of something his father might have left. His mother admitted to him that he had a father and people said his father went to the woods. So he went there to find where his father had gone.

He came to a place where a big tree stood. It had a hollow base. He looked around and found an abalone shell with a hole in it. He continued to wander around in the woods but finally he returned home to his mother.

"Where have you been?" his mother asked.

"I tried to find out what happened to my father," said the child. "I went to the woods to look for traces of him and I found this abalone shell."

The mother said, "I am willing to tell you what happened."

She told her son about the death of his father. She ended her story by saying, "It was your father's punishment because he didn't believe the things his mother told him. His mother told him that hunting or gathering slugs was forbidden but he gathered them anyway. He said he didn't believe any harm would come to him. Your father was taken away to show that people are punished if the laws of our people are broken. Now you will understand that your father died because he broke the law about hunting after the birth of a baby."

"It must be so," said the boy. "I found where my father went and stayed in a hollow tree. I will never do that kind of thing."

"Remember this well," his mother continued, "as the sickness may be visited upon you when your wife has a baby. Don't go wandering around in the woods and do like your father did. Don't hunt deer, don't gather slugs and don't fish."

"Alright, I'll remember," replied the boy.

The boy cared for his mother until he was grown. He then took a wife and in time they had a baby.

The young father obeyed the rules. His children grew up to be good. They had children who obeyed the laws of the Indian way. The family lived at Timber's Edge for many generations.

This is the end of the Slug Woman Story.

"A Description of Slug Woman" and "A Story About the Slug Woman" (which in this paper I refer to as one story or text) were taken from Robert Oswalt's *Kashaya Texts*.[6] In the early seventies non-Indian educators working at YA-KA-AMA, a newly established Indian education and resource center in Sonoma County, collected stories from Pomo elders and various published collections of Pomo stories, such as *Kashaya Texts*, and presented the stories individually in pamphlets for schoolchildren. Each story was illustrated with drawings by Jim Blackhorse, an Indian from an east coast tribe who was working at the center. Bishop gave the Kashaya students the pamphlet with the Slug Woman story. "I didn't know anything about the story," Bishop said. "I just found the pamphlets at the school."

I must mention, if only briefly, the ways the YA-KA-AMA educators edited Oswalt's English translation. Most apparent is their editing of Oswalt's translation that suggests Kashaya patterns of speech, such as the predominance of the verb, specifically the Kashaya verb *mensi* "to do so," which is often used, as Oswalt notes, to begin a second sentence, thus tying the verb or action in the preceding sentence to the second sentence (18–19). Thus, you might have in English a translation that reads: She picked huckleberries. Having done so, she continued on. Continuing on, she found a spring. Note in the YA-KA-AMA text:

> He gathered a lot of them [slugs] and carried them by stringing them on broken-off hazel twigs.

Now see Oswalt's translation:

> He found slugs there in the woods. Then when it had grown dark, he had gathered a lot. While doing so, he strung them. Having broken off hazel twigs, he strung them on that and carried them around. (139–141)

Also, the educators at YA-KA-AMA omitted all of James's narrative commenting, most notably his lines asserting the truth(s) of the story in the present context. In Oswalt note: "We say that the retribution is like that even now. We still remember that now. It really happens like that when those who don't believe do such things. Slug Woman would set fire to them [internally] and abandon them" (143). And again, at the end of James's narration as presented by Oswalt, see: "Those things we still believe nowadays. . . . Therefore we still believe the things they did in ancient times. . . . These words that I have spoken are true" (145). The YA-KA-AMA version is presented without a visible narrator, a first person speaker. Nor is James identified as the storyteller anywhere on the copies of the pamphlet Bishop made and gave to the students. Sidney Parrish, who was working as a consultant and who told some stories used in other pamphlets, is listed as the storyteller on the cover of the pamphlet, even though in the case of the Slug Woman material this is clearly not the case. (Oswalt is not even listed as a source by the YA-KA-AMA editors.) Bishop did not copy the pamphlet cover. So the student readers did not see any name connected with the written words. The story, subsequently, is located in an ahistorical past.

Oswalt's translation, like any translation, is not pure, without bias. A common feature of the Kashaya narrative in a variety of storytelling events is the frequent use of *mulído* "and then, they say." In the untranslated Kashaya Pomo text James uses the phrase sixteen times. Neither the YA-KA-AMA educators nor Oswalt use it once in their translations. Oswalt suggests he kept much of the extensive repetition of verbs and the phrase "and then, they say" out of his English translation because such features of the Kashaya language, if presented as often as in Kashaya, would be annoying to an English reading audience (19).

Before moving on to a discussion of the classroom and issues of reading, specifically reading in the Kashaya classroom, I have to remind the reader that Oswalt and certain well-meaning educators are not the only ones who edited the text. Both Essie Parrish, who gave the description of Slug Woman, and Herman James, who gave the story, undoubtedly edited what they told Oswalt, both in content and form. Just recently Violet Chappell, daughter of Essie Parrish, again remarked: "Mom just told the stories like that for the language. He [Oswalt] wanted to collect stories to study the language and put in a book. We kids heard the stories different." I have never heard one of my elders begin a story with "Now I am going to tell about" and close with "This is the end of that." This framing device, used by the Kashaya narrators in virtually all of the texts given to Oswalt, was emergent in the context of Oswalt's recording. There is an interesting inter-cultural interaction or dialogue within many of James's narratives. James, a Mormon at the time, may have assimilated aspects of Christianity to vari-ous stories to impress Oswalt, a white man surely perceived as a Christian. My point, however, is that the text used in the Kashaya classroom is a text mediated by the Kashaya narrators mediated by Oswalt mediated by the educators at YA-KA-AMA. The thrice mediated text appears with illustrations representing the characters and action of the story.

I am not suggesting the YA-KA-AMA text of Slug Woman is invalid, that it should be discarded. The text does not exist alone. As Boyarin observes about the rabbis' inscribed midrash, the text remains only poten-tial without the reader (212). David Bleich notes that a text is not just a rep-resentation of interaction but also an occasion for interaction (1986:418).[7] And that is exactly what I am looking at: interactions with a text. I briefly discussed the text of the YA-KA-AMA Slug Woman story because the par-ticular presentation of the text, like the presentation of any text, can affect meaning and the ways in which the text might be received, or interacted with, by readers.

When I first read the text on Slug Woman in Oswalt's *Kashaya Texts* I was an undergraduate at UCLA. A professor mentioned the book to me. He thought I might be interested. Actually, I had seen a copy of *Kashaya Texts* in the old schoolhouse on the reservation. It was in a pile with other "Indian" books. I wasn't particularly interested, even though someone men-tioned that it was "a book with Auntie Essie in it." As a child I watched the old timers working with "the scientists" from universities. I saw how they edited information. I heard familiar stories told in new ways. I heard stories that I had never heard, and then waited for the elder's trickster wink as the scientist wrote madly, seriously. Two things seemed clear: university people weren't Indians and what was Indian wasn't in books.

I have had to qualify that which was so clear then. I am a university person who is Indian. I realize now that what is in the books is Indian, even if it is Indian in contact with non-Indian.

I remember paging through *Kashaya Texts* in the UCLA library. I looked at the pictures, or plates as they are called, of Essie Parrish and others from home. I was immediately homesick. I read all eighty-two texts, which

Oswalt divided into four genres: "Myths," "The Supernatural," "Folk History," "Miscellany." I thought of stories, people, places, and the time and manner in which I heard this or that. Though I could not articulate my feelings at the time I sensed what bothered me when reading "Indian books" for "Indian courses" at the university. Objectivism and text positivism, which influenced pedagogical practices at the time, hardly encouraged readers to think of people and places outside the actual text. I was not encouraged to engage my personal experience as I was at home when hearing stories. The text was supposedly complete, self-contained, a thing to dissect rather than to have a relationship with.

I can't think when I first heard about Slug Woman. She seems always to have been there in stories, on trails below Tin Barn Road, in the hands and hearts of certain men and women. That afternoon in the UCLA library I don't remember what I thought when I read about her. But I must have thought of stories, just as I did the day Mollie Bishop telephoned and informed me "most of the students hated the story."

As Bishop related the various student responses, I became agitated then angry. I was not angry with her, but with the students. Their responses hit a nerve. Their repudiation of the story was in effect a condemnation of my beliefs. As Bishop talked on, telling how she read slowly so all the students could follow, "even those who had to just listen," I thought to myself, those little no-good bastards. Well, what do you expect, I said to myself. Look at their parents. I felt sorry for the children from my family who surely were silenced, made to feel ashamed of their parents' ideas and stories by the others. By my family I mean of course those of us who adhere to Essie Parrish's teachings, those of us who are not Mormon or Pentecostal and do not participate in the new Roundhouse activities.

This is when I thought of what happened to my cousin along Tin Barn Road. Two or three of the most raucous protesters in the classroom were from a family closely connected to the woman who my aunts suspected of having poisoned my cousin. In fact, shortly before Bishop related her failure with the story, I had been on the reservation and seen the aforementioned woman in a neighbor's garden. I had heard her aunt, the old poison woman, had died. I wanted to express my condolences. I was sorry. When an old person dies a kind of relationship with the community, no matter what its nature, ends. But now I was angry. I felt insulted by the students. And yet with Bishop, just as with the woman pruning her friend's rose bushes, I said nothing.

I felt I would lose my credibility with Bishop. If I said anything just then, if I mentioned how I felt about the students' responses, I might be seen as biased, not an objective or educated observer. Still, what I could have said—what I am saying in this paper—could help Bishop understand the community and her position in it. I was—after all my experience in the community, after receiving a Ph.D., and after countless lectures and essays about challenging the canon with personal experience—assimilating my experience to what I perceived to be the expectations of Bishop and the classroom. I was an undergraduate at UCLA again. I uttered some platitude to Bishop regarding the importance of active engagement with classroom materials for students. I was, nonetheless, silent.

Bishop comes from the east coast where she was raised and educated. She is a Quaker. She came to California with her husband and young daughter "to find peace, tranquility." Not exactly what she found among the majestic redwoods at Kashaya. Her background positions her in certain ways; her history and education account in large part for her lack of knowledge regarding the Kashaya community and the ways in which the community may see her.

To the Kashaya, Bishop is an outsider. She is white and she is the teacher and principal of the Kashaya reservation school. The way students and parents respond to her may be different. But she is still seen in the seventy-year history of the school as the latest representative of the dominant society who has come with authority to teach and reinforce what that society values. As suggested earlier, the students' elders' experiences with the school have not been particularly good. There was a time when students were physically punished for speaking their language. The Kashaya became so quiet about their lives and culture that one teacher worked for fourteen years without ever knowing the Kashaya spoke a language besides "sub-standard" English. Some teachers have been more sensitive than others. Bishop wants to turn the situation around; she wants the students to feel empowered. Yet the only thing that seems to have changed, at least when I visited the classroom six months ago, is that students now manifest their discontent openly and disrespectfully.

The classroom today is typical of any contemporary gradeschool classroom. It is in a relatively modern building built in the early sixties (the old schoolhouse building was deemed unsatisfactory by the county school district). The building contains the one room class complete with teacher's desk, tables and chairs, blackboard, maps, calendars, and so forth. There is also a teacher/principal's office which serves simultaneously as a library. Books, student records, and school accounts are kept locked in this room. Outside the building are recreational facilities: basketball courts, swings, a slide. Nothing in the classroom or on the school premises reflects in any way the Kashaya people. Books and other materials about Indians, such as the Slug Woman pamphlets, are kept with other books in the teacher's office.

Until this fall, when a second teacher was hired, grades 1–8 functioned as one class. A teaching assistant from the county school district taught the kindergartners separately. Now Bishop teaches K–2 students and the second teacher teaches 3–8. The 3–8 group functions just as they had with Bishop: students read together and then are given individual assignments dependent on their respective competencies as readers. (Math is taught the same way: group work and individual projects.) The younger K–2 students work primarily as one group without much individual activity.

Bishop uses a phonics approach to teach reading. There has been much debate regarding the merit of a phonics approach. Yet most approaches, those that I know of anyway, meet on common ground in terms of what students are eventually asked to do as readers. The difference is that one approach may work faster or more efficiently than another. But they both work to get students to read in certain ways. As C. Jan Swearingen notes about our schooling in general, the practice of reading, in association with other classroom activities, "tends to teach children, among other things, to decontextualize language, spell out the implicit and assumed, formalize explanations, transform the 'impersonal' into the 'communicative,' the interactive contextual 'meaning' into the autonomous iterated 'sense.' Children are taught to distinguish what was said from what (they think) was meant" (1986:152). This begins, or at least reinforces, that chasm-forming process where the students, if they are to succeed in the classroom, must shelve personal experience, the necessary ingredient for "interactive contextual meaning," and adapt the norms and definitions prescribed by the teacher and classroom activities. A certain kind of approach to reading yields a certain kind of response to the text(s) being read, and the students are expected to learn the former in order that they might give the latter. By establishing a chasm between the readers' personal experience and classroom norms, the approach to, or practice of, reading as such robs students of the means to interact with the text in a way the text can be contextualized and, hence, the means to criticize or remake the text as they see fit.

The teaching of reading, then, can be an effective colonizing device. Gabriele Schwab observes: "Only when the colonized's own native culture has been relegated to the political unconscious and becomes internalized as Other, only then is the process of colonization successfully completed" (1986:130). Reading can encourage readers, particularly those from backgrounds different from the dominant society, to internalize life experience as Other. The first teachers at Kashaya were strict. They beat students. They preached Protestant values of cleanliness, orderliness, and clear thinking. Unbeknownst to them, their pedagogy, especially their teaching of reading, might have been as effective, if not more effective, than the content of their speeches in breaking the Kashaya. Certainly pedagogy reinforced ideology. The Kashaya, however, had an exceptional leader during those years. As mentioned earlier, Annie Jarvis preached resistance. The students feigned acceptance with silence. They became poor readers, "too ignorant to learn" as one teacher said, and dropped out by second or third grade.

Today the situation is much different. Religious forces have succeeded in influencing and splintering the community in a number of ways. It is not only community against teacher and school, but community members against one another. Now the reading process, rather than just working to break and convert the community, fosters and maintains the breaks that exist. The content of what is read, such as those representations of life in the students' readers, has little to do with the lives of Kashaya people. The story about going to the store in their *Basal Reader*, complete with its pictures, like the *Dick and Jane* story of old, is hardly a facsimile of what students know as home. The discrepancies are not questioned, since, according to the tacitly understood contract of reading, readers keep their lived experience separate from what is being read. Because the Kashaya students' lives are so complex and diverse they might not only be able to inform a story about going to the store, or whatever it is they are reading, that is, contextualize the text and their own readings, but, in doing as much, they also might see what constitutes their lives as members of a single community in terms of what is similar and different about them, spoken and unspoken. Because their reading does not enable or encourage them to do this, it reinforces the silence, indeed becomes a mechanism for maintaining silence, about the fear, frustration, anger, and confusion experienced by a people splintering in the face of cultural flux, rather than creatively reorganizing in a community determined manner. Reading might never have been more useful as a colonizing tool. It is safe for everyone, Indian and non-Indian.

On the surface Bishop appeared to break the tacitly understood contract that stipulates lived experience be kept separate from what is being read, that lived experience be kept outside the classroom. She introduced a story that probably was in one way or another related to many of the Kashaya students' experience outside of the class and then asked the students to talk about the story. The students were asked to talk about a representation of their experience as Kashaya by engaging and relating their own experiences. But the representation was created by someone other than, and independent from, themselves, at least as far as they could tell from the pamphlet, and it was handed to them by someone who was an outsider with perceived authority over them in a context where representations are engaged, or read, in ways that exclude personal experience. In this sense, the students were asked to consider Bishop's idea of themselves in a way Bishop prescribed. Bishop's explicit command that students use what they know from home to discuss the Slug Woman story conflicted with the inherent commands of the classroom environment, which Bishop maintains, and the practice of reading, which Bishop teaches.

This conflict no doubt effected a double bind situation for the students. Should they respond to Bishop's explicit command or to the inherent commands of the classroom and their practice of reading? Certainly the entire situation must have tweaked the sensitive nerve of Kashaya identity for many of the students. Confusion over what to do and anxiety over the subject matter are likely to have influenced their responses to the text. Denial, conscious and unconscious, appears to be a method for Kashaya to deal with confusion and anxiety, particularly around issues of how we constitute ourselves as Kashaya Indians. Failure of communication between people and different factions of people is the result. And so is anger. With remarks such as "That's all devil worship" and "I don't want to read about no savages," students denied any association with Slug Woman, whether there was any association or not, and foreclosed the opportunity for discussion. And, as Bishop mentioned, the students' responses were angry. This particular reading activity, then, as I see it, replicated alienating, community splintering practices on the reservation. It gave the students practice in the classroom context.

To further explore the students' responses, I must come back to the text they read. If the students were angry, their anger had to be about more than mixed messages and anxiety over the subject matter. Surely their responses had something to do with *what* they read, with what the text suggested to them as readers, which means that to some extent the students did engage the text with their experiences as Kashaya individuals. Here I must mention that, while I have talked about chasms and reading practices that may be chasm causing, the notion of a chasm, or a boundary as such, say between school life and home life, should not be of something set, rigid, impenetrable. Rather there may be processes, such as those I have been describing, that people use, consciously and unconsciously, that they may have been taught or that they may teach, that work with varying degrees of success to keep things fixed, or at least to create the illusion that things can be fixed and safely stored in one place or another. Maintaining the illusion is often what causes dis-ease both within the individual and within the community.[8] So I am not suggesting that students do not use personal experience when encountering a text. Home life and school life need not be mutually exclusive. As I have presumed above, school life may reinforce patterns in home life. I am suggesting that there may be patterns associated with certain reading practices, and whatever else, that make for limited engagements that are ineffectual in terms of positive change. As I stated, I do not purport to unmask each student's reading or response. I do not have that knowledge or power. I can suggest processes associated with the students and their reading and features of the text that I think influence certain reactions that impede change.

I was first struck by the flat language of the text. Note the persistent subject-verb-object sentence structure: "It began to get dark. He looked around in the forest for a place to spend the night. He walked toward a big

upright tree. The tree had a hollow base. He prepared his bed there."
Again, the educators at YA-KA-AMA omitted features of Oswalt's English
version that suggested Kashaya patterns of speech. For whatever reason—
perhaps the notion that schoolchildren can read only simple sentences—
they used an insipid English.

Another feature of the text that I noticed immediately, and that I have
noted above, was the absence of a first person narrator. Except for the line
"Maybe somebody else knows more about her but I never heard it" found
in "A Description of Slug Woman," the text appears without any sense of a
speaker, a distinct voice. This line remains probably because of an editorial
oversight on the part of the YA-KA-AMA editors. And as I also noted earlier, Herman James's narrative commenting in Oswalt's version of the story
has been cut in the YA-KA-AMA version and neither Essie Parrish (who
narrated the description of Slug Woman to Oswalt) nor Herman James is
identified as a storyteller on Bishop's copies of the YA-KA-AMA pamphlet.
(And, again, Bishop did not copy the cover of the pamphlet where Sidney
Parrish is wrongly identified as the storyteller.) Parrish and James were related in one way or another to most of the Kashaya students; certainly the
students would recognize the names. Of course the absence of a voice, or
rather the presence of an anonymous storyteller, would not seem unusual to
the students. Who is telling the story about going to the store in their *Basal
Reader*? And isn't the language there flat also? There is, in fact, someone
telling the story; what seems a void, an absence of voice, is really a ubiquitous presence. The voice, or language if you will, in the story in their
Basal Reader, is from the world of some Other people, the world of the classroom teacher, the world of the dominant society. The voice in the text is
that voice of the adult in the room, of Bishop, the teacher. The words are
authoritative, just as they are presented, without a distinct, identifiable
speaker. That they are authoritative is given, and to question the text is not
merely to question Bishop but to question the context of the text's presentation and the text itself, which is not, as I have said, something encouraged
in the classroom or in the practice of reading. The students would need to
use their personal experiences to do that, at least in a way that promoted,
rather than foreclosed, discussion. Since the Slug Woman story is presented
in the same manner and was given to the students in the same context,
the students were probably further perplexed. The story, as such, com-
plemented the double bind where the students were caught between
Bishop's explicit command and those that inhere in the classroom and
given reading practices. The story was about them in a way that was not
them.

To what extent the students were conscious of the paradoxical situation
in which they were placed, and to what extent their verbal protestations of
the story were associated with the situation, is not clear, nor can it be.

What is likely to have bothered them on a more conscious level, and what in turn may have provided them the opportunity to express a more general frustration and dissatisfaction, was the representations of Kashaya Pomo Indians and the moralizing associated with those representations. The students may not have been able to sense consciously the ways in which the voice of the text was not a Kashaya voice. They could understand, and apparently did understand, that Indians who search for and eat slugs and sleep in hollow trees are not Indians they know. Further, the drawings, which illustrate the written text, depict Indians in loincloths running about the woods. Note that admonitions regarding the breaking of "ancient Indian laws" are repeated throughout the story. The story is a moral tale. It opens with a warning. The protagonist disregards the warning and is punished. His son hears the story, heeds the warning, and lives happily ever after. James's version in *Kashaya Texts* is moral also. But there is at least an identifiable speaker admonishing, someone the students might more easily respond to.

The story closes with an abrupt frame: "This is the end of the Slug Woman story." No questions. No discussion. Presented to the students by Bishop in the classroom context, the story tells the students what an Indian is (i.e., a person in a loincloth who eats slugs and has rules about the birth of babies and hunting) and that if they are not this Indian they "will be punished." And the story's authority is associated, as I have noted, with Bishop. In a variety of ways, then, the students may have been challenging and denouncing Bishop at the same time they were masking their connections with Slug Woman. No, we won't obey you. No, we won't be savages. No, we know nothing about Slug Woman. And that was the end of Slug Woman in the classroom. That was the end of the Slug Woman story. No questions. No discussion.

I said I think of stories whenever I hear or read about someone or something at Kashaya. The stories mix and mingle. I make sense of them. My making sense, of course, has much to do with my experience, my family, and my education. Sometimes I fancy myself a distanced observer, a fantasy that is strengthened by my education. I believe I see things for what they are at Kashaya. I believe I can move beyond my limitations as a person so deeply rooted in the community.

After I heard that the old poison woman had died, I kept thinking of the stories people told about her. I won't tell the stories here, lest the woman be identified. The stories are remarkable. Not just about her poison work. About her life and history. They say so much about our people. I thought I would cover the stories in fiction, in a novel. That way I would not have to cross boundaries. I would not identify the woman. I would not have to talk to her family. But who would read the novel? The conventions of contemporary fiction and the sheer length of a novel would prohibit most Kashaya from reading my book. If I am a distanced observer, if I see certain things about my people as a result, I cannot talk with all my people about what I see. I would, for the most part, be talking to others, to non-Indians who read books. So much for my distance. Silence, again. Like my cousin under a spell, like most everyone on the reservation, I move about unable to talk about what is happening. Slug Woman.

Little is known about so-called precontact storytelling among the Kashaya Pomo. Essie Parrish and other elders maintained that certain stories, especially those about Coyote, those from the time when the animals were still human, could be told only during winter. Essie Parrish remembered an old man who told stories "in the old way," full of songs, and by impersonating the various characters in the stories. He called the children to his home on winter nights and asked them to lie down in the dark before he began his stories.[9] Violet Chappell says of her mother Essie Parrish: "Mom used to imitate the characters in the stories, too. She'd make her voice sound different ways." Many stories surely had to do with šaba·du (teachings). Many stories, then, were moral. But how they were rendered moral, how they were told, received, and understood must have varied, depending on the individual storyteller, the listener(s), and the storytelling context. It is no different today. Mabel McKay, a Cache Creek Pomo, tells stories that are šaba·du, but not in a way that the story or the moral that may be associated with it is fixed, understood on the spot. "Don't ask me what it means the story," Mabel McKay says. "Life will teach you about it the way it teaches you about life."

Neither Essie Parrish nor Mabel McKay are precontact Indians. In looking at how the Kashaya students read stories as opposed to how they hear stories, a scholar might want to compare and contrast precontact storytelling events with reading events, particularly in terms of oral versus literate dynamics. First off, there is no way of *knowing* a precontact situation. And the current situation regarding oral storytelling and associated learning styles varies so greatly from home to home on the Kashaya reservation that it would be impossible to generalize. Second, and more generally, orality is not necessarily something distinct from literacy. Something may be written, or printed, and something may not be. Beyond that, essential distinctions become debatable. The work of many scholars (Tannen 1982; Erickson 1984; Scollon and Scollon 1984) suggests there are different kinds of nonliteracies, just as there are different kinds of literacies.[10] Further, there is often an "interplay in spoken and written discourse in various settings" (Tannen 1982:4). This is particularly true in situations where written texts may influence the form and presentation of oral texts, and vice versa (Heath 1983; Swearingen 1986). And as Boyarin has pointed out, "there is no reason to assume a priori that forms of authority grounded in an interaction between text and speech are any more repressive than those which are exclusively based in orality" (214). My aunts' oral story-telling and dialogue about people and events surrounding the poisoning of my cousin did not necessarily encourage open, nonrepressive exchange with community members outside our family. As it was, their talk framed the woman in given ways and thus sustained political and religious rivalries be-tween our family and friends and hers. This was so whether the woman was guilty of poisoning my cousin or not. Remember, also, that those younger Kashaya students, those who could not read well or at all, were in many ways hearing just as the other students were reading. There existed the same conditions in the classroom with Bishop as authority figure. These younger students just had not quite learned the practice of reading, but they already knew to keep life experience separate from what they do in the classroom. The questions that should concern scholars and others should be about the nature of the relationship students have with texts of any kind, whether written or oral or any combination thereof. Is the text and its pre-sentation authoritative? Can the student talk back, reinvent, exchange with others?

Of course discussions of what constitutes orality or literacy in particular cultural, social, and political contexts are likely to consider these questions in some way. Boyarin suggests that the dynamic, dialogical relationship Jewish people can have with the Bible enables them the opportunity "to dispute and recreate what Judaism is" (229). They are able to "interpret their lifeworld in a way that satisfies their desire for personal integrity, their sense of belonging to the group, their connection to past and future, and their place in the world" (229). Likewise, Michael M. J. Fischer, in his study of contemporary ethnic minority autobiography, points out that for the autobiographers "ethnicity is something reinvented and reinterpreted" (1986:195). Boyarin notes that "the means of appropriation of the ongoing tradition is reflective" (228). The Jews Boyarin discusses are empowered as disputants; they can talk back, challenge the text. The ethnic minority autobiographers Fischer discusses are writers, likewise empowered, partly because of their educations, to reflect upon and dispute given notions of their ethnic identities.

The Kashaya Pomo schoolchildren are not empowered disputants. In the classroom and, I would argue, in other parts of their lives, they cannot actively invent or reinvent their identities as Kashaya Pomo Indians, at least not openly, not away from their immediate families, not with others in the classroom. Reading, as I have described it in terms of the students' cultural and historical community, the classroom environment, and the particular practice of reading in the classroom, separates the students from their ongoing histories and traditions and the processes of identity formation associated with their histories and traditions. Instead of engaging the students, instead of empowering them with a cultural base—their own—from which to work, as Bishop had hoped, the Slug Woman story served to further distance, or redistance, the students from their cultural base and identities. Here, as Boyarin observed in a healthier context, "the strategies employed in reading [were] part of the general strategies of personhood in a world of multiple and conflicting cultural demands" (215).

My family and members of the Kashaya schoolboard wanted any suggestions I might have for improving the state of affairs at the school. I have not made suggestions. Rather, I have described some of what impedes positive change, particularly as I see impediments located in the students' reading of the Slug Woman story. Given what I have described in this paper, I will offer criteria for what reading, and other classroom activities for that matter, should work to accomplish. First, reading must engage the students in a way that encourages them to feel they have power equal to that of the text they are reading and to that of the teacher who has given them the text to read. This does not mean that the students should be in any way disrespectful. Rather, they must feel knowledgeable and able in an encounter with a text and when responding to it. Second, reading, and all classroom activity, must be seen and promoted as something that continues and recreates culture both in the ways its practices alter and maintain previous methods for continuing and recreating culture and in the ways it helps individuals negotiate personhood "in a world of multiple and conflicting demands." In a reciprocal turn, reading should evoke responses from the students that in given ways will inform, continue, and recreate its very practice, classroom pedagogy, and the teacher's notions of logic, critical thought, and so forth. Finally, the practice of reading must work to engage the parents, the entire community. If the parents are not involved, if they do not know or understand what is going on in the classroom, another chasm forms over which there will be limited communication. This means the teacher must get out of the classroom if she is ever going to gain a clearer sense of the community. In both the classroom and the community at large she must position herself as a learner, and in a way students and parents can tell.

AFTERWORD

Victoria Kaplan Patterson has worked with Indian students for over fifteen years. Specifically, she has worked with the central Pomo tribes of Ukiah and Hopland in Mendocino County. She knows the Pomo people of the area well. (Her late husband, Scott Patterson, was an ethnographer and photographer who worked with these and other Pomo tribes and was well respected by them.) As a teacher and consultant for the Ukiah Unified

School District, she saw Indian students' dissatisfaction and alienation in the public schools. Her ideas and programs to rectify the problems associated with student dissatisfaction and alienation are encouraging.

One project that is particularly interesting to me is the *Pomo Supernaturals Coloring Book* created by the students of the sixth, seventh, and eighth grade Title VII classes at Pomolita School. Title VII is a state funded program for Indian students who wish to work with teachers and others on education related projects, such as tutoring for basic skills development. "I wanted to do something more," said Patterson. "Something that would be more than a job of catching these students up with the non-Indian students."

Patterson copied several stories from S. A. Barrett's *Pomo Myths*, a collection of stories recorded and gathered by Barrett in 1933. The stories taken from the central Pomo tribes are often about "mythic" figures such as Coyote. The students were given the stories and asked to make drawings that could be colored in with crayons. The purpose was to create a reader and coloring book for the younger Indian children. Patterson gave no other instructions. The students could choose whatever story they wanted. They could work together or individually. They could ask their parents, grandparents, or anyone else in their community for help.

The students organized themselves. They were responsible for their own recreations of the stories. Patterson said the students divided the work, consulted family and friends, and then brought their respective illustrations back to the group. They examined one another's work. They checked that the illustrations would be accessible to the younger Title VII students. As Patterson noted, "the students were responsible for continuing these stories, for keeping them alive for others, in whatever way they wanted." And that is what they did. One illustration depicts Coyote as a low-rider, a hoodlum, with an accompanying story about Coyote's tricky ways and how "You never know where he will turn up or what he will do." In the introduction Patterson writes: "We never know when the Supernaturals will reveal themselves. To be safe, we must always act courteously to our environment and take good care of it."

As Patterson observed, "the illustrations extended into other stories that are modern stories. The students told them in a way that called up the present, in a way the students could see the stories in the here and now, as real. Fire has power. Water has power. You could burn or drown. These things are real. Coyote can be seen in a low-rider." The illustrations they drew became the texts for other students. The younger students would in turn begin remaking the texts by reading them and coloring in the illustrations as they see fit. And of course the next step was to have the students write the text for their illustrations.

Here it seems the criteria I set forth have been met. The students felt empowered; they were responsible for making sense of what they read based on what they knew or could find out. The drawing continued their culture in a way they determined, and it was done as a community project, with one another, family, and friends. Unfortunately, funding was cut. The project ended. Perhaps the spirit remains for the students. Perhaps in the Ukiah Unified School District there are Indians who are empowered disputants.

It is important for Kashaya Pomo people to know stories, to keep the stories alive. We talk with stories; we know things about one another with stories. We can know things about ourselves with stories.

Throughout the writing of this paper I have been thinking about Slug Woman. Earlier I said that for my family and me Slug Woman is alive. She got into my cousin, poisoned him so that he did not know what he was doing or where he was going. The medical doctors could not detect her. We had to take care of the problem our way.

Slug Woman is alive on the Kashaya reservation. In the writing of this paper, both with my stories and with my schoolish analysis, I found her in us. I found her in our silence. She has lured us there, so we don't know what we are doing as a people, where we are going, so we can't talk about it with one another. Will we come home? Or will we be trapped, left out in a hollow tree with our insides on fire?

This paper is my attempt to doctor and to heal. Can it sing medicine songs? Can it lift Slug Woman up, singing right before our eyes?[11]

NOTES

1. Bishop also gave the students the story "A Pubescent Girl Turns into a Rock," which Bishop copied directly from Robert Oswalt's *Kashaya Texts*. In this paper I will only refer to the Slug Woman story. Though the student response to the Slug Woman story and to the story about the Pubescent Girl was basically the same, the students did say more about the Slug Woman story. Also, the Slug Woman story is meaningful to me as I illustrate in this paper. From here on I will refer to the Slug Woman story as one story or text, even though it is broken into two narratives, "A Description of Slug Woman" and "A Story About the Slug Woman." Bishop presented these narratives as one story. They are collected together in one pamphlet about Slug Woman published by YA-KA-AMA, a local Indian education and resource center.

2. See my article "Storytelling in the Classroom: Crossing Vexed Chasms."

3. Oswalt notes: "Any figure given for the aboriginal population of the Kashaya can only be a rough guess; Kniffen (1939:388) suggests 550; Stewart (1943:51) quotes an Indian's estimate of 800" (3).

4. In some areas entire tribes of Pomo vanished; in other areas only a few in-

dividuals of a tribe survived. Mabel McKay, for instance, is today the last living representative of the Long Valley Cache Creek Pomo tribe.

5. Jonathan Boyarin has seen tradition in the same light in his study of reading in his "Voices Around the Text: The Ethnography of Reading at Mesivta Tifereth Jerusalem." I am indebted to him for his clear statement of this principle: "Tradition is not a thing but a process" (228).

6. In September 1958, Essie Parrish gave a description of Slug Woman to Oswalt, which he titled "Description of Slug Woman" (Oswalt, 139). A month earlier, Herman James told a Slug Woman story, which Oswalt titled "Slug Woman Abducts a Man" (Oswalt, 139–145). Oswalt, in *Kashaya Texts*, presents both the transcribed version of the narratives and his English translations. The YA-KA-AMA story of Slug Woman presented in a single pamphlet was obviously taken from Oswalt's two English translations.

7. Bleich notes this in his astute criticism of Bakhtin. Bleich observes that "when he [Bakhtin] studies literature, he views the texts as *representations* of interaction rather than the *occasion for* interaction" (418).

8. This reminds me of what Gregory Bateson noted many years ago in his study of culture contact patterns. Gabriele Schwab sums up his observations thus: "In *Steps to an Ecology of Mind* Gregory Bateson reveals a tendency of the mind retrospectively to project epistemological independence onto those partialized closed systems of thought. General interaction patterns show, according to Bateson, that all forms of culture contact that tend to rigidify boundaries in order to maintain an unchanged internal coherence lead to an increase of external conflict and hostility ultimately destructive for all agents involved" (134). See Gabriele Schwab's (1986) Reader Response and the Aesthetic Experience of Otherness." Also see Bateson's "Culture Contact and Schismogenesis."

9. Parrish also related this about storytelling to Oswalt (Oswalt, 119). There the old man is identified as Salvador (ca. 1840–1915) (Oswalt, 119).

10. Scollon and Scollon, for example, note: "We feel that this [Northern Athabaskan] oral tradition is strikingly unlike the bard-and-formula oral tradition [i.e., the Homeric tradition studied by Parry and referred to by Ong via Parry] so often advanced as the representative of oral traditions" (182).

11. I am grateful to the people who tell me stories, especially Mabel McKay, Violet Chappell, and Anita Silva. Without them I could not have written this paper. I am also grateful to Judy Bare who listened to this paper over and over again and offered helpful suggestions each time.

REFERENCES

Barret, S. A.
1933   "Pomo Myths." *Bulletin of the Public Museum of Milwaukee* 15.
Bateson, Gregory
1972.   "Culture Contact and Schismogenesis." In *Steps to an Ecology of Mind*, pp. 61–72. New York: Ballantine Books.
Bishop, Mollie
1990   Personal Communication. Stewart's Point, California.

Bleich, David
 1986   "Intersubjective Reading." *New Literary History* 17(3):401–422.
Boyarin, Jonathan
 1989   "Voices Around the Text: The Ethnography of Reading at Mesivta
              Tifereth Jerusalem." *Cultural Anthropology*, 399–421.
Chappell, Violet Parrish
 1990   Personal Communication, Stewart's Point, California.
Clifford, James
 1988   *The Predicament of Culture: Twentieth Century Ethnography, Literature, and
              Art.* Cambridge, Mass.: Harvard University Press.
Erickson, Frederick
 1984   "Rhetoric, Anecdote, and Rhapsody: Coherence Strategies in a
              Conversation Among Black American Adolescents." In *Coherence in
              Spoken and Written Discourse.* Ed. Deborah Tannen, pp. 81–154.
              Norwood, N.J.: Ablex.
Fischer, Michael M. J.
 1986   "Ethnicity and the Post-Modern Arts of Memory." In *Writing Cul-
              ture*, pp. 194–233. Berkeley: University of California Press.
Heath, Shirley Brice
 1983   *Ways With Words.* New York: Cambridge.
Kashaya students
 1990   Personal Communication, Stewart's Point, California.
Kniffen, F. B.
 1939   "Pomo Geography." *UCPAAE* 36:343–400.
McKay, Mabel
 1958   Personal Communication. Santa Rosa and vicinity.
Oswalt, Robert
 1964   *Kashaya Texts.* Publications in Linguistics, vol. 36. Berkeley: Uni-
              versity of California.
Patterson, Victoria Kaplan
 1990   Personal Communication. Berkeley, California.
Pomolita School Title VII students
 1983   *Pomo Supernaturals Coloring Book.* Ukiah Unified School District.
Rosaldo, Renato
 1989   *Culture and Truth.* Boston: Beacon Press.
Sarris, Greg
 1990   "Storytelling in the Classroom: Crossing Vexed Chasms." *College
              English* 52(2):169–185.
Schwab, Gabriele
 1986   "Reader Response and the Aesthetic Experience of Otherness."
              Stanford Literature Review Spring:107–136.
Scollon, Ron. and Suzanne B. K. Scollon
 1984   "Cooking It Up and Boiling It Down: Abstracts in Athabaskan
              Children's Story Retellings." In *Coherence In Spoken and Written Dis-
              course.* Ed. Deborah Tannen, pp. 173–197. Norwood, N.J.: Ablex.
Stewart, O. C.
 1943   "Notes on Pomo Ethnography." *UCPAAE* 40:29–62.

Swearingen, C. Jan
  1986   "Oral Hermeneutics During the Transition to Literacy: The Con-
              temporary Debate." *Cultural Anthropology* 1:138–156.
Tannen, Deborah
  1982   "The Oral/Literate Continuum in Discourse." In *Spoken and Written
              Language: Exploring Orality and Literacy*. Ed. Deborah Tannen, pp. 1–
              16. Norwood, N.J.: Ablex.
YA-KA-AMA Indian Education and Development Inc.
  1974   "A Description of Slug Woman" and "A Story About the Slug
              Woman." Pamphlet. Santa Rosa, Calif.: YA-KA-AMA. (Copy-
              right by Sidney and Essie Parrish).

TWELVE

Afterword

Brian Stock

The ethnography of reading is so timely an idea that one is tempted to ask why it has taken so long for students of society, history, and literature to come around to it.

There are a number of reasons for the relatively late development, as contrasted with studies of orality and literacy, some of which are now well over a century old. One of them arises from the very nature of silent, visual reading, which absorbs our attention so fully that, while we are working through a text, it is very difficult for us to focus our thoughts on what reading is: we just read, making use of procedures lodged in our memories, just as, when we speak, we draw on our linguistic competence without consciously applying the rules of grammar. As a result, it is the facts we read about that appear to be the variables in the experience, not the mental operations we perform: these have a timeless, unchanging quality, as if a mechanical act were being repeated again and again. If we wish to think abstractly about reading, we have to stop reading and direct our attention to what we have been doing. As the focus of our interests shifts, we recognize something fundamental to all "modern" reading: it simultaneously involves us and detaches us from the objects being read about.

It is common knowledge that reading practices have evolved over time. It is also reasonably well known that Western assumptions about the place of reading in relation to the individual and society are not shared by non-Western cultures. As academic readers, we are seldom inconvenienced by these details. When we gather facts through reading, we bracket the history and ethnography of reading and direct our attention singlemindedly to the task before us. However, the moment we step back from what we are doing and think about reading analytically, we have to acknowledge that no aspect of such a basic literate skill can be investigated by literates like us without the observers becoming participants in the phenomenon they are trying to understand (see Fabian in this volume). Reading may open a window onto social experience: but the way in which individuals read is shaped by some of the same experiences that reading is supposed to tell them about. An "ethnography" of reading will not resolve the theoretical dilemma. But it can tackle the issues from another direction. The only way to move beyond the limits of our present understanding is to expand the archive of known reading practices; and this knowledge is perhaps the best guarantee that contemporary practices will not be made the standard for evaluating the different roles that reading plays elsewhere.

Universalist assumptions underlie our nontheoretical approaches to reading for another reason. This can be called cognitive fallacy: the view that, reading, because it is coordinated in the brain, cannot, in its causal mechanisms, be understood through historical or anthropological analysis. Unlike oral or literate communication, which can be studied through what is heard or seen, reading, in its internal aspects, would appear to leave us little or nothing to observe. However, to take this view is to misconceive the issues. What the neurosciences teach is that the brain does not recognize the notion of reading at all. What we call reading is the sum of innumerable small operations of thinking. Some of these can be studied experimentally, like the speed of the eye's movements across a line of text. But no one actually knows what goes on inside the head when a text is read. When the matter is eventually sorted out, the concept of reading will likely not play a large role in the description, except as "folk psychology." So our ignorance of a scientific appreciation of reading is not an obstacle to the historical and anthropological analysis of reading. It is a thinly disguised ideological constraint on our understanding of what is almost entirely a cultural construct.

Historical forces have buttressed the cognitive view. Summarized briefly, they fall under four headings:

1. *The format of reading materials.* Since the eighteenth century, popular reading material has had a standardized book format, which, due to the publishing industry, has spread from Europe and North America to many other countries. This has helped to create the illusion that, while societies may consist of different linguistic groupings, there is something unified, or unifying, about the experience of reading. Because all reading material looks the same, all reading is assumed to be the same. The act of reading is part of a model of society, which assumes that differences between communities can be reduced, or even eliminated, by a common experience of the text.

2. *The rise of general education.* Since the nineteenth century, Western nations have been committed to programs of universal literacy, as have many non-Western countries engaged in "modernization." The adoption of common goals has in itself furthered the view that education has an objec-

tive shared by all individuals, despite their differences in social, economic, or cultural background. Education has likewise contributed to a utopian view of reading's potential by attaching unified goals to the engine of moral and economic progress. During the twentieth century, literacy largely replaced Protestantism as a secular gospel for promoting such views.

3. *The way in which learning to read among children has been experimentally studied.* This has normally been done with control groups of Western children reading books in modern languages and in standard formats. The child's learning experience in oral societies (see Sarris in this volume) or in non-Western literate ones, such as China, India, or Japan, has only recently entered the pedagogical picture. Nor have the roles that reading plays in the socialization of male and female readers, beginning in youth, been the subject of systematic study (see Horton in this volume). The bias of experimental methods appears in the assumption that children with widely differing social experiences, when they are placed in Western style schools, will all emerge with similar values.

4. *The growth of university departments of literature, and, in particular, of literary theory.* The rise of theory, it can be argued, has the same roots as universalist ideas about education and moral development. Theory merely translates practical concerns into reasoned positions, which are universalized, at least to the degree they furnish the non-Western world with a model for higher education. Even theories that purport to undermine theory, like "deconstruction," presume a classroom setting as the institutional backdrop against which literature is "interpreted." This body of knowledge assumes there is a theory that applies generally to such writings, just as there is a "universal grammar" of speech.

There is a good deal of debate nowadays among students of higher culture on the assumptions that lie behind such views—and rightly so. Much of the criticism of "triumphalist" interpretive schemes and inflexible canons of texts has come from within literature departments originally set up expressly to defend them. It is likewise recognized by historians and anthropologists that the notion of literature, as a type of discourse accessible through reading written texts for their nonvisible, allegorical, or spiritual significance, is largely a Western invention. The implied connection between writings and inner realities since Plato is one of the successful fictions that antiquity and the Middle Ages perpetrated on the modern world. Unwittingly, the post-print age has perpetrated the same philosophy on many nonmodern worlds.

It is appropriate to ask when it was that reading became the social and cultural force we nowadays acknowledge it to be. The best way to approach the issues is not to look backward from the age of print—this has the effect of seeing all earlier forces as converging in a single, momentous event—but to look forward, to the degree records permit, from the ancient world, when, with the problematical exception of Jewish culture (see D. Boyarin in this volume), the role we assign to reading was largely taken up by speech. In the Christian West, no one before Augustine successfully elaborated a theory that placed reading above speaking; and he did so principally for interpreting God's Word, which happened to be handed down to him in a written and translated form. There is no hard and fast line between speaking and reading in theories of interpretation among the three chief ancient schools, the Platonists, Aristotelians, and Stoics. In the school system shared by Greeks and Latins in late antiquity, reading was mainly an oral skill; and so it appeared logical to commentators such as Donatus, Quintilian, and Priscian that spoken and written sign systems be discussed as a single body of rules. The goals of reading, when they were mentioned at all, were subordinate to those of speech. The orator was Cicero's ideal, the preacher, Augustine's.

If we examine the uses of reading toward the end of the Middle Ages, it is clear that much had changed. First of all, in the Christian West, as in Judaism and Islam, there were a number of genuine theories of reading and interpretation in which textual concerns were placed at the forefront of the discussion. In the West, silent, visual reading occupied a far more important place than it ever did in the ancient world. Reading in turn promoted new ways of classifying and organizing knowledge: the gloss, the commentary, the footnote, and the index provided aids to the reader, as did the premodern punctuation of the Latin or vernacular texts. The past became the subject of reading and of archival memory: the intellectual experience of the ancient world was written up in a manner only accessible to the eye. Paintings in manuscripts likewise ceased to imitate ancient exemplars and took on narrative functions of their own, thereby emphasizing another aspect of the visual. Also, the displacement of reading praxis away from the voice meant that reading was no longer a commemorative activity. Both reading and writing were widely recognized as modes for the discovery of new knowledge, especially among "scholastic" philosophers and theologians, who looked upon the reading process as an intermediary between divine and human modes of understanding. Above all, writing and reading became official interpreters of social experience. Rules for behavior in society acquired legitimacy because they were written down and open to discussion by those who could read them. As the age of print neared, one saw the appearance, for the first time in large numbers, of the leisured reader, the individual, who read for pleasure rather than for moral improvement. This long complex history is veiled by the Latin terms for reading, *lectio* and *legere*, whose meanings do not greatly change, but can be partly retrieved through the study of the Anglo-Saxon *rædan* (see Howe in this volume).

From the fourteenth century, and well before the advent of printing on a large scale, the reading public was "deinstitutionalized." The individual, male or female, no longer felt the real or invisible presence of a collectivity—a religious order, a courtly circle, or a school of thought—against which his or her interpretations were automatically measured. One of the assumptions of hermeneutics for Montaigne and Erasmus is that readers are united chiefly by their common agreement on the meaning of a text. However, the emergence of the individual as the model reader brought with it problems as well as benefits. Interpretation was freed from real or felt constraints; but the isolated reader of the Renaissance, who was frequently a silent reader, particularized reading while suppressing, or disguising, its group dynamics. Individualization made reading the symbol of privacy and privacy the symbol of reading. Reading became the West's most powerful icon of self-absorption. Yet somewhere in this transformation, the social dimension of reading, which, after all, we share as speakers of the language we read or write, was buried in ill-defined notions like "tradition." And, since the Reformation, we have been unable to relocate it permanently within our culture. For models of social praxis involving reading, we are obliged to look at unmodernized societies—ancient Greece, the Middle Ages, Judaism, and Islam, all of them literate but none of them literate as our society is. At the same time, in the public imagination, the assumption of universality prevails: for instance, at a time of deep political division between the Muslim world and the West, our political leaders consistently fail to understand how the oral reading of the Koran functions as the principle source of social cohesion in Islam, prophetically transcending Western institutions whenever the need arises.

One aspect of this problem has been discussed at length in contemporary criticism. This is the study of the changing criteria for evaluating texts within academic communities engaged in a struggle for hegemony over the interpretation of cultural tradition (see Long in this volume). But there are other issues that likewise merit a more extensive discussion. Two of these are suggested between the lines of several essays in this book: the investing of places with the qualities of readable texts, and the varied roles played by memory within different reading communities.

Among societies that do not have written texts, and within many that do, it is often places—sacred groves, temple complexes, and pilgrimage sites—that are "read." The text is inscribed in the landscape. Among the Kayasha Pomo of northern California, Sarris notes, "all features of the landscape were named and stories were associated with each of them" (Sarris in this volume). On Tidore, in eastern Indonesia, Baker writes, the spirits (jins) communicate with humans at specific sites, and, despite the presence of Islam, the failure to engage in continuous ritual conversations with the beings who live there can preface grave misfortune (Baker in this volume). As Western readers, we automatically linearize such spatial arrangements as an adjustment to the way in which we have been taught to read. It would be more logical to realign our notion of reading to something more prevalent in many non-Western societies, namely the integration of narrative and landscape. There are numerous versions of this type of reading both within Western medieval and eastern literate religious traditions, which James Duncan discusses at length in his powerful study of landscape and textuality in historic Kandy, Sri Lanka: they include the manner in which landscapes encode and sacralize political ideas, archivize and reproduce collective memory, and incorporate competing mythologies about social origins and developments (Duncan 1990).

Such communities utilize social memory in ways that our culture once did. Reading frequently has a commemorative function that it has all but lost in the West, except in the liturgy (see D. Boyarin in this volume; also J. Boyarin). Among the North Moluccans of Tidore, the Koran is accurately recited, even though the natives understand little of the text. How are we to characterize what is taking place? It is not orality, because it is textually based, but it is not literacy either, since meaning does not arise from the text. Written traditions are embedded in "socially reproduced experience" that includes oral recitation and ancestor worship (Baker in this volume). It is here that the Western notion of reading, which begins and ends with the written, needs its most serious revision. For, in all Islamic societies, the mastery of the "sciences" of how to live begins with the memorization and verbatim recitation of the Koran. The role of reading, Dale Eickelman notes, is largely "conservational" (Eickelman 1985:58). In the West, such behaviorally oriented reading was best incorporated into cenobitic monasticism. However, well before the end of the Middle Ages, the readerly asceticism that was originally designed to transform the self became a vehicle of innerworldliness. That part of the story of Western reading and society remains to be written.

REFERENCES

Duncan, James S.
  1990   *The City as Text: The Politics of Landscape Interpretation in the Kandyan Kingdom.* Cambridge: Cambridge University Press.
Eickelman, Dale F.
  1985   *Knowledge and Power in Morocco: The Education of a Twentieth-Century Notable.* Princeton: Princeton University Press.

INDEX

Designer:	U.C. Press Staff
Compositor:	Asco Trade Typesetting Ltd.
Text:	10/12 Baskerville
Display:	Baskerville
Printer:	Maple-Vail Book Manufacturing Group
Binder:	Maple-Vail Book Manufacturing Group